MODERN PLAYS
SHORT AND LONG

MODERN PLAYS

SHORT AND LONG

BY

FREDERICK HOUK LAW

Play Anthology Reprint Series

BOOKS FOR LIBRARIES PRESS

PLAINVIEW, NEW YORK

First Published 1924

Reprinted 1974

Library of Congress Cataloging in Publication Data

Law, Frederick Houk, 1871-1957, ed.
  Modern plays, short and long.

  (Play anthology reprint series)
  Reprint of the 1924 ed. published by the Century Co.,
New York.
  CONTENTS: Jefferson, J. Rip Van Winkle.--Mackay, C.
D. Benjamin Franklin, journeyman.--Macmillan, M. The
pioneers.--[Etc.]
  1. American drama--20th century.   I. Title.
PS634.L35 1974   812'.5'208   73-5501
ISBN 0-8369-8250-9

PREFACE

This is a book especially designed for class reading, class study, and class practice, a book in which every play will interest young people.

The aim is to center interest, not on any one division of the drama but on the drama as a whole. For that reason the book gives examples of different types of one-act plays; of short plays of more than one act; and of full-length plays.

To lead by pleasant paths to an appreciative interest in the modern drama; to an understanding of some of the principles that control the writing of modern plays, both short and long; to information concerning some of the leading modern writers of plays, and some of the principal modern movements for the uplift of the drama; to provide suitable and interesting dramatic material for literary study in the classroom; and to awaken some interest, at least, in original dramatic construction—those are the purposes of this book.

To supplement the plays of Shakespeare, which are always studied in school, and to show that the drama is still a powerful form for the giving of pleasure and for the presentation and criticism of human life, there is need for the study of modern plays. Shakespeare's plays always will be valuable for school study. They contain far-reaching character studies, great moral truths, highly dramatic situations, and passages of exquisite poetic beauty. Nevertheless, the technique of Shakespeare's plays is not modern; and the language, from the point of view of young people, is often obscure.

To study Shakespeare alone is to forget modern times; to study full-length plays alone is to ignore the short play, one of the most interesting and potential literary forms; to study the one-act play alone is to limit one's study of the drama.

v

To study the drama as a whole is to gain a new insight into literature and into life.

The teacher of the drama must train pupils to sympathize keenly, and to visualize vividly. Reading a play always supplements the pleasure of seeing one on the stage; acting a play, or part of a play, always develops new understanding of characters, situations, and effects.

As an aid to awakening sympathy and to stimulating visualization and imagination, this book gives, before every play, introductory problems parallel with those in the play that follows. The problems call for the use of similar dramatic material, the development, from similar themes, of similar situations, and the awakening of like emotions.

Suggestive questions direct pupils to the points of highest interest or of greatest worth in the plays themselves. The intention is not to encourage formal class study but to awaken interest, to give pleasure, to develop appreciation, and to lead to some understanding of the work of the dramatist as a conscious artist.

In accordance with the acknowledged fact that actual class presentation is essential to understanding and sympathy, suggestions for oral work in class accompany every play.

Work along the lines suggested throughout the book, conducted with the purpose of giving pleasure and of awakening sympathy, will prove altogether delightful.

Since the writing of a limited and purposeful series of written imitations will do much to awaken lively appreciation, there are given numerous suggestions and directions for written work in play construction. It is a custom of the day for people to write plays. Why should not the schools do something to teach people to write plays intelligently? The suggestions are simple. They call for the finding and use of a limited amount of dramatic material; for the preparation of preliminary scenarios; and for the writing of parts of plays rather than of entire plays.

CONTENTS

MODERN PLAYS: SHORT AND LONG

MODERN PLAYS:
SHORT AND LONG

I

THE NATURE OF A PLAY

A play is a representation of life. Through action and dialogue it unfolds an interesting story centered around one theme, one group of persons, and one closely related series of events; and through the unfolding of the story it has the power to arouse emotion.

A play lifts us from our ordinary surroundings, permits us to see complete units in the lives of human beings, and deeply arouses our emotions.

In a short story or in a novel the author tells about his characters, comments on their appearance, explains their motives, and points out the results of actions.

In a play the dramatist merely shows life; he gives the opportunity to see for ourselves, to draw our own conclusions, to make our own comments. He himself says nothing, adds nothing, makes no explanations, and gives no comments except through the lips and the actions of his characters. He exhibits life. This principle of play writing holds true in spite of the fact that George Bernard Shaw and a few other modern dramatists, in what may be called subjective plays strongly centered on problems of life in which the authors are intensely interested, have somewhat departed from it, by making almost every person in their plays speak with the authors' own brilliance, rather than in accordance with truth to character.

3

1. A good play compresses into the space of part of an afternoon or evening a representation of a completely unified series of events that awaken emotion.
2. It introduces a group of interesting persons.
3. It shows the beginning of some definite course of action.
4. It leads clearly and surely through a series of events that thereupon develop.
5. It rises to a point of intense interest.
6. It comes to a natural and satisfying conclusion.

Purposeful selection of material, action, character portrayal, condensation, power of suggestion, and power to awaken emotion, are characteristics of all good plays.

A play is much more than a mechanical arrangement of events, and a series of clever dialogues and group scenes. It is first of all the product of a highly developed art that has its own technique; secondly, it is a study of human character, an analysis of the human soul.

THE DRAMA IN ANCIENT TIMES

Nearly two thousand, five hundred years ago the Greeks, with a natural instinct for dramatic effect, wrote plays that we still study as masterpieces. In those plays the Greeks presented situations of such deeply tragic nature, and of such human appeal, that they aroused the greatest sympathy.

Perhaps the most notable influence of the Greek dramatists was toward what is called "The Three Unities," unity of action, unity of time, and unity of place. Their effort to limit the action of a play to a single highly centered series of events, the time to a single brief period, and the scene of action to one place, did much to give the art of play writing great power.

The greatest of the ancient Greek dramatists were men of the highest dramatic power. They were:

Æschylus (525–456 B. C.)
Sophocles (495–406 B. C.)

Euripides (480–406 B. C.)

Aristophanes (450–380 B. C.)

Shortly after the time of the great Greek dramatists the keen-minded philosopher, Aristotle (384–322 B. C.), the first to lay down the principles on which great plays are based, became the first great critic of the theater. He pointed out that a play is a unity in which every part is strictly necessary; that it must have, above everything else, interesting action; that it must have high probability; that the hero will produce the greatest effect when he is neither entirely good, nor entirely bad; and that the highest type of play, a great tragedy, is one that purifies the soul through pity and fear.

The Romans did not equal the Greeks in writing plays. Nevertheless, two Roman writers, Plautus (?——184 B. C.) and Terence (185–159 B. C.) wrote comedies that we read with admiration, and Seneca (4 B. C.–65 A. D.), the philosopher, wrote at least nine tragedies that strongly influenced the dramatists in England fifteen hundred years later.

THE DRAMA IN EUROPE

In Europe the drama grew naturally with the development of civilization, every land producing great plays.

In Spain, Lope de Vega (1562–1635), by writing no less than 1800 plays, won great popularity. Pedro Calderon (1600–1681), another Spanish dramatist, by writing numerous highly successful plays, likewise won lasting fame.

In France, in the seventeenth century, a number of great dramatists wrote remarkable plays.

Three great writers of classic French plays were:

Pierre Corneille (1606–1684)

Molière (Jean Baptiste Poquelin 1622–1673)

Jean Baptiste Racine (1639–1699)

Molière, the author of numerous comedies of character, among which are *Tartuffe, The Miser, The Learned Ladies,* and *The Physician in Spite of Himself,* holds a place in French literature somewhat comparable to the place that

Shakespeare holds in English literature. Like Shakespeare, Molière was both actor and manager, a skillful adapter of plots, and a man who won popular approval.

Nearly two hundred years after Molière, Victor Hugo (1862–1908), turning away from the restrictions of classic form, gave impetus to the development of romantic drama. In more recent times, French dramatists like Alexander Dumas (1824–1895), Victorien Sardou (1831–1908), and Edmond Rostand (1869–1920), the author of *Cyrano de Bergerac, L'Aiglon*, and *Chantecler*, continued the great dramatic work of the past.

In Germany the poetic drama gained power in the work of Johann Wolfgang von Goethe (1749–1832), the author of *Faust;* in the poetic dramas of Friedrich von Schiller (1759–1805), and in the powerful operas of Richard Wagner (1813–1883). Important and more recent German dramatists are Herman Suderman (1857–   ), and Gerhart Hauptmann (1862–   ).

In Scandinavian lands dramatists showed great love of realism, power of critical analysis of character, and high ability in craftsmanship. Henrik Ibsen (1828–1900), a Norwegian, wrote plays that have peculiarly searching power, and that make masterly presentations of human character. Björnstjerne Björnson (1832–1910), also a Norwegian, wrote plays of almost equal force. August Strindberg (1849–1912), a Swede, wrote a number of gloomy but powerful plays.

In all lands, in fact, dramatists did important work. In ancient India, in China, in Japan, and in lands remote from Europe, people developed forms of the drama.

The Drama in England

In England the church encouraged the giving of short dramatic pieces called Mystery Plays, Miracle Plays, and Moralities. The aim of all these was religious instruction: the Mystery Plays portrayed Scriptural stories, often events in the life of Christ; the Miracle Plays usually dealt with miraculous episodes in the lives of saints; the Moralities, by means of characters representing abstract virtues and vices, taught moral truths. *Everyman* is the best known play of this last group. The gradual introduction of humor into these plays led to writing about ordinary life.

John Heywood (1500?–1587?) wrote Interludes, short plays in which he dealt entirely with real people. One of these is the celebrated *Four P's*, a play about a Palmer, a Pardoner, a Poticary, and a Pedlar. Then Nicholas Udall (1505–1556) wrote *Ralph Royster Doyster*, a rollicking comedy, and Thomas Sackville (1536–1608) wrote *Gorboduc*, a tragedy.

Before the time of Shakespeare many men wrote plays, some based on history, some on literary stories, and some on daily life.

Christopher Marlowe (1564–1593), born in the same year as Shakespeare, wrote with remarkable dramatic power, his *Jew of Malta* and *Dr. Faustus* having a force that dramatists before had not been able to achieve. His work deeply influenced Shakespeare.

In the Elizabethan Age, when the people of England were prosperous, the theatres flourished. That was the period of the world's greatest dramatist, William Shakespeare (1564–1616), of rare Ben Jonson, Shakespeare's friend and literary rival, (1573–1637) and of that partnership of dramatists, Francis Beaumont (1584–1616) and John Fletcher (1579–1625), as well as of many other dramatists of brilliant ability.

The Puritan struggle closed the English theatres for a time; then the writing and the production of plays went on as before. It would be a long list indeed that should name even the most popular playwriters of succeeding years.

John Dryden (1631–1700) won the applause of the playgoing public. Oliver Goldsmith (1728–1774) wrote the delightful play, *She Stoops to Conquer;* Richard Brinsley Sheridan (1751–1816) wrote *The Rivals* and *The School for Scandal;* Bulwer Lytton (1803–1873), author of the famous novel, *The Last Days of Pompeii,* wrote several romantic plays, among them being *Richelieu,* and *The Lady of Lyons.*

William S. Gilbert (1836–1911), in company with Sir Arthur Sullivan (1842–1900), wrote extremely popular comic operas that are worthy of a place in the list of English plays, among them being *H. M. S. Pinafore*, *The Pirates of Penzance*, and *The Mikado*.

In our own times James M. Barrie (1860–   ) has written some of the most charming and most original of plays, *Quality Street*, *The Admirable Crichton*, *Peter Pan*, *Alice Sit-by-the-Fire*, *What Every Woman Knows*, *A Kiss for Cinderella*, *Dear Brutus*, and *Mary Rose*. George Bernard Shaw, with a highly cynical pen, has written numerous plays that make people think, among them being *Man and Superman*, *Androcles and the Lion*, and *Back to Methuselah*. John Galsworthy (1867–   ), in extremely realistic plays, *Joy*, *Strife*, and *Justice*, has called attention to important social problems.

THE DRAMA IN THE UNITED STATES

For a hundred and nine years the people of the seaport of New York, busy with the work of a small, remote settlement on the edge of a wilderness, were without theatres. In 1732 people who had been interested by amateur performances, perhaps by the amateur performances that had been given in the South for a generation or more, erected the first of all the theatres on Manhattan Island.

Twenty-seven years later, in 1759, Thomas Godfrey (1736–1763) of Philadelphia wrote *The Prince of Parthia*, the first American tragedy.

Strangely enough, it was not one of the people of commercial New York, nor of Philadelphia, nor of the more pleasure-loving South, who wrote the first American comedy. It was a man of serious, Puritan New England, where the people for generations had looked upon play-writing and play-producing as works of evil. Soon after the birth of the United States as a nation, Royall Tyler (1757–1826) of Boston, wrote *The Contrast* (1787), the first American play to make people laugh.

With the development of the country, and the founding of theatres, interest in play-writing increased. William Dunlap (1766–1839), meeting with success, became the first professional American playwright, and wrote many more plays than did Shakespeare. John Howard Payne (1791–1852), author of *Home, Sweet Home*, and Washington Irving (1783–1859), united in writing a play called *Charles the Second* (1824). George Washington Parke Custis (1781–1857), the adopted son of George Washington, wrote *Pocahontas, or The Settlers of Virginia* (1830). Nathaniel Parker Willis (1806–1867), a distinguished writer, wrote *Totesa the Usurer* (1839). Julia Ward Howe (1819–1910), author of *The Battle Hymn of the Republic*, wrote *Leonora, or The World's Own* (1857).

Many other writers, less known today, contributed to the entertainment of a public that was beginning to take strong interest in the theatre.

After the days of these beginnings play-writing flourished in the United States. Bronson Howard (1842–1908), with plays like *Saratoga* and *Shenandoah*, appealed to popular taste; Denman Thompson (1833–1911), in *The Old Homestead*, and James A. Herne (1840–1901), in *Shore Acres*, wrote most sympatheticlly about humble life; David Belasco (1859–   ), in *Madame Butterfly*, *The Return of Peter Grimm*, and in many other plays, showed high dramatic ability; Augustus Thomas (1859–   ), with *Alabama* and *The Witching Hour*, drew great audiences; Clyde Fitch (1865–1909), with *Nathan Hale*, *Barbara Frietchie*, and fifty-four other plays, won success after success; William Vaughn Moody (1869–1910), with *The Great Divide;* Percy MacKaye (1875–   ), with *Jeanne D'Arc*, and *This Fine-Pretty World;* Edward Sheldon (1886–   ), with *Romance;* and Eugene O'Neill (1888–   ), with *The Emperor Jones—* these are only a few of the many who wrote American plays that are original, that are strong, and that show that the art of play-writing is a growing art in the United States.

The One-Act Play

In comparatively recent times the development of Little
Theatres and small play-producing organizations gave increased opportunity to present short-length plays. In some
ways, this was a return to the past; for the Mysteries, the
Miracle Plays, the Moralities, and the Interludes, as well as
the Latin school plays that were produced in England before
the time of Shakespeare, are all comparatively short. The
Masks and many privately produced plays are likewise short.
Nevertheless, the modern one-act play, like the modern short
story, is a new form. It differs from the short plays of the
past just as the modern short story differs from the tales, or
short stories, of the past, and in much the same ways.

The best one-act play aims at singleness of effect, just as
does the best short story. It has a single theme, a single
dominant emotion; a limited number of characters; a limited
development and action; and one overmastering event toward
which the entire play moves swiftly and certainly from the
very beginning. The play is a unit: there is nothing that
does not contribute to the one effect; nothing that does not
lead to the conclusion, which is, in a sense, the purpose of
the play.

The one-act play is limited in the highest degree. There
is no opportunity, as in the long play, to include much introductory material; no opportunity to permit slow development; no opportunity to add interesting supplementary or
explanatory events. The one-act play is limited in length,
limited in characters, limited in situations, limited in action,
and limited in purpose. This extreme of limitation makes
the one-act play peculiarly striking and effective, and gives
it an intensely stimulating power. The best one-act play
grips its audience, and produces an effect not to be forgotten.

The conclusion of a one-act play is inevitable, satisfying,
and final. Beyond it one wishes to know no more. It is the
point that the very first of the play foreshadowed, the point
that the dramatist had in mind from the beginning. It is
the one conclusion that answers every question, that mag-

nifies the character of the leading person in the play, and that emphasizes to the full the theme of the play. At its best the one-act play illuminates a strong self-explanatory theme, not necessarily a moral, but a thought that can be expressed in one sentence. The theme is the great essential, the soul of the play. The story that the play enacts illustrates the theme; the conclusion of the play emphasizes it.

The one-act play is so short that the audience realizes it as a unit. The number of lines vary, of course, according to the subject matter and the action of the play.

The following points are worthy of consideration:

1. The opening of the play immediately awakens interest. Without delay it presents characters doing and saying something that strongly appeals to the interest of the audience.

2. The early part of the play, in the fewest words possible, and with the utmost naturalness, as though without intent, explains the situation.

3. A complication of some sort, introduced so that it appears natural and entirely to be expected, and suggesting the possibility of two or more ways of solving the problem presented in the situation, arouses intense interest and leads the audience to wonder what the leading characters will do.

4. The action of the play moves through a definite course of development to a point where the principal characters, face to face with a great emergency, take the final steps for which all the previous part of the play through words, action, and suggestion, has prepared.

5. The play comes to a striking, emphatic ending.

What is Dramatic

Every human action or chance word may be dramatic, or may not be dramatic. In general, an action is dramatic when it is unusual or striking, when it arouses, startles, or stimulates. The dramatic elements that appear in a play are not mere transcripts from life: they are the results of purposeful selection and adaptation by the dramatist. The material found in life is like raw ore taken from the ground; the material presented in a play is like keen-edged steel made from the ore. It is the same, and yet it is different. The dross has been removed; the material has been re-worked and transmuted into something new and different; nevertheless, it is the product of the earth as well as of skill. The dramatist is one who, seeing the value of the raw material of life, has the ability and the art to use that material for dramatic purposes.

THE THEME

The theme is the idea that the play develops. It is any conception that can be expressed in a single sentence. It is the thought that gives unity of purpose, that produces unity of effect, and that enriches the play. It is suggested and enforced rather than stated.

THE PLOT

Plot is the story by means of which the theme is developed. In the one-act play the plot is extremely simple and direct; in the long play the plot is often complex in nature, as in *The Merchant of Venice,* involving two or three related stories, all of which work toward one climax. Plot is the unfolding of action that emphasizes the idea of the play.

In all plays the action is selective, rather than complete: that is, much that would appear in actual life is omitted, although the omissions are not noticeable. The action includes all that is essential to the full development of the theme.

CHARACTERS

The characters are the persons represented in the play. In the one-act play the characters are few in number. If this were not so, the attention of the audience would be distracted from the plot, from the theme, and from the emotion. In the long play the number of characters is greater than in the one-act play, but even then the number is limited. There are just enough characters to carry the action, and no more.

In all plays there may be characters of slight importance, or silent characters, presented for the purpose of background or setting.

All characters are presented as truthfully as possible, so that they appear genuine. Natural speeches and natural actions reveal inner life, thoughts, motives, and mental conflicts.

DIALOGUE

A novel includes many pages of description, of explanation, and of comment. A play gives description through stage setting, costuming and make-up; and explanation and comment through the speeches of the persons in the play. This makes the dialogue, the talk that forms a play, utterly important. The characters speak as they do in life, but with a difference. In life, people speak carelessly, without regard for effect. In a play the characters speak as little as possible, even when they appear to speak without restraint; they speak as pointedly as possible, even when they appear to speak carelessly; actually, they speak with the perfection of art; apparently they speak with the thoughtlessness of life.

In life people hold long conversations, or one person speaks at great length. In a play long conversations or long speeches are tiresome. The dramatist, compressing all that is said, makes every sentence, every phrase, every word, while apparently natural and careless, count toward the action, the theme, and the emotion of the play.

SETTING

Setting is the background of a play, the scene and the circumstances under which the action takes place. Setting is made known by stage scenery, costuming, and make-up, and also by the way in which the characters speak, by the dialect or language that they use, or by what they say, their apparently chance words indicating the place, the time, and the circumstances about them. Many of the poetic passages in Shakespeare's plays were written, in an age when scenery was not employed, as a means of giving setting.

ATMOSPHERE

Atmosphere is the pervading spirit, the mood, the emotion, of a play. It is produced by a combination of all that is in a play: by stage setting; by stage effects such as may be produced by lighting, by music, and by various devices; by the dialogue; by the action, and by the entire development of the play. Today modern plays make much appeal to the eye, whereas in the past plays made appeal principally through language.

SITUATION

The situation is the condition of affairs at the beginning of a play, the event or problem from which the play develops. Naturally, the situation is given in the very first of a play, as soon as the characters have been introduced.

OPENING

The opening of a good play is natural, is interesting, and is such that it leads quickly to an understanding of the situation. It indicates the scene of action, the time of action, and the nature of the persons who are to take important part in the action. It does all this with the fewest words possible but with every appearance of naturalness. A long play may use several scenes, or even the entire first act, to introduce the characters, the setting and the situation; a one-act play makes the opening exceedingly brief.

DEVELOPMENT

In a good play the development of the action that takes place as the result of the situation, is entirely clear, well-proportioned, logical, and increasing in interest. The action leads steadily and surely to a point of supreme interest, where the persons of the play are forced to solve the problem presented in the situation. The development is the unfolding of the story, the growth toward the climax. Everything leads so naturally toward the final resolution of the play that the resolution is in full harmony with all that has gone before. Other lines of action may be suggested, but they will be turned aside as false hopes, as unwarrantable wishes, or as utterly impossible. The development shows the principal characters involved by force of circumstances in some intense struggle, driven at last, after what is called the moment of final suspense, a moment when their fate seems to hang in the balance, into acceptance of the one solution that the play presents.

ENDING

As soon as the development has led to the point of highest interest, the play draws to a quick conclusion, the characters entering at once into the circumstances demanded.

COLLECTIONS OF SHORT PLAYS

Baker, George Pierce	Plays of the 47 Work- shop	Brentano's, New York
Barnum, Madalene D.	School Plays for All Oc- casions	Barse and Hopkins, New York
Clark, Barret H.	Representative One-Act Plays by British and Irish Authors	Little, Brown, Boston
Cohen, Helen Louise	One-Act Plays by Mod- ern Authors	Harcourt, Brace, New York
Cohen, Helen Louise	The Junior Play Book	Harcourt, Brace, New York
Cook, George C., and Frank Shay	The Provincetown Play- ers	Appleton, New York

Dunsany, Lord	Five Plays	Mitchell Kennerley, New York
Dunsany, Lord	Plays of Gods and Men	Putnam's, New York
Dickinson, Thomas H.	Wisconsin Plays	Huebsch, New York
Gerstenberg, Alice	Ten One-Act Plays	Brentano's, New York
Eliot, Samuel A., Jr.	Little Theatre Classics (4 volumes)	Little, Brown, Boston
Gregory, Lady	Seven Short Plays	Putnam's, New York
Knickerbocker, Edwin Van B.	Plays for Classroom Interpretation	Holt, New York
Koch, Frederick H.	Carolina Folk Plays	Holt, New York
Leonard, Sterling A.	The Atlantic Book of Modern Plays	Atlantic Monthly Press, Boston
Lewis, Roland B.	Contemporary One-Act Plays	Scribner's, New York
Mackaye, Percy	Yankee Fantasies	Duffield, New York
MacMillan, Mary	Short Plays	Appleton, New York
MacMillan, Mary	More Short Plays	Appleton, New York
MacMillan, Mary	Third Book of Short Plays	Appleton, New York
Mayorga, Margaret	Representative One-Act Plays by American Authors	Little, Brown, Boston
Moses, Montrose J.	Representative One-Act Plays by Continental Authors	Little, Brown, Boston
Moses, Montrose J.	A Treasury of Plays for Children	Little, Brown, Boston
Schafer, Barbara Louise	Book of One-Act Plays	Bobbs-Merrill, Indianapolis
Shay, Frank	A Treasury of Plays for Men	Little, Brown, Boston
Shay, Frank	A Treasury of Plays for Women	Little, Brown, Boston
Shay, Frank, and Loving, Pierre	Fifty Contemporary One-Act Plays	Appleton, New York
Smith, Alice	Short Plays by Representative Authors	Macmillan, New York
Webber, James Plaisted, and Webster, Hanson Hart	One-Act plays for Secondary Schools	Houghton Mifflin, Boston

COLLECTIONS OF LONG PLAYS

Baker, George Pierce	Modern American Plays	Harcourt, Brace, New York

Cohen, Helen Louise	Longer Plays by Modern Authors	Harcourt, Brace, New York
Dickinson, Thomas H.	Chief Contemporary Dramatists	Houghton Mifflin, Boston
Mantle, Burns	The Best Plays of 1919 and 1920	Small, Maynard, Boston
Mantle, Burns	The Best Plays of 1920 and 1921	Small, Maynard, Boston
Mantle, Burns	The Best Plays of 1921 and 1922	Small, Maynard, Boston
Mantle, Burns	The Best Plays of 1922 and 1923	Small, Maynard, Boston
Mathews, Brander	Chief European Dramatists	Houghton Mifflin, Boston
Moses, Montrose J.	Representative Plays by American Dramatists	Dutton, New York
Quinn, Arthur Hobson	Representative American Plays	Century, New York
Quinn, Arthur Hobson	Contemporary American Plays	Scribner's, New York
Tatlock, John S. P., and Martin, Robert G.	Representative English Plays	Century, New York

NOTABLE MODERN PLAYS

AUTHOR	PLAY	YEAR OF PRODUCTION
Barrie, James Matthew	What Every Woman Knows	1908
Zangwill, Israel	The Melting Pot	1909
Galsworthy, John	Strife	1909
Maeterlinck, Maurice	The Blue Bird	1910
Rostand, Edmond	Chantecler	1911
Parker, Louis N.	Disraeli	1911
Belasco, David	The Return of Peter Grimm	1911
Knoblauch, Edward	Kismet	1911
Bennett, Arnold, and Knoblauch, Edward	Milestones	1912
Benrimo, J. Harry, and Hazelton, George C.	The Yellow Jacket	1912
Gates, Eleanor	The Poor Little Rich Girl	1913
Sheldon, Edward	Romance	1913
Cohan, George M., and Biggers, Earl Derr	Seven Keys to Baldpate	1913

AUTHOR	PLAY	YEAR OF PRODUCTION
Housman, Laurence, and Barker, Granville	Prunella	1913
Barrie, James Matthew	The Legend of Leonora	1914
Shaw, George Bernard	Androcles and the Lion	1915
Galsworthy, John	Justice	1916
MacKaye, Percy	Caliban by the Yellow Sands	1916
Barrie, James Matthew	A Kiss for Cinderella	1916
Moody, William Vaughn	The Great Divide	1917
Asche, Oscar, and Norton, Frederick	Chu Chin Chow	1917
Thomas, Augustus	The Copperhead	1918
Smith, Winchell, and Bacon, Frank	Lightnin'	1918
Barrie, James Matthew	Dear Brutus	1918
Ervine, St. John	John Ferguson	1919
Tarkington, Booth	Clarence	1919
Drinkwater, John	Abraham Lincoln	1919
Craven, Frank	The First Year	1920
Gale, Zona	Miss Lulu Bett	1920
O'Neil, Eugene	The Emperor Jones	1920
Shaw, George Bernard	Back to Methuselah	1922
Capek, Karel	"R.U.R."	1922
Dane, Clemence	Will Shakespeare	1923
Davis, Owen	Icebound	1923
Vollmer, Lula	Sun Up	1923
Vollmoeller, Karl	The Miracle	1924

Books on the Technique of Play Writing and Play Production

Andrews, Charlton	The Technique of Play Writing	Home Correspondence School, Springfield, Mass.
Archer, William	Playmaking	Small, Maynard, Boston
Archer, William	Old Drama and the New	Small, Maynard, Boston
Baker, George Pierce	Dramatic Technique	Houghton, Mifflin, Boston
Belasco, David	The Theatre through its Stage Door	Harpers, New York

Burton, Richard	How to See a Play	Macmillan, New York
Cannon, Fanny	Writing and Selling a Play	Holt, New York
Clark, Barret H.	British and American Drama of Today	Appleton, New York
Eaton, Walter Prichard	Plays and Players	Appleton, New York
Freytag, Gustav	The Technique of the Drama	Scott, Foresman, Chicago
Hale, Edward Everett, Jr.	Dramatists of Today	Holt, New York
Lewis, Roland B.	Technique of the One-Act Play	John W. Luce, Boston
Lewisohn, Ludwig	The Modern Drama	Huebsch, New York
Macgowan, Kenneth	The Theatre of Tomorrow	Boni & Liveright, New York
Mackay, Constance D'Arcy	The Little Theatre in the United States	Holt, New York
Mathews, Brander	The Principles of Playmaking	Scribner's, New York
Mathews, Brander	The Development of the Drama	Scribner's, New York
Mathews, Brander	Playwrights and Playmaking	Scribner's, New York
Phelps, William Lyon	The Twentieth Century Theatre	Macmillan, New York
Price, William T.	The Technique of the Drama	Brentano's, New York
Sayler, Oliver H.	Our American Theatre	Brentano's, New York
Wilde, Percival	The Craftsmanship of the One-Act Play	Little, Brown, Boston
Woodbridge, Elisabeth	The Drama, Its Laws and Technique	Allyn & Bacon, Boston

BOOKS ON THE RELATION BETWEEN EDUCATION AND THE DRAMA

Burleigh, Louise	The Community Theatre	Little, Brown, Boston
Chubb, Percival	Festivals and Plays	Harper's, New York
Curtis, Elnora Whitman	The Dramatic Instinct in Education	Houghton Mifflin, Boston
Finaly-Johnson, Harriet	The Dramatic Method of Teaching	Ginn, New York
Fry, Emma Sheridan	Educational Dramatics	Noble, New York
Herts, Alice Minnie	The Children's Educational Theatre	Harper's, New York

| Hillard, Evelyne | Amateur and Educational Dramatics | Macmillan, New York |
| Wise, Claude Merton | Dramatics for School and Community | Appleton, New York |

Books on the Staging of Plays

Clark, H. B.	How to Produce Amateur Plays	Little, Brown, Boston
Johnson, Gertrude E.	Choosing a Play	Century, New York
Platt, Agnes	Practical Hints on Training for the Stage	Dutton, New York
Stratton, Clarence	Producing in Little Theatres	Holt, New York
Taylor, Emerson	Practical Stage Directing for Amateurs	Dutton, New York
Wise, Claude Merton	Dramatics for School and Community	Appleton, New York

Oral Work in Class

1. From plays that you saw produced on the stage tell what you learned concerning manners and customs.
2. From plays that you saw produced on the stage tell what you learned about the costumes of different periods of history.
3. From plays that you saw produced on the stage tell what you learned 'hat will be of service to you in life.
4. Read any one chapter in any of the books named in the list of books on the technique of play writing. Give a talk concerning the contents of the chapter.
5. Consult any one of the books named in the list of books on the technique of play writing. Then apply to any one of the plays in this book the principles of criticism that you learned concerning any one technical point, such as inciting moment, characterization, moment of final suspense, denouement, plot, development of action, climax, dialogue, setting, theme, or any other topic under the head of dramatic technique.

RIP VAN WINKLE

As Played by Joseph Jefferson

The story of Rip Van Winkle, the delightful ne'er-do-well who slept for twenty years in the Catskill Mountains, and then returned to his native village to find himself not recognized, was written in England by Washington Irving some time before that writer was thirty-six years old, and published in New York, May 15, 1919, as part of the first of the seven instalments of the *Sketch-Book* papers. Later in 1819 the story was re-printed in England.

Rip Van Winkle so immediately captured the popular fancy that people began to look for the exact places that Irving had in mind. As a matter of fact, Irving did not visit the scenes of the story until thirteen or more years after he had written it.

As a play *Rip Van Winkle* appeared first on the stage of the Tottenham Street Theatre in London, perhaps six years or so before Washington Irving returned to the United States. The *Rip Van Winkle* play then produced was written by an actor named John Kerr. In October, 1829, the same crude play was acted in Philadelphia, with a certain "J. Jefferson" playing a part.

The first American play based on Irving's story of *Rip Van Winkle* was written by some person in Albany, New York, and acted in that city, May 26, 1828. The name of the writer is not now known.

Other versions of *Rip Van Winkle* appeared, every one more and more emphasizing character. Finally Joseph Jefferson, the actor, gaining the help of Dion Boucicault

(1822–1890), the dramatist, brought about the first version of the present famous play. In a period of thirty years Mr. Jefferson continued to change, revise, subtract from, and add to what had been written, thus making the play his life work. The present version of the play was published in 1895. *Rip Van Winkle* is certainly one of the most notable of all American plays.

For a hundred years the Jefferson family has been connected with *Rip Van Winkle*. "J. Jefferson" played a part in the first Philadelphia play. Without doubt "J. Jefferson" was Joseph Jefferson (1774–1832), the grandfather of the famous Joseph Jefferson of modern times. His son, Joseph Jefferson (1804–1842), also played in *Rip Van Winkle*. The grandson, Joseph Jefferson (1829–1905), made himself so nearly identical with Rip Van Winkle, that he can not be dissociated from the play. Thomas Jefferson (1857–   ) a great-grandson, also took part in the famous old play with which his family had been so notably connected.

Joseph Jefferson (1829–1905), only three years old when he first appeared on the stage, was an actor for seventy-three years! In 1859, having played in various parts with great success, in the United States, in England, and in Australia, Mr. Jefferson took up the old play of *Rip Van Winkle*, which he first presented in Washington. After he had had the play revised by Dion Boucicault he made it such a success that it ran in London for 170 nights.

For the greater part of his life Joseph Jefferson *was* Rip Van Winkle. Once in a country town the cashier of a bank refused to honor a check Mr. Jefferson presented, because the cashier thought the actor had not sufficiently proved his identity. "Vat!" said Mr. Jefferson, "you don'dt know me! Mine leetle dog Schneider, he knows me!" A man who was present at once vouched for Mr. Jefferson. He knew that there was no one else in the world who could speak as Joseph Jefferson, or Rip Van Winkle, spoke!

Joseph Jefferson won success in other plays, notably in Sheridan's *The Rivals,* but to the public at large he was always a re-incarnation of Rip Van Winkle of the Catskills.

Without doubt, Joseph Jefferson was the greatest of all American comedians of his time. *Rip Van Winkle* shows the weakness and the foibles of a man who is his own worst enemy. Incidentally, the play calls attention to the humor and the goodness that often lies more or less dormant in a seemingly worthless person. Dickens chose to make out of the drunkard, Sidney Carton, one of the noblest, most self-sacrificing of heroes; Joseph Jefferson made out of Rip Van Winkle, the village drunkard and good-for-nothing, a simple, kindly man, whom we love, not because he is good, but because he is essentially human.

Even when one admits that most of the characters in the play are caricatures rather than realities, and that much of the plot is conventional, he recognizes that there is a homely simplicity in the dramatized version of the old legend that brings the play close to the world of folk-lore, and therefore close to the sympathies of ordinary people.

The brisk, everyday dialogue, with its rough humor, proved immensely appealing to the popular audiences of Joseph Jefferson's time.

In all respects *Rip Van Winkle* is a typically American play.

INTRODUCTORY PROBLEMS

1. Think of some lovable, peculiar, interesting person whom you have known. Write a scenario for a play that will bring out strongly his eccentricities and his lovable characteristics.
2. Write a scenario of a play in which you make use of Washington Irving's *Legend of Sleepy Hollow*. Plan to make considerable use of the supernatural.

PERSONS OF THE PLAY

RIP VAN WINKLE	JACOB STEIN
DERRICK VON BEEKMAN	GRETCHEN
NICHOLAS VEDDER	MEENIE
HENDRICK	KÄTCHEN
COCKLES	DEMONS AND VILLAGERS
SETH SLOUGH	

ACT I.

SCENE 1. *The village of Falling Waters, set amid familiar and unmistakable Hudson River scenery, with the shining river itself and the noble heights of the Kaatskills visible in the distance. In the foreground, to the left of the stage, is a country inn bearing the sign of George III. In the wall of the inn, a window closed by a solid wooden shutter. To the right of the stage, an old cottage with a door opening into the interior; before the cottage stands a bench holding a wash-tub, with a washboard, soap and clothes in the tub. In the centre of the stage, a table and chairs, and on the table a stone pitcher and two tin cups.*

As the curtain rises, GRETCHEN *is discovered washing, and little* MEENIE *sitting near by on a low stool. The sound of a chorus and laughter comes from the inn.*

GRETCHEN. Shouting and drinking day and night. [*Laughter is heard from the inn.*] Hark how they crow over their cups while their wives are working at home, and their children are starving.

[*Enter* DERRICK *from the inn with a green bag, followed by* NICK VEDDER. DERRICK *places his green bag on the table.*]

DERRICK. Not a day, not an hour. If the last two quarters' rent be not paid by this time tomorrow, out you go!

NICK. Oh, come, Derrick, you won't do it. Let us have a glass, and talk the matter over; good liquor opens the heart. Here, Hendrick! Hendrick!

[*Enter* HENDRICK.]

HENDRICK. Yes, father.

DERRICK. So that is your brat?

NICK. Yes, that is my boy.

DERRICK. Then the best I can wish him is that he won't take after his father, and become a vagabond and a penniless outcast.

NICK. Those are hard words to hear in the presence of my child.

HENDRICK. Then why don't you knock him down, father?

GRETCHEN. I'll tell you why——

DERRICK. Gretchen!

GRETCHEN [wiping her arms and coming to front of tub]. It is because your father is in that man's power. And what's the use of getting a man down, if you don't trample on him?

NICK. Oh, that is the way of the world.

GRETCHEN [to HENDRICK]. Go in, boy. I want to speak to your father, and my words may not be fit for you to hear. Yonder is my little girl; go and play with her.

[HENDRICK and MEENIE exeunt into the cottage.]

GRETCHEN. Now, Derrick, Vedder is right; you won't turn him out of his house yonder.

DERRICK. And why not? Don't he owe me a year's rent?

GRETCHEN. And what do you owe him? Shall I sum up your accounts for you? Ten years ago, this was a quiet village and belonged mostly to my husband, Rip Van Winkle, a foolish, idle fellow. That house yonder has since been his ruin. Yes; bit by bit, he has parted with all he had, to fill the mouths of sots and boon companions, gathered around him in yonder house. And you, Derrick—you supplied him with the money to waste in riot and drink. Acre by acre, you've sucked in his land to swell your store. Yonder miserable cabin is the only shelter we have left; but that is mine. Had it been his, he would have sold it you, Derrick, long ago, and wasted its price in riot.

[VEDDER, who has been enjoying DERRICK'S discomfiture during this speech, is unable to control himself, and at the end of the speech, bursts into a loud laugh.]

GRETCHEN. Aye, and you too, Nick Vedder; you have ruined my husband between you.

NICK. Oh, come, Mrs. Van Winkle, you're too hard. I couldn't refuse Rip's money in the way of business; I had my rent to pay.

GRETCHEN. And shall I tell you why you can't pay it?

it is because you have given Rip credit, and he has ended by
drinking you out of house and home. Your window-shutter
is not wide enough to hold the score against him; it is full
of chalk. Deny it if you can.

NICK. I do deny it. There now!

GRETCHEN. Then why do you keep that shutter closed?
I 'll show you why. *[Goes to inn, opens shutter, holds it
open, pointing at* RIP'S *score.]* That 's why, Nick Vedder,
you 're a good man in the main, if there is such a thing.
[DERRICK *laughs.*] Aye, and I doubt it. *[Turning on him.]*
But you are the pest of this village; and the hand of every
woman in it ought to help pull down that drunkard's nest of
yours, stone by stone.

NICK. Come, Dame Van Winkle, you 're too hard entire;
now a man must have his odd time, and he 's none the worse
for being a jolly dog.

GRETCHEN. No, none the worse. He sings a good song;
he tells a good story—oh, he 's a glorious fellow! Did you
ever see the wife of a jolly dog? Well, she lives in a kennel.
Did you ever see the children of a jolly dog? They are the
street curs, and their home is the gutter.

*[Goes up to the wash-tub, and takes revenge on the clothing
she scrubs.]*

NICK *[getting up and approaching* GRETCHEN *timidly].* I
tell you what it is, Dame Van Winkle, I don't know what
your home may be, but judging from the rows I hear over
there, and the damaged appearance of Rip's face after having escaped your clutches—[GRETCHEN *looks up angrily;*
NICK *retreats a few paces hastily]*—I should say that a gutter
was a luxurious abode compared with it, and a kennel a peace-
ful retreat.

[Exit hurriedly, laughing, to the inn. GRETCHEN *looks up
angrily, and throws the cloth she has been wringing after
him, then resumes washing.* DERRICK *laughs at* VEDDER'S
exit, walks up to GRETCHEN, *and puts one foot on the bench.]*

DERRICK. Is it true, Gretchen? Are you truly miserable
with Rip?

GRETCHEN. Ain't you pleased to hear it? Come then and

DERRICK. The imp is right. Rip must be made to sign this paper. But how—how?

COCKLES. How? How? "How 's" a big word sometimes, ain't it, Nunky?

DERRICK. Rip would not do it if he knew what he was about. But he can't read—nor write, for the matter of that. But he can make his cross, and I can cajole him.

COCKLES. Look sharp, Nunky. The man that 's looking round for a fool and picks up Rip Van Winkle, will let him drop again very quick.

DERRICK. He is poor; I 'll show him a handful of money. He 's a drunkard; I 'll give him a stomachful of liquor. Go in, boy, and leave me to work this; and let this be a lesson to you hereafter; beware of the fatal effects of poverty and drink.

COCKLES. Yes,—and parting with my money on bad security.

[Exit. Laughter outside.]

DERRICK. Here he comes now, surrounded by all the dogs and children in the district. They cling around him like flies around a lump of sugar.

[RIP enters, running and skipping, carrying one small child pickaback, and surrounded by a swarm of others hanging on the skirts of his coat. He is laughing like a child himself, and his merry blue eyes twinkle with delight. He is dressed in an old deerskin coat, a pair of breeches which had once been red, now tattered, patched, and frayed, leather gaiters and shoes equally dilapidated, a shapeless felt hat with a bit of the brim hanging loose—the whole stained and weather-worn to an almost uniform clay-color, except for the bright blue of his jean shirt and the scarlet of his long wisp of a necktie. One of the boys carries his gun.]

RIP [taking his gun from the boy]. There, run along mit you; run along.

[The children scamper off.]

DERRICK. The vagabond looks like the father of the village.

Rip [*who has stood laughing and watching the children, suddenly calls after them*]. Hey! You let my dog Schneider alone there; you hear that, Sock der Jacob der bist eine for donner spits poo—yah——

Derrick. Why, what 's the matter, Rip?

Rip [*coming down and shaking hands with* Derrick]. Oh, how you was, Derrick? how you was?

Derrick. You seem in trouble.

Rip. Oh, yah; you know them fellers. Vell, I told you such a funny thing. [*Laughing.*] Just now, as me and Schneider was comin' along through the willage— Schneider 's my dawg; I don 't know whether you know him? [Rip *always speaks of Schneider as if he were a person, and one in whom his hearer took as profound an interest as he does himself.*] Well, them fellers went and tied a tin kettle mit Schneider 's tail, and how he did run then, mit the kettle banging about. Well, I did n 't hi' him comin'. He run betwixt me and my legs, an' spilt me an' all them children in the mud;—yah, that 's a fact.

[Rip *leans his gun against the cottage.*]

Derrick [*aside*]. Now 's my time. [*Aloud*]. Vedder! Vedder! [Vedder *appears at the door of the inn.*] Bring us a bottle of liquor. Bring us your best, and be quick.

Nick. What 's in the wind now? The devil 's to pay when Derrick stands treat!

[*Exit. Re-enters, with bottle and cups in left hand. Hands bottle to* Derrick. Rip *lounges forward, and perches on the corner of the table.*]

Derrick [*rising and approaching* Rip]. Come, Rip, what do you say to a glass?

Rip [*takes a cup and holds it to be filled.*] Oh, yah; now what do I generally say to a glass? I say it 's a fine thing— when there 's plenty in it. (Ve gates! Ve gates!) [*Shakes hands with* Nick.] And then I says more to what 's in it than I do to the glass. Now you would n 't believe it—that 's the first one I 've had today.

Derrick. How so?

Rip [*dryly*]. Because I could n 't get it before, I suppose.

DERRICK. Then let me fill him up for you.

RIP. No, that is enough for the first one.

NICK. Come, Rip, a bumper for the first one.

RIP. That is enough for the first one.

DERRICK. Come, Rip, let me fill him up for you.

RIP [*with ludicrous decision and dignity*]. I believe I know how much to drink. When I says a thing, I mean it.

DERRICK. Oh, well——

[*Turns aside, and starts to fill his own cup.*]

RIP. All right; come along. [*Holding out his glass, and laughing at his own inconsistency.*] Here's your good health and your families', and may they live long and prosper!

[*They all drink. At the end, NICK smacks his lips and exclaims "Ah!" DERRICK repeats the same and RIP repeats after DERRICK.*]

RIP [*to NICK, sadly*]. Ah, you may well go "Ah!" and smack your chops over that. You don't give me such schnapps[1] when I come. Derrick, my score is too big now. [*Jerking his head towards the shutter, he notices for the first time that it is open.*] What you go and open that window for?—that's fine schnapps, Nick. Where you got that?

NICK. That's high Dutch, Rip—high Dutch, and ten years in bottle. Why, I had that in the very day of your wedding. We broached the keg under yonder shed. Don't you recollect?

RIP. Is that the same?

NICK. Yes.

RIP. I thought I knowed that licker. You had it ten years ago? [*Laughing suddenly.*] I would not have kept it so long. But stop, mein freund; that's more than ten years ago.

NICK. No, it ain't.

RIP. It's the same day I got married?

NICK. Yes.

RIP. Well, I know by that. You think I forgot the day I

---

1 Whiskey.

got married? Oh, no, my friend; I remember that day long
as I live.

[*Serious for a moment. Takes off his hat, and puts it on
the table.*]

DERRICK. Ah! Rip, I remember Gretchen then, ten years
ago.—Zounds, how I envied you!

RIP [*looking up, surprised*]. Did you? [*Winks at* NICK.
Then, suddenly remembering.] So did I. You did n't know
what was comin', Derrick.

DERRICK. She was a beauty.

RIP. What, Gretchen?—Yes, she was. She was a pretty
girl. My! My! Yah, we was a fine couple altogether.
Well, come along.

[*Holding out his cup to* DERRICK, *who fills it from the
bottle.*]

NICK. Yes, come along.

[*Takes water pitcher from the table, and starts to fill up*
RIP'S *cup.* RIP *stops him.*]

RIP [*who has been lounging against the table, sits on it,
and puts his feet on the chair*]. Stop! I come along mitout
that, Nick Vedder. [*Sententiously.*] Good licker and water
is like man and wife.

DERRICK and NICK. How 's that, Rip?

RIP [*laughing*]. They don't agree together. I always
like my licker single. Well, here 's your good health, and
your families', and may they live long and prosper!

[*They all drink.*]

NICK. That 's right, Rip; drink away, and drown your
sorrow.

RIP [*drolly*]. Yes; but she won't drown. My wife is my
sorrow, and you cannick drown her. She tried it once, but
could n't do it.

DERRICK and NICK. Why, how so?

RIP [*puts down his cup and clasps his knee, still perched
on the corner of the table.*] Did n't you know that Gretchen
like to got drown?

DERRICK and NICK. No.

RIP [*puts hat on*]. That 's the funniest thing of the whole of it. It's the same day I got married; she was comin' across the river there in the ferry-boat to get married mit me——

DERRICK and NICK. Yes.

RIP. Well, the boat she was comin' in got upsetted.

DERRICK and NICK. Ah!

RIP. Well, but she wasn't in it.

DERRICK and NICK. Oh!

RIP [*explaining quite seriously*]. No, that's what I say; if she had been in the boat what got upsetted, maybe she might have got drowned. [*More and more reflective.*] I don't know how it was she got left somehow or other. Women is always behind that way—always.

DERRICK. But surely, Rip, you would have risked your life to save such a glorious creature as she was.

RIP [*incredulously*]. You mean I would yump in and pull Gretchen out?

DERRICK. Yes.

RIP. Oh, would I? [*Suddenly remembering.*] Oh, you mean then—yes, I believe I would then. [*With simple conviction.*] But it would be more my duty now than it was then.

DERRICK. How so?

RIP [*quite seriously*]. Why, you see when a feller gets married a good many years mit his wife, he gets very much attached to her.

NICK [*pompously*]. Ah, he does indeed.

RIP [*winks at DERRICK, and points at NICK with his thumb*]. But if Mrs. Van Winkle was a-drowning in the water now, an' she says to me, "Rip, come an' save your wife!" I would say, "Mrs. Van Winkle, I will just go home and think about it." Oh, no, Derrick, if ever Gretchen tumbles in the water, she's got to swim now, you mind that.

DERRICK. She was here just now, anxiously expecting you home.

RIP. I know she's keeping it hot for me.

NICK. What, your dinner, Rip?

RIP. No, the broomstick.

[*Exit* NICK *into house, laughing.*]

RIP [*confidentially*]. Derrick, whenever I come back from the mountains, I always stick the game-bag in the window and creep in behind.

DERRICK [*seating himself on the table by the side of* RIP]. Have you anything now?

RIP [*dropping into the chair* DERRICK *has just left. Leaning back, and putting hands behind his head*]. What for game? No, not a tail, I believe, not a feather. [*With humorous indifference.*]

DERRICK [*touching* RIP *on the shoulder and shaking a bag of money*]. Rip, suppose you were to hang this bagful of money inside, don't you think it would soothe her down, eh?

RIP [*sitting up*]. For me, is that?

DERRICK. Yes.

RIP [*with a shrewd glance*]. Ain't you yokin' mit me?

DERRICK. No, Rip, I've prospered with the lands you've sold me, and I'll let you have a loan on easy terms. I'll take no interest.

RIP [*getting up and walking forward, with decision*]. No, I'm afraid I might pay you again some day, Derrick.

DERRICK. And so you shall, Rip, pay me when you please. [*Puts the bag in* RIP'S *hands, and forces his fingers over it, turns, and goes to the table, speaking as he goes.*] Say in twenty years—twenty years from this day. Ah, where shall we be then?

RIP [*quizzically, and half to himself*]. I don't know about myself; but I think I can guess where you'll be about that time. [*Takes chair and sits down.*]

DERRICK. Well, Rip, I'll just step into the inn and draw out a little acknowledgment.

RIP [*who has been sitting, leaning forward with his elbows on his knees, softly chinking the bag of money in his hand, looks up suddenly*]. 'Knowledgment—for what is that?

DERRICK. Yes, for you to put your cross to.

RIP [*indifferently*]. All right; bring it along.

DERRICK. No fear of Gretchen now, eh, Rip?

RIP [*plunged in thought*]. Oh, no.

DERRICK. You feel quite comfortable now, don't you, Rip?
[*Exit to inn.*]

RIP. Oh, yah! [*Suddenly becoming serious and much
mystified at* DERRICK'S *conduct.*] Well, I don't know about
that Derrick! Derrick! [*Holding up the bag and chinking
it.*] It don't chink like good money neither. It rattles like
a snake in a hole. [*Grimly.*]

GRETCHEN [*inside the cottage*]. Out with that lazy, idle
cur! I won't have him here. Out, I say!

RIP. I'm glad I'm not in there now. I believe that's
Schneider what she's lickin'; he won't have any backbone
left in him. [*Sadly.*] I would rather she would lick me
than the dog; I'm more used to it than he is. [*Gets up, and
looks in at the window.*] There she is at the wash-tub.
[*Admiring her energy, almost envying it.*] What a hard-
workin' woman that is! Well, somebody must do it, I suppose. [*With the air of a profound moral reflection.*] She's
comin' here now; she's got some broomstick mit her, too.

[RIP *snatches up his gun and slinks off around the corner
of the house.*]

[*Enter* GRETCHEN *with broomstick, followed by* HENDRICK
and MEENIE, *carrying clothes-basket.*]

GRETCHEN. Come along, children. Now, you take the
washing down to Dame Van Sloe's, then call at the butcher's
and tell him that my husband has not got back yet, so I will
have to go down myself to the marsh, and drive up the bull
we have sold to him. Tell him the beast shall be in his stable
in half an hour; so let him have the money ready to pay me
for it. [*During this,* RIP *has crept in and sat on the bench
by the side of the tub behind* GRETCHEN.] Ah, it is the last
head of cattle we have left. Houses, lands, beasts, everything gone—everything except a drunken beast whom nobody would buy or accept as a gift. Rip! Rip! wait until
I get you home! [*Threatening an imaginary* RIP *with
broomstick. With a comical grimace,* RIP *tiptoes back behind the house*]. Come, children, to work, to work! [*Exit.*]

[*Re-enter* RIP, *cautiously.*]

RIP [*laughing to himself*]. She gone to look after the

bull. She better not try the broomstick on him; he won't stand it. [*Drops into the chair, with his back to the audience.*]

HENDRICK. Oh, Meenie, there 's your father.

RIP [*holds out his arms, and* MEENIE *runs into them. Taking her in his arms, and embracing her with great tenderness*]. Ah, little gorl, was you glad to see your father come home?

MEENIE. Oh, yes!

RIP [*holding her close*]. I don't believe it, was you? Come here. [*Getting up and leading her to the chair by the side of the table.*] Let me look at you, I don't see you for such a long time; come here. I don't deserve to have a thing like that belong to me. [*Takes his hat off as if in reverence.*] You 're too good for a drunken, lazy feller like me, that 's a fact. [*Bites his underlip, looks up, and brushes away a tear.*]

MEENIE [*kneeling by him*]. Oh, no, you are a good papa!

RIP. No, I was n't: no good father would go and rob his child; that 's what I 've done. Why, don't you know, Meenie, all the houses and lands in the village was mine—they would all have been yours when you grew up? Where they gone now? I gone drunk 'em up, that 's where they gone. Hendrick, you just take warnin' by that; that 's what licker do; see that? [*Holds up the skirt of coat.*] Brings a man to hunger and rags. Is there any more in that cup over there? Give it to me. [*Drinks.*]

[RIP *makes this confession with a childlike simplicity. The tears come, and he brushes them away once or twice. When he asks for the cup, at the end, it seems but the natural conclusion of his speech.*]

HENDRICK [*hands his cup*]. Don't cry, Rip; Meenie does not want your money, for when I 'm a big man I shall work for her, and she shall have all I get.

MEENIE. Yes, and I 'll have Hendrick too.

RIP [*greatly amused*]. You'll have Hendrick, too. [*With mock gravity.*] Well, is this all settled?

HENDRICK. Yes, Meenie and me have made it all up.

RIP. I did n't know, I only thought you might speak to me about it, but if it 's all settled, Meenie, then git married mit him. [*Laughing silently, and suddenly.*] You goin' to marry my daughter? well, now, that 's very kind of you. Marry one another? [*The children nod.* RIP, *with immense seriousness.*] Well, here 's your good health, and your family, may they live long and prosper. [*To* HENDRICK.] What you goin' to do when you get married, and grow up and so? [*Leans forward.*]

HENDRICK. I 'm not going to stop here with father; oh, no, that won 't do. I 'm going with Uncle Hans in his big ship to the North Pole, to catch whales.

RIP. Goin' to cotch wahales mit the North Pole? That 's a long while away from here.

HENDRICK. Yes, but uncle will give me ten shillings a month, and I will tell him to pay it all to Meenie.

RIP. There! He 's goin' to pay it all to you; that 's a good boy, that 's a good boy.

MEENIE. Yes, and I 'll give it all to you to keep for us.

RIP [*with one of his little explosive laughs*]. I would n't do that, my darlin'; maybe if you give it to me, you don 't get it back again. Hendrick! [*Suddenly earnest.*] You shall marry Meenie when you grow up, but you must n't drink.

HENDRICK [*slapping* RIP *on the knee*]. I 'll never touch a drop.

RIP [*quite seriously*]. You won 't, nor me either; shake hands upon it. Now we swore off together. [*With a change of tone.*] I said so so many times, and never kept my word once, never. [*Drinks.*]

HENDRICK. I 've said so once, and I 'll keep mine.

DERRICK [*outside*]. Well, bring it along with you.

RIP. Here comes Derrick; he don 't like some children; run along mit you.

[*Exit children with basket.*]

[*Enter* DERRICK *from inn with document.*]

DERRICK. There, Rip, is the little acknowledgment. [*Handing it to him.*]

RIP. 'Knowledgment. [*Putting on hat.*] For what is that?

DERRICK. That is to say I loaned you the money.

RIP [*lounging back in his chair*]. I don't want that; I would lose it if I had it. [*Fills his cup from the bottle.*] I don't want it. [*Blandly.*]

DERRICK. Don't you? But I do.

RIP [*with simple surprise*]. For what?

DERRICK. Why, for you to put your cross to. Why, bless me, I 've forgotten my pen and ink. [*Enter* COCKLES.] But luckily here comes my nephew with it. [*Aside.*] And in time to witness the signature.

RIP. Say, Derrick, have you been writing all that paper full in the little time you been in the house there? [*Turns the paper about curiously. Pours out more schnapps.*]

DERRICK. Yes, every word of it.

RIP. Have you? Well, just read it out loud to me. [*With an air of great simplicity.*]

DERRICK [*aside*]. Does he suspect? [*Aloud.*] Why, Rip, this is the first time you ever wanted anything more than the money.

RIP [*clasping his hands behind his head with an air of lordly indifference.*] Yes, I know; but I got nothing to do now. I 'm a little curious about that, somehow.

COCKLES [*aside to* DERRICK]. The fish has taken the ground bait, but he 's curious about the hook.

DERRICK [*aside*]. I dare not read a word of it.

COCKLES [*aside*]. Nunkey 's stuck.

DERRICK. Well, Rip, I suppose you don't want to hear the formalities.

RIP. The what?

DERRICK. The preliminaries.

RIP [*indolently*]. I 'll take it all—Bill, Claws, and Feathers. [*Leans forward and rests his head on his hand, and looks at the ground.*]

DERRICK. "Know all men by these presents, that I, Rip Van Winkle, in consideration of the sum of sixteen pounds received by me from Derrick Von Beekman"—[*Looks around at* COCKLES; *they wink knowingly at each other. Continues as if reading. Watching* RIP.]—"Do promise and undertake to pay the same in twenty years from date." [RIP *looks up; as he does so,* DERRICK *drops his eyes on document, then looks as if he had just finished reading.*] There, now are you satisfied?

RIP [*takes the document. In childlike surprise*]. Well, well, and does it take all that pen and ink to say such a little thing like that?

DERRICK. Why, of course it does.

COCKLES [*aside to* DERRICK]. Oh, the fool! he swallows it whole, hook and all.

RIP [*spreading the paper on the table*]. Where goes my cross, Derrick?

DERRICK [*pointing*]. There, you see I've left a nice little white corner for you.

RIP [*folds up paper in a leisurely manner and puts it in game-bag*]. W-e-l-l, I'll yust think about it. [*Looks up at* DERRICK *innocently.*]

DERRICK. Think about it? Why, what's the matter, Rip, isn't the money correct?

RIP. Oh, yes, I got the money all right. [*Chuckling.*] Oh! you mean about signing it. [*Rising. At a loss for a moment.*] Stop, yesterday was Friday, wasn't it?

DERRICK. So it was.

RIP [*with an air of conviction*]. Well, I never do nothing like that the day after Friday, Derrick.

[RIP *walks away toward his cottage.*]

DERRICK [*aside*]. The idiot! what can that signify? But I must not arouse his suspicions by pressing him. [*Aloud.*] You are right, Rip; sign it when you please; but I say, Rip, now that you're in funds, won't you help your old friend Nick Vedder, who owes me a year's rent?

RIP [*coming back to the table*]. Oh, yah, I will wipe off my schore, and stand treat to the whole willage.

DERRICK. Run, boy, and tell all the neighbors that Rip stands treat.

RIP [*leans on back of chair*]. An', Cockles, tell them we 'll have a dance.

COCKLES. A dance! [*Runs off.*]

DERRICK. And I 'll order the good cheer for you. [*Exit.*]

RIP. So do! so do! [*Cogitating dubiously.*] I don't understand it. [*Re-enter* HENDRICK *with the basket over his head, followed by* MEENIE.] Oh, you 've come back?

HENDRICK. Yes, we 've left the clothes.

RIP. Meenie, you take in the basket. [*Exit* MEENIE *with the basket into the cottage.* HENDRICK *is following.*] Hendrick, come here. [HENDRICK *kneels between* RIP'S *knees.*] So you are going to marry my daughter? [HENDRICK *nods.*] So, so. That 's very kind of yer. [*Abruptly.*] Why you don't been to school today, you go to school some times, don't you?

HENDRICK. Yes, when father can spare me.

RIP. What do you learn mit that school,—pretty much something? [*Laughing at his mistake.*] I mean, everything?

HENDRICK. Yes; reading, writing and arithmetic.

RIP. Reading, and what?

HENDRICK. And writing, and arithmetic.

RIP [*puzzled*]. Writing and what?

HENDRICK. Arithmetic.

RIP [*more puzzled*]. What meticks is that?

HENDRICK. Arithmetic.

RIP [*with profound astonishment and patting* HENDRICK'S *head*]. I don't see how the little mind can stand it all. Can you read?

HENDRICK. Oh, yes!

RIP [*with a serious affectation of incredulity*]. I don't believe it; now, I 'm just goin' to see if you can read. If you can't read, I won't let you marry my daughter. No, sir. [*Very drolly.*] I won't have nobody in my family what can't read. [*Taking out the paper that* DERRICK *has given him.*] Can you read ritmatics like that?

HENDRICK. Yes, that 's writing.

RIP [*nonplussed*]. Oh! I thought it was reading.

HENDRICK. It 's reading and writing, too.

RIP. What, both together. [*Suspiciously looking at the paper.*] Oh, yes; I did n't see that before; go long with it.

HENDRICK [*reads*]. "Know all men by these presents"——

RIP [*pleased, leaning back in his chair*]. Yah! that 's right, what a wonderful thing der readin' is; why you can read it pretty nigh as good as Derrick, yes you do; go long.

HENDRICK. "That I, Rip Van Winkle"——

RIP [*taking off his hat, and holding it with his hands behind his head*]. Yah, that 's right; you read it yust as well as Derrick; go long.

HENDRICK. "In consideration of the sum of sixteen pounds received do hereby sell and convey to Derrick Von Beekman all my estate, houses, lands whatsoever"—— [*Hat drops.*]

RIP [*almost fiercely*]. What are you readin', some ritmatics what ain't down there: where you got that? [*Looking sharply at HENDRICK.*]

HENDRICK [*pointing*]. There. Houses! Lands, whatsoever.

RIP [*looking not at the paper but at HENDRICK very earnestly, as if turning over in his mind whether the boy has read it correctly. Then satisfied of the deception DERRICK has practiced upon him and struck by the humor of the way in which he has discovered it, he laughs exultantly and looks towards the inn-door through which DERRICK disappeared a short time before.*] Yes, so it is. Go long mit the rest. [*He leans forward, and puts his ear close to HENDRICK, so as not to miss a word.*]

HENDRICK. "Whereof he now holds possession by mortgaged deeds, from time to time executed by me."

RIP [*takes paper, and looks towards the inn fiercely exultant*]. You read it better than Derrick, my boy, much better. [*After a moment's pause, recollects himself. Kindly to HENDRICK.*] That will do, run along mit you. [*Exit HENDRICK.*]

RIP. Aha, my friend, Derrick! I guess you got some snakes in the grass. Now keep sober, Rip; I don't touch another drop so long what I live; I swore off now, that 's a fixed fact.

[*Enter* DERRICK, VEDDER, STEIN, *and villagers.*]

DERRICK. Come, Rip, we 'll have a rouse.

RIP [*seriously; half fiercely still*]. Here, Nick Vedder, here is the gelt; wipe off my score, and drink away. I don't join you; I swore off.

NICK. Why, Rip, you 're king of the feast.

RIP [*absently, still intent on* DERRICK]. Am I dat?

OMNES. Swore off? What for?

RIP. I don't touch another drop.

JACOB STEIN [*coming down towards* RIP *with cup*]. Come, Rip, take a glass.

RIP [*turning on him, almost angry*]. Jacob Stein, you hear what I said?

STEIN. Yes.

RIP [*firmly*]. Well, when I said a thing, I mean it. [*Leans back in his chair with his hands behind his head.*]

STEIN. Oh, very well. [*Turns away;* NICK *comes down and holds cup under* RIP'S *nose.* RIP *looks to see if they are watching him. He can resist no longer, and takes the cup.*]

RIP [*laughing*]. Well, I won't count this one. Here 's your good health and your families', may they all live long and prosper.

DERRICK. Here come the fiddlers and the girls.

[*Enter girls.*]

[RIP *walks over and closes the shutter which has held his score, then returns and seats himself on a low stool, and keeps time to the music as the villagers dance. Finally, the rhythm fires his blood. He jumps to his feet, snatches one of the girls away from her partner, and whirls into the dance. After a round or two, he lets go of her, and pirouettes two or three times by himself. Once more he catches her in his arms, and is in the act of embracing her, when he perceives* GRETCHEN *over her shoulder. He drops the girl, who falls*

on her knees at GRETCHEN'S *feet. There is a general laugh
at his discomfiture, in which he joins halfheartedly. As the
curtain descends,* RIP *is seen pointing at the girl as if seeking, like a modern Adam, to put the blame on her.*]

ACT II

SCENE 1. *The dimly lighted kitchen of* RIP'S *cottage.
The door and window are at the back. It is night, and
through the window a furious storm can be seen raging, with
thunder, lightning, and rain. A fire smolders on the hearth,
to the right, and a candle gutters on the table in the center;
a couple of chairs, a low stool, and a little cupboard,
meagrely provided with cups and plates, complete the furniture of the room. Between the door and the window a
clothes-horse, with a few garments hanging on it, forms a
screen. To the left is a small door leading to the other
rooms of the cottage.*

[*As the curtain rises,* MEENIE *is seen sitting by the window, and* GRETCHEN *enters, takes off cloak, and throws a
broomstick on the table.*]

GRETCHEN. Meenie! Has your father come yet?

MEENIE. No, mother.

GRETCHEN. So much the better for him. Never let him
show his face in these doors again—never!

MEENIE. Oh, mother, don't be so hard on him.

GRETCHEN. I'm not hard; how dare you say so.
[MEENIE *approaches her.*] There, child, that father of yours
is enough to spoil the temper of an angel. I went down to
the marsh to drive up the bull. I don't know what Rip has
been doing to the beast; he was howling and tearing about.
I barely escaped with my life. [*A crash outside.*] What
noise is that?

MEENIE. That's only Schneider, father's dog.

GRETCHEN [*picking up broomstick*]. Then I'll Schneider

him. I won't have him here. [*Exit through the door leading to the rest of the cottage.*] Out, you idle, vagabond cur;
out, I say!

MEENIE [*following her to the door, and crying*]. Oh,
don't, don't hurt the poor thing!

[*Re-enter GRETCHEN.*]

GRETCHEN. He jumped out of the window before I could
catch him. He's just like his master. Now, what are you
crying for?

MEENIE. Because my poor father is out in all this rain.
[*A peal of thunder is heard.*] Hark, how it thunders!

GRETCHEN. Serve him right—do him good. Is the supper
ready?

MEENIE. Yes, mother; it is there by the fireside. [*Pointing to the soup-bowl by the fire.*] Shall I lay the table?

GRETCHEN. Yes. [*Again it thunders.*] It's a dreadful
night; I wonder where Rip is?

MEENIE [*bringing the cups and platters from the side-
board, together with a loaf of bread*]. Shall I lay the table
for two, mother, or for three?

GRETCHEN. For two, girl; he gets no supper here to-
night. [*Another peal of thunder.*] Mercy, how the storm
rages; the fool, to stop out in such a down-pour. I hope he's
found shelter. I must look out the old suit I washed and
mended for him last week, and put them by the fire to air.
The idiot, to stop out in such a down-pour! I'll have him
sick on my hands next; that's all I want to complete my
misery. [*She fetches clothes from the horse and hangs
them on the back of the chair in front of the fire.*] He
knows what I am suffering now, and that's what keeps him
out. [*Lightning.*] Mercy, what a flash that was! The
wretch will be starved with the cold! Meenie!

MEENIE. Yes, mother.

GRETCHEN. You may lay the table for three. [*There is
a knock at the outer door.*] There he is now! [*Enter HEN-
DRICK, who shakes rain from his hat.*] Where's Rip? Is he
not at your father's?

HENDRICK. No; I thought he was here.

GRETCHEN. He 's gone back to the mountain. He 's done it on purpose to spite me.

HENDRICK [*going to the fire*]. Shall I run after him, and bring him home? I know the road. We 've often climbed it together.

GRETCHEN. No; I drove Rip from his house, and it 's for me to bring him back again.

MEENIE [*still arranging the supper table*]. But mother— [*She pauses, with embarrassment.*] If he hears your voice behind him, he will only run away the faster.

GRETCHEN. Well, I can't help it; I can't rest under cover, while he is out in the storm. I shall feel better when I 'm outside sharing the storm with him. Sit down, and take your suppers. I 'll take my cloak along with me.

[*Exit.* MEENIE *has seated herself by the window.* HENDRICK *carries stool to the center of the stage, in front of the table.*]

HENDRICK. Meenie! Meenie!

MEENIE. Eh?

[HENDRICK *beckons to her. She runs to him. He stops her suddenly, then puts the stool down with great deliberation, and sits on it, while* MEENIE *kneels beside him.*]

HENDRICK [*in a very solemn tone*]. I hope your father ain't gone to the mountains tonight, Meenie?

MEENIE [*in distress*]. Oh, dear! he will die of the cold there.

HENDRICK [*suddenly*]. Sh! [MEENIE *starts.*] It ain't for that. [*Mysteriously.*] I 've just heard old Clausen, over at father 's, saying, that on this very night, every twenty years, the ghosts——

MEENIE [*catching his wrist*]. The what?

HENDRICK [*in an awed tone*]. The ghosts of Hendrick Hudson, and his pirate crew, visit the Kaatskills above here.

[*The two children look around, frightened.*]

MEENIE. Oh, dear! did he say so?

HENDRICK. Sh! [*Again they look around, frightened.*] Yes; and the spirits have been seen there smoking, drinking, and playing at tenpins.

MEENIE. Oh, how dreadful!

HENDRICK. Sh! [*He goes cautiously to the chimney, and looks up, while* MEENIE *looks under the table; then he returns to the stool, speaking as he comes.*] Yes; and every time that Hendrick Hudson lights his pipe there's a flash of lightning. [*Lightning and* MEENIE *gives a gasp of fear.*] And when he rolls the balls along, there is a peal of thunder. [*Loud rumbles of thunder.* MEENIE *screams and throws herself into* HENDRICK'S *arms.*] Don't be frightened, Meenie; I'm here. [*In a frightened tone, but with a manly effort to be courageous.*]

[*Re-enter* GRETCHEN *with her cloak.*]

GRETCHEN. Here, stop that! [*The children separate quickly.* HENDRICK *looks up at the ceiling and whistles, with an attempt at unconsciousness, and* MEENIE *assumes an innocent and unconcerned expression.*] Now, don't you be filling that child's head with nonsense, but remain quietly here until I return. Hush, what noise is that? There is someone outside the window. [*She steps behind the clothes-horse.* RIP *appears at the window, which he opens, and leans against the frame.*]

RIP. Meenie!

MEENIE and HENDRICK [*trying to make him perceive* GRETCHEN, *by a gesture in her direction*]. Sh!

[RIP *turns, and looks around outside to see what they mean, then, discovering nothing, drops his hat in at the window, and calls again, cautiously.*]

RIP. Meenie!

MEENIE and HENDRICK [*with the same warning gesture*]. Sh!

[GRETCHEN *shakes her fist at the children, who assume an air of innocence.*]

RIP. What's the matter? Meenie, has the wild-cat come home? [RIP *reaches in after his hat.* GRETCHEN *catches him by his hair, and holds his head down.*] Och, my darlin', don't do that, eh!

HENDRICK and MEENIE [*who run towards* GRETCHEN]. Don't, mother! don't, mother! don't!

RIP [*imitating their tone*]. Don't, mother, don't! Don't you hear the children? Let go my head, won't you? [*Getting angry.*]

GRETCHEN. No; not a hair.

RIP [*bantering*]. Hold on to it then, what do I care?

HENDRICK and MEENIE [*catching* GRETCHEN'S *dress*]. Don't, mother! Don't, mother! Don't!

[GRETCHEN *lets go of* RIP, *and turns upon them. They escape, and disappear through the door to the left.*]

RIP [*getting in through the window, and coming forward, apparently drunk, but jolly; and his resentment for the treatment he has just received is half humorous*]. For what you do dat, hey? You must want a bald-headed husband, I reckon!

[GRETCHEN *picks up chair, and bangs it down;* RIP *imitates her with the stool. She sits down angrily, and slaps the table.* RIP *throws down his felt hat with a great show of violence, and it makes no noise, then seats himself on the stool.*]

GRETCHEN. Now, then!

RIP. Now, den; I don't like it den, neider.

[*When* RIP *is drunk, his dialect grows more pronounced.*]

GRETCHEN. Who did you call a wildcat?

RIP [*with a sudden little tipsy laugh, and confused*]. A wildcat—dat 's when I come in at the window?

GRETCHEN. Yes; that 's when you came in the window.

RIP [*rising, and with a tone of finality*]. Yes; that 's the time I said it.

GRETCHEN. Yes; and that 's the time I heard it.

RIP [*with drunken assurance*]. That 's all right; I was afraid you would n't hear it.

GRETCHEN. Now who did you mean by that wildcat?

RIP [*confused*]. Who did I mean? Now, let me see.

GRETCHEN. Yes; who did you mean?

RIP. How do I know who-oo I mean? [*With a sudden inspiration.*] Maybe it 's the dog Schneider, I call that.

GRETCHEN [*incredulously*]. The dog Schneider; that 's not likely.

RIP [*argumentatively*]. Of course it is likely; he 's my dog. I 'll call him a wildcat much as I please. [*Conclusively. He sits down in the chair on which his clothes are warming, in front of the fire.*]

GRETCHEN. And then, there 's your disgraceful conduct this morning. What have you got to say to that?

RIP. How do I know what I got to say to that, when I don't know what I do-a, do-a? [*Hiccoughs.*]

GRETCHEN. Don't know what you do-a-oo! Hugging and kissing the girls before my face; you thought I would n't see you.

RIP [*boldly*]. I knowed you would—I knowed you would; because, because—[*Losing the thread of his discourse.*] Oh-h, don' you bodder me. [*He turns and leans his head against the back of the chair.*]

GRETCHEN. You knew I was there?

RIP [*laughing*]. I thought I saw you.

GRETCHEN. I saw you myself, dancing with the girl.

RIP. You saw the girl dancin' mit me. [GRETCHEN *remembers* RIP's *clothes, and goes over to see if he is wet, and pushes him towards the center of the stage.* RIP *mistakes her intention.*] You want to pull some more hair out of my head?

GRETCHEN. Why, the monster! He is n't wet a bit! He 's as dry as if he 'd been aired!

RIP. Of course I 'm dry. [*Laughing.*] I 'm always dry —always dry.

GRETCHEN [*examines game-bag, and pulls out a flask, which she holds under* RIP's *nose*]. Why, what 's here? Why, it 's a bottle—a bottle!

RIP [*leaning against the table*]. Yes; it 's a bottle. [*Laughs.*] You think I don't know a bottle when I see it?

GRETCHEN. That 's pretty game for your game-bag, ain't it?

RIP [*assuming an innocent air*]. Somebody must have put it there.

GRETCHEN [*putting the flask in her pocket*]. Then, you don't get it again.

RIP [*with a show of anger*]. Now mind if I don't get it again—well—all there is about it—[*Breaking down.*] I don't want it. I have had enough. [*With a droll air of conviction.*]

GRETCHEN. I 'm glad you know when you 've had enough.

RIP [*still leaning against the table*]. That 's the way mit me. I 'm glad I know when I got enough—[*Laughs.*] An' I 'm glad when I 've got enough, too. Give me the bottle; I want to put it in the game-bag.

GRETCHEN. For what?

RIP [*lounging off the table, and coming forward and leaning his arms on* GRETCHEN'S *shoulders*]. So that I can't drink it. Here 's the whole business—[*He slides his hand down to* GRETCHEN'S *pocket and tries to find the bottle while he talks to her.*] Here 's the whole business about it. What is the use of anybody—well—wash the use of anybody, anyhow—well—oh—[*Missing the pocket*]. What you talkin' 'bout? [*Suddenly his hand slips in her pocket, and he begins to pull the bottle out, with great satisfaction.*] Now, now I can tell you all 'bout it.

GRETCHEN [*discovering his tactics, and pushing him away*]. Pshaw!

RIP. If you don't give me the bottle, I just break up everything in the house.

GRETCHEN. If you dare!

RIP. If I dare! Have n't I done it two or three times before? I just throw everything right out of the window.

[RIP *throws the plates and cups on the floor and overturns a chair, and seats himself on the table.* GRETCHEN *picks them up again.*]

GRETCHEN. Don't, Rip; don't do that! Now stop, Rip, stop! [GRETCHEN *bangs down a chair by the table and seats herself.*] Now, then, perhaps you will be kind enough to tell where you 've been for the last two days. Where have you been? Do you hear?

RIP. Where I 've been? Well, it 's not my bottle, anyhow. I borrowed that bottle from another feller. You want to know where I been?

GRETCHEN. Yes; and I will know.

RIP [*good-humoredly*]. Let 's see. Last night I stopped out all night.

GRETCHEN. But why?

RIP. Why? You mean the reason of it?

GRETCHEN. Yes, the reason.

RIP [*inconsequently*]. The reason is why? Don't bother me.

GRETCHEN [*emphasizing each word with a bang on the table*]. Why—did—you—stop—out—all—night?

RIP [*imitating her tone*]. Because—I—want—to—get— up—early—in—the—morning. [*Hiccough.*] Come, don't get so mad mit a feller. Why, I 've been fillin' my game-bag mit game.

[RIP *gets down off the table, and* GRETCHEN *comes towards him and feels his game-bag.*]

GRETCHEN. Your game-bag is full of game, is n't it?

RIP [*taking her hand and holding it away from her pocket*]. That? Why, that would n't hold it. [*Finding his way into* GRETCHEN'S *pocket.*] Now I can tell you all about it. You know last night I stopped out all night——

GRETCHEN. Yes; and let me catch you again. [*He is pulling the bottle out, when* GRETCHEN *catches him, and slaps his hand.*] You paltry thief!

RIP. Oh, you ain't got no confidence in me. Now what do you think was the first thing I saw in the morning? [*Dragging a chair to the front of the stage.*]

GRETCHEN. I don't know. What?

RIP [*seating himself*]. A rabbit.

GRETCHEN [*pleased*]. I like a rabbit. I like it in a stew.

RIP [*looking at her, amused*]. I guess you like everything in a stew—everything what 's a rabbit I mean. Well, there was a rabbit a-feedin' mit the grass,—you know they always come out early in der mornin' and feed mit the grass?

GRETCHEN. Never mind the grass. Go on.

RIP. Don't get so patient; you wait till you get the rabbit. [*Humorously.*] Well, I crawl up——

GRETCHEN. Yes, yes!

RIP [*becoming interested in his own powers of invention*]. An' his little tail was a-stickin' up so—— [*With a gesture of his forefinger.*]

GRETCHEN [*impatiently*]. Never mind his tail. Go on.

RIP [*remonstrating at her interruption*]. The more fatter the rabbit, the more whiter is his tail——

GRETCHEN. Well, well, go on.

RIP [*taking aim*]. Well, I haul up——

GRETCHEN. Yes, yes!

RIP. And his ears was a-stickin' up so—— [*Making the two ears with his two forefingers.*]

GRETCHEN. Never mind his ears. Go on.

RIP. I pull the trigger.

GRETCHEN [*eagerly*]. Bang went the gun and——

RIP [*seriously*]. And the rabbit run away.

GRETCHEN [*angrily*]. And so you shot nothing?

RIP. How will I shot him when he run away? [*He laughs at her disappointment.*] There, don't get so mad mit a feller. Now I 'm going to tell you what I did shot; that 's what I did n't shot. You know that old forty-acre field of ours?

GRETCHEN [*scornfully*]. Ours! Ours, did you say?

RIP [*shamefacedly*]. You know the one I mean well enough. It used to be ours.

GRETCHEN [*regretfully*]. Yes; it used, indeed!

RIP. It ain't ours now, is it?

GRETCHEN [*sighing*]. No, indeed, it is not.

RIP. No? Den I won't bodder about it. Better let somebody bodder about that field what belongs to it. Well, in that field there 's a pond; and what do you think I see in that pond?

GRETCHEN. I don't know. Ducks?

RIP. Ducks! More an' a thousand.

GRETCHEN [*walking to where broomstick is*]. More than a thousand ducks?

RIP. I haul up again——

GRETCHEN [*picking up broomstick*]. Yes, and so will I. And if you miss fire this time—— [*She holds it threateningly over* RIP'S *shoulder.*]

RIP [*looking at it askance out of the corner of his eye, then putting up his hand and pushing it aside*]. You will scare the ducks mit that. Well, I take better aim this time as I did before. I pull the trigger, and—bang!

GRETCHEN. How many down?

RIP [*indifferently*]. One.

GRETCHEN [*indignantly*]. What! only one duck out of a thousand?

RIP. Who said one duck?

GRETCHEN. You did!

RIP [*getting up and leaning on the back of the chair*]. I didn't say anything of the kind.

GRETCHEN. You said "one."

RIP. Ah! *One.* But I shot more as one duck.

GRETCHEN. Did you?

RIP [*crosses over, and sits on the low stool, laughing silently*]. I shot our old bull. [GRETCHEN *flings down the broomstick, and throws herself into the chair at the right of the table, in dumb rage.*] I didn't kill him. I just sting him, you know. Well, then the bull come right after me; and I come right away from him. Oh, Gretchen, how you would laugh if you could see that—[*with a vain appeal to her sense of humor*] the bull was a-comin', and I was a-goin'. Well, he chased me across the field. I tried to climb over the fence so fast what I could,—[*doubles up with his silent laugh*] an' the bull come up an' save me the trouble of that. Well, then, I rolled over on the other side.

GRETCHEN [*with disgust*]. And then you went fast asleep for the rest of the day.

RIP. That's a fact. That's a fact.

GRETCHEN [*bursting into tears and burying her head in her arms on the table*]. O Rip, you'll break my heart! You will.

RIP. Now she's gone crying mit herself! Don't cry, Gretchen, don't cry. My d-a-r-l-i-n', don't cry.

GRETCHEN [*angrily*]. I will cry.

RIP. Cry 'way as much as you like. What do I care? All the better soon as a woman gets cryin'; den all the danger 's over. [RIP *goes to* GRETCHEN, *leans over, and puts his arm around her.*] Gretchen, don't cry; my angel, don't. [*He succeeds in getting his hand into her pocket, and steals the bottle.*] Don't cry, my daarlin'. [*Humorously.*] Gretchen, won't you give me a little drop out of that bottle what you took away from me? [*He sits on the table just behind her, and takes a drink from the bottle.*]

GRETCHEN. Here 's a man drunk, and asking for more.

RIP. I was n't. I swore off. [*Coaxingly.*] You give me a little drop an' I won't count it.

GRETCHEN [*sharply*]. No!

RIP [*drinking again*]. Well, den, here 's your good health, an' your family, and may they live long and prosper! [*Puts bottle in his bag.*]

GRETCHEN. You unfeeling brute. Your wife 's starving. And, Rip, your child 's in rags.

RIP [*holding up his coat, and heaving a sigh of resignation*]. Well, I 'm the same way; you know dat.

GRETCHEN [*sitting up, and looking appealingly at* RIP]. Oh, Rip, if you would only treat me kindly!

RIP [*putting his arms around her*]. Well, den, I will. I 'm going to treat you kind. I 'll treat you kind.

GRETCHEN. Why, it would add ten years to my life.

RIP [*over his shoulder, and after a pause*]. That 's a great inducement; it is, my darlin'. I know I treat you too bad, an' you deserve to be a widow.

GRETCHEN [*getting up, and putting her arms on* RIP'S *shoulder*]. Oh, Rip, if you would only reform!

RIP. Well, den, I will. I won't touch another drop so long as I live.

GRETCHEN. Can I trust you?

RIP. You must n't suspect me.

GRETCHEN [*embracing him*]. There, then, I will trust you. [*She takes the candle and goes to fetch the children.*] Here, Hendrick, Meenie? Children, where are you? [*Exit through door on the left.*]

RIP [*seats himself in the chair to the right of the table, and takes out flask*]. Well, it 's too bad; but it 's all a woman's fault anyway. When a man gets drinkin' and that, they ought to let him alone. So soon as they scold him, he goes off like a sky-rocket.

[*Re-enter* GRETCHEN *and the children.*]

GRETCHEN [*seeing the flask in* RIP'S *hand*]. I thought as much.

RIP [*unconscious of her presence*]. How I did smooth her down! I must drink her good health. Gretchen, here 's your good health. [*About to drink.*]

GRETCHEN [*snatching the bottle, and using it to gesticulate with*]. Oh, you paltry thief!

RIP [*concerned for the schnapps*]. What you doin'? You 'll spill the licker out of the bottle. [*He puts in the cork.*]

GRETCHEN [*examining the flask*]. Why, the monster, he 's emptied the bottle!

RIP. That 's a fac'. That 's a fac'.

GRETCHEN [*throwing down the flask*]. Then that is the last drop you drink under my roof!

RIP. What! What!

[MEENIE *approaches her father on tiptoe, and kneels beside him.*]

GRETCHEN. Out, you drunkard! Out, you sot! You disgrace to your wife and to your child! This house is mine.

RIP [*dazed and a little sobered*]. Yours! Yours!

GRETCHEN [*raising her voice above the storm, which seems to rage more fiercely outside*]. Yes, mine, mine! Had it been yours to sell, it would have gone along with the rest of your land. Out then, I say—[*pushing open the door*] for you have no longer any share in me or mine.

[*A peal of thunder.*]

MEENIE [*running over, and kneeling by* GRETCHEN]. Oh, mother, hark at the storm!

GRETCHEN [*pushing her aside*]. Begone, man, can't you speak? Are you struck dumb? You sleep no more under my roof.

RIP [*who has not moved, even his arm remaining out-stretched, as it was when* MEENIE *slipped from his side, murmurs in a bewildered, incredulous way*]. Why, Gretchen, are you goin' to turn me out like a dog? [GRETCHEN *points to the door.* RIP *rises and leans against the table with a groan. His conscience speaks*]. Well, maybe you are right. [*His voice breaks, and with a despairing gesture.*] I have got no home. I will go. But mind, Gretchen, after what you say to me to-night, I can never darken your door again—never—[*Going towards the door.*] I will go.

HENDRICK [*running up to* RIP]. Not into the storm, Rip. Hark, how it thunders!

RIP [*putting his arm around him*]. Yah, my boy; but not as bad to me as the storm in my home. I will go. [*At the door by this time.*]

MEENIE [*catching* RIP'S *coat*]. No, father, don't go!

RIP [*bending over her tenderly, and holding her close to him*]. My child! Bless you, my child, bless you!

[MEENIE *faints.* RIP *gives a sobbing sigh.*]

GRETCHEN [*relenting*]. No, Rip—I——

RIP [*waving her off*]. No, you have drive me from your house. You have opened the door for me to go. You may never open it for me to come back. [*Leaning against the doorpost, overcome by his emotion. His eyes rest on* MEENIE, *who lies at his feet.*] You say I have no share in this house. [*Points to* MEENIE *in profound despair.*] Well, see, then, I wipe the disgrace from your door. [*He staggers out into the storm.*]

GRETCHEN. No, Rip! Husband, come back!

[GRETCHEN *faints, and the curtain falls.*]

ACT III

SCENE 1. *A steep and rocky clove in the Kaatskill Mountains, down which rushes a torrent, swollen by the storm. Overhead, the hemlocks stretch their melancholy boughs. It is night.*

[RIP *enters, almost at a run, with his head down, and his coat-collar turned up, beating his way against the storm. With the hunter's instinct, he protects the priming of his gun with the skirt of his jacket. Having reached a comparatively level spot, he pauses for breath, and turns to see what has become of his dog.*] '

RIP [*whistling to the dog*]. Schneider! Schneider! What 's the matter with Schneider? Something must have scared that dog. There he goes head over heels down the hill. Well, here I am again—another night in the mountains! Heigho! these old trees begin to know me, I reckon. [*Taking off his hat.*] How are you, old fellows? Well, I like the trees, they keep me from the wind and the rain, and they never blow me up; and when I lay me down on the broad of my back, they seem to bow their heads to me, an' say: Go to sleep, Rip, go to sleep. [*Lightning.*] My, what a flash that was! Old Hendrick Hudson 's lighting his pipe in the mountains tonight; now, we 'll hear him roll the big balls along. [*Thunder.* RIP *looks back over the path he has come and whistles again for his dog.*] Well, I—no— Schneider! No; whatever it is, it 's on two legs. Why, what a funny thing is that a comin' up the hill? I thought nobody but me ever come nigh this place.

[*Enter a strange dwarfish figure, clad all in gray like a Dutch seaman of the seventeenth century, in short-skirted doublet, hose, and high-crowned hat drawn over his eyes. From beneath the latter his long gray beard streams down till it almost touches the ground. He carries a keg on his shoulder. He advances slowly towards* RIP, *and, by his gesture, begs* RIP *to set the keg down for him.* RIP *does so, and the dwarf seats himself upon it.*]

RIP [*with good-humored sarcasm*]. Sit down, and make yourself comfortable. [*A long pause and silence.*] What? What 's the matter? Ain't ye goin' to speak to a feller? I don't want to speak to you, then. Who you think you was, that I want to speak to you, any more than you want to speak to me; you hear what I say? (RIP *pokes the dwarf in the ribs, who turns, and looks up.* RIP *retreats hastily.*] Donner an' Blitzen! What for a man is das? I have been walking over these mountains ever since I was a boy, an' I never saw a queer looking codger like that before. He must be an old sea-snake, I reckon.

[*The dwarf approaches* RIP, *and motions* RIP *to help him up the mountain with the keg.*]

RIP. Well, why don't you say so, den? You mean you would like me to help you up with that keg? [*The dwarf nods in the affirmative.*] Well, sir, I don't do it. [*The dwarf holds up his hands in supplication.*] No, there 's no good you speakin' like that. I never seed you before, did I? [*The dwarf shakes his head,* RIP, *with great decision, walking away, and leaning against a tree.*] I don't want to see you again, needer. What have you got in that keg, schnapps? [*The dwarf nods.*] I don't believe you. [*The dwarf nods more affirmatively.*] Is it good schnapps? [*The dwarf again insists.*] Well, I 'll help you. Go 'long; pick up my gun, there, and I follow you mit that keg on my shoulder. I 'll follow you, old broadchops.

[*As* RIP *shoulders the keg, a furious blast whirls up the valley, and seems to carry him and his demon companion before it. The rain that follows blots out the landscape. For a few moments, all is darkness. Gradually, the topmost peak of the Kaatskill Mountains becomes visible, far above the storm. Stretching below, the country lies spread out like a map. A feeble and watery moonlight shows us a weird group, gathered upon the peak,—Hendrick Hudson, and his ghostly crew. In the foreground, one of them poises a ball, about to bowl it, while the others lean forward in attitudes of watchful expectancy. Silently he pitches it; and, after a momentary pause, a long and rumbling peal of thunder reverberates among the valleys below. At this moment, the demon, carrying* RIP'S *gun, appears over the crest of the peak in the background, and* RIP *toils after with the keg on his shoulder. Arrived at the summit, he drops the keg on his knee, and gasps for breath.*]

RIP [*glancing out over the landscape.*] I say, old gentleman, I never was so high up in the mountains before. Look

down into the valley there; it seems more as a mile. I—
[*Turning to speak to his companion, and perceiving another
of the crew.*] You 're another feller! [*The second demon
nods assent.*] You 're that other chap's brother? [*The
demon again assents.* RIP *carries the keg a little further,
and comes face to face with a third.*] You 're another
brother? [*The third demon nods assent.* RIP *takes another
step, and. perceives* HENDRICK HUDSON *in the center, surrounded by many demons.*] You 're his old gran'father?
[HUDSON *nods.* RIP *puts down the keg in perplexity, not
untinged with alarm.*] Donner and Blitzen! here 's the
whole family; I 'm a dead man to a certainty.

[*The demons extend their arms to* HUDSON, *as if inquiring
what they should do. He points to* RIP, *they do the same.*]

RIP. My, my, I suppose they 're speakin' about me!
[*Looking at his gun, which the first demon has deposited on
the ground, and which lies within his reach.*] No good
shootin' at 'em; family 's too big for one gun.

[HENDRICK HUDSON *advances, and seats himself on the keg
facing* RIP. *The demons slowly surround the two.*]

RIP [*looking about him with growing apprehension.*] My,
my, I don't like that kind of people at all! No, sir! I don't
like any sech kind. I like that old gran'father worse than
any of them. [*With a sheepish attempt to be genial, and appear at his ease.*] How you was, old gentleman? I did n't
mean to intrude on you, did I? [HUDSON *shakes his head.*]
What? [*No reply.*] I 'll tell you how it was; I met one of
your gran'children, I don't know which is the one— [*Glancing around.*] They 're all so much alike. Well— [*Embarrassed and looking at one demon.*] That 's the same kind
of a one. Any way, this one, he axed me to help him up the
mountain mit dat keg. Well, he was an old feller, an' I
thought I would help him. [*Pauses, troubled by their
silence.*] Was I right to help him? [HUDSON *nods.*] I
say, was I right to help him? [HUDSON *nods again.*] If he
was here, he would just tell you the same thing any way,
because— [*Suddenly perceiving the demon he had met below.*] Why, dat 's the one, ain't it? [*The demon nods.*]

Yes; dat is the one, dat 's the same kind of a one dat I met. Was I right to come? [HUDSON *nods approval.*] I did n't want to come here, anyhow; no, sir, I did n't want to come to any such kind of a place. [*After a pause, seeing that no one has anything to say.*] I guess I better go away from it. [RIP *picks up his gun, and is about to return by the way he came; but the demons raise their hands threateningly, and stop him. He puts his gun down again.*] I did n't want to come here, anyhow— [*Grumbling to himself, then pulling himself together with an effort, and facing* HUDSON.] Well, old gentleman, if you mean to do me any harm, just speak it right out— [*Then with a little laugh.*] Oh! I will die game— [*Glancing around for a means of escape, and half to himself.*] If I can't run away.

[HUDSON *extends a cup to* RIP, *as if inviting him to drink.*] RIP [*doubtfully*]. You want me to drink mit you? [HUDSON *nods.* RIP *approaches him cautiously, unable to resist the temptation of a drink.*] Well, I swore off drinkin'; but as this is the first time I see you, I won't count this one— [*He takes the cup.* HUDSON *holds up another cup.* RIP *is reassured, and his old geniality returns.*] You drink mit me? We drink mit one another? [HUDSON *nods affirmatively.* RIP *feels at home under these familiar circumstances, and becomes familiar and colloquial again.*] What 's the matter mit you, old gentleman, anyhow? You go and make so [*imitating the demon*] mit your head every time; was you deaf? [HUDSON *shakes his head.*] Oh, nein. [*Laughing at his error.*] If you was deaf, you would n't hear what I was sayin'. Was you dumb? [HUDSON *nods yes.*] So? You was dumb? [HUDSON *nods again.*] Has all of your family the same complaint? [HUDSON *nods.*] All the boys dumb, hey? All the boys dumb. [*All the demons nod. Then, suddenly, as if struck with an idea.*] Have you got any girls? [HUDSON *shakes his head.*] Don't you? Such a big family, and all boys? [HUDSON *nods.*]

RIP [*with profound regret*]. That 's a pity; my, that 's a pity. Oh, my, if you had some dumb girls, what wives they would make— [*Brightening up.*] Well, old gentleman, here 's your good health, and all your family—[*turning, and waving to them*]—may they live long and prosper.

[RIP *drinks. As he does so, all the demons lean forward, watching the effect of the liquor.* RIP *puts his hand to his head. The empty cup falls to the ground.*]

RIP [*in an awed and ecstatic voice*]. What for licker is that! [*As he turns, half reeling, he sees* HUDSON *holding out to him another cup. He snatches it with almost frantic eagerness.*] Give me another one! [*He empties it at a draught. A long pause follows during which the effect of the liquor upon* RIP *becomes apparent; the light in his eyes fades, his exhilaration dies out, and he loses his grasp on the reality of his surroundings. Finally, he clasps his head with both hands, and cries in a muffled, terrified voice.*] Oh, my, my head was so light, and now, it 's heavy as lead! [*He reels, and falls heavily to the ground. A long pause. The demons begin to disappear.* RIP *becomes dimly conscious of this, and raises himself on his elbow.*] Are you goin' to leave me, boys? Are you goin' to leave me all alone? Don't leave me; don't go away. [*With a last effort.*] I will drink your good health, and your family's—— [*He falls back heavily, asleep.*]

CURTAIN

ACT IV

SCENE 1. *As the curtain rises, the same high peaks of the Kaatskills, and the far-stretching valley below, are disclosed in the gray light of dawn.*

RIP *is still lying on the ground, as in the last act, but he is no longer the* RIP *we knew. His hair and beard are long and white, bleached by the storms that have rolled over his head during the twenty years he has been asleep.*

As he stirs and slowly rises to a half-sitting posture, we see that his former picturesque rags have become so dilapidated that it is a matter of marvel how they hold together. They have lost all traces of color, and have assumed the neutral tints of the moss and lichens that cover the rocks.

*His voice, when he first speaks, betrays even more distinctly
than his appearance the lapse of time. Instead of the full
round tones of manhood, he speaks in the high treble of
feeble old age. His very hands have grown old and weather-
beaten.*

RIP [*staring vacantly around*]. I wonder where I was.
On top of the Kaatskill Mountains as sure as a gun! Won't
my wife give it to me for stopping out all night? I must get
up and get home with myself. [*Trying to rise*]. Oh, I feel
very bad! Vat is the matter with my elbow? [*In trying to
rub it, the other one gives him such a twinge that he cries
out.*] Oh! the other elbow is more badder than the other
one. I must have cotched the rheumatix a-sleepin' mit the
wet grass. [*He rises with great difficulty.*] Och! I never
had such rheumatix like that. [*He feels himself all over,
and then stands for a moment pondering, and bewildered by
a strange memory.*] I wasn't sleeping all the time, needer.
I know I met a queer kind of a man, and we got drinkin' and
I guess I got pretty drunk. Well, I must pick up my gun,
and get home mit myself. [*After several painful attempts,
he succeeds in picking up his gun, which drops all to pieces
as he lifts it. RIP looks at it in amazement.*] My gun must
have cotched the rheumatix too. Now, that's too bad.
Them fellows have gone and stole my good gun, and leave me
this rusty old barrel. [*RIP begins slowly to climb over the
peak towards the path by which he had ascended, his memory
seeming to act automatically. When he reaches the highest
point, where he can look out over the valley, he stops in surprise.*] Why, is that the village of Falling Waters that I
see? Why, the place is more than twice the size it was last
night. I— [*He sinks down.*] I don't know whether I am
dreaming, or sleeping, or waking. [*Then pulling himself
together with a great effort, and calling up the image of his
wife to act as whip and spur to his waning powers, he says,
with humorous conviction, as he gets up painfully, again:—*]
I go home to my wife. She'll let me know whether I'm
asleep or awake or not. [*Almost unable to proceed.*] I

don't know if I will ever get home, my k-nees are so stiff. My backbone, it's broke already.

[*As the curtain falls,* RIP *stands leaning on the barrel of his gun as on a staff, with one hand raised, looking out over the valley.*]

SCENE 2. *A comfortable-looking room in* DERRICK'S *house. As the curtain rises,* MEENIE *and* GRETCHEN *enter.* MEENIE *is a tall young woman of twenty-six, and* GRETCHEN *is a matronly figure with white hair. They are well dressed, and have every appearance of physical and material prosperity.*

GRETCHEN. I am sent to you by your father, Meenie.

MEENIE. Oh, don't call him so; he is not my father! He is your husband, mother; but I owe him no love. And his cruel treatment of you——

GRETCHEN. Hush, child! Oh, if he heard you, he would make me pay for every disrespectful word you utter.

MEENIE. Yes; he would beat you, starve and degrade you. You are not his wife, mother, but his menial.

GRETCHEN. My spirit is broken, Meenie. I cannot resent it. Nay, I deserve it; for as Derrick now treats me, so I treated your poor father when he was alive.

MEENIE. You, mother? You, so gentle? You, who are weakness and patience itself?

GRETCHEN. Yes; because for fifteen years I have been Derrick's wife. But it was my temper, my cruelty, that drove your father from our home twenty years ago. You were too young then to remember him.

MEENIE. No, mother, I recollect dear father taking me on his knee, and saying to Hendrick that I should be his wife; and I promised I would.

GRETCHEN. Poor Rip! Poor, good-natured, kind creature that he was! How gently he bore with me; and I drove him like a dog from his home. I hunted him into the mountains, where he perished of hunger or cold, or a prey to some wild beast.

MEENIE. Don't cry, mother!

[*Enter* DERRICK, *now grown old and bent over his cane, and infinitely more disagreeable than before. He, too, has thriven, and is dressed in a handsome full suit of black silk.*]

DERRICK. Sniveling again, eh? Teaching that girl of yours to be an obstinate hypocrite?

MEENIE. Oh, sir, she——

DERRICK. Hold your tongue, Miss. Speak when you 're spoken to. I 'll have you both to understand that there 's but one master here. Well, mistress, have you told her my wishes; and is she prepared to obey them?

GRETCHEN. Indeed, sir, I was trying to——

DERRICK. Beating about the bush, prevaricating, and sneaking, as you usually do.

MEENIE. If you have made her your slave, you must expect her to cringe.

DERRICK [*approaching her threateningly*]. What 's that?

GRETCHEN. Meenie! Meenie! For Heaven's sake, do not anger him!

DERRICK [*raising his cane*]. She had better not.

MEENIE [*defiantly*]. Take care how you raise your hand to me, for I 'll keep a strict account of it. And when Hendrick comes back from sea, he 'll make you smart for it, I promise you.

DERRICK. Is the girl mad?

MEENIE. He thrashed your nephew once for being insolent to me. Go and ask him how Hendrick pays my debts; and then when you speak to me you 'll mind your stops.

DERRICK [*To* GRETCHEN]. Oh, you shall pay for this!

GRETCHEN. No, Derrick, indeed, indeed I have not urged her to this! O, Meenie, do not speak so to him; for my sake forbear!

MEENIE. For your sake, yes, dear mother. I forgot that he could revenge himself on you.

DERRICK. As for your sailor lover, Hendrick Vedder, I 've got news of him at last. His ship, the *Mayflower*, was lost three years ago, off Cape Horn.

MEENIE. No, no. Not lost?

DERRICK. If you doubt it, there 's the *Shipping Gazette*,

in on my office table. You can satisfy yourself that your sailor bully has gone to the bottom.

GRETCHEN. Oh, sir, do not convey the news to her so cruelly.

DERRICK. That 's it. Because I don't sneak and trick and lie about it, I 'm cruel. The man 's dead, has been dead and gone these two years or more. The time of mourning is over. Am I going to be nice about it this time of day?

MEENIE. Then all my hope is gone, gone forever!

DERRICK. So much the better for you. Hendrick's whole fortune was invested in that ship. So there 's an end of him and your expectations. Now you are free, and a beggar. My nephew has a fancy for you. He will have a share of my business now, and my money when—when I die.

GRETCHEN. Do not ask her to decide now!

DERRICK. Why not? If she expects to make a better bargain by holding off, she 's mistaken.

GRETCHEN. How can you expect her to think of a husband at this moment?

DERRICK. Don't I tell you the other one is dead these two years?

GRETCHEN [leading MEENIE away]. Come, my child. Leave her to me, sir; I will try and persuade her.

DERRICK. Take care that you do; for if she don't consent to accept my offer, she shall pack bag and baggage out of this house. Aye, this very day! Not a penny, not a stitch of clothes but what she has on her back, shall she have! Oh, I 've had to deal with obstinate women before now, and I 've taken them down before I 've done with them. You know who I mean? Do you know who I mean? Stop. *Answer me! Do you know who I mean?*

GRETCHEN [submissively]. Yes, sir.

DERRICK. Then why did n't you say so before? Sulky, I suppose. There, you may be off [Exeunt.]

SCENE 3. *The village of Falling Waters, which has grown to be a smart and flourishing town, but whose chief features remain unchanged.*

To the left, as of yore, is the inn, bearing scarcely any mark of the lapse of time, save that the sign of George III has been replaced by a portrait of George Washington. To the right, where RIP'S *cottage used to stand, nothing remains, however, but the blackened and crumbling ruins of a chimney. A table and chairs stand in front of the inn porch.*

Into this familiar scene RIP *makes his entrance, but not as before,—in glee, with children clinging about him. Faint, weak, and weary, he stumbles along, followed by a jeering, hooting mob of villagers; while the children hide from him in fear, behind their elders. His eyes look dazed and uncomprehending, and he catches at the back of a chair as if in need of physical as well as mental support.*

KATCHEN [*as* RIP *enters*]. Why, what queer looking creature is this, that all the boys are playing——

SETH. Why, he looks as though he's been dead for fifty years, and dug up again!

RIP. My friends, *Kanst du Deutsch sprechen?*

FIRST VILLAGER. I say, old fellow, you ain't seen anything of an old butter-tub with no kiver [1] on, no place about here, have you?

RIP [*bewildered, but with simplicity*]. What is that? I don't know who that is.

SECOND VILLAGER. I say, old man, who's your barber?

[*The crowd laughs, and goes off repeating, "Who's your barber?" Some of the children remain to stare at* RIP; *but when he holds out his hand to them, they, too, run off frightened.*]

RIP. Who's my barber; what dey mean by dat? [*Noticing his beard.*] Why is that on me? I didn't see that before. My beard and hair is so long and white. Gretchen won't know me with that, when she gets me home. [*Looking towards the cottage.*] Why, the home's gone away!

[RIP *becomes more and more puzzled like a man in a dream who sees unfamiliar things amid familiar surroundings, and cannot make out what has happened; and as in a*

1 Cover.

dream a man preserves his individuality, so RIP *stumbles along through his bewilderment, exhibiting flashes of his old humor, wit, and native shrewdness. But with all this he never laughs.*]

SETH. I say, old man, had n't you better go home and get shaved?

RIP [*looking about for the voice*]. What?

SETH. Here, this way. Had n't you better go home and get shaved?

·RIP. My wife will shave me when she gets me home. Is this the village of "Falling Waters" where we was?

SETH. Yes.

RIP [*still more puzzled, not knowing his face*]. Do you live here?

SETH. Well, rather. I was born here.

RIP [*reflectively*]. Then you live here?

SETH. Well, rather; of course I do.

RIP [*feeling that he has hold of something certain*]. Do you know where I live?

SETH. No; but I should say you belong to Noah's Ark.

RIP [*putting his hand to his ear*]. That I belong mit vas?

SETH. Noah's Ark.

RIP [*very much hurt*]. Why will you say such thing like that? [*Then, with a flash of humor, and drawing his beard slowly through his fingers.*] Well, look like it, don't I? [*Beginning all over again to feel for his clue.*] My friend, did you never hear of a man in this place whose name was Rip Van Winkle?

SETH. Rip Van Winkle, the laziest, drunken vagabond in the country?

RIP [*somewhat taken aback by this description, but obliged to concur in it*]. Yah, that is the one; there is no mistaking him, eh?

SETH. I know all about him.

RIP [*hopefully*]. Do you?

SETH. Yes.

RIP [*quite eagerly*]. Well, if you know all about him; well, what has become of him?

SETH. What has become of him? Why, bless your soul, he's been dead these twenty years!

RIP [*looking at* SETH]. Then I am dead, I suppose. So Rip Van Winkle was dead, eh?

SETH. Yes; and buried.

RIP [*humorously*]. I'm sorry for that; for he was a good fellow, so he was.

SETH [*aside*]. There appears to be something queer about this old chap; I wonder who he is. [*Rising and taking chair over to* RIP.] There, old gentleman, be seated.

RIP [*seating himself with great difficulty, assisted by* SETH]. Oh, thank you; every time I move a new way, I get another pain. My friend, where is the house what you live in?

SETH [*pointing at inn*]. There.

RIP. Did you live there yesterday?

SETH. Well, rather.

RIP. No, it is Nick Vedder what live in that house. Where is Nick Vedder?

SETH. Does he? Then I wish he'd pay the rent for it. Why, Nick Vedder has been dead these fifteen years.

RIP. Did you know Jacob Stein, what was with him?

SETH. No; but I've heard of him. He was one of the same sort as Rip and Nick.

RIP. Yes, them fellows was all pretty much alike.

SETH. Well, he went off the hooks a short time after Rip.

RIP. Where has he gone?

SETH. Off the hooks.

RIP. What is that, when they go off the hooks?

SETH. Why, he died.

RIP [*with an air of hopelessness*]. Is there anybody alive here at all? [*Then, with a sudden revulsion of feeling, convinced of the impossibility of what he hears.*] That man is drunk what talks to me.

SETH. Ah, they were a jolly set, I reckon.

RIP. Oh, they was. I knowed them all.

SETH. Did you?

RIP. Yes, I know Jacob Stein, and Nick Vedder, and Rip Van Winkle, and the whole of them. [*A new idea strikes him, and he beckons to* SETH, *whom he asks, very earnestly.*] Oh, my friend, come and see here. Did you know Schneider?

SETH. Schneider! Schneider! No, I never heard of him.

RIP [*simply*]. He was a dog. I thought you might know him. Well, if dat is so, what has become of my child Meenie, and my wife Gretchen? Are they gone, too? [*Turning to look at the ruins of the house.*] Yah, even the house is dead.

SETH. Poor, old chap! He seems quite cast down at the loss of his friends. I 'll step in and get a drop of something to cheer him up. [*Exit.*]

RIP [*puzzling it out with himself*]. I can't make it out how it all was; because if this here is me, what is here now, and Rip Van Winkle is dead, then who am I? That is what I would like to know. Yesterday, everybody was here; and now they was all gone. [*Very forlorn.*]

[*Re-enter* SETH, *followed by the villagers.*]

SETH [*offering* RIP *the cup*]. There, old gent, there 's a drop of something to cheer you up.

RIP [*shaking hands with* SETH *and* KATCHEN]. Oh, thank you. I—I—I swore off; but this is the first time what I see you. I won't count this one. [*His voice breaks.*] My friend, you have been very kind to me. Here is your good health, and your family's, and may they all live long and prosper!

SETH. I say, wife, ain't he a curiosity fit for a show?

RIP [*aside*]. That gives me courage to ask these people anodder question. [*He begins with difficulty.*] My friend, I don't know whether you knowed it or not, but there was a child of Rip,—Meenie her name was.

SETH. Oh, yes; that 's all right.

RIP [*with great emotion, leaning forward*]. She is not gone? She is not dead? No, no!

SETH. No; she is alive.

Rip [*sinking back with relief*]. Meenie is alive. It 's all right now,—all right now.

Seth. She 's the prettiest girl in the village.

Rip. I know dat.

Seth. But if she wastes her time waiting on Hendrick Vedder, she 'll be a middle-aged woman before long.

Rip [*incredulously*]. She 's a little child, only six years old.

Seth. Six-and-twenty, you mean.

Rip [*thinking they are making fun of him*]. She 's a little child no bigger than that. Don't bodder me; I don't like that.

Seth. Why, she 's as big as her mother.

Rip [*very much surprised that* Seth *knows* Gretchen]. What, Gretchen?

Seth. Yes, Gretchen.

Rip. Is n't Gretchen dead?

Seth. No. She 's alive.

Rip [*with mixed emotions*]. Gretchen is alive, eh! Gretchen 's alive!

Seth. Yes; and married again.

Rip [*fiercely*]. How would she do such a thing like that?

Seth. Why, easy enough. After Rip died, she was a widow, was n't she?

Rip. Oh, yes. I forgot about Rip's being dead. Well, and then?

Seth. Well, then Derrick made love to her.

Rip [*surprised, and almost amazed*]. What for Derrick? Not Derrick Von Beekman?

Seth. Yes, Derrick Von Beekman.

Rip [*still more interested*]. Well, and then?

Seth. Well, then her affairs went bad; and at last she married him.

Rip [*turning it over in his mind*]. Has Derrick married Gretchen?

Seth. Yes.

Rip [*with a flash of his old humor, but still with no*

laughter]. Well, I did n't think he would come to any good;
I never did. So she cotched Derrick, eh? Poor Derrick!
SETH. Yes.

RIP. Well, here 's their good health, and their family's,
and may they all live long and prosper! [*Drinks.*]

SETH. Now, old gent, had n't you better be going home,
wherever that is?

RIP [*with conviction*]. Where my home was? Here 's
where it is.

SETH. What, here in this village? Now do you think
we 're going to keep all the half-witted strays that choose
to come along here? No; be off with you. Why, it 's a
shame that those you belong to should allow such an old
tramp as you to float around here.

VILLAGERS [*roughly, and trying to push him along*]. Yes;
away with him!

RIP [*frightened, and pleading with them*]. Are you going to drive me away into the hills again?

FIRST VILLAGER. Yes; away with him! He 's an old
tramp.

[*Enter* HENDRICK, *with stick and bundle, followed by
some of the women of the village.*]

VILLAGERS. Away with him!

HENDRICK [*throwing down bundle*]. Avast there, mates.
Where are you towing that old hulk to? What, you won't?
[*Pushing crowd aside, and going forward.*] Where are you
towing that old hulk to?

SETH. Who are you?

HENDRICK. I 'm a man, every inch of me; and if you
doubt it, I 'll undertake to remove the suspicions from any
two of you in five minutes. Ain't you ashamed of yourselves? Don't you see the poor old creature has but half
his wits?

SETH. Well, this is no asylum for worn out idiots.

VILLAGERS [*coming forward*]. No, it ain't!

HENDRICK. Ain't it?

OMNES. No, it ain't.

HENDRICK. Then I 'll make it a hospital for broken heads if you stand there much longer. Clear the decks, you lubberly swabs! [*Drives them aside. Turns to* RIP, *who stands bewildered.*] What is the cause of all this?

RIP [*helplessly*]. I don't know, do you?

HENDRICK [*to villagers*]. Do any of you know him?

FIRST VILLAGER. No; he appears to be a stranger.

HENDRICK [*to* RIP]. You seem bewildered. Can I help you?

RIP [*feebly*]. Just tell me where I live.

HENDRICK. And don't you know?

RIP. No; I don't.

HENDRICK. Why, what 's your name?

RIP [*almost childishly*]. I don't know; but I believe I know vat it used to be. My name, it used to be Rip Van Winkle.

VILLAGERS [*in astonishment*]. Rip Van Winkle?

HENDRICK. Rip Van Winkle? Impossible!

RIP [*pathetically feeble, and old*]. Well, I would n't swear to it myself. I tell you how it was: Last night, I don't know about the time, I went away up into the mountains, and while I was there I met a queer kind o' man, and we got drinkin'; and I guess I got pretty drunk. And then I went to sleep; and when I woke up this morning, I was dead. [*All laugh.*]

HENDRICK. Poor old fellow; he 's crazy. Rip Van Winkle has been dead these twenty years. I knew him when I was a child.

RIP [*clutching at a faint hope*]. You don't know me?

HENDRICK. No; nor anybody else here, it seems.

[*The villagers, finding that there is to be no amusement for them, straggle off to their occupations.*]

SETH [*as he goes into the inn*]. Why, wife, he 's as cracked as our old teapot.

RIP [*with simple pathos*]. Are we so soon forgot when we are gone? No one remembers Rip Van Winkle.

HENDRICK. Come, cheer up, my old hearty, and you shall

share my breakfast. [*Assists* RIP *to sit at the table.* RIP *has fallen into a dream again. To* KATCHEN.] Bring us enough for three, and of your best.

KATCHEN. That I will. [*Exit into inn.*]

HENDRICK. So here I am, home again. And yonder 's the very spot where, five years ago, I parted from Meenie.

RIP [*roused by the name*]. What, Meenie Van Winkle?

HENDRICK. And she promised to .remain true to Hendrick Vedder.

RIP. Oh, yah; that was Nick Vedder's son.

HENDRICK [*turning to* RIP]. That 's me.

RIP [*resentfully*]. That was you! You think I 'm a fool? He 's a little child, no bigger than that,—the one I mean.

HENDRICK. How mad he is! [*Enter* KATCHEN *from inn with tray, on which is laid a breakfast. She puts it on table, and exit into inn.*] There, that 's right. Stow your old locker full while I take a cruise around yonder house, where, five years ago, I left the dearest bit of human nature that was ever put together. I 'll be back directly. Who comes here? It 's surely Derrick and his wife. Egad, I 'm in luck; for now the old birds are out, Meenie will surely be alone. I 'll take advantage of the coast being clear, and steer into harbor alongside. [*Exit.*]

[*Enter* DERRICK, *followed by* GRETCHEN.]

DERRICK. So you have come to that conclusion, have you?

GRETCHEN. I cannot accept this sacrifice.

RIP [*starting from his reverie, and turning to look at her*]. Why, that is Gretchen's voice. [*As he recognizes her, and sees how aged she is.*] My, my! Is that my wife?

DERRICK. Oh, you can't accept! Won't you kindly allow me a word on the subject?

RIP [*aside, humorously*]. No, indeed, she will not. Now, my friend, you are going to cotch it.

GRETCHEN. There is a limit even to my patience. Don't drive me to it.

RIP [*aside, drolly*]. Take care, my friend; take care.

DERRICK. Look you, woman; Meenie has consented to

marry my nephew. She has pledged her word to do so on condition that I settle an annuity on you.

GRETCHEN. I won't allow my child to break her heart.

DERRICK. You won't allow? Dare to raise your voice, dare but to speak except as I command you, you shall repent it to the last hour of your life.

RIP [*expectantly*]. Now she'll knock him down, flat as a flounder.

DERRICK [*sneeringly*]. You won't allow? This is something new. Who are you; do you think you are dealing with your first husband?

GRETCHEN. Alas, no; I wish I was.

RIP [*lost in wonderment*]. My, my, if Rip was alive, he never would have believed it!

DERRICK. So you thought to get the upper hand of me, when you married me; did n't you?

GRETCHEN. I thought to get a home for my little girl— shelter, and food; want drove me to your door, and I married you for a meal's victuals for my sick child.

DERRICK. So you came to me as if I was a poor-house, eh? Then you can't complain of the treatment you received. You sacrificed yourself for Meenie, and the least she can do now, is to do the same for you. In an hour, the deeds will be ready. Now, just you take care that no insolent interference of yours spoils my plans; do you hear?

GRETCHEN. Yes, sir.

DERRICK. Why can't you be kind and affectionate to her, as I am to you. There, go and blubber over her; that's your way. You are always pretending to be miserable.

GRETCHEN. Alas, no sir! I am always pretending to be happy.

DERRICK. Don't cry. I won't have it; come now, none of that. If you come home today with red eyes, and streaky cheeks, I'll give you something to cry for; now you know what's for supper. [*Exit.*]

RIP [*still amazed*]. Well, if I had n't seen it, I never would have believed it!

GRETCHEN [*absorbed in her grief*]. Oh, wretch that I am,

I must consent, or that man will surely thrust her out of doors to starve, to beg, and to become— [*Seeing* RIP.] Yes, to become a thing of rags and misery, like that poor soul.

RIP. She always drived the beggars away; I suppose I must go. [*Getting up, and starting to go.*]

GRETCHEN [*taking penny from her pocket*]. Here, my poor man, take this. It is only a penny; but take it, and may God bless you, poor wanderer, so old, so helpless. Why do you come to this strange place, so far from home?

RIP [*keeping his face turned away from her*]. She don't know me; she don't know me!

GRETCHEN. Are you alone in the world?

RIP [*trying to bring himself to look directly at* GRETCHEN]. My wife asks me if I 'm alone.

GRETCHEN. Come with me. How feeble he is; there, lean on me. Come to yonder house, and there you shall rest your limbs by the fire.

[GRETCHEN *takes his arm, and puts it in her own. As they move towards her house,* RIP *stops, and, with an effort, turns and looks her full in the face, with a penetrating gaze, as if imploring recognition, but there is none; and, sadly shaking his head, he shrinks into himself, and allows her to lead him tottering off.*]

SCENE 4.   *The same room in* DERRICK'S *home as in Scene 2.*

[*Enter* DERRICK.]

DERRICK. I don't know what women were invented for, except to make a man's life miserable. I can get a useful, hardworking woman to keep my house clean, and order my dinner for me, for half that weak, sniveling creature costs me.

[*Enter* COCKLES.]

COCKLES. Well, uncle, what news; will she have me?

DERRICK. Leave it to me; she must, she shall.

COCKLES. If she holds out, what are we to do? It was all very well, you marrying Rip's widow, that choked off all inquiry into his affairs; but here 's Meenie, Rip's heiress, who rightly owns all this property; if we don't secure her, we 're not safe.

DERRICK. You 've got rid of Hendrick Vedder; that 's one obstacle removed.

COCKLES. I 'm not so sure about that. His ship was wrecked on a lonely coast; but some of the crew may have, unfortunately, been saved.

DERRICK. If he turns up after you 're married, what need you care?

COCKLES. I 'd like nothing better; I 'd like to see his face when he saw my arm around his sweetheart—my wife. But if he turns up before our marriage——

DERRICK. I must put the screw on somewhere.

COCKLES. I 'll tell you, Meenie will do anything for her mother's sake. Now you are always threatening to turn her out, as she turned out Rip. That 's the tender place. Meenie fears more for her mother, than she cares for herself.

DERRICK. Well, what am I to do?

COCKLES. Make Gretchen independent of you; settle the little fortune on her, that you are always talking about doing, but never keeping your word. The girl will sell herself to secure her mother's happiness.

DERRICK. And it would be a cheap riddance for me. I was just talking about it to Gretchen this morning. You shall have the girl; but I hope you are not going to marry her out of any weak feeling of love. You 're not going to let her make a fool of you by and by?

COCKLES. I never cared for her until she was impudent to me, and got that sailor lover of hers to thrash me; and then I began to feel a hunger for her I never felt before.

DERRICK. That 's just the way I felt for Gretchen.

COCKLES. 'T ain't revenge that I feel; it 's enterprise. I want to overcome a difficulty.

DERRICK [chuckling]. And so you shall. Come, we 'll put your scheme in train at once; and let this be a warning to you hereafter, never marry another man's widow.

COCKLES. No, uncle; I 'll take a leaf out of your book, and let it be a warning to her. [Exeunt.]

SCENE 5. *A plain sitting-room in* DERRICK'S *house. A table stands in the centre with several chairs around it. There are cups, a jug, and a workbasket on the table. As the curtain rises,* MEENIE *is discovered seated by the table.*

MEENIE. Why should I repine? Did my mother hesitate to sacrifice her life to make a home for me? No; these tears are ungrateful, selfish. [*The door at the back opens.*]

[GRETCHEN *enters, leading* RIP, *who seems very feeble and a little wild.*]

GRETCHEN. Come in and rest a while.

RIP. This your house, your home?

GRETCHEN. Yes. Meenie, Meenie, bring him a chair.

RIP [*turning aside so as to shield his face from* MEENIE]. Is that your daughter?

GRETCHEN. That is my daughter.

RIP [*looking timidly at* MEENIE, *as* GRETCHEN *helps him into a chair*]. I thought you was a child.

GRETCHEN [*crossing to go into another room, and speaking to* MEENIE, *who starts to follow her*]. Stay with him until I get some food to fill his wallet. Don't be frightened, child, he is only a simple, half-witted creature whose misery has touched my heart.

[*Exit.* MEENIE *takes her workbasket and starts to follow.*]

RIP [*holding out his hand to detain her, and speaking with hardly suppressed excitement*]. One moment, my dear. Come here, and let me look at you. [*Pathetically.*] Are you afraid? I won't hurt you. I only want to look at you; that is all. Won't you come? [MEENIE *puts down her workbasket; and* RIP *is relieved of his great fear that she might leave him. His excitement increases as he goes on in his struggle to make her recognize him.*] Yes, I thought you would. Oh, yah, that is Meenie! But you are grown! [MEENIE *smiles.*] But see the smile and the eyes! That is just the same Meenie. You are a woman, Meenie. Do you remember something of your father? [*He looks at her eagerly and anxiously, as if on her answer hung his reason and his life.*]

MEENIE. I do. I do. Oh, I wish he was here now!

RIP [*half rising in his chair, in his excitement*]. Yah? But he isn't? No? No?

MEENIE. No; he's dead. I remember him so well. No one ever loved him as I did.

RIP. No; nobody ever loved me like my child.

MEENIE. Never shall I forget his dear, good face. Tell me——

RIP [*eagerly and expectantly*]. Yah?——

MEENIE. Did you know him?

RIP [*confused by her question, and afraid to answer*]. Well—I thought I did. But I— When I say that here, in the village, the people all laugh at me.

MEENIE. He is wandering. [*She starts to go.*]

RIP [*making a great effort of will, and resolved to put the question of his identity to the test*]. Don't go away from me. I want you to look at me now, and tell me if you have ever seen me before.

MEENIE [*surprised*]. No.

RIP [*holding out his arms to her*]. Try, my darlin', won't you?

MEENIE [*frightened*]. What do you mean? Why do you gaze so earnestly and fondly on me?

RIP [*rising from his chair, in trembling excitement, and approaching her*]. I am afraid to tell you, my dear, because if you say it is not true, it may be it would break my heart. But, Meenie, either I dream, or I am mad; but I am your father.

MEENIE. My father!

RIP. Yes; but hear me, my dear, and then you will know. [*Trying to be logical and calm, but laboring under great excitement.*] This village here is the village of Falling Waters. Well, that was my home. I had here in this place my wife, Gretchen, and my child Meenie—little Meenie—[*a long pause, during which he strives to reassemble his ideas and memories more accurately*] and my dog Schneider. That's all the family what I've got. Try and remember me, dear, won't you? [*Pleadingly.*] I don't know when it was— This night there was a storm; and my wife drived me from my house; and I went away—I don't remember any more till I come back here now. And see, I get back now, and my wife is gone, and my home is gone. My home is gone, and my child—my child looks in my face, and don't know who I am!

MEENIE [*rushing into his arms*]. I do! Father!

RIP [*sobbing*]. Ah, my child! Somebody knows me now! Somebody knows me now!

MEENIE. But can it be possible?

RIP. Oh, yah; it is so, Meenie! [*With a pathetic return of his uncertainty.*] Don't say it is not, or you will kill me if you do.

MEENIE. No. One by one your features come back to my memory. Your voice recalls that of my dear father, too. I cannot doubt; yet it is so strange.

RIP. Yah, but it is me, Meenie; it is me.

MEENIE. I am bewildered. Surely mother will know you.

RIP [*smiling*]. No, I don't believe she 'll know me.

MEENIE. She can best prove your identity. I will call her.

RIP. No. You call the dog Schneider. He 'll know me better than my wife.

[*They retire to a sofa in the background, where* RIP *sits with his arm around* MEENIE.[1]]

[*Enter* DERRICK, *with documents.*]

DERRICK. What old vagabond is this?

---

1 In reply to a question why "Rip" should sit with his arm around "Meenie," during the next scene, when the other persons in the drama are still present, and are still ignorant of his identity, Mr. Jefferson said: "The other persons are occupied with their own affairs, and are not supposed to see this. It is natural that 'Rip' should embrace his daughter whom he has just found, but the others are not supposed to see this. It is like a side speech on a stage. I went to a Chinese theatre once, and after the Chinese lady got through with her song, they brought her a glass of gin; she turned her back to the audience, and drank it, as much as to say, 'That's not in the play.' We are dealing with the impossible all the time on the stage; and we have got to make it appear possible. Dramatically, things may often be right, when, realistically, they are wrong. What we do is often the result of averaging the thing, determining how far good taste will admit of an error, you see; like the discord in music,—not good in itself, but good in its place."

[MEENIE *starts to resent insult.*]

RIP. Don't you say a word.

DERRICK. Here, give him a cold potato, and let him go. [*To* GRETCHEN, *who has entered, followed by* COCKLES. GRETCHEN *seats herself in the chair at the right of the table.*] Come you here, mistress. Here are the papers for the young couple to sign.

COCKLES [*aside*]. And the sooner, the better. Hush, Uncle, Hendrick is here.

DERRICK. Young Vedder? Then we must look sharp. [*To* GRETCHEN.] Come, fetch that girl of yours to sign this deed.

GRETCHEN. Never shall she put her name to that paper with my consent. Never.

DERRICK. Dare you oppose me in my own house? Dare you preach disobedience under my roof?

GRETCHEN. I dare do anything when my child's life's at stake. No, a thousand times, no! You shall not make of her what you have of me. Starvation and death are better than such a life as I lead.

DERRICK [*raising cane*]. Don't provoke me.

GRETCHEN [*kneeling*]. Beat me, starve me. You can only kill me. After all, I deserve it. [*Rising.*] But Meenie has given her promise to Hendrick Vedder, and she shall not break her word.

COCKLES [*seated at right of table*]. But Hendrick Vedder is dead.

[*The door is flung open, and* HENDRICK *enters.*]

HENDRICK. That's a lie! He's alive!

GRETCHEN *and* MEENIE [*rushing to him*]. Alive!

HENDRICK [*to* MEENIE]. I've heard all about it. They made you believe that I was dead. [*To* DERRICK.] Only wait till I get through here. [*Embracing* MEENIE.] What a pleasure I've got to come! [*To* DERRICK.] And what a thrashing I've brought back for you two swabs.

DERRICK [*angrily*]. Am I to be bullied under my own roof by a beggarly sailor? Quit my house, all of you. [*Seizes* GRETCHEN, *and drags her away from the crowd.*]

As for you, woman, this is your work, and I 'll make you pay for it.

GRETCHEN.   Hendrick, save me from him. He will kill me.

HENDRICK.   Stand off!

DERRICK [*raising cane*].   No; she is my wife, mine.

GRETCHEN.   Heaven help me, I am!

[RIP *has risen from the sofa, and come forward, and leans against the centre of the table, with one hand in his game-bag. He is fully awake now, and has recovered all his old shrewdness.*]

RIP.   Stop.   I am not so sure about that.   If that is so, then what has become of Rip Van Winkle?

COCKLES.   He 's dead.

RIP.   That 's another lie.   He 's no more dead than Hendrick Vedder.   Derrick Von Beekman, you say this house and land was yours?

DERRICK.   Yes.

RIP.   Where and what is the paper what you wanted Rip Van Winkle to sign when he was drunk, but sober enough not to do it?   [*Taking an old paper out of game-bag, and turning to* HENDRICK.]   Have you forgot how to read?

HENDRICK.   No.

RIP.   Then you read that.

[HENDRICK *takes the document from* RIP, *and looks it over.*]

DERRICK.   What does this mad old vagabond mean to say?

RIP.   I mean, that is my wife, Gretchen Van Winkle.

GRETCHEN [*rushing to* RIP].   Rip! Rip!

COCKLES.   I say, uncle, are you going to stand that? That old impostor is going it under your nose in fine style.

DERRICK.   I 'm dumb with rage.   [*To the villagers, who have come crowding in.*]   Out of my house, all of you! Begone, you old tramp!

HENDRICK.   Stay where you are.   [*To* DERRICK.]   This house don't belong to you.   Not an acre of land, not a brick in the town is yours.   They have never ceased to belong to Rip Van Winkle; and this document proves it.

DERRICK. 'T is false. That paper is a forgery.

HENDRICK. Oh, no, it is not; for I read it to Rip twenty years ago.

RIP. Clever boy! Clever boy! Dat's the reason I didn't sign it then, Derrick.

DERRICK [*approaching* HENDRICK]. And do you think I'm fool enough to give up my property in this way?

HENDRICK. No. You're fool enough to hang on to it, until we make you refund to Rip every shilling over and above the paltry sum you loaned him upon it. Now, if you are wise, you'll take a hint. There's the door. Go! And never let us see your face again.

RIP. Yah; give him a cold potato, and let him go.

[*Exit* DERRICK *in a great rage. All the villagers laugh at him.* HENDRICK *follows him to the door.*]

COCKLES [*kneeling to* MEENIE]. O, Meenie! Meenie!

HENDRICK [*coming down, and taking him by the ear*]. I'll Meenie you! [*Takes him and pushes him out. All the villagers laugh.* MEENIE *gives* RIP *a chair.*]

GRETCHEN [*kneeling by the side of* RIP]. O, Rip! I drove you from your home; but do not desert me again. I'll never speak an unkind word to you, and you shall never see a frown on my face. And Rip——

RIP. Yah.

GRETCHEN. You may stay out all night, if you like.

RIP [*leaning back in his chair*]. No, thank you. I had enough of that.

GRETCHEN. And, Rip, you can get tight as often as you please.

RIP [*taking bottle, and filling the cup from it*]. No; I don't touch another drop.

MEENIE [*kneeling by the other side of* RIP]. Oh, yes, you will, father. For see, here are all the neighbors come to welcome you home.

[GRETCHEN *offers* RIP *the cup.*]

RIP [*with all his old kindness and hospitality*]. Well, bring in all the children, and the neighbors, and the dogs, and— [*Seeing the cup which* GRETCHEN *is offering to him.*]

I swore off, you know. Well, I won't count this one; for this will go down with a prayer. I will take my cup and pipe and tell my strange story to all my friends. Here is my child Meenie, and my wife Gretchen, and my boy Hendrick. I 'll drink all your good health, and I 'll drink your good health, and your families', and may they all live long and prosper!

CURTAIN

Suggestive Questions

1. In the older versions of *Rip Van Winkle* there were more characters. What advantage did the dramatist gain by limiting the number of characters in the later play?

2. What means did the dramatist adopt in Act I, to reveal the story of the past?

3. Point out evidences of Gretchen's different characteristics. What does most to awaken interest in her?

4. Point out evidences of Rip Van Winkle's characteristics. Why do we sympathize with him?

5. What makes Rip's first appearance effective?

6. What does Rip's dog contribute to the play?

7. Distinguish the plot elements in *Rip Van Winkle*.

8. What dramatic values do some of the minor characters contribute to the play?

9. Point out unusually effective stage business.

10. Point out different effects given by stage setting.

11. What gives Act II its greatest dramatic value?

12. In Act III Rip is the only person who speaks. What effect does that limitation produce?

13. Explain how stage setting and stage business add to the dramatic value of Act III.

14. What different emotional appeals does Act IV make?

15. What foreshadows the conclusion of the play?

16. What are the causes that aided in making Rip Van Winkle such a popular character on the stage?

Subjects for Written Imitation

1. Write a dialogue in which you show the character of some eccentric but lovable person.
2. Write a dialogue in which you show a seemingly stupid person outwitting one who thinks himself exceedingly sharp and clever.
3. Write a dialogue in which you show character, through conversation between a father and a son, or between a mother and a daughter.
4. Without departing too far from reality write a farcical scene of domestic life.
5. Write a pathetic scene of domestic life.
6. Write a scene, including stage directions, in which you make effective use of the supernatural.
7. Write a dialogue in which you tell of the unexpected return of some wanderer.
8. Dramatize the return of Odysseus, emphasizing his meeting with his old shepherd, his dog, and his nurse.

Directions for Writing

Use the simplest everyday speech and dialect. Include full stage directions. Aim to produce broad effects of humor or of pathos, and to awaken sympathy.

Oral Work in Class

1. Read effectively one of the dialogues that you wrote.
2. Arrange with others to act any short section of *Rip Van Winkle*.
3. Select what you believe is the most humorous section of the play. Arrange with others to act that section.
4. Select what you believe is the most pathetic section of the play. Arrange with others to act that section.
5. Read aloud, or act, Act III of *Rip Van Winkle*. Make full use of facial expression, and of dramatic gesture, and movement.
6. Follow, in pantomime, some of the directions for "stage business,"—such as, "Gretchen looks up angrily; Nick retreats a few paces hastily,"—while someone else reads the lines and the directions.

BENJAMIN FRANKLIN, JOURNEYMAN

By Constance D'Arcy Mackay

Constance D'Arcy Mackay, by birth in St. Paul, Minnesota, a citizen of the West, and by education in Boston University, Massachusetts, a citizen of the East, has done notable work in helping to make the drama expressive of civic and national life.

Miss Mackay's *Pageant of Patriots*, presented in Prospect Park, Brooklyn, N. Y., in 1911, was the first children's patriotic pageant ever given in the United States. On various occasions she aided important cities in the celebration of their founding and development. Thus she wrote *The Historical Pageant of Schenectady*, in 1912; *The Historical Pageant of Portland, Maine*, in 1913; *William of Stratford*, the Shakespeare tercentenary pageant for Baltimore, in 1916; *The Victory Pageant*, for New York, in 1918; and *The Patriotic Christmas Pageant*, for San Francisco, in 1918. She also wrote *The Pageant of Sunshine and Shadow*, expressive of popular feeling against child labor, in 1916; and a *Memorial Day Pageant*, in 1916.

In particular, Miss Mackay has interested herself in showing young people how they may make the drama express their own emotions. She has written plays that have been produced in many of the most important schools in the country; and she has written various articles and books to show how schools may make use of plays as an aid to teaching historical facts and ways of right living.

Among her works are *The House of the Heart, and Other Plays for Children*, 1909; *The Silver Thread, and Other*

Folk Plays for Young People, 1910; *Patriotic Plays and Pageants*, 1912; *How to Produce Plays for Children*, 1915; *Plays of the Pioneers*, 1915; *Costumes and Scenery for Amateurs*, 1915; *The Beau of Bath, and Other One-Act plays*, 1915; *The Forest Princess, and Other Masks*, 1916; *The Little Theatre in the United States*, 1917; *and Patriotic Drama in Your Town*, 1918.

In 1918 and 1919 Miss Mackay was Director of the Department of Pageantry and Drama for the War Camp Commission Service.

Benjamin Franklin, Journeyman. is taken, by special permission of the author, and of the publisher, from Miss Mackay's *Patriotic Plays and Pageants for Young People* (Holt, New York).

Benjamin Franklin, Journeyman, tells of the youth of Benjamin Franklin; of his arrival in Philadelphia at the age of seventeen; and of his dramatic meeting with Deborah Read, whom he promptly loved at first sight, and whom he married seven years later. The play tells of an amusing tilt between a proud, vivacious girl, and a sober, practical-minded New England boy, a contest of words that will be understood by every young person.

The dramatist cleverly makes the sprightly Deborah Read, who does not know that Benjamin Franklin is near, ridicule Franklin at a time when he cannot help but hear her. The author then turns the play on the girl's embarrassment, and the boy's irritation; shows the good spirit that is fundamental in both Deborah and Benjamin; and ends the play with Franklin's suggestive meditation, prophetic of the future: "Count thyself rich when thou hast found a friend."

INTRODUCTORY PROBLEMS

1. Write a scenario for a play that you might write concerning the youth of some person famous in the history of your State.
2. Write a dialogue in which you indicate a false judgment made on the basis of clothing, personal appearance, or actions.

3. Write a dialogue in which two persons talking about another, are overheard by the one of whom they talk. Bring the dialogue to an appropriate ending.

CHARACTERS

BENJAMIN FRANKLIN, *a young printer*
ROGER BURCHARD, *a Quaker*
ELIZABETH BURCHARD, *his wife*
DEBORAH READ
WILLIAM, *an inn boy*

SCENE: *A room in a tavern. Place: Philadelphia. Time, October, 1723.*

The room is a private one in the tavern known as The Crooked Billet. It has a neat, cheerful, welcoming aspect. At left a small fire glimmers on the brass andirons of a well-kept hearth. A brass kettle rests on a hob. On the shelf above the hearth candles are alight.

All across the background are a series of small windows curtained in chintz. By these windows a table set for supper, with a white linen cloth and delicately sprigged china. Quaint chairs with spindle legs.

Against the right wall a secretary with a shelf full of handsomely-bound books. Near this two chairs with high backs that would screen from view any one sitting in them.

There is a door at right background opening into the hall.

Another door at left near background, opening into another room.

At the rise of the curtain ROGER BURCHARD is discovered seated at the table, on which a generous supper lies spread; while ELIZABETH, his wife, is bending at the hearth.

ELIZABETH. The kettle hath not yet boiled for thy second cup, Roger. 'T is slow, yet I do not worry, for 't is only twilight, and there is a good hour yet ere we are due at the special meeting of the Friends, and Deborah Read is to come with us. Does thee know, Roger, I sometimes think that for all her saucy ways Mistress Deborah Read is half a Friend at heart. When I do speak she listens to me most attentively.

ROGER. Thee should not *force* belief upon another, Elizabeth.

ELIZABETH [*demurely*]. I did not force: I did but talk to her, Roger. Thee knows I am not over eloquent. How should a worldly maid of Philadelphia give ear to me? [*Crosses to* ROGER: *the kettle lies forgotten.*]

ROGER. How, indeed! Does thee know, Elizabeth, that in so quiet a room as this I can scarce believe that a great city lies about us? 'T is so still that I can hear the ticking of the clock.

ELIZABETH. For myself, I am glad of a little rest after our journey up from Brookfield to the city. I find myself scarce used to city ways.

ROGER. No more do I, Elizabeth, no more do I. I cannot think this lavish life is seemly. This table, now! Does thee note its profusion? More bread and honey and cheese and chicken pie than we can eat. Sheer waste—unless we can share it. If there was but some poor traveler in this inn whom we might bid to supper, and——

[*A knock on the door leading to hall.*]

ELIZABETH. 'T is William, the inn boy, with tea cakes.

[ELIZABETH *opens the door.* WILLIAM *enters with tea cakes on tray. He deposits the plate of cakes on table.*]

ROGER. As I was saying—if there was but some traveler in this inn to share our evening meal—some one with pockets that were well-nigh empty——

ELIZABETH. Perhaps the inn boy knows of such a one. [*To* WILLIAM.] Does thee not, William? Some one whose purse is not too over-burdened?

WILLIAM [*sturdily*]. Aye, that I do. A lad came here this noon from Boston. A journeyman printer so he says he is, and I 'll warrant he has not above four shillings with him. [*To Roger.*] He 's come to search for work in Philadelphia, and says he was directed to this tavern by a—by a Quaker, sir.

ELIZABETH. Directed here by a Quaker—! [*To* ROGER.] Then, Roger, all the more reason why we should bid him in. What is his name?

WILLIAM. He says his name is Franklin.

ROGER. Then ask friend Franklin if he'll sup with us. Tell him we, too, would hear the news from Boston—that he'll confer a favor if he'll come. And mind, no hint about an empty purse! I fear at first I put the matter clumsily. Give him my later message. That is all.

WILLIAM. I will, sir. [*Exit, with a flourish, right background.*]

ROGER. I hope he comes.

ELIZABETH [*fondly*]. 'Tis ever like thee, Roger, to have a care for the friendless and forlorn.

WILLIAM [*knocking, opening door from hall, and announcing*]. Benjamin Franklin, Journeyman!

[*Enter* FRANKLIN, *shabby, travel-stained, and boyishly appealing. Exit* WILLIAM.]

ROGER [*stepping hospitably forward*]. I bid thee welcome, friend Franklin. I hear thee is from Boston, and come to search for work in Philadelphia. Will thee not sup here? We are ever anxious for news such as travelers may bring. This is my wife, Elizabeth Burchard, and she will make thee welcome. I mind me of the time when I was once a stranger. Will thee not do us the pleasure to sup with us?

FRANKLIN. I scarcely, sir, know how to thank you for such kindness. All Quakers must be kind, I think, for it was a Quaker who directed me hither.

[FRANKLIN *crosses to fire,* ROGER *taking his hat from him. In brief pantomime behind* FRANKLIN'S *back* ROGER *has indicated that* FRANKLIN *is to take his place at table, and that he himself will sup no further. During the conversation that follows* ELIZABETH *is taking fresh silver out of a quaint basket that is on the table,* FRANKLIN *stands at fire, and* ROGER *is seated at right.*]

ELIZABETH. Perhaps my husband can advise thee further where best to look for work upon the morrow.

FRANKLIN. I thank you. I will hear him gladly. He that cannot be counseled cannot be helped.[1]

ROGER. Thee means to seek for work at once, I see.

FRANKLIN. Lost time is never found again,[1] and since time is of all things the most precious, I am loth to lose it.

ROGER. There is a wise head upon thy shoulders, friend. [*Indicates table, and rises.*] Sit thee down, lad. Sit thee down.

ELIZABETH [*hurrying to hearth where kettle stands*]. Alas! I have forgotten the kettle! The tea is not yet ready. [*To* ROGER.] Do thee and Benjamin Franklin talk while I prepare it. Show him the volumes lately come from London. Thee knows the print and paper is most pleasing.

[ROGER BURCHARD *and* BENJAMIN FRANKLIN *sit at right in the high-backed chairs, the volumes upon their knees. That they are true book-lovers is instantly apparent. They are lost to everything that goes on about them. They sit with their backs towards the door at left, quite screened from the view of any one entering there. There is a pause. Then* DEBORAH READ *taps softly at the door at left.* ELIZABETH *turns and opens the door.*]

DEBORAH [*finger on lip*]. S-ssh! Not a word! [*Glances towards the back of* ROGER'S *chair.*] I 've crept up the stairs on tip-toe!

ELIZABETH. Sweet rogue! Thee startled me to the point of dropping the kettle! Yonder is my husband so deep in a book that the crack o' doom would scarce rouse him. And with him is a young printer whom we have bid to be our guest. Roger and I have finished our evening meal, so perhaps thee will keep our young guest company while I prepare for meeting.

DEBORAH [*holding up warning finger*]. Primp not too much for meeting, fair friend Elizabeth! A grave demeanor goes with Quaker bonnets! [*Laughs.*] Yes, yes, I 'll serve your printer, play hostess, or aught else that will please you, and you can call me when 'tis time to leave him. [*Throws*

1 From Franklin's "Poor Richard's Almanac."

off her cloak, and sits by hearth on footstool.] La! such a
day! This very morn I saw the strangest sight! I went
to the door to get a breath of air, and as I stood there what
should I see approaching down the street but a lad with
dusty clothes and bulging pockets—nay, wait, Elizabeth!
The drollest part is yet to come! I vow he had stuffed one
pocket full of *stockings,* and from the other protruded a loaf
of bread! And in his hand was a great fat roll, and he was
eating it! Gnawing it off, an you please, as if there were no
one to see him! Then he looked up, and——

ELIZABETH [*shocked*]. Deborah! Thee did not laugh at
him! Thee did not mock at him!

DEBORAH [*wiping tears of mirth from her eyes*]. Mock
at him? Oh, lud! I laughed till my sides ached! [*Rises,
as she happens to see that* ROGER BURCHARD *and his guest are
rising, yet continues gaily*]. And when he caught sight of
my face——

[*Just as* DEBORAH *utters these words she and* FRANKLIN
perceive each other. DEBORAH *is utterly taken aback and
quite speechless.*]

ROGER [*seeing nothing amiss*]. Welcome, Deborah Read.
I present to thee Benjamin Franklin.

[FRANKLIN *bows.* DEBORAH *drops a fluttering courtesy,
and then clings to* ELIZABETH BURCHARD.]

DEBORAH [*quaveringly*]. I—I feel somewhat faint,
Elizabeth.

ELIZABETH [*seeing nothing amiss*]. Then sit at the table,
dear Deborah, and a cup of tea will revive thee.

DEBORAH [*protesting*]. No—! No—! I—I will help
you to dress.

ELIZABETH. Then who will serve Benjamin Franklin?
Thee promised that thee would be hostess, so unless aught is
amiss——

DEBORAH [*recovering herself, and suddenly displaying a
haughty self-possession*]. Naught is amiss, Elizabeth. I will
serve tea if you bid me.

[DEBORAH *sits at one end of the table,* FRANKLIN *at the
other.*]

ELIZABETH.   Thee knows the Friends' special meeting to-night is at the same hour as that of the other churches, so when thee hears the church-bells ringing 'twill be time to prepare, sweet Deborah.

DEBORAH [*with a gleam*]. I 'll not forget the time. I promise you that, Elizabeth.

ELIZABETH.   Come, Roger. Thee must wear a fresh neck-cloth.

[ROGER *and* ELIZABETH *exeunt left. There is a very long pause.*]

DEBORAH.   Will you have tea, Master Franklin?

FRANKLIN.   If it pleases you, Mistress Read.

DEBORAH.   Cream? Sugar?

FRANKLIN.   I thank you.

[*She passes him his cup. There is another long pause.*]

FRANKLIN [*with a great sigh*]. 'T is a silent place, Philadelphia! [*Another pause.*]

FRANKLIN.   Will you have some bread, Mistress?

DEBORAH [*coldly*]. I thank you, no.

FRANKLIN [*bluntly*]. Have you ever pondered, Mistress, that pride that dines on vanity sups on contempt?[1]

DEBORAH [*outraged*]. Master Franklin!

FRANKLIN.   I know right well that my poor coat offends you; yet in truth, Mistress Deborah, why should I dress in finer cloth when silks and satins put out the kitchen fire.[1]

DEBORAH.   'T is not your coat offends me, 't is——

FRANKLIN.   'T is that I am neither the son of a gold-laced governor nor a wealthy merchant but only a poor journey-man printer. Then, Mistress, you have yet to learn that he who hath a trade hath an estate, and he who hath a calling hath an office of profit and honor.[1]

DEBORAH [*with spirit*]. There you read me wrong, Master Franklin. I have supped with printers before this.

FRANKLIN.   Then 't was the printer's loaf you mocked this morning, Mistress Deborah; and not the printer. Yet in truth, why should eating in the street displease you, since 't was a matter of necessity. Ere fancy you consult, consult

1 From "Poor Richard's Almanac."

your purse,[1] and my purse was not over full. But—diligence
is the mother of luck, and heaven gives all things to industry.[1]
DEBORAH [*with a toss*]. You speak as if you and Industry
were boon companions.
FRANKLIN. And what better companion could I have?
Heaven helps them that help themselves.
DEBORAH [*witheringly*]. 'T is a fine thing to have high
hopes, I doubt not.
FRANKLIN [*blithely*]. Oh, I have more than hopes, Mis-
tress Deborah; for he that lives upon hope will die fasting.[1]
To apply one's self right heartily is to do more than hope.
Sloth makes all things difficult; but industry all things easy.[1]
You are not eating, Mistress Deborah. [*She rises.*] Have
my blunt ways offended you? Have I again displeased you?
DEBORAH [*with chilling dignity*]. You could not an you
tried, Master Franklin. I was but going to fetch the tea-
kettle.
FRANKLIN [*starting up*]. If I can help you——
DEBORAH [*still frostily*]. I thank you, I am in no need of
help. A-ah! [*With a cry she drops the kettle.*]
FRANKLIN. You have burned yourself, Mistress Deborah!
The poor little hand! [*He tears up his handkerchief.*] Let
me bandage it for you! It is sorely blistered!
DEBORAH [*tears in her voice the while she submits her hand
to him*]. I can tolerate blisters, Master Franklin. They are
far less irksome than—than——
FRANKLIN [*gravely bandaging her hand*]. Than journey-
men printers who eat their bread in the street. Perhaps you
are right, Mistress Deborah. I trust that the blisters will
soon heal; and that the memory of the journeyman printer
will not trouble you further.
DEBORAH [*as the church-bells begin to ring without*]. The
memory of a chance traveler is easily forgot, Master Franklin.
ELIZABETH [*outside door left*]. Come, Deborah, we shall
be late! Come quickly, child! [DEBORAH *snatches up her
cloak.*] Bid Benjamin Franklin to wait my husband's

1 From "Poor Richard's Almanac."

return. He would talk to him further concerning books. Come, Deborah!

[*Exit* DEBORAH, *left, without a glance at Franklin.*]

FRANKLIN [*dropping into chair by secretary, right*]. Do blisters burn as keen as words, I wonder? "Chance travelers . . . easily forgot!" [*Sits with bowed head.*]

[DEBORAH *stands again in doorway at left, sees him, comes to him swiftly and remorsefully.*]

FRANKLIN [*raises his head; sees her*]. Is it——

DEBORAH. 'T is naught—naught but Deborah Read come to say to you—to say to you—that she should have remembered that you were a stranger in a city full of strangers. [*Pleadingly.*] Indeed, indeed I did not mean to hurt you! I do not mind your rusty clothes; I do not mock your—your faded hat. I—I have been full of foolish pride. Will you forgive me?

FRANKLIN [*rising; amazed*]. Deborah!

DEBORAH [*hurrying on*]. I had not meant to laugh at you this morning. Will you forgive that, too?

FRANKLIN [*moved*]. Deborah!

DEBORAH. I know I sometimes judge by foolish standards. Will you forgive?

FRANKLIN. With all my heart, my friend. [*They clasp hands on it.*] And will you, Deborah, forgive me my blunt speeches? I knew not how to please you. I meant no harm.

DEBORAH [*earnestly*]. I forgive all.

FRANKLIN. And we are friends for life—for all our lives, Deborah.

ELIZABETH [*speaking somewhat impatiently from beyond the door at left*]. Deborah! Child!

DEBORAH [*prettily*]. Yes! Yes! I'm coming!

[*Hastens out the door with a friendly backward glance at* FRANKLIN. *He stands for a moment where she has left him.*

Crosses to secretary, takes book, seats himself, opens it slowly, looking after her. Then sits a-dream in the fading fireglow. Presently he looks at the book again, and reads the first line upon which his eye chances to fall.]

FRANKLIN [*reading*]. "Count thyself rich when thou hast found a friend."
[*The curtain slowly falls.*]

COSTUMES

BENJAMIN FRANKLIN. Travel-stained suit of dark-brown, guiltless of braid or ruffles, coat and knee-breeches being of the same color. The material either of corduroy or homespun (woolen). A white vest flowered with brown roses. A white neckcloth. Black stockings. Low black shoes. A three-cornered black hat, which he carries under his arm. Hair worn long and unpowdered.

ROGER BURCHARD. Coat and knee-breeches of the same style as Franklin's, made of homespun, and Quaker-gray in color. A Quaker-gray vest. White neckcloth. Gray stockings. Low black shoes with silver buckles. Unpowdered hair.

ELIZABETH BURCHARD. Dress of gray satin, simply made, with a crossed kerchief of snowy white lawn. Gray stockings. Gray slippers with silver buckles. Hair worn simply, and unpowdered. (Gray glazed cambric for her dress if satin cannot be had.)

DEBORAH READ. Quilted petticoat of pale-blue satin. Colonial overdress and bodice of white, brocaded with pale-blue roses. Fichu of white lawn. Black picture hat with black plume. Black cloth cloak lined with pale-blue. Black stockings. Low black shoes with gold buckles. Unpowdered hair, worn pompadour. (If satin and brocade cannot be had, have blue glazed muslin and cretonne instead. Or flowered muslin worn over a white dress.) Black patches. Black velvet ribbon at neck. White lace mitts, or black gloves coming to the elbow.

WILLIAM. Maroon suit, of a heavy woolen material. Gold buttons down the front and two in back. Cream-colored vest. Neither braiding nor ruffles. Black stockings. Low black shoes without buckles. A white neckcloth. Unpowdered hair worn in a cue.

Suggestive Questions

1. By what details does the dramatist suggest the early days of the United States?
2. Point out the speeches that do most to reveal character.
3. Name the principal characteristics of every person in the play.
4. What part of the dialogue is most effective? What makes that part most effective?
5. What is the most dramatic moment of the play? Explain why that moment is most dramatic.
6. What gives force to the conclusion of the play?
7. What part of the play is most true to life?
8. What part of the play shows greatest dramatic art?
9. How much does stage setting add to the effect of the play?
10. How much does the dramatist suggest? What are the relative advantages of suggestion, and of plain statement?

Suggestions for Written Imitation

1. What incident in the life of one of the following persons might you use as the basis for a play? Abraham Lincoln; General U. S. Grant; Nathan Hale; General Robert E. Lee; Christopher Columbus.
2. Write directions for the stage setting of a play concerning the youth of one of the persons named in question one.
3. Write that part of the dialogue that will tell about the first appearance of the principal character in the historical play that you might write.
4. Write a short part of the dialogue for your proposed play. Give stage directions that will increase the effect of the dialogue.
5. Write one important speech for your play.
6. Write the closing dialogue, and the final stage directions, for your play.
7. Write a complete list of the characters who might appear in such a play. Tell what characteristics you would emphasize in every character.
8. What theme will you emphasize?
9. What emotions will you try to arouse?
10. Write a short scenario for the entire play.

DIRECTIONS FOR WRITING

Do not attempt to write an entire play. Be content with writing only a little, perhaps no more than will fill one side of a sheet of paper slightly larger than the pages of this book. Write on only one of the suggestions given above. Later you may attempt to complete what you now begin.

ORAL WORK IN CLASS

1. Read aloud the written work that you prepared. Ask for class criticisms.
2. Select the most amusing section of the play. Assign parts, and act that section.
3. Select the most powerful section of the play. Assign parts, and act that section.

THE PIONEERS

By Mary MacMillan

Mary MacMillan has written a number of delightful short plays, all showing keen sense of sympathy, quick enjoyment of life, and the spirit of laughter. At one moment she satirizes the production of a play by amateurs, as in *The Dress Rehearsal of Hamlet;* at another she writes a pathetic Christmas Eve tragedy, as in *The Shadowed Star;* at another, she turns to the romance of the past, as in *The Pioneers.*

Her plays, gathered in such volumes as *Short Plays*, 1913, *More Short Plays*, 1917, and *Third Book of Short Plays*, 1922, are much esteemed by schools, by clubs, and by non-professional organizations. They include such suggestive titles as *A Fan and Two Candlesticks, The Gate of Wishes, The Dryad,* and *When Two 's Not Company.*

The Pioneers is a play of the Middle West about 1791. The play concerns the simple life, the hardships, the dangers, and the heroism of the American pioneers of the West. It reveals the spirit of the past, but it deals with a theme that is living: ''Do unto others as you would have others do unto you.''

The frontier characters, presented simply, without any subtlety, take part in a series of events that unfold the consequences of harshness, and the saving power of sympathy. The dialogue is simple and unaffected.

Mary MacMillan, as her name indicates, is of Scotch

descent. Through her mother she is a descendant of the early pioneers of America. She was born in Ohio, where her great-grandfather had cleared and cultivated some two thousand acres of land.

Mary MacMillan is a graduate of Wells College, and of Bryn Mawr College. She has devoted herself to literary work, in which she has had remarkable success. In addition to many plays, she is the author of numerous poems, many of which have been set to music, or re-published in anthologies; of many historical articles; and of various short stories.

INTRODUCTORY PROBLEMS

1. A gypsy woman comes to your house and begs for food or money. A member of your family angrily drives her away. Write a dialogue that will tell the story. Give stage directions.
2. You speak sympathetically with a vagrant whom you happen to meet under peculiar circumstances. Imagine a condition of affairs in which the vagrant, influenced by your expression of sympathy, might do you a great service. Write a scenario for a play that will tell the story.
3. Write a scenario for a play based on the story of the lion and and the mouse. Plan to use human characters.

PREFATORY NOTE TO THE PLAY

The scene of this play is the first settlement of what is now a great city of the Middle West. The time is about 1791. In writing the play I have introduced characters and described things as I liked to imagine them. If in the exigencies of presentation some of these seem difficult, alterations are easy. For instance, if a larger cast is desired, more pioneers and Indians may be added; if a smaller one, several of the parts may be doubled or omitted entirely. I have made it flexible in that respect purposely. The play has two scenes. The one in the Indian camp may be made possible for amateurs to give by hanging green curtains just inside the other scene. If this seems not to be managed, the act may be made to take place with comparatively little change also inside the pioneer's cabin—that is, there need be no change of scene. Naturally I do not expect the brook to be, or even to be heard, on the stage but have described it for the benefit of the actor's imagination. Additions or changes are altogether permissible. For, in my experience with amateur stagecraft, I have found not only that circumstances alter cases but that cases must alter circumstances and that every one alters plays.

CHARACTERS IN THE ORDER OF THEIR APPEARANCE:

PIONEERS

ALISON CARMICHAEL
ABAGAIL CARMICHAEL, *her sister-in-law*
EDWARD,
SARAH, } *the Carmichael children*
LITTLE NANCY,
EUNICE MORTON
ARTHUR, } *the Morton children*
LUCY,
GEOFFREY BAXTER, *brother of Eunice*
JOHN MORTON, *her husband*
WILLIAM CARMICHAEL, *husband to Abagail, brother to Alison*
MRS. WORTHINGTON
THE GENERAL
MRS. KING

INDIANS

WHITE FEATHER   RED FOX
THE BEAVER   THE EAGLE
GRAY CLOUD

ACT I

[*It is late afternoon on the thirteenth of February. The scene is the interior of a pioneer's log cabin. On one side of the room—in stage directions the right—there is a big open wood fire-place. At the side of this toward the front is the door opening into another room. On the other side of the room is a window towards the front, behind that against the wall a rude bed and near it a baby's crib. At the back there is a door not quite in the center but nearer the side where the bed stands; at the side of the door and towards the fire-place there is a window. A settee is in the corner between the window and the fire-place, a spinning-wheel and chair on the other side of the window rather in front of it. A deal table and some rude chairs compose the rest of the furniture. Some guns, kitchen utensils, and strings of drying herbs—red peppers, hops, and so on—hang on the walls. There are holes—closed now—in the outer door and window shutters for the insertion of guns. Over the door into the inner room a ladder goes up to the loft above. A pretty girl of eighteen or so sits by the wheel and spins, humming a little tune to herself.*]

ABAGAIL [*from within in a mournful complaining voice*]. If the spring does n't come soon the children's bare feet will be upon the snow-covered ground.

ALISON [*smiling and answering in a gay and very sweet voice*]. Oh, when their shoes wear out they can wear moccasins.

ABAGAIL [*coming from the inner room with her knitting of coarse gray yarn in her hand*]. It is not so much their shoes as their stockings that are worn out. I 've darned and darned till they won't hold the stitches any longer. There is scarcely enough yarn left for another pair and that is the last of the wool. [*Sighing, with a glance at the spinning-wheel.*]

ALISON [*hopefully*]. I think the spring will come soon.

If it does n't [*laughing*] we will have to tie their legs up in hay till they can go barefoot.

ABAGAIL. They are not your children, Alison, or you would not jest about it.

ALISON. Oh, you know I love them, Abagail.

ABAGAIL. You take this hard, frontier life as a joke but I am accustomed to the greatest luxuries and all the delicacies of aristocratic society in Trenton.

ALISON. Oh, sister, I left as many pleasant things in Philadelphia as you did in Trenton, of your beloved Jersey. But I am willing to give them all up for this wonderful new land. It has been a long cold winter but for that very reason I think the spring will be early. There are signs. Yesterday I heard a robin.

ABAGAIL [*sitting down by the table and knitting*]. More like it was an Indian. William says they imitate birds for signals. Maybe they are up to some of their devilish tricks.

ALISON [*smiling and shaking her head*]. No, it was no Indian though his breast was red. I saw him. The color was gay against the snowy branch where he sat.

ABAGAIL. Yet I do not think he had come for good. William says they fly up from the south and if it be cold they go back and stay.

ALISON. Will says a great many unpleasant things. This little robin is the advance guard sent by his clan to reconnoiter. He sang to me and said he felt the tingling sweetness of spring in the air despite the snow, and that he would go back to tell the others and they would at once make ready for their journey.

ABAGAIL [*smiling forlornly*]. I can not feel as you do. I am depressed by this rough life.

SARAH [*from within*]. Mother, we can't do these problems Aunt Alison gave us.

ALISON. Work at them a little longer.

EDWARD [*coming out, followed by* SARAH]. But they are too hard.

ALISON [*to* EDWARD]. Read yours over carefully and you will see how to do it.

EDWARD [*reading from his slate. Both children have slates*]. "If it takes an ounce of meal to make a little hoe-cake, and a boy eats six little hoe-cakes for breakfast, dinner, and supper, how long will it take him to eat up a bushel of meal?" It 's too hard, and besides no boy would eat nothing else but hoe-cakes.

ALISON. Suppose he had nothing else to eat?

EDWARD [*grinning*]. His father would go out and shoot wild turkeys.

ALISON. Suppose his father did n't dare go far enough to get wild turkeys because the Indians were on the war-path?

EDWARD. Then the boy would eat some of his sister's apples. Ask *her* for *her* puzzle.

SARAH [*reading*]. "If each blossom in the spring means an apple in the fall and there are three trees, one with a thousand pink and white blossoms, one with two thousand, and one with three thousand, how many red apples will there be in October?" I am going out to see if the little new apple trees have any blossoms coming.

EDWARD. I 'm going out to play.

ABAGAIL. No, no. I am afraid to have you go.

[*There is a knock at the door,* ABAGAIL *looks frightened,* ALISON *stops her wheel and goes to answer the knock.*]

ALISON [*calling out*]. Who is there?

EUNICE [*from without*]. Oh, it is I, Alison. Open up, I 'm not an Indian.

[ALISON *laughs, unbolts the door, swings it wide, and in walks the neighbor,* EUNICE MORTON, *a pleasant, jolly soul, with her two children,* ARTHUR *and* LUCY.]

ALISON. I did n't think you were an Indian, but sister Abagail is so timid we always ask who 's there before opening, to satisfy her.

ABAGAIL. It is best to be on the safe side.

ALISON [*laughing*]. Of the door.

EUNICE [*to* ABAGAIL]. You are so sure of Indians, they will come and get you some day.

ALISON. Sit here. [*She pulls up her chair to the fire,* EUNICE *takes it,* ALISON *herself balances on the edge of the*

table, for a few moments, gracefully swinging her foot.]
ABAGAIL. I do fully expect them. I would not be surprised nor unprepared.

ALISON. Oh, dear. I should be surprised and scared out of my wits.

EUNICE. The ones who think they will be frightened are the ones who will be brave. [*To the children who are sidling about, talking to each other, half embarrassed.*] You children run outdoors and play.

ABAGAIL. No, no. I am afraid to have them outside alone. I fear Indians and snakes and animals. I can't bear to see them out of my sight.

EUNICE [*laughing*]. You see too much out of your sight! Don't imagine unpleasant things for fear they'll come. Run along, children.

ABAGAIL. For a little, then. But if anything happens, come right in.

[*The children go out.*]
EUNICE. You'll make them cowardly, Abagail. Where are the others?

ABAGAIL. Little Alison and the baby are asleep in there. [*Pointing to the inner room. She sighs.*]

EUNICE. Abagail, why do you torment yourself so always with the thought of Indians? A mouse does n't sit down and repine all day about the cat that may eat it up. Perhaps the cat won't come. If it is in my stars to be scalped by Indians, I shall be scalped and it can't be helped. I am not going to make myself miserable thinking about how it will feel. Sometimes I almost believe fear will bring Indians.

ALISON. More like the white man's bad treatment of them will bring them.

EUNICE. In either case worry does n't help.

ABAGAIL. Oh, you are very brave, Eunice, but I am not so blessed. The Lord has not made me valiant.

EUNICE. Well, Abagail, I do think if you did n't leave so much to the Lord and tried to help yourself a little, you would be much more comfortable.

ABAGAIL. But our house is so far away from the rest of

the settlement, and there is the creek between. William
preferred this land over here—it was n't *my* choice.

ALISON. The gardens and orchard are starting excellent
well.

ABAGAIL. We could all be scalped over here and the rest
of the settlement none the wiser. Especially in winter.

EUNICE. Well, winter is nearly over. It is getting much
warmer, real St. Valentine's weather and thawing fast. The
ice in the creek will be gone by morning.

ALISON. Oh, then the ice in the river must have broken
and the boats from above will be coming soon with supplies.

EUNICE. We are almost in dire need of supplies. I
understood a messenger was dispatched from the fort yesterday to Mr. Armatage begging him to hasten them as fast as
possible.

ABAGAIL [*sighing*]. I do wish we were not so far from
the fort.

EUNICE. Why don't you wish you were back in Jersey?
But I am forgetting my errand. We are going to kill our
pigs tomorrow and I came to ask if we might borrow your
big kettle?

ABAGAIL. Yes, and welcome. I hear your pigs are very
fine and fat.

EUNICE. We fed them on beech and hickory nuts the
children gathered in the fall. I must be going. [*She rises,
goes to the door and calls the children who all come troop-
ing in.*]

ARTHUR. You have spoiled our game. The boys were
just going to scalp the girls.

EUNICE. It 's well I interrupted them—just in the nick
of time to save the girls' lives. I 'll send over for the kettle
later. Perhaps my brother Geoffrey will like to come to
carry it. [*With a laughing glance at* ALISON.]

ALISON. Perhaps he would not, Mistress Eunice, like to
carry a great heavy iron kettle.

EUNICE. Oh, a light heart makes a light kettle. Oh, fie,
Mistress Alisón Carmichael, I know very well why he is
always finding an excuse to cross the creek. [ALISON *makes*

a little face at her, smiling.] Come along with me a little way. [*To* ABAGAIL.]

ABAGAIL. I am afraid.

EDWARD. Can't we go, too?

LUCY. Oh, yes, please, can't we?

EUNICE. Yes, all of you.

[*They say good-by and are about to go out.*]

ALISON. Come over this evening and I'll have some apples and nuts, maybe popcorn and cider.

EUNICE. Very well, we'll come. Shall I bring Geoffrey and Geoffrey's fiddle?

[ABAGAIL *opens the door, the children rush out,* EUNICE *is just going through, when she exclaims.*]

EUNICE. Well, well, well, well! Where did you come from? [*To* ABAGAIL *and* ALISON.] Here are two visitors. [*The two men,* JOHN MORTON *and* GEOFFREY BAXTER, *her husband and brother, enter jovially and greet* ABAGAIL *and* ALISON.] Wasn't there men's work for you two to do without your coming visiting in the afternoon like women?

JOHN. No, dear wife, we felt drawn to follow you.

EUNICE. Keep your compliments, John, for those that will swallow them.

JOHN. Well, then, to tell the truth, I came to borrow and bring home the Carmichaels' big iron kettle and Geoffrey, knowing how weak my arms are, felt he must come along to help me carry it. [*With a grin.*]

GEOFFREY [*half blushing*]. I was just starting out to see if I could find a squirrel and thought I might as well come this way with him.

EUNICE. Well, get along, then. For I am just starting for home.

ABAGAIL. The kettle is outside behind the house.

JOHN. We'll find it there then. [*He starts out.*]

EUNICE. I'm glad you came. We'll all go home together. [*She goes out and* ABAGAIL *follows her.*]

GEOFFREY. If I get a squirrel, sweetheart, may I bring it back to you?

ALISON. If you are in truth after a squirrel, Geof, you'd

better be off at once, for the dark will fall fast and it will be gray in the woods.

GEOFFREY. Then I 'll be coming back this way with it.

ALISON. Oh, you can bring it over tonight, if you like. I think they are all coming over to spend the evening with us. Now be off with you, sir.

GEOFFREY [*trying to kiss her, but she evades him*]. Goodby, sweetheart.

[ALISON *follows him to the door, stands there a few moments, comes in, leaving the door open, goes to the fire where she warms her hands a little while and then is about to place a log on the fire when a young Indian suddenly and in absolute silence appears at the door. He stands stock-still watching her, and* ALISON *as if by intuition turns about and sees him. She is startled into dropping the log of wood but otherwise shows no trepidation.*]

WHITE FEATHER. How!

ALISON. How!

WHITE FEATHER [*they take plenty of time between their speeches, the Indian for lack of nerves and possessing a large mental leisure,* ALISON *because of her unseen kinship to him*]. Me come to see Chief Carmichael.

ALISON. He is not at home. Perhaps he will be back soon. Won't you come in?

WHITE FEATHER. See him. Trade.

ALISON. Are there others with you?

WHITE FEATHER [*standing perfectly still in the doorway*]. No.

ALISON. Won't you come in?

[*The Indian stands silent a few moments, then enters and takes the chair* ALISON *places for him before the fire. She stands. He is tall and handsome, a splendid young brave, and his movements are all quick, adroit, graceful.*]

WHITE FEATHER. Cold.

ALISON [*closing the door*]. It is.

WHITE FEATHER. Me no cold—young white squaw. [*He does not look at her, keeping his eyes on the fire.*]

ALISON. Mr. Carmichael will be back any moment, but perhaps I can tell you what you want to know.

WHITE FEATHER. Indians want meal. Trade skins.

ALISON. Oh, there is so little meal left in the settlement. It has been such a cold, hard winter. Have n't your people felt it?

WHITE FEATHER. Indians hungry. No meal.

ALISON. No meal at all?

WHITE FEATHER. No meal.

ALISON. Oh, I am so sorry.

WHITE FEATHER. Indians hunt. Eat game. No meal. Plenty skins. No meal. Indians all hungry—some sick—some dead.

ALISON [*exclaiming*]. Oh! [*Taking a step toward him.*] I know Mr. Carmichael will do all he possibly can for you. I am so sorry. I would help you if I could.

WHITE FEATHER [*looking at her directly for the first time*]. Indians no hurt young white squaw.

[*The door opens and* WILLIAM *and* ABAGAIL CARMICHAEL *and their children enter. At sight of the Indian* ABAGAIL *gives a scream and hurries the children into the other room.*]

WILLIAM [*a raw-boned and severe young pioneer*]. How, chief!

WHITE FEATHER. How!

ALISON. Brother, he has come to see if he can effect a trade with you. The Indians are greatly in need of meal. He says they have furs they want to give you for meal.

WILLIAM [*grimly*]. He 's brought his pigs to a poor market.

WHITE FEATHER. Indians no meal. Hungry. Sick. Starving. Indians have plenty furs. Good furs. Mink, beaver, otter, good furs.

WILLIAM [*roughly*]. I don't want any of your furs.

WHITE FEATHER [*insinuatingly*]. Good furs! Fine!

WILLIAM. I can't help it how good they are, I don't want 'em. We 've little enough grain. We 've got to keep it all to last the season through. I can't spare any to you.

ALISON. Oh, Will, give him some if you possibly can. Some of his people are sick and dying for want of food.

WILLIAM. That's like enough, but it's not my fault. [*To the Indian.*] Why didn't you go to the fort to trade?

WHITE FEATHER. No good. Big chief there say "yes" one day, say "no" another day. No keep word with Indians. In summer promise meal, in winter no trade. Chief Carmichael good man. In summer he promise meal to Indians. He keep word. Indians like him.

WILLIAM [*uneasily*]. Oh, they do, do they? Well, I've always tried to deal fairly with them, but I can't let them have any meal now.

WHITE FEATHER. Last summer Chief Carmichael promise meal.

WILLIAM. I can't help it if I did. There's not enough.

ALISON. Oh, Willie, give him a little. Give him my share.

WILLIAM. No, I'll not. You go back to your people and tell them what the big chief at the fort said is true and that he is a good chief. Tell them I have no meal for them. Your people better plant enough corn this year to last the winter out. You ought to learn your lesson.

[WHITE FEATHER *rises and walks with dignity to the door.* ALISON *looks much distressed.*]

WHITE FEATHER. Me tell.

ALISON. Brother, at least ask him to stay for supper.

WILLIAM [*condescendingly*]. Why yes, chief, won't you stay and eat with us?

WHITE FEATHER. No, Indians waiting. Me no stay.

ALISON [*detaining him*]. We would be so glad to have you stay and share our food with us, chief.

WHITE FEATHER. Me go.

ALISON. Good-by, then. [*She impulsively offers him her hand. He takes it, looking at her intently, and then with dignity walks out.* WILLIAM *closes the door after him, bolts it and then places his gun, which he has kept all the while on his arm, in a corner.*]

WILLIAM. You can't do anything with those people. They 're shiftless. You can't help them.

ALISON. I think you can.

WILLIAM. They 're all a pack of scoundrels.

ABAGAIL [*coming in with all the children, carrying the baby, and with little* ALISON *holding to her dress*]. The redskins are all like devils. I am so afraid they will come and wreak their vengeance on us now. Alison, why did you let him in? Why did you allow him to enter?

ALISON. The door was open and he walked in. I did n't let him. He did n't ask to be allowed. [*Laughing*]. I suppose he never dreamed he was n't welcome. I think he understands we can't spare the meal, but whether he will be able to make the other Indians understand when he tells them of brother William's refusal—I don't know.

WILLIAM. Oh, don't bother your head about it. He was probably lying all the time. And they 're always begging. We 're well rid of him. I 'm as hungry as a bear. How soon will supper be ready?

ABAGAIL. In my fright I totally forgot supper.

ALISON [*bustling about and taking down a pan*]. It won't take long.

[*The curtain falls.   End of Act I.*]

ACT II

[*It is evening of the same day and in the same room. The family have just had their supper. A roaring fire is burning in the fireplace and candles are lighted.* WILLIAM CARMICHAEL *is cleaning his gun, his wife is putting the baby to bed in its crib,* ALISON *is just finishing washing the dishes,* EDWARD *and* SARAH *wiping them for her, and little* ALISON *is playing with a rag-doll on the floor.*]

ALISON. I can't get those poor Indians out of my mind. I wonder if they are having any supper.

WILLIAM [*laughing*]. No corn meal! But they 'll have game. Trust an Indian always to be able to find plenty of game. I can go out hunting and never see a rabbit, not to mention a wild turkey, much less a deer, but an Indian can scare up a deer most any time, the way a robin gets a worm.

ALISON. Robins can't get worms out of frozen ground in the winter. Birds starve to death in the forest.

[*There is a knock at the door*, WILLIAM *jumps to his feet, strides to the door and calls out.*]

WILLIAM. Who 's there?

EUNICE. It 's us! We 've come to scalp you!

[WILLIAM *unbolts the door and* JOHN MORTON *and* EUNICE, *and her brother*, GEOFFREY BAXTER, *come in. Both men carry guns and* GEOFFREY *a violin. There are greetings.*]

GEOFFREY [*to* ALISON]. I 've brought you a present. [*He stands his gun against the wall and takes out of his pocket a strand of red beads which he gives her.*] I got them from an old sailor at the fort today.

ALISON [*delightedly*]. Oh, Geoffrey, they are beautiful!

GEOFFREY. Do you know that tomorrow is St. Valentine's Day?

ALISON. No, in this wilderness I had clean forgotten it.

GEOFFREY. Will you be my valentine? Will you say "yes" at last? [*He speaks very low to her and the others are busy and pay no attention to them.*]

ALISON. Oh, Geoffrey! I 'll tell you tomorrow.

GEOFFREY. Well, at least, may I put these on you? [*He puts the beads over her head and they drop down about her neck. He leans over and tries to kiss her but she escapes him and runs back to her dishes.*]

WILLIAM [*as they take off their wraps*]. You are welcome, neighbors, but you are the only family in the settlement that goes out at night.

EUNICE. A lusty heart goes all the day, a timid stops at night.

ALISON. There are Indians about.

EUNICE [*derisively*]. Dear me, I shall have to lock up my chicken coops.

ABAGAIL. Eunice, you are foolhardy.

EUNICE. Abagail, care killed a cat.

[*As they take off their heavy garments,* JOHN MORTON *examines* WILLIAM'S *gun,* GEOFFREY *follows* ALISON *who throws a dish-towel to him and he wipes the last dish,* EUNICE *leans over the crib looking at the baby, and then speaks to little* ALISON.]

EUNICE. Up yet? Such a late little girl.

ABAGAIL. I must put her to bed. [*She takes little* ALISON *by the hand.*]

EUNICE. I am afraid we got here too early.

ABAGAIL. Oh, no, but we were late starting supper.

ALISON. We had a visitor.

GEOFFREY [*quickly*]. Who?

ALISON [*laughing and shrugging her shoulders*]. A young Indian. [*She hands him a pan, telling him where to hang it on the wall.*]

GEOFFREY. I don't like even an Indian here calling on you. I am jealous of everything.

ALISON [*saucily*]. He is a very fine young man.

WILLIAM. I've seen the fellow before. He is a young brave, going to be one of the wise men in the council some day. He has some education, been to school and with the white men a great deal. But I don't trust any of them. He said he came to trade furs for meal but he came to the wrong diggings.

JOHN. I reckon he was just nosing around.

ALISON. Edward, get the apples, and, Sarah, get the cider.

[*The boy climbs the ladder to the loft and the girl goes with a pitcher into the other room.* ALISON *takes down some tin-cups and hands them to* GEOFFREY *to put on the table.*]

WILLIAM. They've got a lot of curiosity.

EUNICE [*sitting down in a chair and getting out her knitting*]. They're human.

ABAGAIL [*coming out of the other room with her knitting*].

The way that child sleeps! The way she falls asleep and the way she keeps on sleeping!

EUNICE. She's a healthy child. She would sleep through an Indian attack.

[EDWARD *lowers a rope with a basket of apples which* GEOFFREY *takes and, setting it on the floor, picks out a large one, red and shining, and begins peeling it.* SARAH *brings a pitcher of cider which* ALISON *places on the table by the cups.*]

ALISON. Now, Edward, dear, the nuts—and, Sarah, the popcorn. Will you have some cider now or later? [*To the guests.*]

JOHN [*laughing*]. I'll take some cider now and later.

[ALISON *pours a cup of cider for him and* EDWARD *brings a basket of nuts.*]

ALISON. Brother Will, will you crack the nuts? I'm going to roast some apples.

JOHN. Let me crack the nuts while he finishes with his gun.

[ALISON *gives him a smoothing iron and a hatchet and he goes to work. The women knit.* SARAH *has brought the pop-corn and* EDWARD *and she sit on the floor and shell it.* ALISON *is also sitting on the floor selecting apples to roast.*]

GEOFFREY [*just finishing the peeling of his apple*]. Here you are, Alison. [*He hands it to her on the point of his knife and then the peeling.*] It's a whole unbroken rind. Do you want to throw it over your head? Will you name it? Will you name it right?

ALISON [*getting up laughing and taking the rind*]. Yes, I'll name it, but I won't tell you who. [*She looks at him roguishly, takes the apple rind and standing in the middle of the floor, swings it round her head three times after the old custom and then drops it over her shoulder behind her on the floor.*]

GEOFFREY [*leaning over anxiously to examine the apple rind on the floor*]. It is a G!

ALISON [*leaning over with him, mischievously*]. Indeed, sir, it is nothing of the sort. It is quite another letter.

GEOFFREY. It *is* a G. It could n't be anything else.

ALISON. It looks much more like an F. or a W.

GEOFFREY. It is a plain G.

ALISON. If it were a G at all, it ought to be a handsome G. But is is n't a G—it is a true W.

[*He tries to catch her hand but she eludes him. The others have been paying no attention to them but following their own occupations and talking to each other.* JOHN *has taken up the violin and tuning it now calls out.*]

JOHN. Take your partners! [*He plays a rollicking old-fashioned tune.* WILLIAM *with great flourishes invites* EUNICE *to dance and* GEOFFREY *seizes* ALISON. *The four of them dance old-fashioned figures and the dancing continues gayly for some time. Suddenly there is heard the whistle of a red-bird.*]

ALISON. Listen!

[*The whistle is repeated.*]

ALISON [*startled*]. At night!

[*They start apart and are silent listening.*]

JOHN [*laying down the violin*]. The redskins are at their tricks.

[*They are still listening. Again the whistle is heard louder.*]

WILLIAM. It 's the red rascals. What are they up to?

[*There comes the sharp report of a musket, the sharp crack of a bullet against the door. They all start, the little girl runs to her mother.* WILLIAM *grabs his gun and quickly loads it, the other two men seize theirs from the corner where they stand. Other bullets are heard cracking against the house in quick succession.*]

ABAGAIL [*whimpering*]. Oh, dear! Heaven preserve us! The red-skins have come!

EUNICE. You 've got what you have been looking for so long.

ALISON. Be quiet.

[ABAGAIL *is panic-stricken.* WILLIAM *goes to the door, opens the hole and after peering through cautiously, thrusts in his gun and fires. There is heard a shriek from with-*

*out followed by the weird cries of the Indians. Bullets be-
gin to rain against the house.*]

JOHN. Have n't you got other guns to load?

WILLIAM. Yes, I have. Son, get the carbine.

EDWARD. Yes, father. [*He climbs up and gets down the
gun from the wall.*]

WILLIAM. Alison, the old musket and the pistols.
There 's a hole. [*To* GEOFFREY, *indicating the shutter.*
GEOFFREY *inserts his gun and fires. There is a yell from
without.*]

GEOFFREY. I do believe that 's one less.

WILLIAM. John, go in and fire through the shutter-hole
and watch.

EDWARD [*with a carbine*]. Here, father.

EUNICE. Oh, I 've got to be doing something! [*She picks
up the carbine.*] I 'm going to the loft and fire from the
loop-hole there. [*She climbs the ladder with her gun and
soon is heard firing from up there.*]

SARAH. Oh, mother!

ABAGAIL [*moaning and holding the little girl*]. Oh, my
child! Oh, dear.

WILLIAM. Edward.

EDWARD. Yes, father.

WILLIAM. Get me the cutlasses and the knives. They
won 't get in here [*grimly*], but we 'd best be ready for a
hand-to-hand fight. [*To the women.*] Keep loading the
guns and pistols.

[ALISON *loads the guns and pistols, handing them to the
men.* ABAGAIL *tries to assist but gets in the way and runs
about moaning and wringing her hands. She goes into the
other room and comes out.*]

ABAGAIL. Little Alison sleeps through it all.

WILLIAM [*grimly*]. She would sleep through an Indian
attack.

EUNICE [*calling from above*]. I hit one then, I know I
did, I know it.

[ABAGAIL *goes to the cradle, starts to take the baby out,
puts it back, weeps, and becomes more helpless and distracted.*

The bullets crash against the house and the weird yells of the Indians are heard. Within the men shoot and ALISON *arms them.* EUNICE *shouts from above and calls to them encouragingly. This continues for some time.*]

GEOFFREY [*fires and then quickly extracts his gun, looks through the loop-hole and speaks excitedly*]. I hit one then in the ankle. He fell like a deer. I saw him in the moonlight. [*He takes another gun from* ALISON, *thrusts it in the hole and fires again. A bullet hits the window where he stands, he utters an exclamation, retreats a moment, then returns and fires again.* ALISON *comes to him, touches him on the arm as if to make sure he is all right, then returns and loads another gun.*]

INDIAN [*from without*]. Surrender.

WILLIAM [*shouting back*]. Never. We have big garrison.

GEOFFREY. Run while you have the chance, you dogs. We'll be out on top of you in a jiffy.

JOHN [*coming out of the other room and yelling loudly*]. The whole fort will be on your trail by morning.

EUNICE [*from above, imitating a man's voice, and climbing down the ladder enough to show her smiling face*]. We've got more soldiers here than at the fort, even. [*She climbs back and fires again. There is an answering yell.*] I got him in the leg.

WILLIAM [*seizes a pistol, peers through the loop-hole, then thrusts in the pistol and fires. There is a prolonged yell and scuffling of feet on the outside.*] I hit one that time, I think. [*Peers through the hole.*] I did. They are carrying him off and another one, too. Eunice did bring down her man, sure enough. [*He puts in a gun and fires again as* GEOFFREY *does, too. There are one or two more yells and bullets in answer and then silence.*]

GEOFFREY. They are going away.

WILLIAM [*after a pause*]. They are gone.

GEOFFREY [*after another anxious, listening silence*]. At least several of them were wounded.

WILLIAM [*rubbing his hand down the barrel of his gun*]. Good work, old lady.

EUNICE [*climbing down the ladder*]. It's all over now and we must start for home.

ABAGAIL. Oh, you can't go tonight.

EUNICE. My children are there.

WILLIAM. They are all right. They are within the settlement.

EUNICE. Oh, they are safe enough, but they will be frightened. I must go to them. The Indians have gone back to their village and the going in the opposite direction will be safe enough back in our settlement.

ABAGAIL. Oh, indeed they may be lurking behind trees.

EUNICE. Never fear. It wasn't a large band. I could almost count them in the moonlight and they've all gone to carry home their wounded.

JOHN. Eunice thinks right. We must go back to our little fellows. The red-skins won't be back and won't be near for they'd never think of any of us going out again to-night. They won't be back—they've had their night's work. But have a signal ready. In case of need, fire three times in rapid succession and I will come and bring all the men of the settlement over with me.

GEOFFREY [*to* ALISON]. Let me stay with you to guard you. I can't bear to leave you.

ALISON. Your sister needs more than one man to protect her on the way home. You must go.

GEOFFREY. But I think I *must* stay.

ALISON. No, no, I will not let you.

WILLIAM. We will be safe enough now. But I will fire the gun for signal if necessary. [*He unbolts the door and peers out cautiously.*] There is not a sign of them. They've had their dose. I think it is as safe for you to go as if you were walking the streets of Philadelphia. If I didn't I'd make you stay.

EUNICE. We would have to go even if it were not safe.

WILLIAM. But I know the customs and tricks of these varmints pretty well. They'll not be back tonight.

JOHN. Some time later, maybe.

[*They get ready to go.*]

GEOFFREY [*holding* ALISON'S *hand*]. I can't bear to leave you. No telling what may happen before I may see you again.

ALISON. You must go now. Are n't you coming to-morrow? [*She pushes him out after the others.* WILLIAM *comes in from without where he has proceeded with the* MORTONS, *shuts the door and bolts it.*]

[*The curtain falls. End of Act II.*]

ACT III

[*It is after breakfast the next morning in the same room.* ABAGAIL *has put the baby into its crib.* SARAH *sits on a low stool sewing. Little* ALISON *plays with her rag-doll on the floor.* ALISON *hangs up some pans and so on after washing the dishes.*]

ALISON. Where was brother Will going this morning?

ABAGAIL. To help clear away Cyrus Halloway's new field.

EDWARD. It 's wet to burn stumps.

ABAGAIL. They have n't got the trees cut down yet, let alone burning the stumps.

SARAH. Father went away and left us all alone and maybe the Indians will come and get us.

EDWARD. He knew they would n't come or he would n't have gone away. Father knows all about the ways of savages.

ALISON. He thinks there is no possibility at all of their coming in the daytime and that they will not come even at night for a long time, if ever, because so many of them were wounded and they have n't a very strong force now and believe we will be prepared for them and they are afraid of the soldiers at the fort.

ABAGAIL [*sits disconsolately*]. I don't think they are afraid of anything. That attack last night was enough to make us all die of shock. I wonder any of us survived. Oh, I wish we had never left Jersey. For all they say this land is so rich I 'd rather be poor and safe and back in Jersey. And we were n't so poor there, either, but lived like kings and queens compared to this.

ALISON. In a few years, sister, this land will flow with milk and honey and bloom with peach trees and roses, and you will have forgotten you were ever afraid of an Indian.

EDWARD. I 'm not afraid of them now.

SARAH. I am—almighty afraid.

ABAGAIL. Little maids don't say "almighty"—only rough men say that.

SARAH. But I am that.

EDWARD. What? A rough man? [*Laughing uproariously.*]

SARAH. No, but almighty afraid.

ALISON. I am going down to Mary Hopkins'. I promised to help her this morning with her quilting.

ABAGAIL. You 're going to leave me all alone?

EDWARD. You are n't alone, mother.

ALISON. If Will had n't said it is now perfectly safe, I would n't leave you. But you know he truly thinks so. *He* has gone.

EDWARD. The creek is melted and full of floating ice this morning.

SARAH. You can't cross it.

ABAGAIL. 'Tis very cruel for you all to go away and leave me when I am so unnerved.

ALISON. But, Abagail, dear, I promised to go to Mary and you know Will said it is all safe now. [*She is tying on her hood and putting on her shawl.*] I shall not have to cross the creek, I can go down all the way on this side. [*To the children.*] I am going in the opposite direction from the Indian camp. We will all be back for dinner. You know it is St. Valentine's day. I think—perhaps—Geoffrey will be over this afternoon. [*Smiling and blushing a little.*]

ABAGAIL. I don't see why you don't marry him and make him take you back to Philadelphia.

ALISON. Perhaps I don't want to go back to Philadelphia. [ALISON *goes.* ABAGAIL *sits down with her mending.*]

ABAGAIL. Edward, will you bring in some wood. Don't go further than the wood-pile against the house.

EDWARD. I reckon I will do that, mother. [*He goes out and brings in a log of wood.*] Are n't big log fires fine, mother? In one way it would be nicer to have winter last nearly all summer so as to have the big fires. We have so much wood.

ABAGAIL. It is a good thing we have something. Wood seems to be about the only thing we do have.

EDWARD [*after going out and bringing in some more wood*]. Aunt Alison is quite out of sight. She runs like a deer. You know, mother, she can run as well as a boy can? [*He goes out again but comes in a few moments later without any wood and much frightened.*] Oh, mother, there are Indians out there! The woods are full of them! [*He shuts the door and bolts it behind him.*]

ABAGAIL. Oh, Edward!

EDWARD. They are creeping up behind the house. They are hiding behind the trees. They are coming from tree to tree.

SARAH. Oh, mother! [*Running to her mother and crying.*]

ABAGAIL. They 'll scalp us all. They 'll break in and murder us all.

EDWARD. Let 's try to run for the settlement. Maybe they won't see us with the house between us and them and we can escape. Come on.

[ABAGAIL *catches up the baby in her arms and takes* SARAH *by the hand.*]

ABAGAIL [*to* EDWARD]. Bring little Alison.

[*He catches the child by the hand, pulls her up from the floor, she resists, but he drags her along and together they all hurry out, leaving the door open. As they go there is heard the whistle of a red-bird, followed by the whistle of a quail or bob-white. In a few moments little* ALISON *comes running in again and sits down on the floor, picks up her rag-doll and begins to play with it. In a few moments more an Indian appears at the door, looks cautiously in, and then*

*enters. Another comes and another till five have entered.
They are in full war-paint with tomahawks, guns, and knives.
They utter their guttural expressions, then begin dancing
about, giving their weird yells. Other Indians on the outside keep up a din of strange cries. The ones on the inside
run in and out, break furniture, throw things down, hunt
for the bag of meal which they find and with laughs and
cries of satisfaction they play with it. One of them catches
sight of the little girl who has been sitting staring at them
in fascinated terror, and seizes her.]*

RED FOX. Ugh! Papoose. Kill!

GRAY CLOUD. Scalp little white squaw.

WHITE FEATHER [*entering*]. No, no, give me.

*[The others cry "Kill" and "Scalp" and dance about her.
One of them, RED FOX, seizes her by the hair and they are
about to scalp or kill her outright when WHITE FEATHER interposes, knocks them away, catches the child, and takes her
away in his arms.]*

WHITE FEATHER. No, no. Me keep. My prize. Me keep
papoose. She *mine*. [*He lifts her to his shoulder. The
others yell and dance about, run into the other room and out
again, pulling things about and in the general mêlée WHITE
FEATHER escapes, running.*]

[*Curtain to Act III.*]

ACT IV

*[It is early afternoon of the same day. The scene is in the
Indian encampment in the deep woods where the eye travels
as far as it can see among great oaks, elms, beeches, and syca-
mores. A brook is heard singing among its grasses and peb-
bles. On one side is an Indian wigwam with others extending off behind it. Two Indians, THE BEAVER and GRAY
CLOUD, sit on the ground near the center, wrapped in blankets
and smoking pipes. They sit in silence for a little bit when
the young Indian, WHITE FEATHER, comes running in followed by little ALISON. He runs about, followed by her,
catches her and lets her go, finally picks her up and dances*

*about with her and then sits down on the ground with her
in his lap. The others sit stolidly smoking their pipes without lifting their eyes.*]

WHITE FEATHER. White papoose! Little white squaw!
White papoose like Indian?

LITTLE ALISON. Yes, I like you, but I want to go home.

[*Another Indian, RED FOX, comes in, looks at WHITE
FEATHER with the child, shrugs his shoulders, grunts, and
sits down on the ground near the other two Indians.*]

WHITE FEATHER. Like White Feather?

LITTLE ALISON. I like you but I don't like *them*, and I
want to go home.

[*She is frightened and clings to WHITE FEATHER who continues to play with her, laughing and fondling her.*]

WHITE FEATHER. White papoose! Little white squaw!

RED FOX. White Feather once young buck, now squaw!
[*With the utmost scorn.*] Play with papoose. He no young
buck now, no brave chief. Squaw.

[*The other two Indians grunt and laugh, WHITE FEATHER
looks very angry. An old Indian chief, THE EAGLE, comes
out and slowly and with dignity seats himself on the ground
with the others.*]

RED FOX [*again and derisively*]. White Feather no brave
Indian, he white squaw.

[*The old chief grunts low, and other two grunt and laugh.
WHITE FEATHER breaks out into the Indian tongue, which
may be whatever sounds the actors wish to manufacture and
the audience will be none the wiser—whether they are talking
Choctaw, Chinese or Chili Sauce, though it is really the
tongue of the Miamis whose home was the land of south-
western Ohio. RED FOX, GRAY CLOUD, THE BEAVER, and
WHITE FEATHER talk excitedly, the others evidently taunting
WHITE FEATHER till he gets up angrily and walks off with the
child. The old chief sits stolidly smoking, the other three
grunt, shrug their shoulders, and are amused. They talk to
each other in the Indian language for a few moments, when
ALISON appears. She is terribly frightened but resolute, is*

*very pale, and carries a white cloth tied to a wild cherry limb.
She stands a moment, while the Indians silently watch her,
and then she advances a few steps.*]

ALISON. I—I—am Alison Carmichael. I have come—in
peace. Oh, I am not a spy. I have come in peace. [*She
holds out her flag.*] I have not come to spy on you, to tell
anything, but only for one purpose—only to beg—is this—is
this the big chief? [*To the old Indian. He nods and grunts
assent.*] Oh, I beg you—I *implore* you—to tell me—where
is the little child? [*As she says "where" she impulsively
takes a step towards him, her eyes beseeching him. But the
Indians do not answer her questions, remaining impassive,
staring at the ground.*] Oh, won't you tell me something?
Anything—about her? You know? Is she living? Is she
—is she dead? [*The Indians keep absolute silence, paying
no more attention to her than if she were a red-bud tree or
a stone in the brook.*] Won't you tell me something?
[*Looking from one to the other of them.*] Just one little
thing? [*A pleading pause.*] Only that she is alive! Oh,
please tell me that she is alive! [*Another pause while ALI-
SON stands looking very troubled, pale, and lovely, entreating
the Indians who do not answer nor even notice her. Then she
takes another tack.*] I have come a long way through the
forest alone. My people do not know that I have come. I
am very tired and weary. I am very sad and anxious. I
love the little white child. I would brave anything for
her, to return her safely to her home. I do not fear you,
chief. I do not think you will hurt me. Your people were
hungry, some of them were sick and suffering. Some of
my people treated you badly, you were disappointed and
angry.

THE EAGLE [*at last breaking his silence*]. Young white
squaw no wise. She no see. White braves promise meal.
Break promise.

ALISON. I know they did. Some of them lie and steal
and break their words to each other as well as to you. But
they had no meal to spare. They ought not to have promised it to you.

RED FOX. White squaw fool. Squaws fools, no can counsel. Braves council. Young white squaw go home, cook, work, squaw's work. [*He speaks hotly and derisively, while* GRAY CLOUD *and* THE BEAVER *grunt in laughter.*]

ALISON [*looking quickly from them to the old chief*]. I have not come to argue, nor to fight. Braves do that, red braves and white braves. I am only a squaw, I have come only to beg for the little child.

WHITE FEATHER *appears, is startled and looks anxiously at* ALISON.]

ALISON [*turning impulsively towards the young Indian*]. Oh, White Feather, help me, help me! *You* understand. Make them understand that I have come not to spy on them, that I have nothing against them, that I only want the child. Tell me where she is? Is she—is she alive?

WHITE FEATHER [*looking interrogatively at* THE EAGLE]. Me tell?

THE EAGLE [*nodding assent*]. Umph.

WHITE FEATHER. Little child safe.

ALISON [*with great emotion, almost breaking down*]. Oh, thank you. I knew I could trust you—that you wouldn't let her be hurt. Where is she? Is she here?

[WHITE FEATHER *is about to reply when* RED FOX, *leaping to his feet, suddenly and vehemently protests in the Indian tongue.*]

GRAY CLOUD. Red Fox right. White Feather fool. Talk too much.

ALISON. Oh, he has not told me anything that matters, anything that can injure you if I were to tell it, and I shall not tell a thing. Don't you see? White Feather is only kind to me.

RED FOX White Feather fool. Talk to squaw.

THE BEAVER. Red Fox right. He wise brave. Hold tongue. White Feather talk too much—some fool.

RED FOX. White men promise meal, no keep promise. White Feather say can make keep promise, can get meal. White Feather go, talk to white squaw, no get meal, no keep promise. Talk too much. No wise man, no brave—fool.

GRAY CLOUD. Red Fox right. White Feather talk too much to white squaw.

ALISON. Oh, no, no, no, he is n't a fool. He has n't told me anything that would hurt you.

RED FOX [*who has been stalking about*]. White Feather fool. Umph. [*He gives a sort of angry, nasal, guttural growl like that of an animal.*] White squaw fool, white squaw make trouble. Umph. White squaw go home, stay in wigwam, work, no council with braves. Umph. [*With great aversion and contempt he advances menacingly towards* ALISON *who starts back.* THE BEAVER *and* GRAY CLOUD *grunt* "Umph" *with some rising anger.* WHITE FEATHER *goes towards* ALISON.]

WHITE FEATHER. White squaw no fool, no make trouble. Good.

RED FOX. All squaws fool—white squaw much more fool. White man some fool, no keep word, lie, make trouble. All land [*extending his arm in a sweeping gesture*] all belong to our fathers. White men come, no buy, take. Come, say "brother"—no keep word. Make war, kill Indians. Take land away from Indians, cut trees. Indians have no home, no woods, no hunting-ground. White men take skins, no pay. Take furs—otter, beaver, bear—no pay. Promise—no give —promise—lie. [*He has worked himself up into a passion and has also worked upon* GRAY CLOUD *and* THE BEAVER *till they are greatly excited.*]

WHITE FEATHER. White squaw no make trouble. She no lie.

RED FOX. White Feather fool, no brave. White Feather squaw. Go home with white squaw, work like squaw, cook. [*He begins dancing about and pulls out his tomahawk.*]

WHITE FEATHER [*very angry*]. Red Fox make trouble for whole tribe. White men have fort and many soldiers. White men stronger than Indians. Red Fox fool make trouble.

RED FOX [*tauntingly*]. White Feather no get meal. [*Appealing to the others and trying to incite them against* WHITE FEATHER.] White Feather no do anything. Only talk.

GRAY CLOUD. Red Fox right. Umph.

THE BEAVER. White Feather no get meal. Umph.

RED FOX. White Feather fool. White squaw make trouble. [*He gives one of their peculiar yells and dances from the two Indians towards* ALISON. *They jump to their feet, follow him, leaping and uttering queer guttural, unearthly yells. They dance about brandishing their tomahawks.* WHITE FEATHER *watches them closely, keeping between them and* ALISON *who is terrified. The old* EAGLE *is unperturbed. This continues, becoming more and more exciting, dramatic and menacing to* ALISON, *when* WHITE FEATHER *begins to talk in the Indian tongue excitedly, evidently expostulating with the others and endeavoring to persuade the old Indian to interfere.* RED FOX, THE BEAVER, *and* GRAY CLOUD *reply with derisive yells, threats, and closer drawing towards* ALISON, *while* THE EAGLE *sits as unmoved as a rock. Suddenly* RED FOX *leaps forward, reaching to strike* ALISON. WHITE FEATHER *instantly lunges like a cat towards him, and* THE BEAVER *seizes his chance to make at* ALISON, WHITE FEATHER *leaps back at him and as he eludes* WHITE FEATHER, *jumping away, the latter follows him and* RED FOX *returns, darts at* ALISON, *clutches her in his arms, she screaming, and is about to throttle her, when the old Indian rises to his feet exclaiming in a loud deep tone in the Indian tongue.* RED FOX, *however, does not relax his hold on* ALISON *and* WHITE FEATHER *leaps back from the other Indian to him, grapples and chokes him, he still holding* ALISON, *when, amid the yelling and scuffle,* THE EAGLE *speaks again, louder and more commandingly.* RED FOX *lets go his victim,* WHITE FEATHER *loosens* RED FOX, *the others stop and they all stand suddenly silent and motionless,* ALISON *breathing heavily and trying to recover herself.* THE EAGLE *speaks to them in the Miami tongue and then turns to* ALISON.]

THE EAGLE. Young white squaw go home! [*Majestically raising his right arm and pointing in the direction from which she has come.*] Young white squaw no come back. Young white squaw go home. [*He speaks very slowly as though unaccustomed to English and measuring his words.*

RED FOX, GRAY CLOUD, *and* THE BEAVER *look angry and sullen.* ALISON *turns to go.*]
    WHITE FEATHER. Me go with white squaw to end of woods. [*He watches the three Indians scornfully, then, as if in challenge and with a final contemptuous look at them, he throws back his head and turns away from them and towards* ALISON. *She goes, he following her closely. The old* EAGLE *sits down again, his back towards the retreating figures of* ALISON *and* WHITE FEATHER. *The other three Indians stand watching them with ugly anger and hatred in their faces.*]
    RED FOX. White child! Where find white child? White child alive? [*He laughs, jeers, yells after* ALISON *and* WHITE FEATHER *as they disappear.*] Scalp little white papoose now!
    GRAY CLOUD. White Feather come back soon.
    [RED FOX *laughs, yells, leaps in the air, and runs screaming in the direction* ALISON *and* WHITE FEATHER *have taken. The other two sneak off in the opposite direction, muttering, as if bent on mischief.*]
                    [*Curtain to Act IV.*]

                    ACT V

    [*It is late afternoon of the same day, the fourteenth of February, twenty-four hours after the beginning of the play.* ABAGAIL *is sitting disconsolately in the center of the room, doing nothing, looking woe-begone. The baby lies in its crib.* EUNICE *sits near the spinning wheel by the window and every now and then looks out as if watching for some one to come.* ABAGAIL *weeps, covers her eyes with a handkerchief. The children,* EDWARD *and* SARAH, *sit watching their mother and whenever she weeps,* SARAH *cries, too.*]

    ABAGAIL. Oh, dear! [*She moans and sobs into her handkerchief.*]

EUNICE. Abagail, dear, don't cry so.

ABAGAIL. Oh, it's very well for you to say, "don't cry," but it's not *your* child that's stolen by the Indians.

EUNICE. There, there, Abagail, I did n't mean to hurt you. But it's too hard on the rest of us when you cry so. You see you have other children. Come here, my little bird. [*To* SARAH, *who goes to her*.] Do not be so disconsolate. The little sister is not lost forever. She must be safe and will come back to us—oh, she will be here sooner than the flowers and the birds! Have you seen a bluebird yet, Sarah?

SARAH [*wiping her eyes*]. No.

EDWARD. Robins come before bluebirds.

EUNICE. No, I think bluebirds are supposed to come the very first of all.

EDWARD. But robins *do* come first, for they have come. Aunt Alison and I saw them yesterday and again today and heard them, too.

EUNICE. Then spring is not far away, for he is the sure harbinger of April hopes. And after him come all the flowers.

SARAH [*looking up with interest and a smile*]. Violets?

EUNICE. And what else, Edward?

EDWARD. Spring beauties.

EUNICE [*to* SARAH]. And then?

SARAH. Squirrel-corn.

EUNICE [*to* EDWARD]. And then?

EDWARD. Adder's-tongue.

[EUNICE *looks from one to the other and they answer as if antiphonally*.]

SARAH. Dutchman's-breeches.

EDWARD. Blood-root.

SARAH. Jack-in-the-pulpit.

EDWARD. Wild-carrot.

SARAH. Dandelions.

EDWARD. Dog-tooth violets.

SARAH. Anem—anem——

EUNICE. Anemones. Yes, all springing up in gay little groups out of the dead leaves in different parts of the woods like actors in a grand old-fashioned carnival—the carnival of the coming of summer.

ABAGAIL. I don't see how you can talk and be so flippant and heartless at such a time.

EUNICE. Abagail, dear, don't think I 'm heartless, but it is wiser to keep people cheerful—especially little people. [*She looks out of the window, smiles, and says gayly.*] Ah, there come my little rascals. [*She goes to the door and opens it to her boy and girl,* ARTHUR *and* LUCY.] But I thought I told you to stay at home and mind the house and see that the fire did n't go out.

LUCY. We washed the dishes and tidied up everything and carried in wood and made porridge for supper and then we came over——

ARTHUR. To fetch home our little mother.

EUNICE. You little beggars! But I can't go just yet. Take Edward and Sarah out to play, but don't go far from the house. Stay close where I can see you and call you when I want you.

LUCY. All right, mother.

ARTHUR. Dear little mother!

EUNICE [*to the children*]. Now, run along, lambkins, and have a good time. [*The children all go out, she follows them to the door, and throws kisses after them, then turns and watches* ABAGAIL, *who is silently weeping and mopping her eyes and nose.* EUNICE *goes to her, puts her arms round her, stroking her hair tenderly, and talking to her in a low and tender voice.*] I know it is very hard for thee, poor thing. Do not think I do not sympathize. I love thy little child, and Alison Carmichael is as dear to my heart as a sister could be.

ABAGAIL. But you let her go to those Indians.

EUNICE. She would go. I had no choice.

[*There is a knock at the door and* EUNICE, *answering it, admits two ladies of the settlement,* MRS. KING *and* MRS. WORTHINGTON.]

MRS. KING. We came to express our sympathy and to learn if there is any good news.

ABAGAIL [*weeping*]. No, no, no! No good news nor ever will be again.

MRS. WORTHINGTON. Don't give up hope, neighbor. They stole the child because they liked her, to adopt her, depend upon it. And in that case they will take good care of her and we will get her back, never fear.

ABAGAIL. But Alison's gone, too.

MRS. WORTHINGTON. Alison?

ABAGAIL [*to* EUNICE, *weeping*]. Tell her.

EUNICE. Alison was in an agony about the child and reproached herself that if she hadn't been away from home this morning the dreadful thing some way or another would not have chanced. And she hoped that a woman could do more with the Indians than guns——

ABAGAIL [*breaking in*]. What could she do with those savage butchers?

MRS. WORTHINGTON. Alison didn't go to them?

EUNICE. Yes.

MRS. WORTHINGTON. Oh, mercy! oh, mercy!

MRS. KING. Heaven preserve us!

EUNICE. She has confidence in that young Indian, White Feather. She didn't tell her plan to any one but me and at first I tried to dissuade her, but somehow she overpersuaded me. I have such confidence in her. Anyhow I couldn't dissuade her from her intention—I could only have told and then she would have escaped and run off somehow, for she was determined and she has a will of her own. So I kept still about it till afterwards as she asked me to do. She set out early this afternoon and she has had time to get back by now—more than time—to get back.

MRS. KING. I put no trust in red-skins.

MRS. WORTHINGTON. Nor I.

ABAGAIL. She will never be back! Oh, dear! Oh, dear!

EUNICE. The garrison is taking the matter up. The general is on his way here now to ask Abagail definitely about everything. The rumor is that a scouting party is forming.

MRS. KING [*looking out of the window*]. The General is coming.

[ABAGAIL *is much flurried.* EUNICE *goes to the door and opens it to the* GENERAL, *a red-faced, stout, pompous old fellow in full Revolutionary regimentals. Following him are* WILLIAM, JOHN, *and* GEOFFREY, *all looking very nervous and anxious.*]

GENERAL. Ah, good afternoon, ladies! [*Bowing low to* ABAGAIL.] Good afternoon, Mrs. Carmichael, and ladies!

[*The people dispose themselves about the room, the* GENERAL *seated in the center,* ABAGAIL *near the baby's crib, the men at the back on one side, the women rather on the other. The children have crept in after the* GENERAL, *and, fascinated, are watching him.*]

GENERAL. We are planning to send out a scouting party at once to be headed by our ablest soldier, Captain Hunter, who is much liked by the Indians and has treated with them a great deal. And I am come to ask you for the details of your attack and see if we can find out what Indians committed the deed. Was White Feather among them?

ABAGAIL. Yes, oh, yes, he was one of the prime movers.

EUNICE. Oh, Abagail, you told me that you never looked back, but ran as hard as you could—then how could you tell that White Feather was among them?

ABAGAIL. Well, he must have been.

GENERAL. Now, Mrs. Carmichael, try to be exact. It will help very much. Try to tell me just what happened.

ABAGAIL. Well, White Feather came about this time yesterday afternoon to steal a bag of meal.

EUNICE. Oh, Abagail!

ABAGAIL. I am perfectly sure he came to steal it, but we were all at home, so he decided to beg instead.

EUNICE. Alison said he didn't beg—he wanted to pay for it with valuable skins.

WILLIAM. Of course I couldn't let him have the meal.

GENERAL. Was he angry?

ABAGAIL. Oh, he pretended to be good-natured but he went away and brought back a horde of them to attack the house at night.

EUNICE. There wasn't a horde. There could have been

only a few of them for they gave up the attack so easily.

ABAGAIL. Well, they *did* come, and it *seemed* like a horde.

GENERAL. Yes, yes, I know all that. [*Impatiently. He is an irascible old person and drums with his fingers.*] But what about the child's capture?

ABAGAIL. This morning when my husband said we were perfectly safe—and I don't think any one is perfectly safe with Indians within a thousand miles of you—you 're never perfectly safe, General, you know you never are!

GENERAL [*very impatient and puffy and bored*]. Oh, yes, yes, yes! Go on, go on!

ABAGAIL. Well, this morning when I was left all alone here with the children Edward went out to bring in wood and saw Indians——

EDWARD. They were dodging and hiding and slipping from tree to tree.

GENERAL [*with great severity, pouncing on* EDWARD]. Children should be seen and not heard! Allow your mother to tell her story.

ABAGAIL. I felt that I could not defend the house against them.

GENERAL. I should think likely not.

ABAGAIL. So I caught the baby in my arms, seized little Sarah by the hand, commanded Edward to bring little Alison, and we started to run. We had gone some distance when I found the child had escaped from Edward and gone back, as I suppose, to get her doll. We would all have been slaughtered if we had gone back, so, trusting that the child's tender age might save her in the hearts of the savages, we ran on, plunging into the icy waters of the creek full of floating ice, and finally arrived more dead than alive at the Mortons' house.

GENERAL. You were n't close to any of them, then? Did n't look one in the face?

ABAGAIL. Look a savage in the face? Mercy sakes, I 'd die right there looking one in the face!

GENERAL. And you did n't turn and look back as you ran?

ABAGAIL. Gracious me, no. It's all I can do to run at all.

GENERAL. When the men came over from the settlement, they found the house topsy-turvy and the child gone and the meal? And you didn't see an Indian closely? Very well, madam, that is all. I will send out a company.

[*There is a slight noise at the door, it is opened and* ALISON *comes in extremely pale and tired-looking, her hair rumpled from the tussle with* RED FOX. *They all exclaim and are much excited.*]

EUNICE [*running to* ALISON]. Oh, my dear, my dear, thank God!

[GEOFFREY, *pale and excited, rushes to* ALISON *but gives place to the* GENERAL *who rises and advances to her. With enormous ceremony he bows to her, takes her by the hand and leads her to his own chair.* ALISON *drops into it with a sigh of extreme weariness.*]

GENERAL. Now, my dear young lady, will you tell us exactly what you discovered at the Indian camp and all about your expedition? Shed all the light you can on the mystery.

[*They all range themselves about her in an interested group.* GEOFFREY *edges as close to her as possible.*]

ALISON. Oh, I am so tired! [*Closing her eyes.*] There isn't anything to tell except that little Alison is alive and safe.

ABAGAIL. Oh! [*They all exclaim and* WILLIAM *puts his arm round his wife.*]

GENERAL. But—but! What about the expedition? What did you discover? Tell us all about that.

ALISON. There isn't anything to tell. I went to the Indian encampment—a walk through the woods. [*She opens her eyes and her face lightens into a rather teasing smile.*] You all know what a walk through the woods about here is like. It isn't exactly like a walk along the streets of the town of Philadelphia. The virgin forests are quite different. In the woods there are tangles, briars, underbrush, and at this time of year no birds to make it merry. I found it altogether wearisome. [*She closes her lips and eyes as if that were all she had to say.*]

GENERAL. Yes, yes, my dear young lady. We all know the troubles that would beset your steps in the wilderness. You need not go into details concerning that. But what about the Indians?

ALISON. Oh, the Indians? I found their camp at last.

GENERAL. Yes, yes.

ALISON. I met a number of the Indians. Some of them were polite and [*with a twisted funny smile of recollection*] some of them were distinctly rude.

GENERAL. Yes, yes. Well?

ALISON. That's all.

GENERAL. What? What? Have you nothing more to say?

ALISON. Truly there isn't any more to tell worth the telling.

GENERAL. Very well, I will organize the company at once and send it out immediately.

ALISON [*eying him and thinking*]. Oh, yes, and they told me that the child is safe.

GENERAL. That is really nothing. The company will start at once.

ALISON [*hurriedly*]. Then they advised me to go home and one of them escorted me to the clearing.

GENERAL [*rising*]. Ladies, good afternoon! I will go at once and give the orders.

ALISON. Indeed it would be best not to anger the Indians any further.

GENERAL. I think it necessary to take steps. It unfortunately may mean a bloody war but——

ALISON [*rising and going to him*]. Oh, will you please not start your soldiers right away?

GENERAL. I believe it best to deal with the savages sternly and precipitately.

ALISON. Oh, will you please, sir, give me your word not to do anything before tomorrow morning?

GENERAL [*hesitating*]. Well, upon my soul! Why?

ALISON [*pleading earnestly*]. I can't tell you exactly yet, but you will promise, General, won't you, please? [*Very coaxingly and fetchingly.*]

GENERAL [*giving in to her*]. Well, well, well, though I declare I can't for the life of me see what you are up to, I will wait till tomorrow. And now I must be going. Ladies, good afternoon! [*With great gallantry.*]

JOHN. I will go with you, General. Are you going now? [*To his wife.*]

MRS. WORTHINGTON. We may as well all be going.

EUNICE [*to* GEOFFREY]. Are you coming?

GEOFFREY. In a moment.

[*They all say good-by and follow the* GENERAL *out,* JOHN, EUNICE, MRS. KING, MRS. WORTHINGTON, *and the two children.* GEOFFREY *goes with them, then comes back and hangs about the door.* ABAGAIL *goes into the other room.* ALISON, *who has risen at their departure, drops to the settle.*]

WILLIAM [*to* ALISON]. Are you quite sure the child is safe?

ALISON. Quite.

WILLIAM. What are you planning? This waiting is terrible.

ALISON [*smiling sadly*]. Yes, brother, terrible. Can't you do something to divert her? [*With a gesture in the direction of* ABAGAIL *in the other room.*]

WILLIAM. I will try. Abagail! [*Calling.*] Could you come and help me with the new calf?

SARAH. I want to see the little new calf.

WILLIAM. All right. Come along.

[WILLIAM, ABAGAIL, EDWARD, SARAH *go out.* GEOFFREY *stands and looks at* ALISON *with wonder, almost with reverence in his eyes.*]

GEOFFREY. Alison!

ALISON. Yes, Geoffrey.

GEOFFREY. Are you truly safe and unhurt?

ALISON. Yes, truly safe and unhurt.

GEOFFREY. You don't know what you put me through.

ALISON. Not half what I put myself through. Scratchings and chokings and clawings by briars and brambles and Indians. [*She rubs her neck and arms.*]

GEOFFREY. Did they dare touch you? Did they dare?

ALISON. Oh, did they not? Now, Geoffrey, keep your curiosity to yourself. Some day I'll maybe tell you all about it—when we are a hundred. Not now. Not till this episode is safely over, as I hope it will be soon. It isn't yet.

GEOFFREY. Alison, marry me and we'll go back to Philadelphia to live. [*He seizes her hand.*]

ALISON. Oh, Geoffrey, dear, if you only had a little more of the hero in you—a little more of the Indian brave.

GEOFFREY. Alison, I am in earnest.

ALISON. Geoffrey, so am I.

GEOFFREY. Will you do what I propose, then?

ALISON. I may promise to marry you, but I'll never go back to Philadelphia. With all its hardships I like this free life of the West.

GEOFFREY. But promise me you'll never again undertake an expedition alone to an Indian camp.

ALISON. Oh, yes, I can promise that. You see I wasn't exactly welcome. [*Smiling.*] Now, will you go, please? I am so tired.

GEOFFREY. Poor little girl. But may I come over tonight? You know it is St. Valentine's?

ALISON. I suppose you may come whenever you like now. [*Smiling a little wanly.*] But I am so very tired—I must rest a little. [*He kisses her and goes. She follows him, throws him a kiss as he departs, then comes in, leaving the door open, looks about at the empty and rather disheveled room and throws herself down wearily into the low chair in front of the fire. She sighs aloud and sits there a few moments when* WHITE FEATHER *appears in the doorway with* ALISON *in his arms.*]

LITTLE ALISON. Oh! [*Holding out her arms.*]

ALISON [*starting up with a cry of joy*]. Oh, my precious baby! [*The child runs to her and she catches and hugs and kisses it. Then she speaks to* WHITE FEATHER.] I knew you would bring her back. I was waiting for you.

WHITE FEATHER. Today—morning—me take baby to save her. Indians scalp her—me save her for you. Me do anything for young white squaw.

ALISON. Yes, I know. You are good.

LITTLE ALISON. Mother?

ALISON. Mother and father are out at the stable, looking at the little new calf. Run out to them and give them the nicest surprise they ever had in their whole lives. [LITTLE ALISON *runs out.* ALISON *turns to* WHITE FEATHER.] Won't you come in now and have supper with us?

WHITE FEATHER. No, me go back.

ALISON. But they will want to thank you.

WHITE FEATHER. You thank. 'Nough.

ALISON. Oh, I *do* thank you—you will never know how much. I had faith in you. You are good and very brave. You have much influence with the old chief. You will be a big chief in the council some day.

WHITE FEATHER. Me no like Chief Carmichael. No keep word.

ALISON. He'd give you all the meal he has now.

WHITE FEATHER. Indians angry. Red Fox make trouble. Me no could help attack. Me do anything to save—you.

ALISON. The great chief at the fort was going to send out his soldiers to attack your people for the child. I persuaded him to wait till tomorrow, hoping you could bring her back before then.

WHITE FEATHER. Young white squaw very good, very wise. Me go.

ALISON. There must be no more trouble between your people and my people.

WHITE FEATHER. No more war—peace.

ALISON. Oh, yes, peace.

WHITE FEATHER. My people no stay here much longer. Go west. Go far. Me go far away. No see young white squaw no more.

ALISON [*with feeling*]. Oh, are you going away?

WHITE FEATHER. My people go soon—very soon. No hunting-grounds here no more. Our land all gone from us.

My people must go away. Me go with my people. Me go far away.

ALISON. Oh, won't I ever see you again?

WHITE FEATHER [*with great dignity and sadness*]. No. Never no more. Me go far away.

ALISON [*impulsively and with much emotion*]. Will you let me give you something to thank you for your kindness— something to remember me by? [*She looks about for a second, then quickly takes off the red beads,* GEOFFREY'S *present, which* WHITE FEATHER'S *eyes have been admiring, and gives them to him. He takes them and as she offers him her hand, he takes it slowly, holds it long and tenderly, with a lingering look at her.*]

WHITE FEATHER. Me go far away to the west—me never forget—good-by.

ALISON [*with much feeling and tears in her eyes*]. Good-by.

[*He goes out and as she stands looking after him, the curtain falls.*]

[*End of Act V and of the play.*]

SUGGESTIVE QUESTIONS

1. What effect does the opening scene of the play produce?
2. By what means does the dramatist make the situation clear?
3. Make a list of all references to old times. What is the purpose in making numerous references to the past?
4. Point out various means of revealing character.
5. Study the first three references to Indians. What effect does every reference produce?
6. What is the location of the house in which most of the action takes place? What is the dramatic purpose in naming the location?
7. What gives dramatic force to the first appearance of the young Indian?
8. Point out contrasts in character.
9. Point out contrasts in action.
10. What dramatic purpose does Act I accomplish?
11. What foreshadowing appears in Act I?

12. What is the dramatic value of making use of a small child as a character of the play?
13. What dramatic purpose is accomplished by indicating that the young Indian has had a very different history from that of his fellows?
14. What dramatic purposes are evident in the early part of Act II?
15. What is the dramatic purpose of introducing old-time games, and dancing?
16. Point out action that is merely suggested, not seen? What is the resulting effect? Would it have been better to have presented the action?
17. Point out foreshadowing in Act II.
18. What is the situation in Act III?
19. How did the previous part of the play prepare for the action of the young Indian as shown in Act III?
20. Is Alison's action in Act IV guaranteed by what she did and said before in the play?
21. What is the principal situation in Act IV?
22. What is the value of the stage directions in Act IV?
23. Why is the General introduced?
24. How did the previous part of the play foreshadow the action of the young Indian in Act V?
25. What thoughts, and what emotions, does the conclusion of the play emphasize?
26. Compare *The Pioneers* with the moving picture, *The Covered Wagon*, or with some other moving picture of frontier life.
27. In what ways does the technique of *The Pioneers* differ from the technique of the moving picture?
28. What advantages are gained by stage production?
29. In what ways is stage production limited?
30. What advantages are gained by moving picture production?
31. In what ways is moving picture production limited?
32. Why must each kind of production have a dramatic technique peculiar to itself?
33. Point out all the differences in dramatic technique, between stage production and moving picture production.

SUBJECTS FOR WRITTEN IMITATION

1. Write a short scenario for a somewhat similar play concerning Pocahontas.

2. Write a short scenario for a somewhat similar play concerning kidnapers, tramps, or a Chinese Tong.
3. Write a passage of lively dialogue, introducing and using modern games or indoor amusements.
4. Write a passage of dialogue in which you indicate an unexpected appearance.
5. Write the closing lines of a play, making your last words suggestive of character, or such that they will arouse thought, or stimulate emotion.
6. Write part of the dialogue for the early part of a play, making the dialogue reveal the circumstances of period in history, of season, and of circumstances.
7. Write a short dialogue that will reveal contrasts in character.
8. Write a short dialogue, including full stage directions, for any scene of quick action.
9. Write a passage of dialogue, without stage directions, to indicate action that is not shown on the stage.
10. Write a passage of dialogue, with full stage directions, to indicate highly dramatic action.
11. Write a dialogue between children, or between older people and children.
12. Write a dialogue in which you use dialect, or language peculiarities.

DIRECTIONS FOR WRITING

Say the greatest amount possible in the fewest words possible. At the same time, give your work full evidence of reality. Produce your effects without violating the laws of probability.

ORAL WORK IN CLASS

1. Read aloud a section of the play. Then read aloud a corresponding section of your own work.
2. Read aloud the most pleasure-giving section of the play.
3. Select the part of the play that awakens most intense emotion. Read that part aloud.
4. Select that part of the dialogue that is most compelling in interest. Act that part.
5. Select that part of the play that calls for the greatest action on the part of actors. Act that part.

JUST NEIGHBORLY

By Alexander Dean

Just Neighborly presents action founded on the old theme
of gossip, "Is it best to believe all that our neighbors tell
us?" Students who are familiar with *Mr. Higginbotham's
Catastrophe,* in Hawthorne's *Twice Told Tales,* based on the
same theme, but worked out with an entirely different plot,
will find it interesting to put Hawthorne's story and *Just
Neighborly* side by side, and to notice the different methods
of development of action.

The characters of *Just Neighborly* are simple, country
people, speaking a country dialect, and believing sincerely in
themselves. They have had such slight experience in the
sophisticated world of humankind, that they are ready to become victims of one with a slanderous tongue.

From the first indications of the increasing age and help-
lessness of the old couple, and of their deep-seated longing
for the return of their prodigal son, to the exposition of
their final rejection of the very son for whom they had
longed, the plot is worked out without haste. The words
of the village gossip gradually prove stronger than the words
of the son.

The dialogue has an ease and a naturalness that make it
convincing. Best of all are the suggestions, given in all
parts of the play, that speak far more clearly than do actual
words, concerning the deeper emotions of the father, the
mother, and the son.

Alexander Dean, the author of *Just Neighborly,* is
Associate Professor of Dramatic Literature and Art at

Northwestern University, where he is Head of the University
Theatre, and Head of the Northwestern Playshop. He is
also Director of the North Shore Theatre Guild, an active
group that produces long plays over an extended circuit.
Mr. Dean had remarkable training for his work. After his
graduation from Dartmouth in 1916, and a year in dramatic
study in the "47 Workshop" at Harvard, he played for
several years on the professional stage in the companies of
John Drew, Rose Coglan, Crystal Hearn, and Margaret
Illington, as well as in various stock companies. He then
became Director of Dramatics in the University of Montana,
where he established a University Theatre, and a Traveling
Company. He directed the first American production of
Leonid Andreyev's *He Who Gets Slapped.* He was one of
the first to form a circuit for a Little Theatre group.

Just Neighborly is called by *Little Theatres,* an official
publication of The New York Drama League, "one of the
finest of recent American plays." Since its first production
in 1921, when it won a prize, it has been produced in important cities in many different States. It was first published
in *The Drama,* October, 1921.

INTRODUCTORY PROBLEMS

1. In Hawthorne's *Twice Told Tales* you read the story, *Mr. Higginbotham's Catastrophe.* Outline the plot of that story.
   How does Hawthorne show the cumulative effect of gossip?
   How might the events of that story have led to tragedy?
   What clever development of plot does Hawthorne make?
   Why is Dominicus Pike an ideal character for Hawthorne's
   story?
2. Read *Pippa Passes,* by Browning. What results did Pippa accomplish on her day of freedom from work? How did she
   accomplish these results?
3. Perhaps you have read Thomas Bailey Aldrich's novel, *The
   Queen of Sheba.* If so, tell why the hero of the story was
   unable to identify himself.
4. Write a scenario for a play in which you show that gossip may
   lead to tragedy, or to amusing complications.

5. Write a dialogue in which you show a man, in an unusual situation, making a fruitless effort to prove his identity.
6. What does the game called "Gossip" teach?

THE SCENE OF THE PLAY

It is the kitchen sitting-room of the CARRS *on the Norwich
Road. If you do not already imagine this snug room, if you
do not instantly hear the loud, monotonous ticking of the
clock and the intermittent and hollow sound of the chopping
of wood out-of-doors, then no words of mine can draw the
picture for you. It differs not at all from other gray New
England homes except that a small silver cup shines con-
spicuously on the mantelshelf and seems to be in determined
rivalry to the brilliant, red tablecloth. Nearby this smug
treasure a faded daguerreotype is so placed that we know it
is of equal importance.*

*It is true that there are doors and windows, but indeed I
have forgotten their number and location. When the outer
door is open you will see the distant mountains, but if you
cannot discover them, it is of no consequence, for you will
soon know that this is the hill-country where "humans" are
scarce and "sich few there be"—well, when this neighbor
has had her say, you'll concur with me that neighbors are
not confined to the corners where the occasional postman alone
braves the mud-rutted roads.*

*Here someone hunts, for a double-barreled gun hangs on
the wall. Here someone cooks, for we smell the doughnuts
frying on the stove. These two are* EZRA *and* ADNA CARR.
*Here they have lived and toiled and grown old, thirty years
of it, an unvaried, commonplace, deadening, but for them a
sufficient existence. Tall, spare, slightly bent, his active use-
fulness nearly outgrown,* EZRA *still remains the hard and
domineering master of his household by a naturally quick
and irritable temper. For many years* ADNA *has been his
sole companion, and her meek and forbearing acquiescence
has exaggerated his consciousness of his own importance and
ability. But why should I describe him further, you will*

know him in a moment quite as thoroughly as I. One word of ADNA. *She is quite the antithesis of her husband—a tiny, sweet-faced, lovable mother. The only qualities they share in common are ignorance and simplicity. Now these folks with the neighbor and a—late-comer—can best speak for themselves, so to them I leave the boards.*

It is late afternoon about the middle of September, 1901. The house is empty, but soon ADNA *struggles in with a great basket which she sets by the door. She hurries to the stove, forks out the few doughnuts remaining in the hot fat, and then lifts the heavy kettle to the sink. The back-door is kicked. She hastens to open it, and* EZRA *lugs in a great armful of wood. He drops a piece, and characteristically the wife picks it up. As* EZRA *stoops to deposit the load, he groans, lets fall the wood on the floor, puts his hands on the small of his back and staggers to the rocking chair.*

EZRA. Oh-oh oh! My back! It aches me so!

ADNA. Set a mite, Ezra, catch yer wind.

EZRA. This ain't no work fur a man above seventy years of age anyway.

ADNA. Well I'm five year the younger, but my work's made me feel a good sight the oldest, yet I don't complain.

EZRA. It's a dog's life.

ADNA. It's all the leadin' o' Providence.

EZRA. Ef we'd found gold lyin' right out in our pastures like them New Yorkers, we'd hav our coach an' four, too.

ADNA. We was born on a Sat'day.

EZRA. There ain't no need of our workin', sech as we be with money in the bank.

ADNA. Ezra, you stop.

EZRA [*yelling in a quick temper*]. I've stopped long enough. You think more o' yer money in the bank than you do o' me.

ADNA. Now, Ezra, you know that ain't true; but nobody's goin' ter touch that money till we're flat on our backs with ailments. Ef it warn't fur me a takin' stiddy ter my knittin' o' nights; an' a-gatherin' herbs and simples; an savin', and savin', and savin', there would n't be no sum laid aside. After all my years of toil, I ain't goin', in some flighty spell, ter touch it, and hev it spent an' past like this summer. I ain't, an' you ain't, nor nobody ain't.

EZRA. We 'll die afore we get the good o' it.

ADNA. Then it 'll pay fur our coffins. We ain't got nobody else to do it fur us—now.

EZRA [yelling]. There you go, a-slurrin' at me. You allus do that. Why don't you tell me it 's all my fault, we ain't got our boy with us now, that I drove him out o' my house into the night, an' him only twelve years old. Tell me that I hit him. Carry on like I did n't know it. What are yer waitin' for? That 's just like you.

ADNA. It 's just like you, Ezra, ter boil over so. You go along a pace with no starch in you, an' then git flashy an' het up over some little trifle. I did n't say nothin' about Vyron an' you. I don't talk 'bout him comin' back ter help. Why, from plowin' ter ice-cuttin' and between times, too, you want him here ter work. My lot is plain an' hard workin', and I long fur my boy. But a woman's heart is different. A mother loves her son. She jest wants him 'round. I try not to think on him, but fur thirty years them feelings hev come back an' come back as sure as spring comes with the year.

EZRA. You said it was my fault he war n't here ter pay fur our coffins.

ADNA. No sech a thing. It was his fault, too. He was jest like you. Go along as sweet as milk an' then explode all of a sudden like. Both was that way, the night he run away. [She crosses to the window.] I would n't care anythin' 'bout the past if he 'd only come home to me now, ef he 'd only come home. Our life is just like that plain, rocky garden there, now that the season 's 'bout past. We 're the poor few o' late stalks that 's left combatin' the wind. [She stands silently looking out of the window. He is mute as he sits in the rocking chair, thinking. Outside a woman's loud laugh is heard in the descending scale. This brings the husband and wife to consciousness.]

ADNA. I do believe there 's Neighbor Webb comin' out o' Maria Sharp 's.

EZRA. She 's dreadful good company. Let 's ask her in.

ADNA. She 's kind o' worldly, Rhoda is, but she 's a good friend. [*Calling out of the door*]. Mis' Webb, Mis' Webb. Jest a minute.

RHODA [*a cheery voice outside*]. All right.

EZRA. She knows more news than all the papers this side o' Springfield.

ADNA. She 's real gifted in that line, a-comin' from a most respectable family. My lan's, this dirty apron—tain't decent ter be seen by nobody. I 'll be right back. [*She hastens off*. RHODA WEBB, *a dark-haired and dark-skinned woman, good looking but vixenish, stands in the door. She wears country clothes of an antiquated style, but of brilliant color. Under her arm, she carries a market basket covered with a red cloth.*]

RHODA. Evenin'.

EZRA [*without moving*]. Come right along in.

RHODA. What do you think? Pres'dent McKinley was shot three days ago come eight o'clock tonight.

EZRA. I want ter know.

RHODA [*spying the doughnuts, and crossing to the stove*]. My cousin's husband, Ike Hen Snow, was ter Lebanon yes'ter, and the news came in while he was there. He drove home this afternoon, and I was the fust ter hear 'bout it. [*Looking first at* EZRA *and then at the doughnuts.*] You see— [*She takes a doughnut and slips it into the basket.*] you see—they live in t' other half o' my house. [*Basketing two more doughnuts.*] The party walls in the kitchen has a crack where the house is settling.

EZRA [*helping her out*]. Course you can't help seein' and hearin' all the carryin's on.

RHODA. Who could?

EZRA [*not offering to part with the rocker*]. Hev a chair.

RHODA. Thanks. [*Taking a doughnut.*] But I prefer standin'. [*Taking a sixth.*] Don't know why. They 've been after me—Heavens knows how long—ter hev it fixed.

But somehow I don't seem ter git round ter it. [*By this time she has taken her goodly number and goes to the table.*]

EZRA. I should n't go ter all that work. You would n't do nobody no harm.

[ADNA *returns.*]

RHODA. I was jest a tellin' Ezra, Pres'dent McKinley was shot.

ADNA. What's goin' ter become of us *now?*

EZRA. Any particulars?

RHODA. No—Y-e-s—well, he was way out West.

EZRA. He ought to know better 'n to go out o' civilization.

RHODA. And—and—fifty—[*Seeing she has her audience with her.*] no—one hundred and fifty furrieners attacked him. An' he was killed plumb dead!

ADNA. What turrible times we be livin' in. I would n't feel safe nowhere's outside o' Norwich.

RHODA [*sitting at the table*]. You won't feel secure even ter home when I get thru tellin' yer *all* I know.

EZRA. Can't be wus than losin' our President.

RHODA. No. I s'pose not, but it's nearer home.

ADNA. What can it be!

RHODA. A bank ter St. Johnsburg 's been robbed!

ADNA [*quickly and worried*]. What bank?

RHODA. The Champlain National.

ADNA [*relieved*]. Oh-h.

RHODA. It's not the bank you've got your money in, Adna. Lan's no.

ADNA. How'd you know I've got money in the bank?

RHODA. Oh, I know lots an' lots o' things I don't talk 'bout. Well, the most interestin' part of it all is, that the Reverend Faulkner of the Methodist Episcopal preached a sermon las' Sunday 'bout the wickedness of automobiles. He said them godless instruments are only for the unpious, an' the friends of Satan an' the Devil hisself.

EZRA. That's what I allus said.

RHODA. An' then the very next night four of 'em come right along the turnpike into town. They carried them fiends that robbed the Champlain National.

EZRA. Did n't the sheriff an' constable s'pect 'em when they see 'em come?

RHODA. No. Nobody did.

EZRA. Well, I would n't trust nobody that rides in automobiles.

RHODA. They could n't find 'em the next day, for everyone of them ungodly horseless carriages had gone a different one of the four roads which lead out er the city.

EZRA. It 's their own fault. I 'd known better.

RHODA. Well, that ain't all. One of 'em has took the "come back" road an' everyone 's scared that they 'll clean up Norwich or sleep o' nights in our barns, an' burn 'em when they 're through or murder us in our beds. Maria Sharp, she ain't locked her back dor fur eighteen year, but since I told her, she 's goin' ter do it, not only at night, but in the late afternoon when it gets sort of crawlish out like it is now. Lor! Adna, what you so silent 'bout? You look like you was puttin' up a sort o' silent 'jaculation.

ADNA. I was just a-meditatin'.

RHODA. 'Bout what?

ADNA. How 'd you know I 've got money in the Institution fer Savin's?

RHODA. You poor little dear, you 've been worryin' 'bout that all this while. Well, I seen how anxious you be when I told you, so I know 'd you hed money in the bank, and then you was so relieved when it was the Champlain National that I know'd your bank must be t' other one. Don't give yourself another thought 'bout it. I won't tell nobody.

EZRA. How did you hear all this?

RHODA [with a nervous laugh]. Fan Rundlet hed a communication from her brother-in-law's aunt who lives there. She would n't acquaint me with the news. She held it back jest from spite, an' I vowed she would n't get the best o' me, so when she was outter the room, I investigated the contents for myself. You think I done right, don't you, Ezra?

EZRA. It 's all right fur you women folks.

[ADNA who has been too upset to listen to this and who is

still worrying, goes to the mantel, takes the silver cup and daguerreotype, crosses to the sink. From the cupboard she takes a covered kettle. In this she deposits these tokens, replaces the cover, then the kettle, and finally shuts the cupboard door carefully.]

RHODA [*speaking while* ADNA *is busied*]. Not that I cared what was in it—but.

EZRA. Did they get much of a haul?

RHODA. Most five thousand dollars. Why, what's Adna doin'?

ADNA. There's two things in this house that nobody's goin' ter get. That's my boy's picture, and his silver cup, my sister Lizzie give him when he was born. Jest them two saved, and they can take anything in this house. [*A noise outside of a tin box opening is heard.*] What's that?

EZRA. Now don't get excited, Adna. Ef anybody tries to enter this 'ere house, I'll fix 'em. [*With a look at his gun.*] Don't you worry with me here.

RHODA. Ain't it nice ter hev a smart man like Ezra ter protect yer? My land o' Liberty! It ain't nothin' but the afternoon post.

ADNA. You go, Ezra, will you? [*For the first time* EZRA *moves his hulk and goes out.*] What kin it be? We ain't had a letter since my sister Harriet was took with "near pneumonia." [*With a startled cry.*] Oh-h-h, who has took my doughnuts?

RHODA. Don't look to me. You know ef I touch my lips with a morsel o'nights, I would n't sleep a wink.

ADNA. Yes, I know you would n't rest well.

RHODA. Must hev been Ezra. Men hev such stomics!

[EZRA *returns with great excitement, holding a letter. He hastens to the rocker and sits.*]

EZRA. Somethin' fur me.

ADNA. What kin it be?

RHODA. I do hope it's interestin'. [*She leans over the back of the chair, ready to read it for herself.* EZRA *tears the envelope open, then sees her intention. He looks at her, and holds the gaze, then moves the envelope from her sight.*

*She catches the significance, and withdraws herself, much
disappointed. He, taking his time, produces his spectacles,
and placing them on reads the letter. During which* RHODA
*is suffering from intense excitement and curiosity, keeping
her distance, trying to approach sufficiently near to read for
herself.*]

EZRA [*excited*]. He's comin' home, he's comin'!
Vyron's comin' back!

ADNA. What's that you're——

EZRA [*reading*]. "I'm returning ter take care of you."

ADNA. "Take care of you."

EZRA. Yes, ter do the plowin' fur me, an' the hayin'.
Comin' home soon, he says, tomorrow or the next day.

ADNA. Vyron, my son, Vyron comin'! Comin' ter his
mother, after all these years!

RHODA. My! What grand news! [EZRA *continues to
scan the letter.* RHODA's *inquisitiveness has overcome her
and she is back of the chair earnestly reading over his
shoulder.*]

EZRA [*removing the letter from her vision*]. Just you
keep your eyes ter home.

RHODA. What else'd he say?

EZRA. This letter's mine, not yourn. [RHODA, *keenly
disappointed, and angry, withdraws.*]

ADNA. What else'd he say, Ezra, tell me, please tell yer
wife!

EZRA. Nothin', but I ain't goin' ter hev her an' the
countryside know it. [*But* RHODA *is nursing her anger with
spiteful, contemptuous glances.* EZRA *rises.*] Now le's see.
It's too late now fur the noon train. He won't be here till
the one from Lebanon gits in at eight-thirty.

ADNA. My son, come back! Dear God, I thank thee!

EZRA. Cut yer prayin', Adna; I've got a lot ter do fur
preparation. You jes' set the teakettle on, an' drop in
a good han'ful o' chips. [*He begins to pack the wood-box
with the wood he dropped.*]

RHODA [*caustically*]. Yes, you don't suppose he's hed a
mite o' supper, do you?

ADNA. The poor boy! I s'pose he don't get a good meal o' vi'tuals real often. [*She "builds up" the fire, and puts the kettle on.*]

RHODA [*by the center table*]. Now what kin Neighbor Webb do? Do let me help. What kin I do fur—fur— [*She stops short, changing her tone to excited mystery—as an idea flashes across her imaginative mind.*] Could it be— I do believe——

EZRA. I 'll fetch up a bottle of our dandelion wine.

RHODA [*spitefully*]. My sakes, you 'd better bring up two. This—this—this that 's a-comin' is a man o' the world an' they like twice a mug better 'n once a mug. You watch an' see.

ADNA [*unheeding RHODA*]. I 'd better make up the bed in the best room, too.

RHODA. Seems ter me yer beginning ter take ter him rather soon, ain't yer?

ADNA [*she starts, looks at RHODA, and then too happy to stop to fully comprehend, she goes to the cupboard and takes out the silver cup and the daguerreotype*]. My son, Vyron, a-comin' back to his mother after thirty-two years. [*Placing the silver cup and the daguerreotype back on the shelf. Then she sets a place at the table for him. EZRA is piling wood still. The neighbor gives her wild, tantalizing laugh.*]

RHODA [*with contempt*]. I allus thought, Adna, you cared fur yer son, but now ye leave yer only token of him right where a stranger can help himself to it, I—I——

ADNA [*bewildered*]. Stranger?

RHODA [*cruelly*]. Oh, you think this is really your son that 's a-comin'. 'Scuse me, I forgot.

ADNA. Well, he *is*.

RHODA. Why, sure it 's him. And jest you see how fond he is of that silver cup. He 'll remember that as a-bein' his.

ADNA [*undisturbed*]. I don't know what you 're drivin' at. But I 'm as happy as the robins in the spring. [*She goes about her work, and RHODA, seeing ADNA and EZRA with their backs to her, steps lightly to the table and takes the letter*]

from the envelope. She is just unfolding the letter when
EZRA *turns and sees her.*]

EZRA. Wall?

RHODA [*stammering*]. I—I—I—You said I done right to
inspect Fan Rundlet's.

EZRA. That's a mite different from your investigatin'
mine.

RHODA [*greedily scanning the envelope*]. Where's this
letter come from? [EZRA *rises and grabs the envelope from
her and examines it. She retreats several steps, abashed,
angry, bitter in her disappointment.*]

EZRA. St. Johnsbury.

RHODA. Oh! St. Johnsbury.

EZRA. Why yer askin'?

RHODA. I was jest a-thinkin'.

EZRA. What yer thinkin' on?

RHODA. I didn't know he'd been livin' there.

ADNA. No. No. Course he ain't.

EZRA. He must hev gone there afor' he started for his
home here.

RHODA. Oh yes. Why didn't I understand afore. Course
he'd go way up north fust, instead of comin' right here
direct, through Lebanon.

EZRA. He would ef he wanted to.

RHODA. And then he'd take the fourth road outter the
city, the "come back" road ter Norwich.

ADNA. How else would he be comin'?

RHODA. I guess it's jest as well Maria Sharp's lockin'
her door.

EZRA. What's that you're mutterin'?

RHODA. Nothin'.

EZRA. I heard you sputter.

RHODA. Well, I was reckonin' when he must o' left St.
Johnsbury. Course he didn't leave there Monday night, or
he'd been here long afore this evenin'.

ADNA. That warn't what you parleyed, Rhoda. You
said as how Mis' Sharp was lockin' her door.

RHODA. Did I? Well, I don't know what's the matter with me o' late.

ADNA. I don't see what Ria Sharp's got ter do with my son's comin'. I don't understand what you 're drivin' at. S'pose Vyron was to St. Johnsbury on Monday. What then?

EZRA. Yes. What then? He can travel where and when he likes, my son can. I bet he has his own buggy an' span.

RHODA. Oh fancy!

EZRA. Fancy! He's earned lots o' money, he has.

RHODA. Lots o' money. It's commonly the way with them kind. And they'll show it to you, too. But ain't that nice.

ADNA. The just Lord has made my boy a good man, and smart, and rich. And he's comin' home.

RHODA. Indeed?

EZRA. Indeed! It's aggravatin', you are. [*He turns and goes to the back of the room.*]

RHODA. Then he won't hev no need of your savin's, Mis' Carr, need he? [*She crosses to the mantel.*]

ADNA. Oh, Ezra. [*going to her husband.*] What's she doin'? I 'm almost dizzy. She's upset me so.

EZRA [*to* RHODA]. No. He *won't.*

RHODA. Yes. He won't hev no need of your savin's in the Institution. That's jest what I said, ain't it?

EZRA. Say! But look how you're a-sayin' it.

RHODA. Well, how?

EZRA [*yelling*]. You're tellin' us how this ain't our Vyron. You're tellin' us he's one of them fien's that was ter St. Johnsbury ter steal, and is now a-comin' ter take ourn.

RHODA. Why, Ezra Carr! How can you! I never said nothin' of the kind. You made that all up out o' whole stuff. You know you ain't tellin' the truth, jest now. Did I say all that, Adna?

ADNA [*who is between* EZRA *and* RHODA]. N-n-n-no, but somehow——

RHODA [*to* EZRA]. There you see. Even your wife says I didn't say nothin' like that.

ADNA. But somehow——

RHODA. She admits it right here afore you. She knows
I love her. Don't I, Adna?

ADNA. Yes, but——

RHODA. Look how I allus take the trouble ter go out of
my way ter drop in an' tell you all the news.

EZRA [*yelling*]. You 've told too much this time.

RHODA. . Dear me, after all I 've done fur you! I never
thought I 'd live ter see the day when I was called a liar.

EZRA [*louder*]. You told me jes' now, this war n't my
son, Vyron, that was a-comin'. I don't know the parlance
you employed, but you told me.

RHODA [*weeping at the table*]. I 've allus been a real
good neighbor, I have, and thought you cared fur me, but
now look how yer treatin' an' thankin' me when all 's I done
was ter tell you in so many straight words that yer want ter
be sure it 's him by a-testin' an' a-questionin' him.

EZRA. You never said nothin' of the kind.

RHODA. I did say jest them words.

ADNA. Ezra, don't be too hasty. I hev a feelin' that 's
what she did say atter all.

EZRA. You know she did n't say nothin' of the kind.

ADNA [*turning first from the one then to the other*]. Yes
—no—yes—oh I don't know what 's she sayin'. I 'm all
mixed up.

RHODA [*her head on her arms on the table*]. This is all
the thanks I get fur bein' a good neighbor.

ADNA [*soothing* EZRA]. There, there! This must be our
Vyron. The Lord has surely sent him for us to love in our
old age, to be a comfort fur us after all these years of
prayer.

EZRA. You 're always so plumb full o' doctrine, but I
don't know how good help ye are to me in a situation like
this.

ADNA. You must n't mind what she said. She did n't
mean anythin' bad. Rhoda is a real good neighbor.

EZRA. A place with sech a mess o' women folks ain't
healthy ter live in. It 's a torment, she is. But she can't

keep my boy from fetchin' in the wood o'nights fer his dad.

ADNA [*looking over her shoulder to* RHODA *and then addressing* EZRA]. You really think this is our Vyron, don't yer?

EZRA. Yes, Adna, but—I don't know what ter do 'bout it.

ADNA. I—I—don't know either. I 'm so confused. I 'm so unhappy. Somethin' in me tells me this is Vyron, and then when I think what she said I don't—I don't—know, I—I——

[*Outside there is a noise of a vehicle stopping. It is quite dark.*]

ADNA. Ezra, what 's that?

EZRA. I did n't hear nothin'.

ADNA. Oh Ezra, Ezra, I 'm mortal 'fraid.

EZRA. You 've got me here.

ADNA. Somebody 's comin', and I don't feel like I was able to cope with it.

EZRA. Well, I do. Old 's I be, I 've got 'nough fight in me to handle any of them bank thieves that come snoopin' 'bout us. [*He takes from the wall the shotgun, examines it, and sets it against the wall, directly behind him. Then there is a knock at the door.*] Come. [*A middle-aged man with white hair, tall, good-looking, well dressed, but decidedly the self-made man enters. He, standing at the door, surveys the room, then* RHODA, EZRA, *and* ADNA.]

THE MAN. Mother!

ADNA. Vyron!

[*They rush to one another's arms.* RHODA *retires to the further corner of the room, viewing the scene with suspicion. They hold the embrace for a pause during which only* ADNA'S *sobs are heard.* EZRA *is diffident, smiling inanely, trying not to feel out of it.*]

MAN. Don't, little mother, don't. It hurts too much.

ADNA. For thirty-two years, Vyron, thirty-two years.

MAN. To me more like a thousand. [ADNA *sobs.*] Come, we mus' n't. [*She breaks away and then upon release she rebounds into his arms.*] But this, this is worth a lifetime. More wonderful than I had dared to dream, little mother. [*He kisses her again.*]

EZRA. Ain't you goin' ter say howdy ter yer pa?

MAN. It 's not like me to forget that. [*He holds out his free hand, and they shake.*]

EZRA. I 'm an ailin' man, Vyron, but you 've come jest in time ter help.

MAN. We can settle all that later.

EZRA [*he looks at the man quickly and is worried. Then* RHODA *coughs and he sees the significance*]. You changed yer name, did n't yer?

MAN. Vyron Carr was a good enough name for my mother to give me. It was good enough for me to keep.

ADNA. Vyron! [*And she sobs with her head on his shoulder.*]

MAN. See for yourself if you like. Here 's my business card. [*He produces a card.*]

EZRA. I war n't doubtin' yer word. I don't care 'bout seein' it. [*Thereupon he stares at the proof.*]

MAN. And here 's a better evidence—my check book. There 's my name printed on the end.

EZRA [*taking and looking at the book*]. There ain't no doubt but what you belong to us. And it 's a comfort havin' yer here. [*He hands back the book, but the* MAN *finds it is difficult to return it to his pocket with* ADNA *in his arms, so he lays it on the table.*]

MAN. We mus' n't carry on this way, mother. [*Patting* ADNA.] We ought to be happy.

ADNA. Happy! I 'm almost giddy.

EZRA. You 'll excuse my bein' sort of clever with you. [*A nervous, uneasy laugh.*]

ADNA. Yer pa 's a powerful particular man.

MAN. I belong to you and I belong to Norwich. Why, through all these years, I remember more details. The house where Mattie Turner went crazy——

ADNA [*gently correcting him*]. Not crazy, Vyron, jest sort o' silly.

MAN. And the little white church where Uncle Eleazar was buried.

ADNA. See how well he scares off any 'spicions of his not bein' our Vyron.

EZRA. Yes, yes. [*With a sigh of anticipation.*] With Vyron here, I can lie abed mornin's till sunrise.

MAN. You know I 'd forgotten it—but it all came back to me as I passed by—the incident after his service—when a woman, teary and weepy as if she had lost her own husband, came up to Fan Rundlet and asked whose funeral it was. [*He laughs.* RHODA *steps forward.*]

ADNA [*nervous and trying to change the subject*]. Yes, yes, but you must be tired.

EZRA. I don't recollect nothin' o' the sort.

ADNA. Hev—hev a chair, Vyron. [*She turns the rocker so that he can sit in it, which he does.*]

MAN. *What* was that woman's name——

EZRA. Hold on there. That 's my special settin' place.

ADNA. But Vyron 's got ter hev the best now, Father, the best of everything.

MAN. Her—name——

EZRA. He ought to take us as he finds us.

MAN. I would n't want anything different. [*Rising.*] It 's yours. You shall sit there.

EZRA [*not liking it*]. Be still, be still. I don't want it for some space yet. [*The* MAN *sits, still pondering over the name.*] But in the future, just you keep in mind that that chair is mine.

MAN. I 've got it. Rhoda—Rhoda——

ADNA [*trying to divert him*]. Vyron, you 'll take a taste o' my dandelion wine?

MAN. Rhoda—Rhoda——

ADNA. I made it myself.

MAN. Rhoda Webb—That 's it! Rhoda Webb!

RHODA [*coming forward*]. That 's a white lie. I never did nothin' o' the kind. You 're jest repeatin' gossip you 've picked up 'bout the Center. You 're all lies.

ADNA. Sh-sh. He did n't mean no malice, Rhoda.

MAN [*offering his hand*]. Well, well. Rhoda Webb. My! How you 've changed.

RHODA [*ignoring the hand*]. I ain't changed so much as a certain other I see.

ADNA [*again trying to save the situation*]. You set still—you all—while I step down cellar ter fetch up the wine.

MAN. You rest, little mother. I 'll go.

ADNA. No. You could n't find it.

MAN. Then father 'll go for you.

EZRA. Eh?

ADNA. No! no! [*Upset at the error.*] I 've got to go, Vyron. Yer pa——

MAN. Nonsense. There 's no reason why, with two men in this house, you should. [*With a look at EZRA.*] I know Father will be glad to save you the trouble and work, won't you?

EZRA. Eh? [*They stare at one another, then EZRA rises loathfully.*] Oh-h-h-h ye-s-s.

RHODA [*to EZRA*]. Ain't he goin' ter be sech a comfort an' help? [*Doggedly he goes out, down the cellar steps. To the MAN.*] Ef you know'd yer folks were here all these years why did n't yer trouble to see 'em?

ADNA. How could you keep me worrin' so?

MAN. I was poor, little mother, desperately so. [*There is a short pause.*]

RHODA. Do you mean ter insinuate that you could n't git the car fare?

MAN [*ignoring RHODA and addressing all to ADNA*]. No, no, not that, but I could n't bring myself to come back till I was rich enough to be independent. Then father and I could get along agreeably.

RHODA. That sounds sort-a slim. [*The MAN turns quickly and gives her a severe look.*] Oh, I must hev imagined it.

MAN. I almost got home ten years ago, mother. I had launched a big deal in steel in the Middle West, and it was going through. But my partner and I had a quarrel over a detail. I—I—lost my temper and like a fool quit. That cost me half a million dollars and my home for ten years longer.

ADNA. And did n't you go back an' make up to him again?

MAN. I could n't.

ADNA. Why not?

MAN. No. No. I 'm afraid you don't know *me*, mother.

RHODA. No. Not *yet.* [EZRA *returns with two bottles of dandelion wine. He lays them on the table and sits.* ADNA *gets four glasses and pours out the contents. One has more than the rest.*]

RHODA. A postage stamp only costs two cents.

MAN. Mother, you don't think I didn't *want* to come back?

EZRA. Why did n't you write?

MAN. I was ashamed. [*There is a slight pause.*]

ADNA. I know, Vyron, *I* know. Now wet yer lips with this. It will taste good. [*She hands out the fullest glass of wine for him, but he is lost in thought, and does n't touch it.* EZRA *notices the uneven division.*]

EZRA. Seems ter me ef you 're ter give one more 'n t' other, I ought to be favored. I went and brung it here.

ADNA. But Vyron ain't touched his lips to any fur thurty-two years. Can't you understand?

RHODA. Yes, can't you understand?

MAN. If you *only* knew! Why, when I was taken with fever in Kansas and that burning, barren country seemed to scorch what bit of life I had, all I cried out for in my agony was home and you——

ADNA. You suffered *so?*

[RHODA *inspects the check book.*]

MAN. Look at my hair and then ask me if I suffered. All I dreamed of was my home—New England with her green trees and rocks. The green, the green—these little mountains of the North; and when I recovered—well, it did n't seem as if I could keep away any longer.

EZRA. Well, I can't seem ter cal'late why yer did.

MAN. I was proud.

EZRA. Well, ye 're home now, and it 'll be good havin' yer ter look after the chores, I can tell yer. Come, we 'll give yer a toast. [*The father, mother and* MAN *raise their glasses.*] To the happiness that 's a-comin'. [*They drink.*]

ADNA. Why, Rhoda, you did n't touch yourn.

RHODA. I won't drink no toast to no stranger—to say nothin' of one that carries a pistol in his hip pocket.

ADNA. That ain't so.

MAN [*standing and staring at* RHODA]. Yes—it—is. [*He draws a pistol from his pocket and lays it on the table.*]

ADNA. Vyron!!!

MAN [*watching* RHODA]. It 's different in the West, mother. Different in the cities——

RHODA. Or to a man who with that gun comes from Buffalo right after they 've killed our President.

MAN [*quickly*]. Prove that!

RHODA. On the check book you was so anxious to flounce afore us. [*She is defiant.* EZRA *looks at her, then at the man, then at* ADNA. *He looks as if he feared that perhaps he was n't as clever as his reputation demanded. The* MAN *sees that some trouble is taking place, but what, he is unable to gather. He is silent, and then, believing it best, he throws it off with a jest.*]

MAN [*laughing*]. That 's just an excuse. She 's signed the pledge, and does n't want to admit it. Mother, with your permission. [*He drains* RHODA's *glass.*]

RHODA. There! See that! Did n't I tell you them kind like twice a mug better 'n once a mug— [*She is triumphant.*]

ADNA. Rhoda, ain't you ashamed——

RHODA. Don't Rhoda me——

[*The two women talk at once each trying to drown out the other.* EZRA *is silent, worried, thoughtful, horrified.*]

EZRA [*yelling louder than the women in his sudden excitement*]. Now you women folks keep quiet. I 'm a-commanding this situation. [*They are silent.* EZRA *pauses, restless, uneasy. Then he commences deliberately what he considers*] *a third degree.*] We got your letter all right, but jest a pace back. We cal'lated since you did n't come on the noon train, you would n't arrive here till eight-thirty.

MAN. Well, you see, I came down from St. Johnsbury in my automobile.

ADNA [*a half cry*]. Automobile! [*They look at* RHODA. *She gives a knowing smile.*]

EZRA. "Them godless instruments are only for the unpious, and the fiends of Satin."

MAN. I guess Norwich's a bit behind the rest of the world. But I love her for it. Why, they and telephones are the greatest inventions of the century!

EZRA. Well, I guess that 's a question fur opinions an' character ter settle. Why 'd you go ter St. Johnsbury, stead o' comin' straight through Lebanon. 'T war n't natural, yer know.

MAN. Down to Springfield, they figured the roads were better and I could make time.

EZRA. I guess the roads in our country are as good as t' other.

RHODA. Ain't it nice ter know he ain't connected with other things we 've heard 'bout automobiles an' St. Johnsbury.

EZRA. You shet up.

RHODA [*loudly to* ADNA]. Then too, dearie, he don't know you 've got money in the bank.

ADNA. S-s-sh.

RHODA. Oh, don't tell me to shet up again, Ezra, 'cause I see you settin' up an' takin' notice so I 'm goin'. I know you 're able ter take good care o' Adna, and so she don't need me no longer. Live up ter yer reputation as bein' real clever. Goo' bye, everybody. [*With a look at the* MAN *she bounces out taking her basket with her.*]

EZRA. When did you arrive ter the city?

MAN. Late Monday afternoon. I meant to start for here the next morning, but my single chain drive broke, and I could n't budge until it was mended. You see, machines are just on the market, and they 're not perfect yet.

Ezra. The Lord will see that they won't be.

Man. I know you don't like them now, but after I 've whisked you over the roads at fifteen miles an hour, you 'll think you 're flying.

Ezra. I 'll think they 're heathenish. I would n't step my foot in one of 'em.

Man. But Mother, you will, won't you?

Adna [*pleased at the idea of riding alongside her son*]. I don't know as I dare.

Man. Of course, you can trust me.

Adna [*smiling*]. I s'pose I 'd have to.

Man. My dear little mother. [*He starts to move to her.*]

Ezra. You stay where you are, and don't move till I say.

Man. What do you mean?

Adna. Why, Ezra! There 's no mistake.

Ezra. I 'm a practical man, an' ain't goin' ter be fooled by nobody.

Adna. You see your father 's got a powerful big reputation, Vyron, an' he 's mazin' proud on it.

Ezra. You 've changed considerable, ain't yer?

Man [*laughing*]. Well, I should hope so in thirty-two years.

Ezra. Come, don't see how funny you can be. You used ter favor yer ma—but there ain't no trace of her in yer face.

Adna. And you took after yer father even ter goin' a pace with no starch in him and then——

Ezra. But he don't take after me a-ridin' in horseless buggies. [Adna *takes the daguerreotype from the shelf and scans it.*] No, he don't hev no likeness to that 'ere resemblance of our Vyron.

Man. But I can remember when that was taken.

Ezra. What was the name of him as took it?

Adna. How much did it cost?

Man. You can't expect me to remember those details—his name, how much it cost, or even how old I was, but I was young, very young. I remember, oh so well, driving to town with my best clothes on, and having to be careful that the horsehairs did n't blow on it, for I sat in the front seat. Yes, then I recollect sitting up in a very high place. I don't suppose it was very high, but it seemed so to tiny me. And I looked down and saw you and dad, sitting along a row of seats by the windows. Windows! Why there were hundreds of them—and all were so awfully big, but they did n't give much light. Then don't you remember, the man made faces and jangled a monkey in a red coat to make me laugh. I can see them yet.

EZRA. I never heard of them occurrences. Did you, Adna?

ADNA. I don't know. Let me think real hard.

EZRA. All that folderol don't count anyway.

ADNA. Ef I told you his first name was Ephraim could n't you remember his last?

MAN. No, mother, I was too young.

EZRA. You know'd it at the time.

MAN. Perhaps so, but think of all these years.

ADNA. Yes, Ezra, that's so. You could n't hev——

EZRA. Certain I could. I can retain the name of him as foreclosed on my father's farm when I was only eight.

MAN. But you heard it mentioned afterwards.

EZRA. I don't know as I did. But I don't see how that would alter things.

MAN. Then you hated the name, and it made an enormous impression on your young mind. Mine was just passing knowledge. Surely you can see these points. It's not fair to me.

EZRA. A name's a name.

ADNA. Set a mite, Vyron, and think, think real hard. Pray that it will come to you.

MAN [*he stops, attempts to think, becomes impatient, gets excited*]. Oh, I can't. It's ridiculous. But I proved it once—with my card, with my check book, now with my automobile license. [*He takes out his card.*]

EZRA. You've been smart. I grant that, but not smart 'nough fur me. [*He chuckles.*] All that printed stuff you can hev turned out of the press fur pay. Gotta do better 'n that.

MAN. Good Heavens! you don't honestly feel——

ADNA. Your father don't really suspicion you, Vyron. Hev patience with him.

MAN. But there's a limit, and it's coming.

ADNA. Fur my sake, Vyron.

MAN. Well, fire ahead.

EZRA. He took my chair, drunk more wine, and now he ain't respectful to my age. Now my boy——

ADNA. The house looks natural, don't it?

MAN. Just as it always did. [*He surveys the room.*] Not a thing changed. I recollect it so well. I can remember playing there before the stove in winter, with a little rag policeman, and seeing the sunlight come in through those shutters and making little diamonds on the floor. Then all of a sudden they vanished. It seemed wonderful to me then, but it was because the sun had hidden behind the mountain there. Mount—Mount Piscar, I think we called it.

ADNA. This is Vyron, Ezra, our Vyron.

EZRA. I don't put no stock in all this rubbish. He didn't see we had a new stove, or that we put the pump from outside near the barn inter the sink.

ADNA. It cost a powerful lot o' money, too.

EZRA. Why, anyone could talk as he does, after havin' sort o' shied by the outside here.

MAN. But I am your son. I swear it, and you're my father. Why won't you believe it?

EZRA. Course you'll say an' vow it.

MAN. Little mother, *you* trust me. You know——

ADNA. Yes, yes. [*She goes to him and puts her arms on his shoulder.*] I don't care, Ezra, 'bout you an' your reasonin's. The Lord has given a mother feelin's, an' love, an' she knows her son—she does. And this is mine!

EZRA. He don't move me, and I'm his father.

ADNA. Give him your account as how you left this house.

MAN. It was in October, on a Friday.

ADNA. Yes, yes. I'd al'ays laid the trouble to that. Didn't I, now?

MAN. I was just turning twelve years and loved to play,

but you never would take any excuse for my not getting the chores done. Friday afternoon, a circus passed through Norwich, and I went down to the Center to see it pass, hoping to get back in time to milk. But the teams were very late, and it was dark before I got home. You had been obliged to do the milking and scolded me. I said things I should n't have to my father, even if I was angry. Then you grew furious and hit me with the poker. It hung there beside the stove. I went upstairs, and late that night I came down and went out into the night. I felt you were unfair to always make me work so hard.

[ADNA *is crying. The* MAN *sober.* EZRA *silent, but bitter, suspicious. There is a pause.*]

ADNA. Now I hope you 're satisfied. Ain't he given you proof?

EZRA. Your tale hangs together tolerable well, but there ain't nobody in the hul o' Champlain county that don't know that story every bit as good as you. And there 's some as knows it better.

ADNA. Why do you carry on sech? Let me hev my son. I want my boy. He 's mine, proof or no proof. I know he 's mine. The Lord has sent him to me in my old age, an' I want my boy. [*She rushes past* EZRA *into the arms of the* MAN. *They embrace.*]

MAN. The same dear little mother that you always were. And he the same——

ADNA. Be patient with him, Vyron.

MAN. But he——

ADNA. Fur my sake.

MAN. For your sake, little mother.

EZRA. How big 's the farm?

MAN. Why— Why——

EZRA. Come. You ought to know that.

MAN. It must be miles. Just walking the boundary used to tire me out

EZRA. U-u-um, I thought so. That there shows you never belonged here. It ain't but ten acres, woods an' all.

ADNA. That don't count, I——

EZRA. Women be sech fools. Lucky most of 'em has a man ter take care of 'em. Why, he 's had two hul days since he left St. Johnsbury on that Monday night to find out all 'bout it. Ain't you ashamed o' yourself, Adna, huggin' that stranger— And sech goin's on ain't countenanced by society in these parts. Maybe they is *west*. [*He sits in the rocker.*]

ADNA. He ain't no stranger. He 's Vyron.

EZRA. Well, I 'll set here so long as he hangs around. I guess he won't outdo me. As fur as I 'm concerned, he can clear out any time. I 'm done with him.

MAN. What am I to do? What am I to do? How would you want anyone to prove that he is his father's son?

EZRA. There 's a lot o' queer folks, you can fool in this world, but I ain't one. I guess you'd better clear out soon.

MAN. Mother, tell me how to show him. Help me. You must wait.

EZRA. I noticed when at first you did the talkin', you got along middlin' well. But when I put the askin's, you don't know nothin' that counts fur much.

MAN. I 'll think of something. I 'm bound to. I 've no birth mark. But there must be something. [*He looks about the room.*]

EZRA. On general gossip, you 're pretty good, but when it comes to facts you show clear enough you don't belong here, nor never did.

MAN. Something. Something. Oh! I 've proved it once; but I 'll prove it again and again. How? How? [*He is searching the room, finally his eyes rest upon the silver cup. He lets go his mother and takes the cup off the mantel.*] There! The silver cup!

ADNA [*terrified*]. The silver cup!

MAN. From Aunt Lizzie. I remember— [*There is a pause. He believes himself at last victorious.*]

EZRA [*quietly*]. It 's written right on the cup. Course you can read.

MAN. The silver cup! It 's my own.

EZRA [*to* ADNA]. Seems to me I 've heard the likes of this before, somewhere afore. Hey, Adna?

ADNA. Put it down. [*She goes to the* MAN *to try and take it from him.*]

MAN. But it 's mine! [*He is wild with joy.*]

ADNA. Give it to me.

MAN. It 's mine from my Aunt Lizzie when I was born.

ADNA. Give it to me. [*She tries desperately, wildly, to take it from him, but as he is tall and holds it high, and she is short, she cannot reach it. This makes her more wild.*]

MAN. There! Mother, I 've proved it all! To suit everybody.

ADNA. Give it to me. Ezra, help me. Help me make him put it down. [*She is wild with terror and fright. She continues to grab for it, but without success.*]

EZRA [*standing*]. Put that cup down. [*He takes the gun from behind him and starts to aim it at the* MAN. ADNA *watches the* MAN *slowly put the cup down, and then quickly and timidly grabs it. She hurries around back of* EZRA *for protection.*]

MAN [*after a pause in which he and* EZRA *stare at one another*]. Good Heavens! Father's threatening to shoot me. No, no! Not that! After thirty years of waiting, I come back and just because I was in a city while a bank was robbed and because I came home in an automobile, I 'm suspected of being a thief. What would I want to steal here? Answer me that, will you? I 've got plenty of money. I waited until I had before I allowed myself to come back. I did n't come for your savings in the bank——

ADNA. My savin's! How 'd you know I 've got savin's in the bank?

MAN. How did I know? I can't remember now. Everything has been so confused, so different from what I had expected. Why, you told me yourself.

ADNA. That 's a lie. I never told nobody. There ain't a body in this town as knows it.

MAN. Let me think. Just give me a chance to think. Why, that woman who was here, Rhoda Webb—the neighbor you called her. She told me.

ADNA. No sech a thing.

MAN. Here, before you, she said so.

ADNA. I can't remember.

MAN. But what difference does that make to me? I don't want your money. I 've got plenty of it myself. Why, look. [*He takes from his pocket a wallet and produces a pile of bills. The old couple are spellbound.*]

EZRA. It 's wicked ter hev so much. [*Then he looks at ADNA, and the two grow knowing, and nod to each other, finally suspicious.*]

ADNA. She said them kind always has a awful lot of money, and show it.

EZRA. She said they got a great haul to the city, too.

ADNA. She was right 'bout the cup; right more 'n one way.

MAN. She? Who 's "she?" Rhoda? The neighbor. She started you on this track.

EZRA. She did not. *I* was clever from the fust.

MAN. Mother! Father! Can't you understand. I love you. For thirty years I 've longed to come back, longed for this moment when I should throw myself into your arms.

EZRA. I ain't deaf or hard o' hearin'.

MAN. I wanted to earn money for you, Father, so that you could take it easy. I wanted love, Mother, from you. Think what it meant to live most of one 's life without a mother's love. Why, it 's hell. You know I 'm your son, tell me you know it. [*He goes to her, taking her hand and laying it on her cheek. But she timidly hides behind EZRA, concealing the cup under her apron.*]

MAN. I come home after all these years, offering comfort, and love; but the neighbor got ahead of me. My father threatens to shoot me. My mother thinks I want her silver cup, and her savings, when I could afford to buy hundreds of silver cups. No, no! Say you don't think that. [*There is no answer from ADNA.*] Why, even you 've gone back on me!

ADNA. I 'm afraid you don't belong here.

MAN [*in a quick and violent temper*]. You turn me out into the night for a second time. Well, I 'm glad I 'm going.

You nor nobody else could stop me now. And you can't ever find me when I 'm gone, for I 'm going West again. I 've stood insults with a smile because I knew you were old. I 've been slurred at and mocked. Well, keep on doing it, but let your pains ache, and your love starve. Next time do what you think best, not what your neighbor tells you. Nothing in God's earth could keep me with you ignorant people. [*He dashes out through the door.* EZRA, *standing by the rocking chair, and* ADNA *by the table, look after him.*]

EZRA [*sitting*]. He slipped away as if he was glad of the opportunity.

ADNA [*to herself*]. He went fer so long a pace with no starch in him——

EZRA. He was a dangerous man, he was. Listen how he yelled.

ADNA. And then got fleshy and het up jest like you——

EZRA. I could see he would n't lift his finger to the chores.

ADNA. He got along as sweet as milk.

EZRA. I know 'd all the while, he was after your earnin's. But I saved them fur you.

ADNA. And then exploded all of a sudden like!

EZRA. It 's long late in the afternoon. Le 's hev supper. [*He rises, takes the tea kettle from the stove, crosses to the sink, pumps water to fill the kettle.*]

ADNA. Jest like—Jest like— [*She falls in the chair by the table.*]

EZRA. Oh, my back. Adna, you—I 'm too old to work sech like. [*With his hand on his back, he crosses to the rocker and sits.*]

ADNA [*her head on her arm on the table*]. Jest like—him.

EZRA. Why, Adna, what 's the matter?

ADNA. I 'm wonderin'.

EZRA. Wonderin' 'bout what——

ADNA. Wonderin' ef it 's best to believe our neighbors.

[*In the darkness, the neighbor looks in at the rear window with her hands shading her eyes from the little light there is left without. She sees the yearning mother and the ailing*

*father.   Then we hear her laugh as she goes to spread the
news.*]

SUGGESTIVE QUESTIONS

1. What is the importance of stage setting in relation to plot in
   Just Neighborly?
2. How much of character does the dramatist show by setting,
   and how much by action, before any of the persons in the
   play speak?
3. By what means does the dramatist explain the events that pre-
   ceded the action of the play?
4. Point out indications of the mentality of the various characters.
5. What emotions does the beginning of the play arouse?
6. Point out the different means employed to indicate the character
   of Rhoda Webb.
7. What dramatic purpose does the mention of the bank robbery
   fulfil?
8. What advantage is gained by making the boy's picture, and the
   boy's cup, conspicuous on the mantelshelf, and prominent in
   the dialogue?
9. What dramatic advantage is gained by having the son's letter
   read before the son's arrival?
10. What emotions move the father and the mother when the letter
    is read?   What emotions move the audience?
11. Point out the first suggestion of suspicion.
12. Trace the development of suspicion, from suggestion to final
    result.
13. Summarize the evidence in favor of the theory that the stranger
    is the actual son.   Summarize the evidence against that
    theory.   What dramatic advantage is gained by leaving the
    decision to the audience rather than by stating it?
14. How does the son account for his long absence?
15. Show the gradual yielding of the parents under the suggestions
    given by Rhoda Webb.   What is the effect of making the
    yielding gradual?
16. Point out all the uses of suggestion in the play.
17. What effects does the conclusion of the play produce?
18. Read *Spreading the News,* by Lady Gregory.   Compare or con-
    trast that play and *Just Neighborly.*

Subjects for Written Imitation

1. Write a dialogue based on any part of the story of *The Prodigal Son.*
2. Give directions for the stage setting of a play concerning any definite section of the State in which you live.
3. Write a short dramatic sketch based on any incident at a country post office.
4. Write a dialogue between two old people who live in the city.
5. Write a dialogue in which you emphasize the attitude of ignorant people toward new inventions.
6. Write a dramatic sketch in which you emphasize childhood memories. Make your sketch lead to a climax.
7. Write a dialogue between a father and a mother concerning the punishment of a disobedient child.
8. Write a dramatic sketch in which you make full use of suggestion.
9. Write a dialogue, with full stage directions, emphasizing family resemblances.
10. Write the last words of a play, emphasizing theme.

Directions for Writing

In all the work suggested above, aim at realism of speech and of action. Let the emotions be those of everyday life. Use little exaggeration. Awaken sympathy with character through appeal to fundamental emotions.

Oral Work in Class

1. Select that part of *Just Neighborly* that awakens deepest emotions. Act that part of the play.
2. Select that part of the play that calls for the greatest amount of stage business. Act that part.
3. Select that part of the play that is most true to ordinary life. Act that part.
4. Read aloud the most effective part of your own written work.

MASKS

By Perry Boyer Corneau

Masks is an example both of a fantastic play, and of a satirical play. Being fantastic, that is, highly unusual and whimsical, it gives relief from the commonplace. Nevertheless, fantastic as *Masks* may be, it is founded substantially on what is real. In other words, the author makes the very strangeness of the play, the fantastic nature of the plot, effective by making the action and the dialogue as real as possible. He gives no excuses; he makes no explanations. He shows a man and his wife speaking of wings and of masks as naïvely as though all people wore them. He makes the entire action of the play proceed as though the fantastic plot were a matter of every-day life.

While the dramatist nowhere explains his satire, that is, his biting but humorous criticism of life, he makes his meaning sufficiently pointed to be clear. Who is there who, at all times, displays his real self? Who is there who does not put on masks for various occasions? Who is there who, behind the various masks that he wears, has a self that is thoroughly substantial and worthy? Indeed, the dramatist makes the satire biting enough!

The author makes his play universal by making it represent whole classes of people, not merely one man and his wife, but people in general, "The World and His Wife." Then, having all people in mind, he makes his characters act and talk as though they were simply "Mr. and Mrs. Brown," or "Mr. and Mrs. Anyone!"

Because the writer made the dialogue so natural, and the

plot so simple, involving the most ordinary domestic events
and vexations, he made it most compelling.

The author of *Masks*, Perry Boyer Corneau, has written a
number of plays that have been produced by community
players with marked success. Among these are *Children*,
produced by The Hull House Players; *The Shadow*, produced
by The Play-Shop Players of Chicago; and three distinctly
children's plays produced by The Drama League of Chicago,
two having the honor of being produced in the Chicago
Children's Civic Theatre.

Among Mr. Corneau's plays are *Napoleon and the Sentry;
The Last Voyage of Odysseus; Robin Hood and the Widow's
Three Sons; Little John and the Miller Join Robin Hood's
Band;* and *The Poor Boy Who Became a Great Warrior.*

As the titles indicate, Mr. Corneau has written many of
his plays especially for young people.

Introductory Problems

1. In Hawthorne's *Twice Told Tales* you read the story called *The
   Minister's Black Veil.* Write a dialogue that will dramatize
   the climax of that story. Make the dialogue emphasize the
   theme.
2. Write a dialogue in which you show one person, at one time displaying one side of his character, and at another time displaying an entirely different and somewhat contradictory
   side.

PEOPLE OF THE PLAY:

[A Man and His Wife]

Time: The Present

In the small, pleasantly furnished room in the Man's *house,
a door leads outside and another opens into a room or closet
where the masks are kept. Or possibly there is a chest that*

is used for this purpose. There is a wide window through which are seen only sky and distant mountains, glowing with the approach of sunset. The weather is warm; and the window is wide open. Through it a strong breeze is blowing. There is a couch near the window and a mirror on the opposite wall. The MAN'S WIFE *comes in. She wears a hat which she removes. She goes to the mirror and arranges her hair. She goes to the window and moves back the curtains so that they will not blow so much in the breeze and picks up a paper that the wind has blown on the floor. There is a noise at the door. She turns expectantly. As the* MAN *enters she bursts out laughing. He makes a ridiculous figure. He is dressed in ordinary clothes, but over them he has thrown a white sheet which he has wrapped around himself in the fashion of a toga. On his shoulders are awkwardly fastened two large feathery wings. He wears a mask and a wig of long, curly hair. In one hand he carries a small harp. He is slightly annoyed at his* WIFE'S *laughter.*

WIFE. At it again?

MAN. Can you never be serious?

WIFE. Not when I look at you with that stuff on.

MAN. My dear, can't you see that you pain me by such language? Stuff!

WIFE. Your wings aren't on straight.

MAN [*looking anxiously over his shoulder*]. Oh, dear me! The wind is so strong it must have blown them loose.

WIFE. You didn't fasten them on straight in the first place. You never do— Oh dear! Oh, dear! [*She goes into another paroxysm of laughter.*]

MAN. That's always the way! I get no sympathy from you. I go to address a meeting of the Associated Sunday School Superintendents. I do address them. They are charmed and uplifted. I am uplifted. I come home full of noble thoughts and aspirations. And I am greeted with ridicule. Have you no feeling at all for the higher things of life? [*Unconsciously he begins to accompany himself on his harp.*] Do you never give yourself up to the con-

templation of the good, the beautiful, the true? Look at life
in its larger meaning. The birds, the trees, the flowers, the
purling brooks——

WIFE. Don't be ridiculous. [*Bursting out laughing.*]
Oh, you are so funny!

MAN. The Associated Sunday School Superintendents did
not think me ridiculous or funny.

WIFE. Did n't they notice that your wings were crooked?

MAN. No. I was eloquent. I quite carried them away.
My costume was a compliment to them. And it pleased
them. [*He begins to accompany himself on his harp again.*]
And when I spoke of antelopes and grazing gazelles and little
children they wept. Ah, what a beautiful thing——

WIFE [*interrupting*]. I wish you would not try to play
on that harp. It is horribly out of tune.

[MAN *stops playing and throws the harp angrily on a
chair.*]

MAN. You find fault with everything.

WIFE. Oh, take that stuff off and be yourself.

MAN. To the Associated Sunday School Superintendents
this was myself.

WIFE. The Associated Sunday School Superintendents
can't be very observing.

MAN. They look at me with sympathy.

WIFE. I know you too well. I know how easy those
things are to put on. Now take off that horrid mask and
give your little wife a nice, long kiss.

[MAN *removes his mask. But beneath it is another, less
obviously a mask than the first one. In fact, it is difficult
to distinguish the fact that it is a mask. It is more human
than the first and extremely handsome, but a little cold in its
regularity and the intelligence of its expression. He kisses
her.*]

WIFE. Now let me put away those wings. The feathers
keep coming out and getting all over things. We must have
them fixed before the next Associated Sunday School
Superintendents' meeting. [*She removes his wings and
wig. He unwraps his toga and throws it aside.*]

MAN. That's better. That wig and mask are a little too much in this warm weather.

WIFE. I like your own real face ever so much better.

MAN. Do you?

[*She picks up the wings and wig and mask and puts them in the closet or the chest. An automobile horn is heard outside.*]

WIFE. Oh, I forgot to tell you. Mr. Jenks telephoned he would stop here on his way home. That must be he now. I think he wants you to go out with him to-night.

MAN. You know, darling, I'd much rather stay home with you.

[*The horn sounds again.*]

WIFE. Of course. But he is waiting for you.

MAN. He doesn't expect me to go now?

WIFE. Oh, no. Not till this evening.

MAN. I'll just slip on a mask while I talk to him.

WIFE. How silly!

MAN. It gives me quite a reputation as a joker among my friends. [*He puts on a Mephistophelean mask which he selects from a number. As he puts on the mask his manner changes noticeably.*] I tumbled them about a good deal.

WIFE. Never mind. I'll put them back while you are talking to Mr. Jenks.

MAN. So long, Bright Eyes. [*He goes out with a jaunty manner. She picks up the masks one by one and replaces them.*]

WIFE. Goodness! I haven't seen this one for a long time. It's the one he wears when he goes around to pay our bills. [*She picks up another mask.*] And this one—I wonder what it is—I've never seen him wear this. [*She picks up another mask.*] This mask he wears when we dine out is getting awfully worn.

[MAN *comes in again, humming a popular song. He clasps his* WIFE *in his arms, bending her head back and kissing her long and passionately.*]

WIFE. Oh, don't! Take that horrid mask off.

MAN. Oh, Baby Doll——

WIFE. Take it off. [*She snatches off the mask and puts it away. His manner instantly changes.*]

WIFE. Are you going with Mr. Jenks?

MAN. No. I 'm too tired this evening. I could hardly keep awake at the office this afternoon. You 've been putting the masks in order. That 's nice of you.

WIFE. Your dining-out mask is pretty badly worn. Don't you think if you will persist in wearing one that you had better get a new one?

MAN. That one is good enough. People know it. I don't think they 'd like it if I wore any other. Besides, it harmonizes so perfectly with my dinner conversation.

WIFE. It might n't be a bad idea at that to get some new conversation.

MAN. At my age? Oh dear no! [*He puts on the dining-out mask.*] It 's a pretty good old mask. Yes, I 'm fond of the opera—some operas. I don't know much about music; but I know what I like. That reminds me of a story I heard an Englishman tell on the boat to Honolulu last winter. You know, running off for a little sea voyage now and then has got to be a sort of habit with me. I thought this story was rather clever. Why, you see he——

WIFE [*snatching off the mask*]. For mercy sake, don't!!

MAN. I don't understand your not liking that.

[*Shouts and laughter are heard outside. The* WIFE *goes to the window.*]

WIFE. Oh! There are those children running across my flower beds again! Go out and drive them away.

MAN. Where 's that mask? This one— [*He finds a hideous and imposing mask, something like those worn by the warriors of old Japan, and puts it on.*] I 'll fix the little devils! [*He goes out. He can be heard outside speaking in thunderous and terrifying tones.* MAN *dashes into the room.*]

MAN [*ferociously*]. Get me my business mask.

WIFE. Which one?

MAN. My borrowing mask. Hurry, you fool! The president of the bank is coming down the street. [*He throws off*

the mask he has been wearing and puts on the one his WIFE
*hands to him. It is a mask with an expression of combined
shrewdness and humility.*]

MAN. Oh, thank you. I am negotiating for a loan at the
bank. I don't want the president to see me with a different
mask from the one I wear when I call on him at his office.
It will be good policy to be standing in front of the house as
he goes by—to let him know I live in a pretty good neighbor-
hood. And this is n't a bad-looking house.

[*The* MAN *goes out. His* WIFE *continues to sort and replace the masks. She sits down, holding some of the masks
in her lap and looks at them thoughtfully.*]

WIFE. Masks—masks— Why does he do it—? Am I
the only one that ever sees him without a mask? I—I
wonder— He wore one when he used to come to see me
before we were married. It is broken now. Masks—
masks— Do people never wonder what is behind them?
This mask of flesh? [*She puts her hand to her face.*] What
is behind it? That is the secret that the world has striven to
know—and striven in vain—Oh!!! [*She jumps up, startled,
as the* MAN *comes in. He carries his business mask in his
hand.*]

WIFE. Oh, you startled me. I was talking to myself—
dreaming——

MAN. It seems he knew this was a mask all the time.
He laughed and asked me if I did n't take off my mask even
at home.

WIFE. So you took it off——

MAN. He seemed in a good humor. He laughed again
and said, "Oh, I see. You wear a mask at home, too."
What do you suppose he meant?

WIFE. He meant the mask you 've taken off.

MAN. No, he did n't. Do you suppose he thinks this is a
mask too? [*He puts his hand to his face.*]

WIFE. I would not blame him if he did. Is n't it natural
for him to suspect that if you wear a mask before him, you
wear one before me also?

MAN. Before you—? My dear——

WIFE. I never thought of it before. I thought that when your courtship mask fell and was broken that I saw your true self. But I see it now. That face is a mask! You have been deceiving me.

MAN. My dear—You don't know what you are talking about.

WIFE. I used to laugh when you put on masks and fooled other people—fool myself! To think that you did n't deceive me too.

MAN. I assure you——

WIFE [bitterly]. You have had your joke—but take it off now. It can never deceive me again.

MAN. You are out of your head. This is no mask.

WIFE. No mask? Any fool but me could have seen it long ago.

MAN. Won't you believe me? This is no mask. I tell you this is no mask. I 've never had it off. I mean this is my face—my face. Won't you believe me?

WIFE. Of course. You always tell me the truth.

MAN. I give you my word. Won't you take my word for it?

WIFE. Of course I 'll take your word for it. [She goes up behind him and with a sudden, swift movement attempts to remove the mask. He jumps away from her in alarm.]

MAN. What are you doing?!!

WIFE [sweetly and innocently]. Nothing.

MAN. You tried to see if this was a mask. Did n't you? Did n't I give you my word?

WIFE. Yes.

MAN. Do you still doubt it?

WIFE. Of course not. I never, never doubt you. —But —if it is not a mask why were you afraid I was going to take it off?

MAN. I was n't. You startled me coming up behind me that way.

WIFE. Oh, I see.

MAN [angrily]. What do you see?

WIFE. Nothing—I mean of course.

MAN. I tell you this isn't a mask. It is ridiculous to think it could be.

WIFE. Oh, I believe you. You needn't shout at me. —But——

MAN. Why do you always say "but?"

WIFE. I know you believe what you say. But it might be a mask and you might be so used to it you didn't know it.

MAN. That's ridiculous.

WIFE. You deceive other people with your masks. Perhaps you deceive yourself too.

MAN. That's like a woman. She gets an idea in her head; and all the reasoning and logic in the world can't get it out.

WIFE. I'm not that kind. I know it is not a mask. I was only teasing.

MAN. What is the sense in doing that? When I'm tired out with being at the office all day?

WIFE. Oh, I'm so sorry that I bothered you. Forgive me—Please—Of course it isn't a mask. But——

MAN. There you go again!

WIFE. But wouldn't it be interesting if it were a mask? Mask beneath mask; and beneath the last mask—what?

MAN. Haven't we had enough of this discussion?

WIFE. After every mask is torn away—would we find the soul itself?

MAN. You've been going to some of those crazy highbrow lectures again.

WIFE. You asked me a while ago to look at life in its larger meaning.

MAN. That was when I had my Associated Sunday School Superintendents' costume on. [*He goes over to the couch and lies down.*] Don't bother me. I want to rest and look over the paper. It's getting pretty dark. Let's have a little light.

WIFE. I'll light the lamp. [*She does so, placing it near him. The wind blows it out.*] Oh! I didn't know the wind was so strong. I'll light it again and close the window.

MAN. Don't close the window. It's too hot. I won't read. I'll lie here and rest my eyes. Don't disturb me. I may doze a bit.

[*She puts the rest of the masks away, then goes to the window and stands looking out, now and then furtively watching her husband. He closes his eyes and is soon apparently asleep. It is evident that she has restrained her curiosity with difficulty. After a moment she turns and tiptoes over to the couch. She then takes the lamp, and moving it farther from the window, lights it again. It flickers in the wind, but does not go out. She approaches the couch again, doubtfully, struggling with her curiosity. She is about to touch his face when she hesitates and draws back. Again she approaches. This time she moves her fingers lightly over his face. He stirs. She draws back. Again she approaches.*]

WIFE. Is it, is it a mask—?—What is beneath it—? [*With sudden resolution she goes to him. Her hands are at his face. She gives a pull; and the mask comes off. She gives a cry, half of triumph, half of terror. The* MAN *awakens with a cry of pain. He sits up and looks about as if dazed. The light falls on him revealing a face (a mask) commonplace, dull, wicked except for the fact that it expresses insufficient intelligence for wickedness. She gazes at him, horrified. The mask slips from her hand and is shattered on the floor. She gives a cry of terror. The* MAN *leaps to his feet. His hand goes gropingly to his face.*]

MAN. Heavens! [*He rushes to the mirror. He looks at himself a moment. He trembles and seems to shrink. He turns and faces his* WIFE.]

MAN. It—it was a mask——?

WIFE. It was a mask.

MAN [*dully*]. I—I know myself—at last—! [*He puts his hands to his face.*] This is what I was—after all—this——

[*His* WIFE *begins to cry.*]

MAN. I—did—deceive myself. I thought I was handsome and noble—and—I know—You know— But—but the

world need n't know. Put back my mask—we 'll try—we 'll
try to forget— Where is it? My pretty face—where——?
WIFE. Oh, why did I? Why did I do it? You can
never put it on again.
MAN. Never—? Why?
WIFE. Oh! It is broken.
MAN [*dully*]. Broken——?
[*She points to the fragments on the floor. With a cry he
kneels to pick them up, trying to piece them together. He
throws them down in despair.*]
WIFE. I am sorry—terribly sorry——
MAN. You broke it—you— [*A strange light shines on his
face giving it a tinge of ferocity and brutality.*] I told you
not to touch it. You—you—Do you know I could kill you
for this?! [*He approaches her threateningly.*]
WIFE. Oh—please—please—look— There are plenty of
other masks. Here—this one—Put it on.
[*He takes the mask and tries to fit it on. It falls off.*]
MAN. It—it will not stay.
WIFE. This—— [*She hands him another mask.*]
MAN. No. They were only meant to fit on my pretty
face—my pretty face— It 's broken—broken—— [*He be-
gins to sob. It is like the whining of a whipped animal.*]
WIFE. Don't. Don't. Don't feel bad about it. I love
you just the same. Oh, what can I do?!
MAN. What can you do——
WIFE. This is not your real self. No one's real self is
like that. It can't be.
MAN. It can't be—No—it can't be.
WIFE. I see it all now! That is a mask too.
MAN. A mask too——?
WIFE. We 'll take it off. We 'll find what is beneath
it. There is something beneath every mask. There must be.
There is something deep, deep in each of us—something beau-
tiful—something good—something true——
MAN. Something true——
WIFE. If we could throw aside every mask we could find
it. The world has always sought to know it—to know what

we are—what we really are, deep, deep within ourselves.
There must be something divine there——

MAN. There must be. There must be.

WIFE. And we shall find it. It will be a glorious thing.
The first man and woman to find it, to know what is behind
the last mask of all. Perhaps this mask of yours is the last
one—and behind it—behind it——

MAN. We 'll know. Take it off. You 'll find something
there—something divine—something——

[*She approaches him and is about to take off the mask when
a strong gust of wind extinguishes the light.*]

WIFE. Wait—I 'll light the lamp.

MAN. Hurry. Oh, hurry.—Think. We 'll know now
what man really is.

WIFE. I must have light to see it. [*She lights the lamp.
The* MAN, *now facing the back of the room, has approached
her. She grasps the mask and tears it off. Behind the mask
there is—NOTHING.*] Behind all masks—Nothing?! [*She
stands holding the empty mask in her hand. The figure of
the* MAN *collapses like a house of cards, his clothing falling
in a little heap on the floor. She screams and clutches the
empty mask. A gust of wind extinguishes the light.*]

NOTE.

[*When the wind extinguishes the light the next to the last time, it is
of course to give an opportunity for the actor playing the* MAN *to leave
the stage. In his place there is to be substituted a suit of clothes of
very light material and similar in appearance to those the* MAN *wears,
this with the mask and a wig to be hung on a frame or suspended in
some way from above in such a manner that the* WIFE *in removing the
mask causes the whole thing to collapse and fall to the floor.*
*After the removal of the mask, (the pretty-face mask)—make-up may
take the place of a second mask, as the audience will have no opportunity
to examine closely the last mask removed by the* WIFE.]

SUGGESTIVE QUESTIONS

1. What advantage does the ordinary home setting give?
2. How does the dramatist make the Man's fantastic appearance
   natural?
3. What effects do the first words of the play produce?

4. What characteristics of human life does the play satirize? By what dramatic means does the dramatist present the satire?
5. Point out the different parts of the plot.
6. Trace the development of the action toward the climax.
7. What effects does the conclusion of the play produce?
8. What is the theme?
9. Define "fantasy" and "satire."

SUGGESTIONS FOR WRITTEN IMITATION

1. Write a brisk dialogue between any two people in an ordinary American household.
2. Write a dialogue in which you show important character contrasts in the persons who speak.
3. Write a scenario for a play that will satirize daily life.
4. Write the closing lines for the play suggested in Question 3.

DIRECTIONS FOR WRITING

Write with extreme brevity, aiming always at naturalness of expression, but keeping the theme well in mind. Use short, common words, the idioms of ordinary conversation, the broken expressions, and the half-completed sentences, of daily life. Make your dialogue vigorous and spirited, one quick remark suggesting another.

ORAL WORK IN CLASS

1. Act the most important parts of the play, especially the introduction and the conclusion.
2. Act any part of the play with the purpose of making the satire clear and forceful.
3. Act any part of the play with the purpose of making the dialogue appear the dialogue of everyday life.
4. Read aloud the best part of your own writing.

THE MAID WHO WOULDN'T BE PROPER

A PUPPET PLAY

By Hettie Louise Mick

The Maid Who Wouldn't Be Proper, as its sub-title indicates, is a "puppet play," or "marionette play," a play to be acted by little Punch-and-Judy-like figures, or puppets, or marionettes, moved by almost invisible threads, the operator or his assistants remaining hidden and speaking the words of the play.

There is something peculiarly interesting in seeing puppets move about, imitating or exaggerating the actions of life. *Punch and Judy,* with all its crudeness, has amused people for over three hundred years.

Children of all lands and periods of history have made their dolls imitate life; in a certain sense their elders have followed the children's example; wherever there has been any form of the drama there have been puppet plays, even in India and in China, and in ancient Greece and Rome.

Well before the seventeenth century, puppet plays became popular in England. In later years the development of mechanical skill led to the making of most ingenious puppets, capable of performing almost any action. In recent years, in the United States, Tony Sarg, with marvelously managed puppets, made a great success.

As in *Punch and Judy*, every character speaks briefly, repeats frequently, and acts in some one characteristic way,
the quickness of dialogue, and the constant repetition of
words and actions producing a unique effect.

The Maid Who Would n't Be Proper is an elaborate
example of the modern puppet play, a type of drama that
has stimulated the work even of so great a dramatist as
Maurice Maeterlinck.

Suzanne, the Maid who "Just-won't-be-proper"; Prudence,
who is always "proper"; the "Irate Father"; the "Motherly
Mother"; the "Proper Young Man," and the very gypsy
"Gypsy Boy," are all characteristic puppet personalities.

See all these, not as living beings but as puppets, acting
in the most unnatural-natural manner, and you increase the
enjoyment that you gain from the whimsical play.

Hettie Louise Mick, the author of *The Maid Who Would n't
Be Proper*, by carrying on active work in theatres in Chicago
and in New York, by giving courses of instruction in the
preparation of puppet plays, and by writing articles on how
to make puppets, has made herself an authority on all that
is concerned in the puppet play as a type of drama.

Soon after her graduation from the University of Chicago,
where she had interested herself in undergraduate dramatic
work, she became connected with the Chicago Little Theatre.
There she dramatized *The Frog Prince* and *Little Red Riding
Hood*, and acted in many plays. Later, in New York City,
she gained valuable experience in assisting in the production
of Tony Sarg's famous puppet plays. Later still, she
dramatized Dickens' *A Christmas Carol* for Lilian Owen's
marionettes.

In recent years Miss Mick has worked with The Laboratory
Theatre, a pioneering venture after the methods of the Moscow
Art Theatre.

Her inspiration for writing such a delightful play as *The
Maid Who Would n't Be Proper* came from the chance ob-
servation of an advertisement that showed a little girl dressed
in the quaint, prim costume of our great-great-grandmothers.
The girl in the advertisement seemed to say: "I just *must*

be proper." That suggested the girl of the play, "The Maid
Who *Would n't* Be Proper."

INTRODUCTORY PROBLEMS

1. Describe a *Punch and Judy* show.
2. What characteristic words or actions did you notice in *Punch and Judy?*
3. Why are puppet plays popular?
4. In what ways is a dramatist limited in writing a puppet play?
5. In what ways is a dramatist given greater scope in writing a puppet play?
6. Explain all the differences between the method of presenting a puppet play and the method of presenting an ordinary realistic play.

SCENES:

ACT I—A garden. Morning.
ACT II—Suzanne's bedroom. Afternoon.
ACT III—The woods. Evening.

CHARACTERS:

SUZANNE, *the maid who would n't be proper*
PRUDENCE, *her proper sister*
HER IRATE FATHER
HER MOTHERLY MOTHER
THE PROPER YOUNG MAN
THE GYPSY BOY

ACT I

*A garden, with a wall at the back, and a house at the right,
showing doorway, and two windows above. The scene is very
conventionalized, hedges are all neatly cut, and trees are
trimmed into geometrical shapes, the whole giving an impression of absolute symmetry, and devotion to form.
Exactly fitting into this picture sits* PRUDENCE, *on a bench to*

the left, sewing. A moment after the curtain goes up a
head appears over the fence and a low whistle is heard. The
head is of SUZANNE. *She is dressed exactly like her sister*
except that her bonnet hangs around her neck by a string
instead of being placed firmly on her head, her hair is di-
sheveled, and her whole air is one of carelessness and freedom,
while PRUE'S *is that of sedateness, neatness, and, above all,*
propriety. SUE *climbs to the top of the wall, swings her*
feet over and sits there whistling.

PRUE [*primly*]. Suzanne, do be proper!
SUE [*chanting*].

Oh, I met a jolly lad a-going out to sea,
And he was as gay as any lad could be,
Oh, he pulled out a lock of hair and gave a lock to
me——
PRUE. Suzanne, be proper!
SUE. Proper, proper, proper, proper, proper, proper,
proper!
PRUE. Yes, proper.
SUE. I am proper.
PRUE. You 're not.
SUE. I am.
PRUE. You 're not.
SUE. What do you mean by proper, anyway?
PRUE. Why—why—you know what I mean well enough.
SUE. Oh, no. Do tell me. [*Jumping down.*]
PRUE. Why, I mean, I mean, as a young girl should be,
regular, not jumping over fences and all.
SUE. But I don't jump over all fences, only this one.
Most of them are too high.
PRUE. Father said he was going to make this one higher,
and then you can't jump over it.
SUE. Now is n't that just like my irate father.
PRUE. Now, Suzanne, you really must be proper.
SUE. Proper, proper, proper, proper, proper, proper,
proper. There it is again. What proper, why proper, when
proper! Are you proper?

PRUE. Dear me, yes. Every young maiden should be proper.

SUE. Then I must be like you. But how? What *is* ''proper?''

PRUE. Now really you must ask papa—or perhaps you would better ask mamma. All I know is that all young maidens should be it.

SUE. And sit and sew like a quiet little mouse in a corner. [*Wagging her head.*] So, so, so.

PRUE [*nodding*]. Quite so.

SUE. So-so. [*She pauses.*] Oh, no.

PRUE. Mother will teach you to sew.

SUE. Dear me, yes, my motherly mother would teach me to sew, I know.

PRUE. So disrespectful. Now you must be——

SUE. Proper, proper, proper, proper, proper, proper, proper. Yes, I 've heard that before. Oh, Prue, can you stand on your head!

PRUE. Suzanne!

SUE. Look I can. See. [*She does so, falling over into* PRUE'S *lap and pushing her off the bench.* SUE *begins to laugh.*] Now, really, I did n't mean to push you over. I must learn to do that better.

PRUE [*starting to cry*]. Oh, dear, why did I ever have such an improper sister?

SUE [*seriously*]. Yes, that was n't proper. Now had I done it properly, I should never have knocked you over, and furthermore, you would have been entranced and would have wanted to do it too, *if* I had done it properly. [PRUE *continues to cry.*] Come, I 'll do it again, and maybe I 'll do it better this time.

PRUE. Oh, Suzanne!

[SUE *tries the stunt again, and her irate* FATHER *and motherly* MOTHER *enter.*]

FATHER. Suzanne, put your feet where they should be, immediately.

MOTHER. Father, dear, would n't it be more proper to tell her to put her head where it should be?

SUE [*waving her feet in the air*]. Father, where should my feet be?

FATHER. Down, always, down.

SUE [*dropping into sitting position*]. But my irate father, yours are always straight out when you are in bed.

ALL. Suzanne!

FATHER [*roaring*]. Suzanne, stand up.

SUE. Father, dear, wouldn't it be much more proper to speak in a tone suitable to the distance which we are apart? Now I am sure I could hear you if you spoke in a teenty-teenty voice.

FATHER. Suzanne, stand up. [PRUE *who has been sitting thunder-struck all this time gets up.*] Yes, Prudence, you too. Why are you in that improper position as well?

SUE [*jumping up*]. Oh, Father, let me tell you. I was showing her how to stand on her head, when I fell over and pushed her down——

FATHER. Enough! Mother, mother, what are we to do?

MOTHER [*wagging her head*]. Father, father, how can I tell? My two darlings, my two chicks, my two pets. So alike. So unlike.

[*They both shake their heads and sigh.* PRUDENCE *shakes her head and sighs.* SUE *giggles.*]

FATHER. Something must be done.

MOTHER. It surely must.

FATHER. They are too old to be locked in their rooms.

PRUE. Oh, Father, me too?

FATHER. Yes, indeed. Don't you see if you were locked in your room Suzanne could not tease you?

PRUE. Yes, that would be quite proper.

FATHER. And they've finished all the schooling young maidens should have.

MOTHER. Oh, yes. There remains but one thing.

FATHER. What's that?

MOTHER. Well—it might not be proper to mention it in their presence.

FATHER. Of course, of course.

SUE [*giggling*]. Prue should get married.

PRUE [*extra horrified*]. Suzanne!

FATHER AND MOTHER. Suzanne!

FATHER. You must not mention such things.

SUE. But are n't you and mother married? Is n't that proper?

FATHER. That 's different.

MOTHER. My poor child!

FATHER. Go into the house at once. Prudence, too. Mother, we must talk.

PRUE. Yes, father. [*She goes out.*]

SUE. Oh, yes, my irate father, and my motherly mother. [*She leaves. In a few minutes her head is seen sticking out of one of the windows in the house.*]

MOTHER [*wagging her head*]. They should get married!

FATHER. Well, yes, maybe they should.

MOTHER. Prudence is older by two years. She should be married first.

FATHER. So she should.

MOTHER. But it would settle Suzanne down so to be married. [SUE *giggles at the window softly, and withdraws. In a moment* PRUE *sticks her head out.*]

FATHER [*sighing*]. She would need a mighty proper husband.

MOTHER. And if Prudence should not happen to get married, she would make a much more dignified old maid than Suzanne. [PRUDENCE *sighs and withdraws.*]

FATHER. So she would. Old maids don't jump over fences, nor stand on their heads.

MOTHER. But, then, neither do young wives.

FATHER. A husband would see to that. [*Both heads appear at the upper windows. They see each other.* PRUE *withdraws hastily.* SUE *giggles.* FATHER *looks up.*] Suzanne, withdraw your head.

SUE. But, Father, I 'm not a turtle.

FATHER. Suzanne, withdraw your head, and set it at something useful.

MOTHER. Sue, dear, run down into the kitchen and see what you find there.

[SUE *withdraws quickly.*]

FATHER. Do you think that quite proper, my dear?

MOTHER. Maybe not. [*A proper* YOUNG MAN *appears at the gate.*] My, my, here's a visitor. Perhaps a prospect!

YOUNG MAN. Good day!

FATHER. Good day, sir! Will you come in, sir!

YOUNG MAN. Yes, sir. [*He enters.*] Mayhap you wonder who I am, sir.

FATHER. Not at all, sir. Sit down, sir.

[PRUDENCE *sticks her head out of the window, registers delight, and withdraws.*]

YOUNG MAN. Yes, sir. [*To* MOTHER.] After you, madame.

MOTHER. Oh, yes, yes, indeed. I'll sit. Do sit down. [*She sits.*]

YOUNG MAN. Thank you, madame. [*He sits.*] I am the young man who lives in the next house.

FATHER. Oh, ho. Quite so, quite so. Quite a proper young man, I hear.

YOUNG MAN. I hope so, sir.

MOTHER. Oh, dear, what a gentleman.

YOUNG MAN. I hope so, madame. [*He clears his throat.*] My good sir, [*again clearing his throat*] may I have the honor—of asking for the—hand of your daughter?

FATHER. Oh, hum.

MOTHER. Dear, dear, so soon.

YOUNG MAN. Pardon me, madame?

MOTHER. Oh, dear, oh, dear, nothing, nothing at all.

FATHER. Which daughter?

YOUNG MAN. The beautiful daughter, the lovely daughter, the daughter who sits with downcast eyes at her work. Prudence, most exquisite of all maidens——

MOTHER. Dear, dear.

FATHER. Young man.

YOUNG MAN. Yes, sir.

FATHER. Have you spoken to my daughter?

YOUNG MAN. *Good sir!*

FATHER. No, no, of course not, of course not. I beg your pardon.

MOTHER. Oh, dear, what a gentleman.

FATHER. Are you in love with my daughter?

YOUNG MAN. Good sir, I have not, as yet, allowed myself that privilege. Nor could I, until I knew that that emotion would be thoroughly proper, and in accord with your wishes.

FATHER. Fortunate, very fortunate. And suppose I tell you you cannot have her?

YOUNG MAN [rising]. Then sir, I bid you good day. I see that I must look elsewhere.

FATHER. Wait a bit. Sit down, young man.

YOUNG MAN [he sits]. Yes, sir.

FATHER. I have another daughter, whom I should like to have you marry.

MOTHER. Very beautiful as well, and, we might say— lively, eh, Father?

YOUNG MAN. Yes, she too is beautiful. But, as you say, "lively"—er—ah!

FATHER. Could you bestow your affections upon her?

YOUNG MAN. Is that your wish, sir?

FATHER. Well, I might say that it is.

YOUNG MAN. And yours, madame?

MOTHER. Oh, dear, yes, yes, indeed, quite.

YOUNG MAN. But she—pardon my hesitancy—she—her —what—her wifely duties you know—sewing, and modesty, and dignity, you know.

FATHER. You should see to that.

MOTHER. She is young. Marriage is sure to settle her.

FATHER. Prudence is, we might say, already settled.

YOUNG MAN. Ah, yes, a perfect wife.

MOTHER. But Suzanne, too, is our daughter.

YOUNG MAN. Quite true, quite true. You think all she needs is settling?

FATHER. That's it, good sir.

YOUNG MAN. And you think I am the proper person?

FATHER. We are sure of it.

MOTHER. Oh dear, yes.

YOUNG MAN. And you would rather have me marry her than Prudence?

MOTHER. Prudence will make such a sweet old maid.

FATHER. You say you have not fallen in love with her?

YOUNG MAN. Alas, how could I, till I knew it was her parents' wish?

FATHER. Why not, then, fall in love with Suzanne?

YOUNG MAN. Very well, then, I shall do as you wish, that is— Good sir, may I have the honor of asking for the hand of your younger daughter, Suzanne?

MOTHER. My, what a gentleman.

FATHER. You may, my boy, and I gladly consent. [FATHER *and* MOTHER *sigh.* SUE *takes a flying leap through the door, and lands at their feet.*]

SUE. I knew I could jump from the inside hall out here if I tried. [*Scrambling up.*] Good heavens, who 's this? Sorry, I 'm sure. [*She starts back into the house.*]

FATHER. Suzanne, this is the young man from across the way. Young man, this is my daughter, Suzanne. [SUE *curtsies.*]

YOUNG MAN [*bowing deeply*]. I am greatly honored. [SUE *giggles and starts to go.*]

FATHER. Suzanne, stay here with your mother and entertain the young man, while I—while I— [*To* MOTHER.] My dear, I have a letter to post. I shall leave you. Haven't you—er—some knitting that you might attend to—er, not too far away?

MOTHER. Oh, yes, of course, of course. [FATHER *bows and goes.*] Now you young people just talk to each other, while I, while I sit here and knit. [*She sits with her back to them.*]

SUE [*to the* YOUNG MAN]. Do you need entertaining?

YOUNG MAN. Well, er, yes, that is—will you sit?

SUE [*sitting on the ground where she is*]. There, I 've sat.

MOTHER [*turning around*]. Suzanne, on the bench. [*To* YOUNG MAN.] I beg your pardon. Excuse me again. [*She turns to her work.*]

SUE [*sighing and sitting on the bench*]. What shall I do to entertain you? I know, I 've just learned to stand on my head. Would that entertain you?

YOUNG MAN.   Well, er——

MOTHER.   Suzanne!   [*To* YOUNG MAN.]   I beg your pardon.   Excuse me again.

SUE.   Mother thinks that would not be proper.

YOUNG MAN.   To tell the truth, Miss Suzanne, there is a question which [*with forced enthusiasm*] I have been longing to ask you.   [MOTHER *sighs contentedly.*]

SUE.   Question?

YOUNG MAN.   Yes.   [*Swallowing and then blurting it out.*] Will you marry me?

[SUZANNE *bursts into laughter and falls over backward on the bench.*]

MOTHER [*coming around quickly*].   Suzanne, Suzanne, get up immediately.   My dear sir, I apologize.   Maybe she does n't feel well.

[SUE *still screaming with laughter runs out the gate.*]

YOUNG MAN.   Well!   [PRUE *enters, hands up.*]

PRUE.   What did I hear?   What is all this?   [*Seeing the* YOUNG MAN.]   Oh, sir, I beg your pardon.

MOTHER.   Oh, dear, oh, dear.   What shall I do?   I must speak to your father.   What shall I do?   It would n't be proper to leave the young man alone, nor would it be proper to leave him with my young daughter.   Oh, dear, oh, dear.

YOUNG MAN.   Madame, you may trust me.

MOTHER.   Well, of course, I know I can, and Prudence is perfectly proper too.   I am sure it would be safe, and I must find Father.   [*She goes.*]

YOUNG MAN [*bowing*].   My dear miss, will you sit?

PRUE.   Oh, sir, you are most kind and polite.   [*She sits on one end of the bench.   He sits upon the other.*]

YOUNG MAN.   Pleasant day.

PRUE.   Oh, very.

YOUNG MAN.   Pleasant day yesterday.

PRUE.   Oh, very.

YOUNG MAN.   Hope it will be pleasant tomorrow.

PRUE.   Oh, yes.

YOUNG MAN [*looking at her*].   Miss Prudence.

PRUE. Oh, sir.

YOUNG MAN. Miss Prudence. [*Edging nearer.*]

PRUE. Yes, sir.

YOUNG MAN [*edging nearer*]. You 're very pretty.

PRUE [*turning away*]. Oh, sir.

YOUNG MAN [*edging away*]. I beg your pardon.

PRUE [*turning back*]. Not at all.

YOUNG MAN [*edging nearer*]. You are very beautiful.

PRUE. Oh no, sir.

YOUNG MAN. Yes, you are. You are the most beautiful girl I have ever met, and I fear I love you.

PRUE. Oh, sir. But is it something to fear?

YOUNG MAN. I fear it is. You see I just gave your father my word that I would marry Suzanne.

PRUE. Then it would be only proper to do so.

YOUNG MAN. But then I did not know that I loved you so madly.

PRUE. If you are to marry my sister you should not say those words to me.

YOUNG MAN [*moving away and looking dejected*]. No, it is most improper.

PRUE. Suzanne must be settled.

YOUNG MAN. So your parents say.

PRUE. Therefore, it is only proper that she should marry.

YOUNG MAN. So your parents say.

PRUE. Then you must marry her.

YOUNG MAN. So your parents say.

[*There is a pause.*]

PRUE [*rising*]. Good day, sir.

YOUNG MAN [*rising*]. Good day. I humbly beg your pardon for those improper words I spoke to you just now.

PRUE. Alas, most improper.

YOUNG MAN [*sighing*]. Good day.

PRUE [*sighing*]. Good day.

[*He goes. She drops on the bench and begins to cry.* SUE *enters.*]

SUE. Hello, crying again. Was the proper young man teasing you?

PRUE. How can you speak so! He is a lovely young man, and he is going to marry you.

SUE. Oh, he is.

PRUE [*crying louder*]. Yes.

SUE. Does he love you?

PRUE. It would be most improper to say so.

SUE. Do you love him?

PRUE. Oh, I must not say so.

SUE. Stuff and nonsense. Here's a pretty situation. You, crying your eyes out over a youth I would n't marry for anything in the world, and who does n't love me. Now is that proper? Three people unhappy, you and me and him! I have n't met the man I would marry, yet, but I am sure it is n't that one—certainly not, if he loves some one else.

PRUE. But you must be settled.

SUE. Oh, so that's it, is it? [*A long low whistle is heard, and the head of the* GYPSY BOY *appears over the fence where* SUE *can see it and* PRUE *cannot.* SUE *motions to him, and he disappears.*] Prue, dear, now dry your eyes, and run into the house. I won't take your young man.

PRUE. I have acted most improperly I know.

[*When she has gone,* SUE *giggles invitingly. The head appears again.*]

SUE. Hello.

BOY. Hello.

SUE. Who are you?

BOY. Gypsy boy, who are you?

SUE. Sue.

BOY. Hello, Sue.

SUE. Hello, gypsy boy.

BOY [*swinging his feet over the fence*]. Zis where you live?

SUE. Sometimes.

BOY. Sometimes?

SUE. When I sleep and eat. Where do you live?

BOY. Everywhere.

SUE. How wonderful!

BOY [*he jumps down and looks around*]. Stiff garden,
is n't it?

SUE. Oh, I don't know.

BOY. Trees don't grow like that.

SUE. Trees must be very improper then.

BOY. What?

SUE. Everything in this garden is proper.

BOY. Proper?

SUE. Yes.

BOY. What 's that?

SUE. What those trees are.

BOY. Stiff, I call it. Are you proper? [*He sits beside
her. She giggles.*] You are n't stiff.

SUE [*with mock primness*]. There is those as thinks I 'm
most improper.

BOY. What are you doing in this garden then?

SUE. My parents live in that house, and my sister.

BOY. Are they proper?

SUE. Oh, very.

[BOY *giggles, and* SUE *giggles with him.*]

BOY. You don't belong in this garden.

SUE. No?

BOY. No. You belong out where the trees are as ragged
as your dress.

SUE. I 've been there once or twice.

BOY. Come again.

SUE. When?

BOY. Now. With me.

SUE. That would be most improper.

BOY [*getting up*]. Oh, all right. Stay here, then.

SUE. You stay, too.

BOY. Nope. Too stiff. Except you. You 're not stiff.

SUE. Neither are you. Nor proper!

BOY. Nope, don't know what that is.

SUE. A proper young man wants to marry me.

BOY. Oh.

SUE. But he loves my proper sister.

Boy [*sitting*]. Do you love him?

Sue. No.

Boy. Are you going to marry him?

Sue. My father thinks so, and my mother thinks so, and my sister thinks so.

Boy. Do you think so?

Sue. That 's different.

Boy. Come with me.

Sue. I might.

Boy. Do. Rugged camp fires, and ragged trees, crooked stars and winding paths.

Sue. And no one to call me improper.

Sue. None. Will you come?

Sue [*suddenly*]. I 'll be over the fence first.

[*They start for the fence, when in come irate* FATHER *and motherly* MOTHER.]

FATHER. Suzanne.

Sue. My irate father!

[*The* BOY *whistles.*]

FATHER. Suzanne, who is this person?

Sue. Friend of mine.

FATHER. He looks distinctly like a gypsy.

Boy. Right you are. At your service.

FATHER. Nothing you can do will be service to me.

MOTHER. Suzanne, Suzanne, how could you be so improper? And you about to be married!

[*The* BOY *whistles and* SUE *giggles.*]

FATHER. Boy, leave this place. [*The* BOY *starts over the fence,* SUE *after him.*] Suzanne! Come down. Boy, go through the gate. Let your exit be more proper than your entrance or your visit here.

Boy. As you say. [*He starts out the gate.*]

SUE. That 's my window up there, don't forget.

Boy. Not I. [*He goes.*]

FATHER. Disgraceful, disgraceful.

MOTHER. My poor child.

[SUE *giggles.*]

FATHER. You must be married at once.

SUE. Father!

MOTHER. But, Father, that would be most improper.

FATHER. She will have time to be proper after she is married. In the meantime, you must be locked in your room. Mother, go fetch the young man, and a minister.

[SUE *bursts into hysterical laughter.*]

ACT II

SUZANNE'S *bedroom gives the appearance of having once been stiff and proper, furnished with the same neatness and geometrical exactness that characterizes the house, the garden, and the inhabitants, but the pictures are awry, clothes are strewn around, chairs crooked, bed unmade.* SUE *is engaged in climbing up over the head of the bed and sliding down the back when the curtain rises. She does this several times, when the irate* FATHER *enters.*

FATHER. Suzanne! How many times do I have to tell you to put your feet where they should be, *down.*

SUE. But Father, that is such a prosy way to be always, feet down. Why, you get only one view of things that way.

FATHER. There is only one view, the proper view. Suzanne, stand up.

SUE [*righting herself*]. But Father, what is the proper view?

FATHER. I know what the proper view is.

SUE. Then what is it?

FATHER. Stay head up, feet down, and you 'll always get the proper view.

SUE. But Father, I see such strange new things with my feet up and my head down.

FATHER. Then they are improper things.

SUE. Not improper, just amusing.

FATHER. Not at all amusing, only improper.

SUE. Oh, but you don't know—let me tell you what you look like upside down. [*She stands on her head again.*] Your feet are very large and your head very small.

FATHER. Suzanne!

SUE. But Father, how funny to see you with a small head. I always thought your head was large.

FATHER. Nothing could be better proof of the impropriety of standing on your head.

SUE. But Father, what is the proper way to stand?

FATHER. As I am standing.

SUE [*pointing*]. Feet that way, head that way.

FATHER. Certainly.

SUE [*in triumph*]. But Father, how about the Chinamen?

FATHER. Did I say that Chinamen were proper?

SUE. Can't say that you did.

FATHER. You will find that my point of view is the only proper one.

SUE. But Father, wouldn't it be terrible if you should find yourself mistaken some day?

FATHER. I shall never find myself mistaken.

SUE. But *just suppose* you should.

FATHER. Then I *suppose* I should stand on my head.

SUE. Oh, Father, then practice it now. You'll want to stand on your head properly I am sure when you have to. [*Starting again to stand on her head.*]

FATHER. Suzanne, less words, more sense.

SUE [*standing up*]. Yes, Father. Feet down, less words, more sense!

FATHER. That's better.

SUE. Yes, Father.

FATHER. Suzanne, I am making all arrangements for your wedding tonight.

SUE [*dropping on the bed*]. Oh, Father, less words, more sense.

FATHER. After your disgraceful conduct yesterday, in fact, your almost continual disgraceful conduct, I feel that we cannot longer delay your marriage to the estimable young man who has done you the honor to ask your hand in marriage.

SUE. But Father, he doesn't wish to marry me.

FATHER. I assure you that he does. Furthermore, he has

assured me that my wish is his law. He is a most estimable young man.

SUE. He must be.

FATHER. He is.

SUE. Does he ever stand on his head?

FATHER. Certainly not.

SUE. Then he does n't know what it is like.

FATHER. I hope not.

SUE. Father, I might teach him to stand on his head.

FATHER. I hope marriage will ease you of your deplorable habit of standing on your head.

SUE. You would n't call it a deplorable habit, if you had ever tried it.

FATHER. Alas, I did try it in my youth.

SUE. Oh, Father, how ecstatic!

FATHER. But I fear my sins are being visited upon me now.

[MOTHER *enters, carrying a pile of white lace and satin.*]

MOTHER. Now, my dear, I have come to talk to you about your wedding dress.

FATHER. I will leave you. I must confer with the minister and the young man. Suzanne, remember, feet down, less words, more sense.

SUE. Yes, Father, feet down, less words, more sense.

FATHER. Very well. I must go now. [*He goes.*]

MOTHER. Dear me, yes, you must learn to be a lady now.

SUE. Does standing on my head make me less of a lady?

MOTHER. Dear me, yes.

SUE. Why?

MOTHER. You 'll have to ask your father. He is sure to have the proper point of view.

SUE. Yes, so he says.

MOTHER. Now, dear, here is the material from my wedding dress. It is with great happiness that I make it up for you. I had thought perhaps it might be made for dear Prudence first, since she is the older, but alas, I fear dear Prudence will remain with us always to grace our old age.

SUE. Mother, when I am married, I won't be married in white.

MOTHER. Not in white! Why, my dear, what would you be married in?

SUE. Red!

MOTHER. Suzanne! But white is the only proper thing to be married in.

SUE. Why?

MOTHER. Dear me, I don't know why. Just because it is. I was married in white. My mother was married in white.

SUE. And her mother was married in white. And her mother was married in white—and so on back! Mother, what were the aborigines married in?

MOTHER. Oh, dear, I am sure it isn't proper for young ladies to think of such things whatever they are.

SUE. They must have been married in red.

MOTHER. Then it must be improper to be married in red, I am sure.

SUE. Red is such a pretty color, and white is just white, sort of flat. Trees don't put on white for their wedding garments, neither do birds and flowers.

MOTHER. Tush, tush, now, white it is to be, for that is the only proper color for matrimony. And just think my dear, Prudence is making you a beautiful wedding cake!

SUE. White, I suppose—angel food! Why couldn't she have made a devil's food?

MOTHER. Suzanne, for a wedding!

SUE. Certainly for my wedding. You wouldn't call me an angel, would you?

MOTHER. Suzanne, go no further!

SUE. But Mother, you wouldn't, would you?

[PRUDENCE enters, carrying a large white cake, crying the while.]

PRUE [between sobs]. Here, dear sister, is a wedding cake I made you. May you live long and happily——

MOTHER. There, there, now. You see how badly your sister feels at parting from you.

SUE. Be careful, don't cry on the cake. Makes it soggy. If I must be an angel, I won't be a soggy one.

PRUE. True, dearest sister, I must dry my tears. They are most improper at such a time.

MOTHER. How sweet! Well, I shall leave you two girls to exchange your last girlish confidence before the sacred veil of matrimony falls between. [*She goes.*]

PRUE [*sinking down on the floor, cake and all, and sobbing*]. Dear Sue, forgive me, I am all unstrung.

SUE. There goes the angel food.

PRUE [*sitting up*]. No, I think it is safe. Oh, dear, oh, dear!

SUE. Listen to me, Prue. I don't want your old young man, and what's more, I don't intend to have him. I am going to run away with the gypsy boy.

PRUE. Oh, you wouldn't bring our parents down in white hairs to the grave!

SUE. No, but I'd pitch the proper young man, black hairs first, into *his* grave the first week, I assure you.

PRUE. Oh, Sue, I beg you, for my sake, make him a good wife. Then I can rejoice in your children, though I may have none of my own.

SUE. I'll make him a good wife, all right. I'll make him the wife he wants.

PRUE. Oh, will you? That will be most proper, I'm sure.

SUE. I'll make him the proper wife.

PRUE. Still, if you make him a good wife, he may forget me.

SUE. He'll have no chance to forget you.

PRUE. Oh, Sue, that would be sweet—but improper.

SUE [*she goes to the window and looks out*]. Look here, Prue, if you will help me run away with the gypsy boy, you will benefit by it, for then there will be nobody to keep you from your young man.

PRUE. Oh, I could not assist in a scheme so nefarious.

SUE. Oh, I don't know. Anybody who hangs out of a window and listens to some one else's conversation isn't proper as she pretends to be.

PRUE. Oh, Suzanne, I——

SUE. Don't deny it, for I saw you.

PRUE. I was only arranging the flowers. Besides, you did it, too.

SUE. Yes, but I don't pretend to be proper.

PRUE. It was most unladylike, and I shall beg my parents' pardon immediately. [*She starts to go.*]

SUE. Oh, come now, Prue, loosen up a bit. You are just like the trees that grow in our garden. Do you know what the gypsy boy called them yesterday? Stiff! Stiff, too stiff and proper to— [*A whistle is heard.*] There, there is the gypsy boy! I knew he 'd come.

PRUE. Oh, Sue, you would n't really run away with him!

SUE. Keep my irate father from following me, and the proper young man, whom you love, is yours. [*She whistles in return, and goes to the window. The* GYPSY BOY *appears.*]

BOY. Hello, Sue.

SUE. Hello, Gypsy Boy.

BOY. Fine day out.

SUE. Is it? I have n't been out.

BOY. Pshaw, you don't know what you 've missed.

SUE. Oh, yes, I do. You see my irate father locked me in.

BOY. No? Just like he threatened.

SUE. Yes. He says I 'm to marry tonight, the proper young man, whom this, my sister loves.

BOY. Does he *say* that?

SUE. Oh, yes.

BOY. Oh, no!

[*They both giggle.*]

SUE. My motherly mother is making me a white, white dress, and my bereaved sister has just baked me a white, white cake, and my irate father is talking to the white, white minister.

BOY. All on account of a black, black wedding.

SUE. Do you think so?

BOY. No, I don't, exactly.

SUE. How are the rugged camp fires, and the ragged trees, and the crooked stars, and the winding paths?

BOY. Waiting.

SUE. Waiting?

BOY. Waiting.

SUE. Waiting for you?

BOY. And for you.

SUE. Waiting for us.

BOY. Come, then.

PRUE. Sue!

SUE. So you think it proper to thwart true love?

PRUE [*doubtfully*]. No-o-o.

SUE. This is true love. Your love for the young man is true love.

PRUE. Yes.

SUE. If I go with my true love, you can have your true love.

PRUE. Ye-es.

SUE. And all would be quite proper.

PRUE. Proper? Perhaps it would.

SUE. Then keep them from following me, till we can fly, fly away.

PRUE. Well—I 'll—try—that is, if that is really the proper thing to do.

SUE. Oh, Prue, dear, then the lovely young man is yours. I am going out where the trees are as ragged as my dress.

PRUE. But what will Father and Mother say?

SUE. It won't be long before you know.

PRUE. But what shall I tell them?·

SUE. Tell them—tell them it would be most improper to run after me.

[*A whistle is heard below, and she goes out through the window.*]

PRUE [*running to the window and looking out*]. Oh, Sue, take the cake with you. You may need it in the woods!

[*Irate* FATHER *enters.* YOUNG MAN *stands at the door and peeps in.*]

FATHER. Now, young man, I must apologize for bringing

you to this room. I realize it is most improper. But under
the circumstances—you see I cannot let my daughter leave
it; she might run away. But we can talk at this door.
[*Turning around.*] Suzanne, the young man wishes to make
arrangements for the wedding. [PRUE *turns around.*] Oh,
Prudence. I thought it was Suzanne. [*In dawning fear.*]
Where is Suzanne?

PRUE. Oh, Father. [*To the* YOUNG MAN.] Oh, sir.

FATHER. Prudence, is Suzanne under the bed?

PRUE. No, Father.

FATHER. Behind it?

PRUE. I—think not, Father.

FATHER. Then, where is she?

PRUE. Oh, Father!

FATHER. The Gypsy!

YOUNG MAN [*stepping into the room*]. Pardon me, sir,
but I believe I saw a gypsy boy flit past the door below. I
thought he might be the gardener's son.

FATHER [*sinking to the floor.*] Gone with the gypsy boy!
[MOTHER *enters, still piled high with white stuff.*]

MOTHER. Dear, dear, what has happened? Father, *you*
on the floor! What a shocking place for you to be.

FATHER [*jumping up*]. Yes, yes, I beg your pardon.
Young man, I beg your pardon. Prudence, I beg your pardon. Mother, Suzanne has run away with the gypsy boy.

MOTHER. Dear, dear, and I was just ready to fit her
dress.

FATHER. She must be found and brought back. I must
go after her. Mother, we must go after her.

PRUE. Oh, Father, you and mother running through the
streets! How terribly improper!

FATHER. True, true. But we 'll try not to run.

YOUNG MAN. Good sir, since the young miss is to be my
bride, and since it seems she is running away from me, I believe it would be only proper for me to pursue her.

[PRUE *sinks onto a chair.*]

FATHER. Quite so, quite so.

MOTHER. My, what a gentleman!

YOUNG MAN. I suppose I should take the most direct path. Ah—did she go through this—ah, window?

PRUE [*jumping up and standing in front of it*]. Would n't it be more proper for you to leave sedately and slowly by the front door, good sir?

YOUNG MAN. Oh yes. I forgot myself, Miss Prudence. Ah, would I *could* forget myself. [*He goes by the door.*]

PRUE. Oh, dear, oh, dear, what shall I do? He must not find her. I 'll run after her myself! [*She suddenly jumps out of the window.*]

FATHER. My word!

MOTHER. Good heavens!

BOTH. Prudence!!

FATHER. I believe we would better follow after all.

MOTHER. I believe we would.

FATHER. At a distance, and quite sedately.

MOTHER. Yes, quite.

[*They walk slowly, goose-step, toward the door.*]

ACT III

The woods. The gypsy camp fire is in the center of the stage front. Large ragged trees are at the back. The stage is empty for a few minutes after the curtain rises. Shortly, SUE and the Gypsy BOY run in giggling.

SUE [*standing on her head*]. Really I must celebrate!

BOY. Bravo! Me, too. [*He stands on his head.*]

SUE. Don't you get a funny view of things.

BOY. Yes.

SUE. Father says that 's not the proper view.

BOY. How does he know?

SUE. Oh, Father knows everything—everything proper, that is. [*Dropping down.*] Now, you must tell me once in a while to be proper, just to keep me from being lonesome. [*She stands on her head again. He stands on his.*]

BOY. Suzanne, be proper! [*Both fall in a heap, giggling.*] Do you suppose they will pursue us?

SUE. I persuaded Prue that it was entirely proper to hold them back until we got away.

BOY. Never mind, I know the woods, anyway. We can hide.

SUE. Is it true that joining hands over a camp fire constitutes a gypsy wedding?

BOY. So it does, and you shall hereby be my bride, immediately. Take my hand. [*They join hands over the fire.*] We'll have the ragged trees for witnesses.

SUE. And the crooked stars will pronounce a blessing! Sh, I hear some one coming.

BOY. Let's hide. You behind that tree, I behind this.

[*They do so. In a moment, on tip-toes the proper* YOUNG MAN, *looking this way and that,—fearfully comes in.* SUE *giggles, and he looks around. The gypsy gives a wild night call, and he jumps and stands trembling.*]

YOUNG MAN [*calling feebly*]. Miss Suzanne, Miss Suzanne. [*The* BOY *mocks him with a whistle. He draws nearer to the fire and holds out his hands, looking around every once in a while.*] Miss Suzanne, Miss Suzanne. Br-r-r-. [*He shivers. He crosses the stage and looks out, and crosses back, looking back. As he crosses* PRUDENCE *enters, from the direction whence he first came, also looking back. They meet in the middle.*]

PRUE [*squealing*]. Oh, oh.

YOUNG MAN [*also frightened*]. Oh. [*They turn around.*] Miss Prudence!

PRUE. Oh, sir.

YOUNG MAN. Out in these woods alone!

PRUE. No, sir, not alone.

YOUNG MAN. *Not* alone?

PRUE. Oh, no, sir, there's you, sir.

YOUNG MAN. Ah, yes, me. [*He sighs.*] Miss Prudence, I fear I must escort you back to your parental domicile.

PRUE. Oh, no.

YOUNG MAN. It is not proper that you should search for Suzanne. It is only meet that I should, I, who am to marry her. [*He sighs.* SUE *and the* GYPSY BOY *stick their heads*

out from behind the trees and giggle.]   I beg your pardon?
[*To* PRUE.]

PRUE. Nothing, I was just sighing.

YOUNG MAN. So was I.

PRUE. Oh. [*They both sigh.* PRUE *looks around.*]   It
is a terrible place for a young girl to be alone.

YOUNG MAN [*edging nearer*]. But I am here with you.

PRUE. I meant Suzanne.

YOUNG MAN. Oh, yes, of course, Suzanne.

PRUE. But, of course, the gypsy boy must be with *her.*
[SUE *and the* GYPSY BOY *again stick out their heads.*]

YOUNG MAN. Ah, yes, and I must tear her from him.
How sad?

PRUE [*boldly*]. Why?

YOUNG MAN. Becaue he is not a proper young man for
her to marry.

PRUE. Are you, then?

YOUNG MAN. So your parents say. [*They both sigh.*]   I
must take you home to your parents.

PRUE. You don't need to; my parents will be here in a
moment, I feel sure.

YOUNG MAN. Your parents in the woods with the night
coming on!

PRUE. I think I saw them coming at quite a proper gait
as I ran on ahead.

YOUNG MAN. But you should not have come, though with
the estimable motive of persuading your sister to return—
alas, to me.

PRUE. But I don't intend to persuade her to return to
you—or my parents either.

YOUNG MAN. No? Then pray, why did you follow?

PRUE. To detain you.

YOUNG MAN. To detain me?

PRUE. Yes. And let Sue marry the man she loves—which
is entirely proper.

YOUNG MAN. Proper?

PRUE. Yes, that true love should not be thwarted.

YOUNG MAN. True love should be its own reward.

PRUE. That is virtue you are thinking of.

YOUNG MAN [*with a profound sigh*]. Ah, yes, that too.

PRUE. Good sir, mean you yourself?

YOUNG MAN. I fear it is only virtue to wed where one is not loved and loves not.

PRUE. You are determined to wed Sue, then?

YOUNG MAN. Alas, I have given your parents my word, though I find my heart beats for another.

PRUE. Another?

YOUNG MAN. Oh, woe is me, yes.

PRUE. Who?

YOUNG MAN. I may never mention her again.

PRUE. Me?

YOUNG MAN. Yes. [*Suddenly.*] Oh, Prue, how can I marry Suzanne, when you are the most beautiful and the most perfect maiden in all the world!

PRUE. Good sir, you, who have been talking of virtue and propriety!

YOUNG MAN. Propriety be dashed. I will not marry Suzanne.

SUE [*stepping out*]. Nobody asked you, sir.

YOUNG MAN and PRUDENCE. Suzanne!

BOY. How dare you seek to marry my wife?

YOUNG MAN and PRUDENCE. Your wife!

SUE [*giggling*]. His wife. Just made so by authority of the trees and the stars. Gypsy wedding, you know.

PRUE. Oh, Sue, do you think that is quite proper?

SUE. Gypsies think so. We joined hands over the fire, and asked the stars to bless us.

YOUNG MAN [*suddenly and sternly*]. Prudence, give me your hand.

PRUE [*doing so*]. Oh, sir.

YOUNG MAN [*leading her to the fire*]. What are the proper words? Addressing the stars, you know. I 've never done it.

BOY [*standing in front of them*]. Dearly beloved stars, look on while this couple is joined. Trees bear witness. Prudence, do you?

PRUE. Do I what?

BOY. You must say, "I do."

PRUE. I do.

BOY. Young Man, do you?

YOUNG MAN. Must I say, "I do," too?

BOY. Yes.

YOUNG MAN. I do.

BOY. Trees, if you know of any just reason why these two should not be joined in matrimony, speak, or forever after hold your peace. [*There is a slight pause.*] They don't, so it's all right. I pronounce you man and wife.

PRUE. Where did you learn all that?

BOY. I found it in an old black book in a deserted church once. I thought you'd prefer a proper wedding.

PRUE. *Have* I been improper, do you suppose?

SUE. Improper in marrying the man you love?

PRUE. But it was very sudden and the minister didn't marry us.

SUE. What has the minister got to do with a union of hearts? Sh, I believe I hear the patters of my motherly mother, and the pants of my irate father.

PRUE. Oh, dear, I fear my father may not approve a gypsy wedding.

SUE [*giggling*]. It is just possible that he may not!

FATHER [*striding in*]. Here you are, all four!

SUE. Father, how did you guess it!

MOTHER [*panting*]. I tried so hard to keep your father from running—through the streets and all.

FATHER. Prudence, though your somewhat hasty, and decidedly improper exit from your parental domicile was reprehensible, I excuse it on the ground of your haste to seek your sister. Young man, I am glad these two maids have had the favor of your manly protection.

MOTHER. Suzanne, I must try your dress on. I just had it ready when you left.

FATHER. Try it on, when she returns. This will delay the wedding somewhat. But the minister waits at home.

ALL FOUR. But we are already married!

FATHER. What? Who 's married? How?

SUE. I 'm married to the gypsy boy, and Prudence to the proper young man.

FATHER. When? How?

SUE. Just now, over the gypsy fire.

FATHER. Nonsense. That does n't count. Suzanne, you shall come home and marry the young man.

SUE. But I don't want to marry the young man.

PRUE. I don't want Sue to marry the young man. I want to marry him myself.

YOUNG MAN. If you please, sir, I don't wish to marry Suzanne, I wish to marry Prudence.

MOTHER. Oh, dear, Prudence would have made such a proper old maid, the grace of our old age.

FATHER. Young man, which of these young ladies do you love?

YOUNG MAN. Prudence.

FATHER. Prudence, do you love this young man?

PRUE. Yes, Father.

FATHER. But, young man, you promised me to fall in love with Suzanne.

YOUNG MAN. So I did, sir.

FATHER. And you have instead fallen in love with Prudence?

YOUNG MAN. At the dictates of my heart, sir. I find I could not help it.

FATHER. H'm, well, then it is only proper that you should marry Prudence. I am sure I did not know you loved each other. Mother, I think it is only proper that they should marry, since they love each other.

MOTHER. Oh, yes. He 's such a gentleman.

FATHER. But now, Mother, we must find another proper young man for Suzanne‾

SUE. Oh, Father, I am sure you could never find another young man so proper.

PRUE. Oh, Father, I am sure you could not.

YOUNG MAN. No, sir, I fear you could not.

FATHER. Dear, dear, that 's so. Mother, what are we to do with Suzanne?

SUE. But Father, I 'm not proper.

FATHER. No, Suzanne, I fear you are not.

BOY. And I 'm not proper.

FATHER. No, I am sure you are not.

SUE. But, Father, I love the gypsy boy.

BOY. And I love Sue.

MOTHER. Oh dear, both improper.

SUE. Then, Father, dear, and Mother dear, would it not be proper for us two improper people to wed?

FATHER. That is looking at things from a slightly different point of view from the one I have been used to.

SUE. Is there a different point of view?

FATHER. An opposite point of view. I suppose one might call it the improperly proper point of view.

SUE. Then we may wed.

FATHER. H 'm, well, provided you are properly wed.

SUE. Minister if you say so, Father.

MOTHER. Oh dear, which of you is to wear this lovely dress?

SUE. Prue can have it. I prefer red. Father, have n't you changed your point of view a little?

FATHER. Not at all, not at all. Every other point of view has changed, that is all.

SUE. Father, then do you think you should still look at things as you do?

FATHER. Sue, I think I shall try standing on my head. [*He does so.*]

CURTAIN

FOOTNOTES TO *THE MAID WHO WOULD N'T BE PROPER*.

Costumes for *The Maid Who Would n't Be Proper* are in the pantalet. full-skirt, bonnet period. Each puppet has one characteristic gesture, which in the construction of the puppet should be made dominant above all other necessary movement. SUZANNE, for instance, has the very obvious characteristic of standing on her head. She should be made with extra strings on the back of her heels, in order that she may tip forward, instead of backward, the easiest way for a normal puppet to stand on its head. FATHER, in the last act, however, could tip over backwards to lend an element of further surprise to his conduct. SUZANNE should be generally built with great flexibility, in order that her abandon may have full play.

PRUDENCE, on the other hand, while being dressed almost exactly like SUZANNE, should be rather tight and precise in her movements. The expression on her face is one of shocked and modest surprise, and her principal gesture is both arms bent at the elbow and held up at the sides to express her lady-like amazement.

The IRATE FATHER is a stocky individual, who is continually laying down the law with a positive arm, which should be capable of a gesture of emphasis, either with fist or with finger. The MOTHERLY MOTHER, round and plump, should certainly be capable of folding her hands over her tummy. The PROPER YOUNG MAN should be able to bow, profoundly and politely. The GYPSY BOY is a typical story book gypsy with an air even more abandoned than SUZANNE'S, and the ability to rest his hand on his hip in thorough gypsy fashion.

Further suggestions or information concerning the production of this play will be happily furnished by the author upon request. All acting and production rights are reserved by the author.

SUGGESTIVE QUESTIONS

1. Why is the setting for Act I made so extremely conventional?
2. Why did the dramatist suggest three entirely different settings for the three acts?
3. What spirit pervades the entire play?
4. What are the divisions of the plot?
5. What part of the action is most effective?
6. Why is the action not kept within the bounds of probability?
7. Which character is most amusing?
8. What is the effect of repetition?
9. Why is the Gypsy Boy introduced?
10. Prove that the play is, or is not, satirical.

SUGGESTIONS FOR WRITTEN IMITATION

1. Write an outline for a simple play that children might give with ordinary dolls.
2. Write a scenario for a fantastic puppet play based on school life.
3. Write any part of the dialogue for a puppet play based on school life.
4. Write directions for an effective stage setting for a puppet play based on school life.

DIRECTIONS FOR WRITING

Bear in mind that your play is to be acted by puppets, and not by living people. Do not try to keep the action entirely within the bounds of probability, but do not venture too far into the region of the absurd. Try to produce legitimate humor.

ORAL WORK IN CLASS

1. Read aloud any one complete section of *The Maid Who Wouldn't Be Proper,* changing your voice to indicate different characters; using suitable exaggeration; and emphasizing and repeating characteristic effects, as if you were presenting the puppet play in public.
2. In a similar way read aloud part of your own puppet play.

IOLANTHE

By William Schwenk Gilbert

The comic operas by Gilbert and Sullivan are eternally new, having peculiarly individual vitality. From time to time they appear on the stage, and in all times they furnish popular songs, and humorous passages that people quote. Like Lewis Carroll's *Alice's Adventures in Wonderland,* they are delightful examples of nonsense made classical. They represent a type of artistry that is altogether happy.

Iolanthe, whose fairy world reminds one of the fairy worlds of *A Midsummer Night's Dream* and *The Tempest,* is especially suitable for school study. Like all the operas by Gilbert and Sullivan, *Iolanthe* is unique and original in plot, and is filled with the spirit of fun, laughter and frolic.

Iolanthe illustrates what Milton had in mind when he wrote: "Quips and cranks and wanton wiles," for the play is made up of clever twistings of language, quick, bright dialogue, and the bringing about of unexpected and altogether humorous situations.

In great measure, *Iolanthe* produces its fun by opposites. It places fairies where fairies are ridiculously out of place; it places mortals who normally have the highest dignity, in situations where they have no dignity; it turns the whole world upside down. It even makes the fairies laugh at themselves when they sing:

> "Tripping hither, tripping thither,
> Nobody knows why or whither."

While the aim is nonsense, and then more nonsense, the play makes sufficient differentiation of characters to create personalities; and has sufficient plot to make an interesting

216

story. Beneath it all it has kindly satire that never offends. In many ways the play represents art of a most admirable kind. The clever jingle of rhymes, the patter of the verse, and the unique quality of the humor, are inimitable.

Sir William Schwenk Gilbert, the author of *Iolanthe*, was a descendant of the great sixteenth century soldier and sailor, Sir Humphrey Gilbert. Sir Humphrey Gilbert, refusing to seek safety for himself and leave his men in a small ship, called out to those on a larger vessel near by, "We are as near to heaven by sea as by land." On the night of that same day he and all his men were lost. That Sir William Schwenk Gilbert inherited some of the spirit of his famous ancestor is shown by the fact that at the age of seventy-five he plunged into a lake in order to save a woman from drowning, and thus nobly lost his own life.

From his early days W. S. Gilbert was a humorist. As a boy he drew odd pictures to illustrate the novels that his father wrote. Soon after his graduation from the University of London he began the writing of humorous verse, much of which he collected later in *Bab Ballads* and *More Bab Ballads*.

After various experiences in the Civil Service, in the practice of law, and in journalism as dramatic critic, he began the writing of the long list of plays that bear his name. He was thirty when he wrote *Dulcamara*, a Christmas burlesque, his first play.

W. S. Gilbert was thirty-five when he began to collaborate with Arthur Sullivan, the composer, in preparing the series of operas that made both men famous, and that brought to both the honor of Knighthood. The collaboration was one of the happiest; on one side was a great humorous artist, and on the other, one of the most highly gifted of popular musicians. The result was a series of unsurpassed comic operas, universal in charm, fantastic and delightful in humor, clean, clever, brilliantly original, extremely popular, and destined to become classics of the stage. Among the Gilbert and Sullivan operas the most famous are: *H. M. S. Pinafore* (1878); *The Pirates of Penzance* (1880); *Patience* (1880); *Iolanthe*

(1882) ; *Princess Ida* (1884) ; *The Mikado* (1885) ; *Ruddigore* (1887) ; *The Yeomen of the Guard* (1888) ; and *The Gondoliers* (1889). In addition to these operas W. S. Gilbert wrote a great number of other operas and plays.

INTRODUCTORY PROBLEMS

1. Write a scenario for a fantastic play based on *Puss in Boots, Cinderella, Alice's Adventures in Wonderland,* or *Through the Looking-Glass.*
2. Write a scenario for a fantastic play that will satirize modern follies of the lighter sort.
3. Write a dialogue in which you make use of fantastic characters.

DRAMATIS PERSONÆ

STREPHON	IOLANTHE
THE EARL OF MOUNT ARARAT	THE FAIRY QUEEN
THE EARL OF TOLLOLLER	CELIA
PRIVATE WILLIS	LELIA
THE TRAIN-BEARER	FLETA
and	PHYLLIS
THE LORD CHANCELLOR	CHORUS OF FAIRIES
CHORUS OF PEERS	

ACT I—*An Arcadian Landscape*
ACT II—*The Palace Yard, Westminster, at Night*

ACT I

SCENE.—*An Arcadian Landscape. A river runs across the back of the stage.*
[*Enter Fairies, led by* LELIA, CELIA, FLETA. *They trip across the stage, singing as they dance.*]

CHORUS

Tripping hither, tripping thither,
Nobody knows why or whither,

We must dance and we must sing
Round about our fairy ring.

SOLO—CELIA

We are dainty little fairies,
  Ever singing, ever dancing;
We indulge in our vagaries
  In a fashion most entrancing.
If you ask the special function
  Of our never-ceasing motion,
We reply, without compunction,
  That we have n't any notion.
  No, we have n't any notion.
Cho.   Tripping hither, etc.

SOLO—LELIA

If you ask us how we live,
Lovers all essentials give:
We can ride on lovers' sighs,
Warm ourselves in lovers' eyes,
Bathe ourselves in lovers' tears,
Clothe ourselves in lovers' fears,
Arm ourselves with lovers' darts,
Hide ourselves in lovers' hearts.
When you know us, you 'll discover
That we almost live on lover.
Cho.   Tripping hither, etc.

[*At the end of the chorus all sigh wearily.*]

Celia. Ah, it 's all very well, but since our queen banished Iolanthe, fairy revels have not been what they were.
  Lelia. Iolanthe was the life and soul of Fairyland. Why,
she wrote all our songs and arranged all our dances! We
sing her songs and we trip her measures, but we don't enjoy
ourselves.
  Fleta. To think that five-and-twenty years have elapsed

since she was banished! What could she have done to have deserved so terrible a punishment?

Lelia. Something awful: she married a mortal.

Fleta. Oh! Is it injudicious to marry a mortal?

Lelia. Injudicious? It strikes at the root of the whole fairy system. By our laws the fairy who marries a mortal dies.

Celia. But Iolanthe didn't die.

[*Enter* QUEEN *of the* FAIRIES.]

Queen. No, because your queen, who loved her with a surpassing love, commuted her sentence to penal servitude for life, on condition that she left her husband without a word of explanation and never communicated with him again.

Lelia. And that sentence of penal servitude she is now working out at the bottom of that stream?

Queen. Yes. But when I banished her I gave her all the pleasant places of the earth to dwell in. I'm sure I never intended that she should go and live at the bottom of that stream. It makes me perfectly wretched to think of the discomfort she must have undergone.

Lelia. To think of the damp! And her chest was always delicate.

Queen. And the frogs! ugh! I never shall enjoy any peace of mind until I know why Iolanthe went to live among the frogs.

Fleta. Then why not summon her and ask her?

Queen. Why? Because if I set eyes on her I should forgive her at once.

Celia. Then why not forgive her? Twenty-five years! It's a long time.

Lelia. Think how we loved her!

Queen. Loved her? What was your love to mine? Why, she was invaluable to me! Who taught me to curl myself inside a buttercup? Iolanthe!—Who taught me to swing upon a cobweb? Iolanthe!—who taught me to dive into a dewdrop, to nestle in a nutshell, to gambol upon gossamer? Iolanthe!

Lelia. She certainly did surprising things.

Fleta. Oh, give her back to us, great queen—for your sake, if not for ours. [*All kneel in supplication.*]

Queen [*irresolute*]. Oh, I should be strong, but I am weak; I should be marble, but I am clay. Her punishment has been heavier than I intended. I did not mean that she should live among the frogs. And— Well! well! it shall be as you wish.

INVOCATION

Queen.   Iolanthe!
All.   From thy dark exile thou art summoned;
                Come to our call,
                  Iolanthe!
                  Iolanthe!
                  Iolanthe!
                Come to our call,
                  Iolanthe!

[IOLANTHE *rises from the water. She is clad in tattered and somber garments. She approaches the* QUEEN *with head bent and arms crossed.*]

Io.   With humble breast,
                And every hope laid low,
              To thy behest,
                Offended queen, I bow.
Queen.   For a dark sin against our fairy laws
              We sent thee into lifelong banishment;
              But Mercy holds her sway within our hearts:
              Rise, thou art pardoned!
Io.   Pardoned?
All.   Pardoned!
Io.   Ah!

[*Her rags fall from her, and she appears clothed as a fairy. The* QUEEN *places a diamond coronet on her head and embraces her. The others also embrace her.*]

Cho.   Welcome to our hearts again,
            Iolanthe! Iolanthe!
       We have shared thy bitter pain,
            Iolanthe! Iolanthe!
       Every heart and every hand
       In our loving little band
       Welcomes thee to Fairyland,
            Iolanthe!

Queen. And now tell me: with all the world to choose from, why on earth did you decide to live at the bottom of that stream?

Io. To be near my son, Strephon.

Queen. Your son! Bless my heart! I didn't know you had a son.

Io. He was born soon after I left my husband by your royal command, but he doesn't even know of his father's existence.

Fleta. How old is he?

Io. Twenty-four.

Lelia. Twenty-four! No one to look at you would think you had a son of twenty-four? But of course that's one of the advantages of being immortal—we never grow old. Is he pretty?

Io. He's extremely pretty, but he's inclined to be stout.

All [*disappointed*]. Oh!

Queen. I see no objection to stoutness in moderation.

Celia. And what is he?

Io. He's an Arcadian shepherd, and he loves Phyllis, a ward in Chancery.

Celia. A mere shepherd, and he half a fairy!

Io. He's a fairy down to the waist, but his legs are mortal.

Celia. Dear me!

Queen. I have no reason to suppose that I am more curious than other people, but I confess I should like to see a person who is a fairy down to the waist, but whose legs are mortal.

Io. Nothing easier, for here he comes.

[*Enter* STREPHON, *singing and dancing, and playing on a flageolet. He does not see the Fairies, who retire up stage as he enters.*]

SONG—STREPHON

Good-morrow, good mother;
    Good mother, good-morrow!
By some means or other
    Pray banish your sorrow!
    With joy beyond telling
    My bosom is swelling,
    So join in a measure
    Expressive of pleasure,
For I 'm to be married to-day, to-day—
Yes, I 'm to be married to-day.

Cho.   Yes, he 's to be married today, today—
Yes, he 's to be married to-day.

Io. Then the Lord Chancellor has at last given his consent to your marriage with his beautiful ward, Phyllis?

Streph. Not he, indeed! To all my tearful prayers he answers me, "A shepherd lad is no fit helpmate for a ward of Chancery." I stood in court, and there I sang him songs of Arcadee, with flageolet accompaniment, in vain. At first he seemed amused, so did the Bar, but, quickly wearying of my song and pipe, he bade me get out. A servile usher then, in crumpled bands and rusty bombazine, led me, still singing, into Chancery Lane! I 'll go no more; I 'll marry her to-day, and brave the upshot, be what it may!—[*Sees Fairies.*] But who are these?

Io. Oh, Strephon, rejoice with me; my queen has pardoned me!

Streph. Pardoned you, mother? This is good news, indeed!

Io. And these ladies are my beloved sisters.

Streph. Your sisters? Then they are my aunts [*kneels*].

Queen. A pleasant piece of news for your bride on her wedding-day!

Streph. Hush! My bride knows nothing of my fairy-hood. I dare not tell her, lest it frighten her. She thinks me mortal, and prefers me so.

Lelia. Your fairyhood does n't seem to have done you much good.

Streph. Much good? It 's the curse of my existence! What 's the use of being half a fairy? My body can creep through a keyhole, but what 's the good of that when my legs are left kicking behind? I can make myself invisible down to the waist, but that 's of no use when my legs remain exposed to view. My brain is a fairy brain, but from the waist downward I 'm a gibbering idiot. My upper half is immortal, but my lower half grows older every day, and some day or other must die of old age. What 's to become of my upper half when I 've buried my lower half, I really don't know.

Queen. I see your difficulty, but with a fairy brain you should seek an intellectual sphere of action. Let me see: I 've a borough or two at my disposal; would you like to go into Parliament?

Io. A fairy member! That would be delightful.

Streph. I 'm afraid I should do no good there. You see, down to the waist I 'm a Tory of the most determined descrip-tion, but my legs are a couple of confounded Radicals, and on a division they 'd be sure to take me into the wrong lobby. You see, they 're two to one, which is a strong working majority.

Queen. Don't let that distress you; you shall be returned as a Liberal-Conservative, and your legs shall be our peculiar care.

Streph. [*bowing*]. I see Your Majesty does not do things by halves.

Queen. No; we are fairies down to the feet.

ENSEMBLE

Queen.   Fare thee well, attractive stranger.
Fairies.   Fare thee well, attractive stranger.
Queen.   Shouldst thou be in doubt or danger,
                Peril or perplexitee,
                Call us, and we 'll come to thee—
Fairies.   Call us, and we 'll come to thee.
             Tripping hither, tripping thither,
             Nobody knows why or whither,
             We must now be taking wing
             To another fairy ring.

[*Fairies and* QUEEN *trip off,* IOLANTHE, *who takes an affectionate farewell of her son, going off last.*]

[*Enter* PHYLLIS, *singing and dancing, and accompanying herself on a flageolet.*]

SONG—PHYLLIS

Good-morrow, good lover;
    Good lover, good-morrow!
I prithee discover,
    Steal, purchase, or borrow,
Some means of concealing
The care you are feeling,
    And join in a measure
    Expressive of pleasure;
For we 're to be married to-day, to-day—
For we 're to be married to-day.

Both.   Yes, we 're to be married, etc.

Streph. My Phyllis! And to-day we 're to be made happy forever!
Phyl. Well, we 're to be married.
Streph. It 's the same thing.
Phyl. Well, I suppose it is. But oh, Strephon, I tremble

at the step we 're taking. I believe it 's penal servitude for
life to marry a ward of court without the Lord Chancellor's
consent. I shall be of age in two years. Don't you think
you could wait two years?

Streph. Two years! You can't have seen yourself.
Here, look at that [*offering mirror*], and tell me if you think
it 's reasonable to expect me to wait two years?

Phyl. No; you 're quite right; it 's asking too much—
one must be reasonable.

Streph. Besides, who knows what will happen in two
years? Why, you might fall in love with the Lord Chancellor
himself by that time.

Phyl. Yes, he 's a clever old gentleman.

Streph. As it is, half the House of Lords are sighing at
your feet.

Phyl. The House of Lords is certainly extremely
attentive.

Streph. Attentive? I should think they were! Why did
five-and-twenty Liberal peers come down to shoot over your
grass-plot last autumn? It could n't have been the spar-
rows. Why did five-and-twenty Conservative peers come
down to fish in your pond? Don't tell me it was the gold-
fish! No, no. Delays are dangerous, and if we are to marry,
the sooner the better.

DUET—PHYLLIS *and* STREPHON

Phyl.   None shall part us from each other;
       One in love and life are we—
       All in all to one another,
       I to thee and thou to me.

PHYLLIS	STREPHON
Thou the tree, and I the flower;	I the tree, and thou the flower;
Thou the idol, I the throng;	I the idol, thou the throng;
Thou the day, and I the hour;	I the day, and thou the hour;

Thou the singer, I the song;
Thou the stream, and I the willow;
Thou the sculptor, I the clay;
Thou the ocean, I the billow;
Thou the sunrise, I the day.

I the singer, thou the song;
I the stream, and thou the willow;
I the sculptor, thou the clay;
I the ocean, thou the billow;
I the sunrise, thou the day.

Phyl.   Ever thine since that fond meeting,
When in joy I woke to find
Thine the heart within me beating—
Mine the love that heart enshrined.

PHYLLIS

Thou the tree, and I the flower;
Thou the idol, I the throng;
Thou the day, and I the hour;
Thou the singer, I the song;
Thou the stream, and I the willow;
Thou the sculptor, I the clay;
Thou the ocean, I the billow;
Thou the sunrise, I the day.

STREPHON

I the tree, and thou the flower;
I the idol, thou the throng;
I the day, and thou the hour;
I the singer, thou the song;
I the stream, and thou the willow;
I the sculptor, thou the clay;
I the ocean, thou the billow;
I the sunrise, thou the day.

[*Exeunt* STREPHON *and* PHYLLIS.]

[*March. Enter procession of Peers, headed by the* EARL OF MOUNT ARARAT *and* EARL OF TOLLOLLER.]

CHORUS

Loudly let the trumpet bray—
    Tantantara!
Gayly bang the sounding brasses—
    Tzing!
As upon its lordly way
    This unique procession passes!
    Tantantara! tzing! boom!
Bow, ye lower, middle classes!
Bow, ye tradesmen! bow, ye masses!
Blow the trumpets, bang the brasses!
    Tantantara! tzing! boom!
We are peers of highest station,
Paragons of legislation,
Pillars of the British nation!
    Tantantara! tzing! boom!

[*Enter the* LORD CHANCELLOR, *followed by his train-bearer.*]

SONG—LORD CHANCELLOR

The law is the true embodiment
Of everything that 's excellent:
It has no kind of fault or flaw;
And I, my lords, embody the law.
The constitutional guardian I
Of pretty young wards in Chancery.
All are agreeable girls, and none
Are over the age of twenty-one.
A pleasant occupation for
A rather susceptible Chancellor!

All.　　　A pleasant, etc.

But, though the compliment implied
Inflates me with legitimate pride,
It nevertheless can't be denied
That it has its inconvenient side;

For I 'm not so old and not so plain,
And I 'm quite prepared to marry again;
But there 'd be the deuce to pay in the Lords
If I fell in love with one of my wards;
Which rather tries my temper, for
I 'm such a susceptible Chancellor!

All.   Which rather, etc.

And every one who 'd marry a ward
Must come to me for my accord;
And in my court I sit all day,
Giving agreeable girls away—
With one for him, and one for he,
And one for you, and one for ye,
And one for thou, and one for thee;
But never, oh never, a one for me;
Which is exasperating for
A highly susceptible Chancellor!

All.   Which is, etc.

[*Enter* LORD TOLLOLLER.]

Ld. Toll. And now, my lord, suppose we proceed to the
business of the day?
Ld. Chan. By all means. Phyllis, who is a ward of court,
has so powerfully affected your lordships that you have
appealed to me in a body to give her to whichever one of
you she may think proper to select; and a noble lord has
gone to her cottage to request her immediate attendance.
It would be idle to deny that I, myself, have the misfortune
to be singularly attracted by this young person. My regard
for her is rapidly undermining my constitution. Three
months ago I was a stout man. I need say no more. If
I could reconcile it with my duty, I should unhesitatingly
award her to myself, for I can conscientiously say that I
know no man who is so well fitted to render her exceptionally

happy. But such an award would be open to misconstruction, and therefore, at whatever personal inconvenience, I waive my claim.

Ld. Toll. My lord, I desire, on the part of this House, to express its sincere sympathy with your lordship's most painful position.

Ld. Chan. I thank your lordships. The feelings of a Lord Chancellor who is in love with a ward of court are not to be envied. What is his position? Can he give his own consent to his own marriage with his own ward? Can he marry his own ward without his own consent? And if he marries his own ward without his own consent, can he commit himself for contempt of his own court? can he appear by counsel before himself to move for arrest of his own judgment? Ah, my lords, it is indeed painful to have to sit upon a woolsack which is stuffed with such thorns as these.

[*Enter* LORD MOUNT ARARAT.]

Ld. Mount. My lords, I have the pleasure to inform your lordships that I have succeeded in persuading the young lady to present herself at the bar of this House.

[*Enter* PHYLLIS.]

RECITATIVE—PHYLLIS

My well-loved lord and guardian dear,
You summoned me, and I am here.
Cho. of Peers.
Oh, rapture! how beautiful!
How gentle! how dutiful!

SOLO—LORD TOLLOLLER

Of all the young ladies I know,
This pretty young lady 's the fairest;
Her lips have the rosiest show,
Her eyes are the richest and rarest.

Her origin 's lowly, it 's true,
    But of birth and position I 've plenty;
I 've grammar and spelling for two,
    And blood and behavior for twenty.

Cho. Her origin 's lowly, it 's true,
    But he 's grammar and spelling for two;
Of birth and position he 's plenty,
    With blood and behavior for twenty.

SOLO—EARL OF MOUNT ARARAT

Though the views of the House have diverged
    On every conceivable motion,
All questions of party are merged
    In a frenzy of love and devotion.
If you ask us distinctly to say
    What party we claim to belong to,
We reply, without doubt or delay,
    The party I 'm singing this song to.

Cho. If you ask us distinctly to say,
    We reply, without doubt or delay,
That the party we claim to belong to
Is the party we 're singing this song to.

SOLO—PHYLLIS

I 'm very much pained to refuse,
    But I 'll stick to my pipes and my tabors;
I can spell all the words that I use,
    And my grammar 's as good as my neighbor's.
As for birth, I was born like the rest;
    My behavior is rustic, but hearty;
And I know where to turn for the best
    When I want a particular party.

Cho. Though her station is none of the best,
    We suppose she was born like the rest;

And she knows where to look for her hearty
When she wants a particular party.

RECITATIVE—PHYLLIS

Phyl.   Nay, tempt me not:
            To wealth I 'll not be bound:
            In lowly cot
            Alone is virtue found.

All.   No, no, indeed; high rank will never hurt you:
          The peerage is not destitute of virtue.

BALLAD—LORD TOLLOLLER

Spurn not the nobly born
    With love affected,
Nor treat with virtuous scorn
    The well-connected.
High rank involves no shame;
We boast an equal claim
With him of humble name
    To be respected.
        Blue blood!
        Blue blood!
When virtuous love is sought,
Thy power is naught,
Though dating from the Flood,
Blue blood! ah, blue blood.

Cho.   When virtuous love, etc.
        Spare us the bitter pain,
            With stern denials,
        Nor with low-born disdain
            Augment our trials.

Hearts just as pure and fair
May beat in Belgrave Square
As in the lowly air
    Of Seven Dials.
        Blue blood!
        Blue blood!
Of what avail art thou
To serve us now,
Though dating from the Flood,
Blue blood? ah, blue blood!

Cho.　　　　Of what avail art thou, etc.

RECITATIVE—PHYLLIS

My lords, it may not be;
    With grief my heart is riven;
You waste your words on me,
    For, ah! my heart is given.

All.　　　　Given?

Phyl.　　　　Yes, given!

All.　　　　Oh, horror!

RECITATIVE—LORD CHANCELLOR

And who has dared to brave our high displeasure,
    And thus defy our definite command?

[*Enter* STREPHON; PHYLLIS *rushes to his arms.*]

Streph.
'T is I, young Strephon; mine the priceless treasure;
    Against the world I claim my darling's hand.

All.　　　Ah! rash one, tremble!
Streph.　　　A shepherd I—
All.　　　　A shepherd he!

Streph.   Of Arcady—
All.   Of Arcadee!
Streph. and Phyl.   Betrothed are we!
All.   Betrothed are they—
Streph. and Phyl.   And mean to be
                    Espoused to-day.

ENSEMBLE

STREPH.   THE OTHERS

A shepherd I   A shepherd he
Of Arcady;   Of Arcadee;
Betrothed are we   Betrothed is he,
And mean to be   And means to be
Espoused to-day.   Espoused to-day.

Ld. Chan.   Ah! rash one, tremble!

DUET—LORD MOUNT *and* LORD TOLL. [*aside to Peers*].

               'Neath this blow,
                    Worse than stab of dagger,
               Though we mo-
                    mentarily stagger,
               In each heart
               Proud are we innately:
               Let 's depart,
                    Dignified and stately—
All.   Let 's depart,
                    Dignified and stately.

CHORUS OF PEERS

Though our hearts she 's badly bruising
In another suitor choosing,
Let 's pretend it 's most amusing.
Ha! ha! ha! ha! tzing! boom!

[*Exeunt all the Peers, marching round stage with much dig.*

nity. LORD CHANCELLOR *separates* PHYLLIS *from* STREPHON, *and orders her off. Manent* LORD CHANCELLOR *and* STREPHON.]

Ld. Chan. Now, sir, what excuse have you to offer for having disobeyed an order of the court of Chancery?

Streph. My lord, I know no court of Chancery; I go by Nature's acts of Parliament. The bees, the breeze, the seas, the rocks, the brooks, the gales, the vales, the fountains, and the mountains, cry, "You love this maiden; take her, we command you!" 'T is writ in heaven by the bright-barbed dart that leaps forth into lurid light from each grim thunder-cloud. The very rain pours forth her sad and sodden sympathy. When chorused Nature bids me take my love, shall I reply, "Nay, but a certain Chancellor forbids it?" Sir, you are England's Lord High Chancellor, but are you Chancellor of birds and trees, king of the winds and prince of thunder-clouds?

Ld. Chan. No. It's a nice point; I don't know that I ever met it before. But my difficulty is, that at present there's no evidence before the court that chorused Nature has interested herself in the matter.

Streph. No evidence? You have my word for it. I tell you that she bade me take my love.

Ld. Chan. Ah! but, my good sir, you must n't tell us what she told you; it's not evidence. Now, an affidavit from a thunderstorm or a few words on oath from a heavy shower would meet with all the attention they deserve.

Streph. And have you the heart to apply the prosaic rules of evidence to a case which bubbles over with poetical emotion?

Ld. Chan. Distinctly. I have always kept my duty strictly before my eyes; and it is to that fact that I owe my advancement to my present distinguished position.

SONG—LORD CHANCELLOR

When I went to the Bar as a very young man
(Said I to myself, said I),

I 'll work on a new and original plan
　　(Said I to myself, said I),
I 'll never assume that a rogue or a thief
Is a gentleman worthy implicit belief
Because his attorney has sent me a brief
　　(Said I to myself, said I).

I 'll never throw dust in a juryman's eyes,
　　(Said I to myself, said I),
　　Or hoodwink a judge who is not over-wise
　　(Said I to myself, said I),
Or assume that the witnesses summoned in force
In Exchequer, Queen's Bench, Common Pleas, or Divorce
Have perjured themselves as a matter of course
　　(Said I to myself, said I).

Ere I go into court I will read my brief through
　　(Said I to myself, said I),
And I 'll never take work I 'm unable to do
　　(Said I to myself, said I);
My learned profession I 'll never disgrace
By taking a fee, with a grin on my face,
When I have n't been there to attend to the case
　　(Said I to myself, said I).

In other professions in which men engage
　　(Said I to myself, said I),
The Army, the Navy, the Church, and the Stage
　　(Said I to myself, said I),
Professional license, if carried too far,
Your chance of promotion will certainly mar;
And I fancy the rule might apply to the Bar
　　(Said I to myself, said I).　[*Exit* LORD CHANCELLOR.]

[*To* STREPHON, *who is in tears, enters* IOLANTHE.]

Streph.　Oh, Phyllis! Phyllis! To be taken from you just
as I was on the point of making you my own! Oh, it 's too
much! it is too much!

Io. My son in tears, and on his wedding-day?

Streph. My wedding-day! Oh, mother, weep with me, for the law has interposed between us, and the Lord Chancellor has separated us forever!

Io. The Lord Chancellor!—[*Aside.*] Oh, if he did but know!

Streph. [*overhearing her*]. If he did but know—what?

Io. No matter. The Lord Chancellor has no power over you. Remember, you are half a fairy; you can defy him—down to the waist.

Streph. Yes, but from the waist downward he can commit me to prison for years. Of what avail is it that my body is free if my legs are working out seven years' penal servitude?

Io. True. But take heart; our queen has promised you her special protection. I'll go to her and lay your peculiar case before her.

Streph. My beloved mother, how can I repay the debt I owe you?

FINALE

QUARTETTE

[*As it commences the Peers appear at the back, advancing unseen and on tiptoe.* MOUNT ARARAT *and* TOLLOLLER *lead* PHYLLIS *between them, who listens in horror to what she hears.*]

Streph. [*to* IOLANTHE].
      When darkly looms the day,
      And all is dull and gray,
      To chase the gloom away
        On thee I'll call.

Phyl. [*speaking aside to* MOUNT].
      What was that?

Ld. Mount [*aside to* PHYLLIS].
      I think I heard him say
      That on a rainy day

> To while the time away,
> On her he 'd call.

Cho.   We think we heard him say, etc.

[PHYLLIS *much agitated at her lover's supposed faithless-ness.*]

Io. [*to* STREPHON].

> When tempests wreck thy bark,
> And all is drear and dark,
> If thou shouldst need an ark,
> I 'll give thee one.

Phyl. [*speaking aside to* TOLLOLLER].

> What was that?

Ld. Toll. [*aside to* PHYLLIS].

> I heard the minx remark
> She 'd meet him after dark
> Inside St. James's Park,
> And give him one.

Cho.   We heard the minx remark, etc.

Io.   The prospect 's not so bad;

> Thy heart, so sore and sad,
> May very soon be glad
> As summer sun;
> But while the sky is dark,
> And tempests wreck thy bark,
> If thou shouldst need an ark,
> I 'll give thee one.

Phyl. [*revealing herself*].

> Ah!

[IOLANTHE *and* STREPHON *much confused.*]

> Oh, shameless one, tremble!
> Nay, do not endeavor
> Thy fault to dissemble;
> We part, and forever.
> I worshiped him blindly,
> He worships another—

Streph.   Attend to me kindly:
        This lady 's my mother.

Ld. Toll.   This lady 's his—*what?*

Streph.   This lady 's my mother.

Tenors.   This lady 's his—*what?*

Basses.   He says she 's his mother.

[*They point derisively to* IOLANTHE, *laughing heartily at her. She clings for protection to* STREPHON.]

[*Enter* LORD CHANCELLOR; IOLANTHE *veils herself.*]

Ld. Chan.
    What means this mirth unseemly
      That shakes the listening earth?

Ld. Toll.
    The joke is good, extremely,
      And justifies our mirth.

Ld. Mount.
    This gentleman is seen
    With a maid of seventeen,
  A-taking of his *dolce far niente;*
    And wonders he 'd achieve,
    For he asks us to believe
  She 's his mother, and he 's nearly five-and-twenty!

All.   Ha! ha! ha! ha! ha!

Ld. Chan. [*sternly*].
    Recollect yourself, I pray,
    And be careful what you say;
  As the ancient Romans said, *festina lente;*
    For I really do not see
    How so young a girl could be
  The mother of a man of five-and-twenty.

All.   Ha! ha! ha! ha! ha!

Streph.
    My lord, of evidence I have no dearth:
    She is—has been—my mother from my birth.

BALLAD—STREPHON

In babyhood
Upon her lap I lay;
With infant food
She moistenèd my clay;
Had she withheld
The succor she supplied,
By hunger quelled
Your Strephon might have died.

Ld. Chan. [*much moved*].
Had that refreshment been denied,
Indeed our Strephon might have died.
All [*much affected*].
Had that refreshment been denied,
Indeed our Strephon might have died.
Ld. Mount.
But as she 's not
His mother, it appears,
Why weep these hot,
  · Unnecessary tears?
And by what laws
Should we so joyously
Rejoice because
Our Strephon did n't die?
Oh, rather let us pipe our eye
Because our Strephon did n't die.
All.   That 's very true; let 's pipe our eye
Because our Strephon did n't die. [*All weep.*]

[*Exit* IOLANTHE.]

Phyl.   Go, trait'rous one; for ever we must part;
           To one of you, my lords, I give my heart.
All.   Oh, rapture!
Streph. Hear me, Phyllis, ere you leave me.
Phyl.   Not a word; you did deceive me.

All.   Not a word; you did deceive her!

For riches and rank I do not long;
  Their pleasures are false and vain:
I gave up the love of a lordly throng
  For the love of a simple swain;
But now that that simple swain 's untrue,
With sorrowful heart I turn to you—
    A heart that 's aching,
    Quaking, breaking,
As sorrowful hearts are wont to do.

The riches and rank that you befall
  Are the only baits you use;
So the richest and rankiest of you all
  My sorrowful heart shall choose.
As none are so noble, none so rich,
As this couple of lords, I 'll find a niche
    In my heart that 's aching,
    Quaking, breaking,
For one of you two; and I don't care which.

Phyl. [*to Lds. Mount and Toll.*].
        To you I give my heart so rich.
Lds. Mount and Toll. [*puzzled*].
        To which?
Phyl.   I do not care.
        To you I yield; it is my doom.
Lords. To whom?
Phyl.   I 'm not aware.
        I 'm yours for life, if you but choose.
Lords. She 's whose?
Phyl.   That 's your affair.
        I 'll be a countess, shall I not?
Lords. Of what?

Phyl.   I do not care.

Tenors. To them she gives her heart so rich.

Basses. To which?

Tenors.   She won't declare.

Basses. To whom she yields; it is her doom.

Tenors. To whom?

Basses.   I 'm not aware.

Tenors. She 's theirs for life, if they but choose.

Basses. She 's whose?

Tenors.   That 's her affair.

Basses. She 'll be a countess, will she not?

Tenors. Of what?

Basses.   We 're not aware.

All.   Lucky little lady!
    Strephon's lot is shady;
    Rank, it seems is vital;
    "Countess" is the title;
    But of what, I 'm not aware.

Streph.   Can I, inactive, see my fortune fade?
    No, no!—
      No, no!—
Mighty protectress, hasten to my aid!

[*Enter Fairies, tripping, headed by* CELIA, LELIA, *and* FLETA, *and followed by Queen.*]

CHORUS OF FAIRIES

    Tripping hither, tripping thither,
    Nobody knows why or whither;
    Why you want us we don't know,
    But you 've summoned us, and so
    Enter all the little fairies
      To their usual tripping measure.
    To oblige you all our care is;
      Tell us, pray, what is your pleasure!

Streph.   The lady of my love has caught me talking to
    another.

All.   Oh, fie! Strephon is a rogue.

Streph. I tell her very plainly that the lady is my mother.

All.   Taradiddle! taradiddle! tol-lol-lay!

Streph. She won't believe my statement, and declares we
          must be parted,

Because on a career of double-dealing I have started;

Then gives her hand to one of these, and leaves me broken-
          hearted.

All.   Taradiddle! taradiddle! tol-lol-lay!

Queen.

Ah, cruel ones, to part two faithful lovers from each other!

All.   Oh, fie! Strephon is a rogue.

Queen.

You 've done him an injustice, for the lady is his mother.

All.   Taradiddle! taradiddle! tol-lol-lay!

Ld. Chan.

That fable perhaps may serve his turn as well as any other.
[*Aside.*]

I didn't see her face, but if they fondled one another,

And she 's but seventeen, I don't believe it was his mother.

All.   Taradiddle! taradiddle! tol-lol-lay!

Ld. Toll. I 've often had a use
            For a thoroughbred excuse
       Of a sudden (which is English for *"repente"*),
            But of all I ever heard
            This is much the most absurd,
       For she 's seventeen, and he is five-and-twenty.

Fairies.   Tho' she is seventeen, and he is four- or five-and-
                twenty,
                Oh fie! Strephon is no rogue.

Ld. Mount.
            Now listen, pray, to me,
            For this paradox will be
       Carried, nobody at all *contradicente:*
            Her age upon the date
            Of his birth was minus eight,
       If she 's seventeen, and he 's five-and-twenty.
          He says she is his mother, and he 's four- or five-
          and-twenty.

All.   To say she is his mother is an utter bit of folly.
Oh fie! Strephon is a rogue.
Perhaps his brain is addled, and it 's very melan-
[‹]   choly;
Taradiddle! taradiddle! tol-lol-lay!
I would n't say a word that could be construed as injurious,
But to find a mother younger than her son is very curious;
And that 's the kind of mother that is usually spurious.
Taradiddle! taradiddle! tol-lol-lay!

Ld. Chan.   Go away, madam!
I should say, madam,
You display, madam,
Shocking taste.
It is rude, madam,
To intrude, madam,
With your brood, madam—
Brazen-faced!

You come here, madam,
Interfere, madam,
With a peer, madam
(I am one);
You 're aware, madam,
What you dare, madam;
So take care, madam,
And begone!

ENSEMBLE

FAIRIES TO QUEEN	PEERS
Let us stay, madam;	Go away, madam!
I should say, madam,	I should say, madam,
They display, madam,	You display, madam,
Shocking taste.	Shocking taste.
It is rude, madam,	It is rude, madam,
To allude, madam,	To intrude, madam,
To your brood, madam—	With your brood, madam—
Brazen-faced!	Brazen-faced!

We don't fear, madam,   You come here, madam,
Any peer, madam,   Interfere, madam,
Though, my dear madam,   With a peer, madam
    This is one.   (I am one).
They will stare, madam,   You 're aware, madam,
When aware, madam,   What you dare, madam;
What they dare, madam—   So take care, madam,
    What they 've done!   And begone!

Queen [furious]. Bearded by these puny mortals,
    I will launch from fairy portals
    All the most terrific thunders
    In my armory of wonders.

Phyl. [aside]. Surely, these must be immortals.
    Should they launch from fairy portals
    All their most terrific wonders,
    We should then repent our blunders.

Queen.   Oh, Chancellor unwary,
    It 's highly necessary
        Your tongue to teach
        Respectful speech—
    Your attitude to vary.

    Your badinage so airy,
    Your manner arbitrary,
        Are out of place
        When face to face
    With an influential fairy.

All the Peers [aside].   We never knew
        We were speaking to
    An influential fairy.

Ld. Chan.   A plague on this vagary!
    I 'm in a nice quandary:
        Of hasty tone
        With dames unknown

I ought to be more chary.
It seems that she 's a fairy
From Anderson's library;
And I took her for
The proprietor
Of a ladies' seminary.

All.　　He ⎱ took her for
　　　　We ⎰

The proprietor
Of a ladies' seminary.

Queen.　When next your Houses do assemble
You may tremble.

Lelia.　Our wrath, when gentlemen offend us,
Is tremendous.

Celia.　They meet, who underrate our calling
Doom appalling.

Queen.　Take down our sentence as we speak it,
And he shall wreak it [*indicating* STREPHON].
Henceforth, Strephon, cast away
Crooks and pipes and ribbons so gay,
Flocks and herds that bleat and low;
Into Parliament you go.

Fairies.　Into Parliament he shall go.
Backed by our supreme authority,
He 'll command a large majority.
Into Parliament he shall go.

Queen.　In the Parliamentary hive,
Liberal or Conservative,
Whig, or Tory, I don't know;
But into Parliament you shall go.

Fairies.　Into Parliament etc.
Peers.　Ah, spare us!

QUEEN [*speaking through music*].

Every bill and every measure
That may gratify his pleasure,

Though your fury it arouses,
Shall be passed by both your Houses.
You shall sit, if he sees reason,
Through the grouse-and-salmon season;
He shall end the cherished rights
You enjoy on Wednesday nights;
He shall prick that annual blister,
Marriage with deceased wife's sister;
He shall offer to the many
Peerages at three a penny;
Titles shall ennoble then
All the common councilmen;
Earldoms shall be sold apart
Daily at the auction-mart;
Peers shall teem in Christendom,
 And a duke's exalted station
Be attainable by com-
 petitive examination.

PEERS	FAIRIES *and* PHYLLIS
Oh, horror!	Their horror
But we 'll dissemble	They can't dissemble,
The coward fear that makes	Nor hide the fear that makes
us tremble.	them tremble.

ENSEMBLE

PEERS	FAIRIES, PHYL. *and* STREPH.
Young Strephon is the kind	With Strephon for your foe,
of lout	no doubt
We do not care a fig about	A fearful prospect opens out;
We cannot say	And who shall say
What evils may	.What evils may
Result in consequence;	Result in consequence?
But lordly vengeance will	A hideous vengeance will
pursue	pursue
All kinds of common people	All noblemen who venture to
who	

Oppose our views,	Oppose his views,
Or boldly choose	Or boldly choose
To offer us offense.	To offer him offense.

He 'd better fly at humble game,	'Twill plunge them into grief and shame;
Or our forbearance he must claim,	His kind forbearance they must claim
If he 'd escape	If they 'd escape
In any shape	In any shape
A very painful wrench.	A very painful wrench.
Your powers we dauntlessly pooh-pooh!	Although our threats you may pooh-pooh!
A dire revenge will fall on you	A dire revenge will fall on you
If you besiege	Should he besiege
Our high prestige	Your high prestige
(The word "prestige" is French).	(The word "prestige" is French).

Peers.   Our lordly style
           You shall not quench
           With base *naille.*
Fairies.   (That word is French.)
Peers.   Distinction ebbs
           Before a herd
           Of vulgar *plebs.*
Fairies.   (A Latin word.)
Peers.   'Twould fill with joy
           And madness stark
           The οἱ πολλοί.
Fairies.   (A Greek remark.)

PEERS	FAIRIES
You need n't wait:	We will not wait;
Away you fly!	We go skyhigh;
Your threatened hate	Our threatened hate
We thus defy!	You won't defy.

Fairies.	Your lordly style We 'll quickly quench With base *canaille.*
Peers.	(That word is French.)
Fairies.	Distinction ebbs Before a herd Of vulgar *plebs.*
Peers.	(A Latin word.)
Fairies.	'Twould fill with joy And madness stark The οἱ πολλοί.
Peers.	(A Greek remark.)

PEERS

You need n't wait:
Away you fly!
Your threatened hate
We thus defy!

FAIRIES

We will not wait;
We go skyhigh;
Our threatened hate
You won't defy.

[*Peers and Fairies take attitudes of defiance.*]

PICTURE

ACT II

SCENE.—*Palace Yard, Westminster, Westminster Hall, L.*

PRIVATE WILLIS *discovered on Sentry, R. Night.*

SONG—WILLIS

When all night long a chap remains
On sentry-go, to chase monotony
He exercises of his brains;
That is, assuming that he 's got any.

Though never nurtured in the lap
Of luxury, yet, I admonish you,
I am an intellectual chap,
And think of things that would astonish you.
I often think it 's comical (fal, lal, la!)
How Nature always does contrive (fal, lal, la!)
That every boy and every gal
That 's born into the world alive
Is either a little Liberal
Or else a little Conservative.
Fal, lal, la!

When in that house M. P.'s divide,
If they 've a brain and cerebellum too,
They 've got to leave that brain outside
And vote just as their leaders tell 'em to.
But then the prospect of a lot
Of dull M. P.'s in close proximity,
A-thinking for themselves, is what
No man can face with equanimity.
Then let 's rejoice with loud fal, lal, fal, lal, la!
That Nature wisely does contrive (fal, lal, la!)
That every boy and every gal
That 's born into the world alive
is either a little Liberal
Or else a little Conservative.
Fal, lal, la!

[*Enter Fairies, R., tripping, and led by* LELIA, CELIA, *and*
FLETA.]

CHORUS

Strephon 's a member of Parliament,
Carries every bill he chooses;
To his measures all consent,
Showing that fairies have their uses.
Whigs and Tories dim their glories,

Giving an ear to all his stories;
Lords and Commons are both in the blues;
Strephon makes them shake in their shoes—
     Shake in their shoes—
Strephon makes them shake in their shoes!

[*Enter Peers from Westminster Hall.*]

CHORUS OF PEERS

Strephon 's a member of Parliament—
Running amuck of all abuses;
His unqualified assent
Somehow nobody refuses.
Whigs and Tories dim their glories,
Giving an ear to all his stories,
     Carrying every bill he may wish;
Here 's a pretty kettle of fish—
Here 's a pretty kettle of fish!
Chorus of Peers and Fairies.
Strephon 's a member of Parliament—
Carries ev'ry bill he chooses;
To his measures all assent,
     Carrying ev'ry bill he may wish—
     Carrying ev'ry bill he may wish;
Here 's a pretty kettle of fish!

[*Enter* LORDS TOLLOLLER *and* MOUNT ARARAT.]

Ld. Mount. Perfectly disgraceful! disgusting!
Celia. You seem annoyed.
Ld. Mount. Annoyed! I should think so! Why, this ridiculous protégé of yours is playing the deuce with everything! To-night is the second reading of his bill to throw the peerage open to competitive examination.
Ld. Toll. And he 'll carry it, too!
Ld. Mount. Carry it? Of course he will! He 's a Parliamentary Pickford—he carries everything.

Lelia. Yes. If you please, that 's our fault.

Ld. Mount. The deuce it is!

Celia. Yes; we influence the members, and compel them to vote just as he wishes them to.

Lelia. It 's our system; it shortens the debates.

Ld. Toll. Well, but think what it all means! I don't so much mind for myself, but with a House of Peers with no grandfathers worth mentioning the country must go to the dogs.

Lelia. I suppose it must.

Ld. Mount. I don't want to say a word against brains— I' ve a great respect for brains. I often wish I had some myself—but with a House of Peers composed exclusively of people of intellect, what 's to become of the House of Commons?

Lelia. I never thought of that.

Ld. Mount. This comes of women interfering in politics. It so happens that if there is an institution in Great Britain which is not susceptible of any improvement at all, it is the House of Peers.

Song—Lord Mount

When Britain *really* ruled the waves
  (In good Queen Bess's time)
The House of Peers made no pretense
To intellectual eminence
  Or scholarship sublime;
Yet Britain won her proudest bays
In good Queen Bess's glorious days.

Cho.   Yes, Britain won, etc.

When Wellington thrashed Bonaparte,
  As every child can tell,
The House of Peers throughout the war
Did nothing in particular,
  And did it very well;
Yet Britain set the world ablaze
In good King George's glorious days.

Cho. Yes, Britain set, etc.

And while the House of Peers withholds
 Its legislative hand,
And noble statesmen do not itch
 To interfere with matters which
  They do not understand,
As bright will shine Great Britain's rays
As in King George's glorious days.

Cho. As bright will shine, etc.

[*Exeunt Chorus of Peers. Manent* LORDS MOUNT ARARAT
 and TOLLOLLER, *and Fairies.*]

Lelia [*who has been much attracted by the Peers during
the song*]. Charming persons, are they not?

Celia. Distinctly. For self-contained dignity, combined
with airy condescension, give me a British representative
peer!

Ld. Toll. Then, pray, stop this protégé of yours before
it 's too late. Think of the mischief you 're doing!

Lelia [*crying*]. But we *can't* stop him now.—[*Aside to*
CELIA.] Are n't they lovely?—[*Aloud.*] Oh, why did you
defy us, you great geese?

DUET—LELIA and CELIA

Lelia. In vain to us you plead—
  Don't go;
Your prayers we do not heed—
  Don't go.
It 's true we sigh,
 But don't suppose
A tearful eye
 Forgiveness shows;
  Oh, no!
We 're very cross indeed—
 Don't go!

All. It 's true they sigh, etc.

Celia.   Your disrespectful sneers—
                    Don't go!
              Call forth indignant tears—
                    Don't go!
              You break our laws,
                    You are our foe:
              We cry because
                    We hate you so—
                          Oh, no!
              You very wicked peers,
                    Don't go!

FAIRIES	LORDS MOUNT *and* TOLL.
You break our laws,	Our disrespectful sneers—
You are our foe:	Ha! ha!
We cry because	
We hate you so—	Call forth indignant tears—
Oh, no!	Ha! ha!
You very wicked peers,	If that's the case, my dears,
Don't go!	We go!

[*Exeunt* MOUNT ARARAT *and* TOLLOLLER. *Fairies gaze wistfully after them. Enter* FAIRY QUEEN.]

Queen. Oh, shame! shame upon you! Is this your fidelity to the laws you are bound to obey? Know ye not that it is death to marry a mortal?

Lelia. Yes; but it's not death to wish to marry a mortal.

Fleta. If it were you'd have to execute us all.

Queen. Oh, this is weakness! Subdue it!

Celia. We know it's weakness, but the weakness is so strong!

Lelia. We are not all as tough as you are.

Queen. Tough? Do you suppose that I am insensible to the effect of manly beauty? Look at that man [*referring to* SENTRY.] A perfect picture!—[*To* SENTRY.] Who are you, sir?

Sentry. Private Willis, B Company, First Battalion Grenadier Guards.

Queen. You 're a fine fellow, sir.

Sentry. I am generally admired.

Queen. I can quite understand it.—[*To Fairies.*] Now, here is a man whose physical attributes are simply godlike. That man has a most extraordinary effect upon me. If I yielded to a natural impulse I should fall down and worship that man. But I mortify this inclination; I wrestle with it, and it lies beneath my feet. This is how I treat my regard for that man.

SONG—FAIRY QUEEN

Oh, foolish fay,
   Think you, because
His brave array
   My bosom thaws,
I 'd disobey
   Our fairy laws?
Because I fly
   In realms above,
In tendency
   To fall in love
Resemble I
   The amorous dove?

(*Aside.*)   Oh, amorous dove!
Type of Ovidius Naso!
   This heart of mine
   Is soft as thine,
Although I dare not say so.

Cho.   Oh, amorous dove, etc.

On fire that glows
   With heat intense
I turn the hose
   Of common sense,
And out it goes
   At small expense.
We must maintain
   Our fairy law;

That is the main
On which to draw;
In that we gain
A Captain Shaw.

(*Aside.*)   Oh, Captain Shaw!
Type of true love kept under!
Could thy brigade
With cold cascade
Quench my great love, I wonder?

Cho.   Oh, Captain Shaw! etc.

[*Exeunt Fairies sorrowfully, headed by* FAIRY QUEEN.]

[*Enter* PHYLLIS.]

Phyl. [*half crying*]. I can't think why I'm not in better
spirits. I'm engaged to two noblemen at once. That ought
to be enough to make any girl happy; but I'm miserable.
Don't suppose it's because I care for Strephon, for I hate
him! No girl would care for a man who goes about with
a mother considerably younger than himself.

[*Enter* LORD MOUNT ARARAT.]

Ld. Mount. Phyllis! my own!
Phyl. Don't! How dare you? But perhaps you are one
of the noblemen I'm engaged to?
Ld. Mount. I'm one of them.
Phyl. Oh! But how came you to have a peerage?
Ld. Mount. It's a prize for being born first.
Phyl. Oh, I see—a kind of Derby cup.
Ld. Mount. Not at all. I'm of a very old and distin-
guished family.
Phyl. And you're proud of your race? Of course you
are; you won it. But why are people made peers?
Ld. Mount. The principle is not easy to explain. I'll
give you an example.

Song—Mount Ararat

De Belville was regarded as the Crichton of his age;
His tragedies were reckoned much too thoughtful for the
    stage;
His poems held a noble rank, although it 's very true
That, being very proper, they were read by very few;
He was a famous painter, too, and shone upon the line,
And even Mr. Ruskin came and worshiped at his shrine;
But, alas! the school he followed was heroically high,
The kind of art men rave about, but very seldom buy;
    And ev'rybody said,
    "How can he be repaid—
This very great, this very good, this very gifted man?"
But nobody could hit upon a practicable plan.

He was a great inventor, and discovered, all alone,
A plan for making everybody's fortune but his own;
For in business an inventor 's little better than a fool,
And my highly-gifted friend was no exception to the rule.
His poems—people read 'em in the sixpenny Reviews;
His pictures—they engraved 'em in the *Illustrated News;*
His inventions—they perhaps might have enriched him by
    degrees,
But all his little income went in Patent-Office fees.
    So everybody said,
    "How can he be repaid—
This very great, this very good, this very learned man?
But nobody could hit upon a practicable plan.

At last the point was given up in absolute despair,
When a distant cousin died, and he became a millionaire,
With a county seat in Parliament and a moor or two of
    grouse,
And a taste for making inconvenient speeches in the House.
Then Government conferred on him the highest of rewards:
They took him from the Commons and they put him in the
    Lords.

And who so fit to sit in it—deny it if you can—
As this very great, this very good, and very gifted man?
　　　Though I 'm more than half afraid
　　　That it sometimes may be said
That we never should have reveled in this source of proper
　　　pride,
However great his merits, if his cousin had n't died.

[Enter Lord Tolloller, L.]

Ld. Toll. Phyllis! my darling! [*embraces her.*]

Phyl. Here 's the other! Well, have you settled which
it 's to be?

Ld. Toll. Not altogether; it 's a difficult position. It
would be hardly delicate to toss up. On the whole, we would
rather leave it to you.

Phyl. How can it possibly concern me? You are both
earls, and you are both rich, and you are both plain.

Ld. Mount. So we are. At least I am.

Ld. Toll. So am I.

Ld. Mount. No, no!

Ld. Toll. Oh, I am indeed very plain.

Ld. Mount. Well! well! perhaps you are.

Phyl. There 's really nothing to choose between you. If
one of you would forego his title and distribute his estates
among his Irish tenantry, why, then I should see a reason
for accepting the other.　　　　　　　[Phyllis *retires up.*

Ld. Mount. Tolloller, are you prepared to make this sacrifice?

Ld. Toll. No!

Ld. Mount. Not even to oblige a lady?

Ld. Toll. No!

Ld. Mount. Then the only question is, Which of us shall
give way to the other? Perhaps, on the whole, she would be
happier with me? I don't know; I may be wrong.

Ld. Toll. No, I don't know that you are. I really think
that she would. But the painful part of the thing is, that if
you rob me of the girl of my heart, one of us must perish.

Ld. Mount. Again the question arises, Which shall it be?
Do you feel inclined to make this sacrifice?

Ld. Toll. No!

Ld. Mount. Not even to oblige a gentleman?

Ld. Toll. Impossible! The Tollollers have invariably
destroyed their successful rivals. It 's a family tradition
that I have sworn to respect.

Ld. Mount. I see. Did you swear it before a commis-
sioner?

Ld. Toll. I did, on affidavit.

Ld. Mount. Then I don't see how you can help yourself.

Ld. Toll. It 's a painful position, for I have a strong regard for you, George [*shake hands*].

Ld. Mount [*much affected*]. My dear Thomas!

Ld. Toll. You are very dear to me, George. We were
boys together—at least *I* was. If I were to destroy you, my
existence would be hopelessly embittered.

Ld. Mount. Then, my dear Thomas, you must not do it.
I say it again and again: if it will have this effect on you,
you must not do it. No, no! If one of us is to destroy the
other, let it be me.

Ld. Toll. No, no!

Ld. Mount. Ah, yes! By our boyish friendship I implore you [*shake hands*].

Ld. Toll. [*much moved*]. Well! well! be it so. But no,
no! I cannot consent to an act which would crush you with
unavailing remorse.

Ld. Mount. But it would not do so. I should be very sad
at first—oh! who would not be?—but it would wear off. I
like you very much [*shakes hands*], but not, perhaps, as
much as you like me.

Ld. Toll. George, you 're a noble fellow, but that tell-tale
tear betrays you. No, George, you are very fond of me,
and I cannot consent to give you a week's uneasiness on
my account.

Ld. Mount. But, dear Thomas, it would not last a week.
Remember, you lead the House of Lords; on your demise I

shall take your place. Oh, Thomas! it would not last a day!

Ld. Toll. It's very kind and thoughtful of you to look at it in that light, but there's no disguising it, George—we're in a very awkward position.

Phyl. [*coming down*]. Now, I do hope you're not going to fight about me, because it really isn't worth while.

Ld. Toll. I don't believe it is.

Ld. Mount. Nor I. The sacred ties of friendship are paramount. No consideration shall induce me to raise my hand against Thomas.

Ld. Toll. And in my eyes the life of George is more sacred than love itself.

QUARTETTE—PHYLLIS, LORD TOLLOLLER, LORD MOUNT, *and* SENTRY

Ld. Toll.
> Tho' p'raps I may incur your blame,
> The things are few I wouldn't do
> In Friendship's name.

Ld. Mount.
> And I may say I feel the same;
> Not even Love should rank above
> True Friendship's name.

Phyl.
> Then free me, pray; be mine the shame;
> Forget your craze and go your ways,
> In Friendship's name!

All.
> Oh, many a man in Friendship's name
> Has yielded fortune, rank, and fame,
> But no one yet in the world so wide
> Has yielded up a promised bride.
> Accept, O Friendship, all the same,
> Our sacrifice to thy dear name.

[*After Quartette, exeunt* PHYLLIS *and* LORDS TOLLOLLER *and* MOUNT ARARAT.]

[*Enter* LORD CHANCELLOR, *very miserable.*]

RECITATIVE

Love, unrequited, robs me of my rest;
Love, hopeless love, my ardent soul encumbers;
Love, nightmare-like, lies heavy on my breast,
And weaves itself into my midnight slumbers.

SONG—LORD CHANCELLOR

When you 're lying awake with a dismal headache, and repose is tabooed by anxiety,
I conceive you may use any language you choose to indulge
in without impropriety;
For your brain is on fire—the bedclothes conspire of usual
slumber to plunder you:
First your counterpane goes and uncovers your toes, and
your sheet slips demurely from under you;
Then the blanketing tickles—you feel like mixed pickles, so
terribly sharp is the pricking,
And you 're hot and you 're cross, and you tumble and toss
till there 's nothing 'twixt you and the ticking;
Then your bedclothes all creep to the ground in a heap, and
you pick 'em all up in a tangle;
Next your pillow resigns and politely declines to remain at
its usual angle.
Well, you get some repose in the form of a doze, with hot
eyeballs and head ever aching,
But your slumbering teems with such horrible dreams that
you 'd very much better be waking;
For you dream you are crossing the Channel, and tossing
like mad in a steamer from Harwich;
Which is something between a large bathing-machine and a
very small second-class carriage;
And you 're giving a treat (penny ice and cold meat) to a
party of friends and relations—
They 're a ravenous horde, and they all come on board at
Sloane Square and South Kensington stations;

And bound on that journey you find your attorney (who
    started that morning from Devon);
He 's a bit undersized, and you don 't feel surprised when he
    tells you he 's only eleven.
Well, you 're driving like mad with this singular lad (by-the-
    bye, the ship 's now a four-wheeler),
And you 're playing round games, and he calls you bad names
    when you tell him that "Ties pay the dealer;"
But this you can 't stand, so you throw up your hand, and
    you find you 're as cold as an icicle
In your shirt and your socks (the black silk with gold clocks),
    crossing Salisbury Plain on a bicycle;
And he and the crew are on bicycles too—which they have
    somehow or other invested in—
And he 's telling the tars all the particulars of a company
    he 's interested in:
It 's a scheme of devices to get at low prices all goods from
    cough-mixtures to cables
(Which tickles the sailors) by treating retailers as though
    they were all vegetables.
You get a good spadesman to plant a small tradesman (first
    take off his boots with a boot-tree),
And his legs will take root and his fingers will shoot, and
    they 'll blossom and spread like a fruit tree.
From the greengrocer tree you get grapes and green pea,
    cauliflowers, pineapples, and cranberries,
While the pastry-cook plant cherry brandy will grant, apple
    puffs, and three-corners, and banberries.
The shares are a penny, and ever so many are taken by
    Rothschild and Baring;
And just a few are allotted to you, you awake with a shudder
    despairing.
You 're a regular wreck, with a crick in your neck; and no
    wonder you snore, for your head 's on the floor, and
    you 're needles and pins from your soles to your
    shins; and your flesh is a-creep, for your left leg 's
    asleep; and you 've cramps in your toes, and a fly
    on your nose, and some fluff in your lung, and a

feverish tongue, and a thirst that 's intense, and a
general sense that you have n't been sleeping in
clover;
But the darkness has passed, and it 's daylight at last, and
the night has been long—ditto, ditto, my song—
and thank Goodness they 're both of them over!

[*During the last lines* LORDS MOUNT ARARAT *and* TOLLOLLER
have entered. They gaze sympathetically upon the
LORD CHANCELLOR'S *distress. At the end of his song*
they come forward.]

Ld. Mount. I am much distressed to see your lordship in
this condition.

Ld. Chan. Ah, my lords, it is seldom that a Lord Chancellor has reason to envy the position of another, but I am
free to confess that I would rather be two earls engaged to
Phyllis than any other half-dozen noblemen upon the face
of the globe.

Ld. Toll. [*without enthusiasm*]. Yes. In a way, it 's an
enviable position.

Ld. Mount. Oh, yes—no doubt most enviable. At the
same time, seeing you thus, we naturally say to ourselves,
"This is very sad. His lordship is constitutionally as blithe
as a bird—he trills upon the bench like a thing of song and
gladness. His series of judgments in F sharp, given *andante*
in six-eight time, are among the most remarkable effects
ever produced in a court of Chancery. He is, perhaps, the
only living instance of a judge whose decrees have received
the honor of a double encore. How can we bring ourselves
to do that which will deprive the court of Chancery of one
of its most attractive features?"

Ld. Chan. I feel the force of your remarks, but I cannot make up my mind to apply to myself again. I am here
in a double capacity. Firstly, as a Lord Chancellor entrusted
with the guardianship of this charming girl; and, secondly,
as a suitor for her hand. In my latter capacity I am over-
awed by my dignity in my former capacity; I hesitate to
approach myself—it unnerves me.

Ld. Toll. It 's a difficult position. This is what it is to have two capacities. Let us be thankful that we are persons of no capacity whatever.

Ld. Mount. But take courage! Remember, you are a very just and kindly old gentleman, and you need have no hesitation in approaching yourself, so that you do so respectfully and with a proper show of deference.

Ld. Chan. Do you really think so? Well, I will nerve myself to another effort, and if that fails I resign myself to my fate.

TRIO—LORD CHANCELLOR, MOUNT ARARAT, *and* TOLLOLLER

Ld. Mount.

> If you go in
> You 're sure to win—
> Yours will be the charming maidie;
> Be your law
> The ancient saw,
> "Faint heart never won fair lady."

All.

> Never, never, never, never—
> Faint heart never won fair lady.
> Every journey has an end;
> When at the worst affairs will mend;
> Dark the dawn when day is nigh;
> Hustle your horse and don't say die.

Ld. Toll.

> He who shies
> At such a prize
> Is not worth a maravedi;
> Be so kind
> To bear in mind,
> "Faint heart never won fair lady."

All.

> Never, never, never, never—
> Faint heart never won fair lady.
> While the sun shines make your hay;
> Where a will is, there 's a way;

Beard the lion in his lair;
None but the brave deserve the fair.

Ld. Chan.

I 'll take heart
And make a start,
Though I fear the prospect 's shady;
Much I 'd spend
To gain my end—
"Faint heart never won fair lady."

All.

Never, never, never, never—
Faint heart never won fair lady.
Nothing venture, nothing win;
Blood is thick, but water 's thin;
In for a penny, in for a pound;
It 's love that makes the world go round.

[Dance, and exeunt arm-in-arm together.]

[Enter STREPHON.]

RECITATIVE

My bill has now been read a second time;
His ready vote no member now refuses;
In verity I wield a power sublime,
And one that I can turn to mighty uses.
What joy to carry, in the very teeth
Of Ministry, Cross-Bench, and Opposition,
Some rather urgent measures, quite beneath
The ken of patriot and politician!

SONG—STREPHON

Fold your flapping wings,
Soaring legislature!
Stoop to little things—
Stoop to human nature!
Never need to roam,
Members patriotic;

Let 's begin at home—
Crime is no exotic.
Bitter is your bane,
Terrible your trials,
Dingy Drury Lane!
Soapless Seven Dials!

Take a tipsy lout
Gathered from the gutter,
Hustle him about,
Strap him to a shutter;
What am I but he,
Washed at hours stated,
Fed on filigree,
Taught and titivated?
He 's a mark of scorn;
I might be another
If I had been born
Of a tipsy mother.

Take a wretched thief
Through the city sneaking
Pocket-handkerchief
Ever, ever seeking;
What is he but I
Robbed of all my chances,
Picking pockets by
Force of circumstances?
I might be as bad—
As unlucky, rather—
If I 'd only had
Fagin for a father.

[*Enter* PHYLLIS.]

Phyl. [*starting*]. Strephon!
Streph. [*starting*]. Phyllis! But I suppose I should say,
"My lady." I have not yet been informed which title your
ladyship has pleased to elect.

Phyl. I haven't quite decided. You see, *I* have no *mother* to advise *me*.

Streph. No; I have.

Phyl. Yes, a *young* mother.

Streph. Not very—a couple of centuries or so.

Phyl. Oh, she wears well.

Streph. She does; she 's a fairy.

Phyl. I beg your pardon—a what?

Streph. Oh, I 've no longer any reason to conceal the fact—she 's a fairy.

Phyl. A fairy! Well, but—that would account for a good many things. Then I suppose you 're a fairy?

Streph. I 'm half a fairy.

Phyl. Which half?

Streph. The upper half—down to the waist.

Phyl. Dear me! [*prodding him with her fingers*]. There is nothing to show it. But why didn't you tell me this before?

Streph. I thought you would take a dislike to me. But as it 's all off, you may as well know the truth—I 'm only half a mortal.

Phyl. [*crying*]. But I 'd rather have half a mortal I do love than half a dozen I don't.

Streph. Oh, I think not. Go to your half dozen.

Phyl. [*crying*]. It 's only two, and I hate 'em! Please forgive me.

Streph. I don't think I ought to. Besides, all sorts of difficulties will arise. You know my grandmother looks quite as young as my mother. So do all my aunts.

Phyl. I quite understand. Whenever I see you kissing a very young lady I shall know it 's an elderly relative.

Streph. You will? Then, Phyllis, I think we shall be very happy [*embracing her*].

Phyl. We won't wait long before we marry; we might change our minds.

Streph. Yes—we 'll get married first.

Phyl. And change our minds afterwards.

Streph. Yes, that 's the usual course.

DUET—STREPHON *and* PHYLLIS

Streph.   If we 're weak enough to tarry
                Ere we marry,
                You and I,
            Of the feeling I inspire
                You may tire
                By and by;
            For peers with flowing coffers
                Press their offers;
                That is why
            I think we will not tarry
                Ere we marry,
                You and I.
Phyl.   If we 're weak enough to **tarry,**
                Ere we marry
                You and I,
            With a more attractive maiden,
                Jewel-laden,
                You may fly.
            If by chance we should be parted,
                Broken-hearted,
                I should die:
            That is why we will not tarry
                Bre we marry,
                You and I.

Phyl. But does your mother know you 're—— I mean
is she aware of our engagement?

(*Enter* IOLANTHE.)

Io. She is, and thus she welcomes her daughter-in-law
[*kisses her*].
Phyl. She kisses just like other people! But the Lord
Chancellor?
Streph. I had forgotten him.—Mother, none can resist
your fairy eloquence. You will go to him and plead for us?

Io. [*aside*]. Go to him?—[*Aloud*]. No, no! impossible!

Streph. But our happiness, our very lives, depend upon our obtaining his consent.

Phyl. Oh, madam, you cannot refuse to do this?

Io. You know not what you ask! The Lord Chancellor is my husband!

Streph. and Phyl. Your husband?

Io. My husband and your father! [STREPHON *overcome.*]

Phyl. Then our course is plain. On his learning that Strephon is his son, all objections to our marriage will be at once removed.

Io. Nay, he must never know. He believes me to have died childless; and, dearly as I love him, I am bound, under penalty of death, not to undeceive him. But see, he comes! Quick! my veil! (*Retires up.*)

[*Enter* LORD CHANCELLOR. IOLANTHE *retires with* STREPHON *and* PHYLLIS.]

Ld. Chan. Victory! victory! Success has crowned my efforts, and I may consider myself engaged to Phyllis. At first I would n't hear of it; it was out of the question. But I took heart. I pointed out to myself that I was no stranger to myself—in point of fact, I had been personally acquainted with myself for some years. This had its effect. I admitted that I had watched my professional advancement with considerable interest, and I handsomely added that I yielded to no one in admiration for my private and professional virtues. This was a great point gained. I then endeavored to work upon my feelings. Conceive my joy when I distinctly perceived a tear glistening in my own eye! Eventually, after a severe struggle with myself, I reluctantly, most reluctantly, consented.

[IOLANTHE *comes down*, STREPHON *and* PHYLLIS *going off.*]

But whom have we here?

RECITATIVE

Io.   My lord, a suppliant at your feet I kneel;
Oh, listen to a mother's fond appeal!
Hear me to-night; I come in urgent need.
'T is for my son, young Strephon, that I plead.

BALLAD—IOLANTHE

He loves! If in the bygone years
    Thine eyes have ever shed
Tears—bitter, unavailing tears—
    For one untimely dead;
If in the eventide of life
    Sad thoughts of her arise,—
Then let the memory of thy wife
    Plead for my boy; he dies!

He dies! If, fondly laid aside
    In some old cabinet,
Memorials of thy long-dead bride
    Lie dearly treasured yet,
Then let her hallowed bridal dress,
    Her little dainty gloves,
Her withered flowers, her faded tress,
    Plead for my boy; he loves!

[*The* LORD CHANCELLOR *is moved by this appeal. After a
pause—*]

Ld. Chan.
    It may not be, for so the Fates decide:
    Learn thou that Phyllis is my promised bride!
Io. [*in horror*].
    Thy bride? no! no!
Ld. Chan.   It shall be so.
    Those who would separate us, woe betide!
Io.   My doom thy lips have spoken—
    I plead in vain.

Chorus of Fairies [*without*].
               Forbear! forbear!
Io.   A vow already broken
               I break again.
Chorus of Fairies [*without*].
               Forbear! forbear!
Io.   For him—for her—for thee,
               I yield my life!
               Behold! it may not be—
               I am thy wife!
Chorus of Fairies [*without*].
               Aiaiah! aiaiah! willaloo!
Ld. Chan. [*recognizing her*].
               Iolanthe! thou livest?
Io.   Ay,
               I live! Now let me die!

[*Enter* FAIRY QUEEN *and Fairies.* IOLANTHE *kneels to her.*]

Queen.   Once more thy vows are broken:
               Thou thyself thy doom hath spoken.
Chorus of Fairies.   Aiaiah! aiaiah!
               Willahalah! willaloo!
               Laloiah! laloiah!
               Willahalah! willaloo!
Queen.   Bow thy head to destiny:
               Death 's thy doom, and thou shalt die!
Chorus of Fairies.   Aiaiah! aiaiah! etc.

[*The Peers and* STREPHON *enter. The* QUEEN *raises her
spear.* LORD CHANCELLOR *and* STREPHON *implore her
mercy,* LELIA *and* CELIA *rush forward.*]

Lelia. Hold! If Iolanthe must die, so must we all, for
as she has sinned, so have we.
    Queen. What? [*Peers and Fairies kneel to her*—LORD
MOUNT ARARAT *with* LELIA; LORD TOLLOLLER *with* CELIA.]

Celia. We are all fairy duchesses, marchionesses, countesses, viscountesses and baronesses.

Ld. Mount. It's our fault; they couldn't help themselves.

Queen. It seems they *have* helped themselves, and pretty freely too!—[*After a pause.*] You have all incurred death, but I can't slaughter the whole company. And yet [*unfolding a scroll*] the law is clear: Every fairy must die who marries a mortal!

Ld. Chan. Allow me, as an old equity draughtsman, to make a suggestion. The subtleties of the legal mind are equal to the emergency. The thing is really quite simple; the insertion of a single word will do it. Let it stand that every fairy shall die who *don't* marry a mortal, and there you are, out of your difficulty at once!

Queen. We like your humor. Very well. [*Altering the MS. in pencil.*]—Private Willis!

Sentry [*coming forward*]. Ma'am!

Queen. To save my life it is necessary that I marry at once. How should you like to be a fairy Guardsman?

Sentry. Well, ma'am, I don't think much of the British soldier who wouldn't ill-convenience himself to save a female in distress.

Queen. You are a brave fellow. You're a fairy from this moment. [*Wings spring from Sentry's shoulders.*]—And you, my lords, how say you? Will you join our ranks?

[*Fairies kneel to Peers, and implore them to do so.*]

Ld. Mount [*to* TOLLOLLER]. Well, now that the peers are to be recruited entirely from persons of intelligence, I really don't see what use *we* are down here.

Ld. Toll. None, whatever.

Queen. Good! [*Wings spring from the shoulders of Peers.*] Then away we go to Fairyland!

FINALE

Phyl.   Soon as we may
                Off and away,

We will start our journey airy;
　　Happy are we,
　　As you can see;
Every one is now a fairy.

PHYLLIS, IOLANTHE *and* QUEEN

Tho', as a general rule, we know
Two strings go to every bow,
Make up your mind that grief 't will bring
If you 've two beaux to every string.
　　CHO.—Tho', as a general rule, etc.

Ld. Chan.　　　　　Up in the sky
　　　　　Ever so high,
Pleasures come in endless series;
　　　Let us arrange—
　　　Pleasant exchange—
House of Peers for House of Peris.

TRIO—LORD TOLLOLLER, LORD MOUNT ARARAT, *and* LORD
CHANCELLOR

Up in the air sky high,
Far from wards in Chancery,
He will be surely happier, far,
For he 's a susceptible Chancellor.
　　CHO.—Up in the air, etc.

SUGGESTIVE QUESTIONS

1. In what ways does the plot of *Iolanthe* resemble the plot of an
   ordinary play?
2. In what ways does the plot of *Iolanthe* differ from the plot
   of an ordinary play?
3. Point out the most important parts of the plot.
4. In what ways do the characters of *Iolanthe* resemble the char‑
   acters of an ordinary play?

5. In what ways do the characters of *Iolanthe* differ from the characters of an ordinary play?
6. In what ways does the general construction of *Iolanthe* differ from the construction of other plays?
7. Point out some of the means of producing humor.
8. What advantages does the dramatist gain by the use of setting?
9. Which of the stage directions are most important?
10. What uniform spirit pervades the play?
11. Point out all the respects in which *Iolanthe* resembles *A Midsummer Night's Dream.*
12. Point out all the respects in which *Iolanthe* differs from *A Midsummer Night's Dream.*
13. Point out all the respects in which *Iolanthe* resembles *The Tempest.*
14. Point out all the respects in which *Iolanthe* differs from *The Tempest.*
15. To what extent are the happy effects of *Iolanthe* produced by plot? By characterization? By phrasing? By verse, rhythm, and rhyme?
16. What is the purpose of the dramatist in *Iolanthe?*
17. What effects are produced by changing from verse to prose?
18. What gives unusual effectiveness to the dialogue?
19. What effects does the dramatist gain by the use of a chorus?
20. To what extent does satire appear in the play?
21. Ask the teachers of music in your school to assist you and your classmates in singing parts of *Iolanthe.*
22. Procure phonograph records of various Gilbert and Sullivan songs, and give a class entertainment.

Suggestions for Written Imitation

1. Write the introductory dialogue for a fantastic play based on the scenario you wrote in answer to Question 1 of Introductory Problems.
2. Write any fantastic, humorous dialogue.
3. Write full directions for the stage setting for the play for which you wrote a scenario.
4. Write a mildly satirical speech, or, if you wish, a satirical song, to form part of your play.
5. Write a dialogue for your play. Make use of a chorus in order to increase humorous effects.

DIRECTIONS FOR WRITING

Make your work as original and as fantastic as possible, but keep within the bounds of good taste. Try to produce humor through unexpected turns of language, or through any unusual use of words, or through placing characters in situations that will be humorously out-of-keeping with their natures.

ORAL WORK IN CLASS

1. Read aloud your own written work.
2. Select associates, and act any part of *Iolanthe*.
3. Select the character in *Iolanthe* who pleases you most. Select associates, and act any dialogue in which that character appears.
4. Select associates, and act any dialogue in which the chorus takes part. Let the class act as chorus.
5. Read aloud, with appropriate dramatic action, one of the long speeches in *Iolanthe*.

WHAT MEN LIVE BY

By Virginia Church

What Men Live By is an allegorical play founded on one of Count Leo Tolstoi's short stories. It emphasizes as its theme the worthiness of self-sacrifice, of charity, of sympathy, and of love. The dramatist, conscious of the freedom of the allegorical form, departs somewhat from strict realism. At the same time, while introducing supernatural characters, she keeps the play sufficiently close to ordinary life to make it intimate and appealing. She makes *What Men Live By* remind one of such a play as *The Servant in the House,* by Charles Rann Kennedy.

The characters of *What Men Live By* are not purely symbolic as are the characters in the old English morality play, *Everyman.* With two exceptions the characters are those of life. The nature of the play permitted the introduction of unearthly characters. Shakespeare chose to introduce three witches, and Hecate, the spirit of Evil, in *Macbeth;* Milton introduces an Attendant Spirit, Comus the enchanter and his fantastic company, and Sabrina, the spirit of the Waters, in his masque of *Comus.* In modern times David Belasco introduced the ghostly in *The Return of Peter Grimm.* Nevertheless, in all plays from Shakespeare's *Hamlet* to James Matthew Barrie's *Mary Rose,* the interest lies in real people, and in what real people do. So it is in *What Men Live By.* More than that, the development of the drama has led to increased interest in the plain ordinary people of daily life. Shakespeare's plays concern kings and queens; modern plays concern all classes of people, often the most humble.

The plot of *What Men Live By,* subordinate to the theme, centers around incidents that exalt the theme. With its atmosphere of peasant life, in far-away Russia, the story is sufficiently real.

The dialogue is simple in the extreme, and is full of touches of local color, indicating the influence of the realism that marks the work of Tolstoi, and of the dramatists of the Russian school.

Virginia Church, the author of *What Men Live By,* is a graduate of Smith College, and also of Boston University, where she won a higher degree. She specialized in dramatic work at Columbia University, and at Harvard University, in the latter institution studying with Professor George P. Baker in the course known as "47 Workshop."

Mrs. Church is the author of *Commencement Days,* a novel (L. C. Page Co.); *Commencement Days,* a three-act comedy written in collaboration with Margaret Mayo; *The Heart Specialist,* a three-act comedy; *The Perverseness of Pamela,* produced by Harvard University in 1916, and later by stock campanies; and various one-act plays, among which are: *The Bee Man; The Revolt of the Dolls; Pierrot by the Light of the Moon; Very Social Service,* and *What Men Live By.*

Mrs. Church has written much for *The Dramatic Mirror, The Theatre Magazine, The Drama,* and other publications.

She is head of the Department of English in the Franklin High School, Los Angeles, California.

INTRODUCTORY PROBLEMS

1. You have read Milton's *Comus.* What theme does Milton emphasize?
2. You have read *Macbeth.* Did Shakespeare gain or lose in dramatic value by introducing supernatural characters? Explain your answer.
3. Tell the story of *The Servant in the House.*
4. Write a scenario based on *The Vision of Sir Launfal.*
5. Write a scenario based on Longfellow's *King Robert of Sicily.*

PREFATORY NOTE TO THE PLAY

(Especially suited to School and Church Production in the
Christmas Season)

CHARACTERS:

SIMON, *the cobbler*
MATRENA, *his wife*
MICHAEL, *his apprentice*
BARON AVEDEITCH, *a wealthy landowner*
THEDKA, *his footman*
SONIA IVANICH, *a lady of means*
BRENIE } *Her two adopted children, little girls of about*
NIKITA } *six years*
ANNA MALOSKA, *a widow and friend of Matrena*
TROFINOFF, *a debtor*
THE GUARDIAN ANGEL
A LITTLE DEVIL

*About four feet below the level of the street, which is
reached by a few stairs at the back leading to an outer door.
is the basement occupied by* SIMON. *At the right of the door
on a line with the pavement is a long narrow window through
which one may see the feet of the passers-by.* SIMON, *who
does most of the cobbling for the village, knows the way-
farers by the boots which he has repaired. Under the window, placed so as to catch the meager light, is a cobbler's
bench with tools on either side. At the left of the stairs are
long gray curtains forming a kind of closet in which outer
wraps are hung. In the corner is a small china closet. In
the left wall is a hearth; here, over the fire, the wife cooks the*

meals. Two old chairs huddle near the fire as though for warmth. A table half concealed by a worn cloth, stands near the fireplace. Opposite the fireplace, is a door leading into the inner room.

SCENE I

[SIMON, *old, slow in movement, kindly of feature, is seated at his table, mending a pair of rough hide shoes. His wife,* MATRENA, *as brown and dry as a chip, is on a stool by the fire, mending a tattered old sheep-skin outer coat. Occasionally one sees the feet of pedestrians pass by the little window.* SIMON *glances up as they throw a shadow on his table.*]

MATRENA. And who was that went by, Simon?

SIMON. It was Thedka, my dear Matrena. Thedka, the footman of the Barina. The side-patch on his boot has lasted well.

MATRENA. Yes, you make them last for so long that they do not need to come to you and so you have little trade.

SIMON. But, Matrena, I could not put on patches that would not last; then I should have no trade at all. I must do my best. That is the kind of man I am.

MATRENA. Yes, yes, Simon, that is the kind of man you are and so this is the kind of home we have, with hardly enough flour in the bin for one baking.

SIMON. Don't fret, Matrena. We shall not starve. God is good.

MATRENA. Aye, God is good, but his handmen are far from the likeness in which He cast them. [*A girl trips by.*] Was that Rozinka went by?

SIMON. No, Rozinka has not such high heels. It was Ulka, the Barina's maid.

MATRENA. I might have guessed it, after Thedka had passed. The minx is as hard on his footsteps as a man's shadow on a sunny day. It's a pity since you shoe all the

servants in the Baron's household that the master would not
let you make boots for him.

SIMON. The boots of the nobilities are brought from Paris,
and are cut from northern leather. Trofinoff told me he
brought five pair from the station on his last trip.

MATRENA. Trofinoff, hum! Did you not tell me Trofinoff
promised to come this afternoon to pay the eight roubles he
has owed you three years coming Michaelmas?

SIMON. Aye, so he said.

MATRENA. So he said, but I 'll warrant we never see a
hair of his beard till he 's come barefoot again. Now [*holding
up the sheepskin*] I 've done all I can to your sheepskin. It 's so thin the cold does n't have to seek the holes
to creep in: it walks through. It 's thankful I 'll be when
we can buy another skin so that I can get out of the house
the same time you go.

SIMON. We 'll buy a skin this very afternoon, my dear.
When Trofinoff brings me the eight roubles, we shall add it
to the three you have saved and that ought to buy a good
skin—if not a tanned one, at all events, a good rough one.

MATRENA. *If* Trofinoff brings the money.

SIMON. He 'll bring it, or by heaven, I 'll have the cap off
his head, so I will. That is the kind of man I am.

MATRENA. If he were to come in and tell you he is hard
up, you would tell him not to worry his head about the
roubles, that God is good.

SIMON. No, I shall say, "Am I not hard up as well?"

MATRENA. Very well, if he comes we shall see what kind
of man you are. Who was that?

SIMON. It was your friend, Anna Maloska, who wears
shoes too small for her.

MATRENA. She wore large shoes after she caught her
husband; but now he is dead, she wears small shoes again
to catch another.

SIMON. I wonder that she did not stop.

MATRENA. She will stop on her way back from market
for there will be more news.

SIMON [*looking out the window and rising happily*]. But see here, Matrena, you wronged the good Trofinoff. He has come to pay the eight roubles as he promised. [*There is a halting knock at the door.*] Coming! Coming! [*He limps slightly as he hastens up the steps.*]

MATRENA [*as she crosses to go into the room at the right*]. Well, Simon, I shall be the last to be sorry if your faith has been rewarded. [*She goes out as* SIMON *opens the door to the street. He comes down with* TROFINOFF, *a middle-aged, sharp-faced little man with gray beard and keen roving eyes. He carries a bundle wrapped in brown cloth.*]

SIMON. Welcome, Trofinoff, I salute you.

TROFINOFF. Welcome, fellow-brother. I wish you every thing that is good.

SIMON. I thank you, brother. Is all well at home?

TROFINOFF. Not as well as might be, alas. Fuel takes much money these days. I have a flat purse.

SIMON. Then it was doubly good of you, friend Trofinoff, to come to settle our account. My good wife has not a kaftan or a sheepskin to wear when it snows.

TROFINOFF. I regret, Simon, I was unable to bring you the roubles, I owed you. I am so hard pressed.

SIMON [*with forced sternness*]. Am I not hard up as well?

TROFINOFF. Aye, but you have not so many mouths to fill, nor cattle to feed, nor grain to dispose of with little profit.

SIMON. Friend Trofinoff, you have a hut and cattle, while I have all on my back. You grow your own bread; I have to buy mine. If you do not pay me, I shall not have money for bread.

TROFINOFF. You are not so grieved as I, brother, and had it been any one but you I should not have dared face him, but I knew the kind of man you were. I have heard you say "Let us love one another."

SIMON. That is so, for love is of God.

TROFINOFF. So I said to my wife: "Anya, if it were any-one but Simon, the good Simon, I would not dare take him our little one's shoes, but I know what kind of man he is:

he loves the children and would not that the least of these should suffer and he could help it.'' [*He unwraps a tattered pair of shoes, belonging to a child.*]

SIMON. Aye, the little Sarah's shoes. They need soles badly and a toe cap.

TROFINOFF. You will repair them for her, Simon?

SIMON. Of course, brother, I— [*He looks nervously toward the door to the inner room.*] Could you not pay me something, Trofinoff?

TROFINOFF. Here are two copecks. They will buy a half loaf for the wife, Simon. [*He goes to the door.*]

SIMON. Thank you.

TROFINOFF. And you shall have your roubles in a day or so as soon as my grain is paid for.

SIMON. I can get along very comfortably. While one of us has a warm coat, why should we fret? I can stay in by the fire. Only, of course, there 's my wife. She keeps worrying about it.

TROFINOFF. Your wife has no cause to be anxious while she has such a kind husband, Simon. I will send for the boots shortly. Good-day.

SIMON. Good-day. God be with you, brother.

[TROFINOFF *goes out.* SIMON *lays the copecks on the bench, and is examining the small shoes when* MATRENA *enters. He puts them behind his back guiltily.*]

MATRENA. Well, what are you hiding there? Did he bring you a gift with your money?

SIMON [*sadly*]. No, he—he assured me, he was quite destitute.

MATRENA [*enraged*]. Do you mean he brought you not even your eight roubles? [SIMON *shakes his head.*] What did I tell you, eh?

SIMON. But he says he will bring them soon—when his money comes in. I railed at him, Matrena. I scored him roundly for not paying his just dues.

MATRENA. And what have you there? [SIMON *produces the shoes and* MATRENA *is further enraged.*] I thought as much. You 've taken more work for the cheater. You let him hoodwink you out of your senses while your old wife may go hungry and cold. What 's this?

SIMON. He gave me two copecks for bread.

[MATRENA *hurls them angrily on the floor at* SIMON's *feet. The old man patiently picks them up.*]

MATRENA. Bread, bah! It would not buy half a loaf. The thief! It is a shame, a shame. [*She rocks herself, crying, then falls into a chair by the fire, her apron thrown over her head and gives way to grief.*]

SIMON [*distressed*]. Come now, Matrena, why will you wag your tongue so foolishly? If we have bread for the day, the morrow will provide for itself. As for the coat, I shall go to Vanya, the vender of skins, and get one on credit.

[*The* LITTLE DEVIL *peers in at the window, then disappears.*]

MATRENA. And who would give the likes of us credit with not a dessiatin of land to our share?

SIMON [*putting the shoes on the bench and preparing for outdoors*]. Vanya will. I have bought many skins from him for my shoes. I have favored him in his turn.

MATRENA. Men forget past favors in the face of present desires. But if you are going out, you had better put my woolen jacket under your kaftan. The wind is bitter cold to-day.

[*She goes to the curtains to the left of the stairs and takes down a close-fitting woolen sack. From a shelf of the cupboard, she lifts a jar and shakes into her hand some money.* SIMON *is drawing on woolen slippers over his shoes. He puts on* MATRENA's *jacket, a woolen kaftan or smock over it, and throws the sheepskin about his shoulders. On his bald head he draws down a fur cap.*]

SIMON [*submitting to* MATRENA's *ministrations*]. Thank you, Matrena, I shall feel quite warm in this old sheepskin. I shan't want a new one in a lifetime. [*He goes up the steps.*]

MATRENA. You won't get one, the way you conduct your

business. Now, Simon, here are our three roubles, give these
to Vanya on account and he should then let you have the
skin.

SIMON. He will, wife, he will.

MATRENA. Now go, and mind you do not stop for vodka
on the way—your tongue is loose enough as it is. And do
not talk aloud to yourself as is your custom, for if a thief
learn you have the roubles, he will not be above killing you
for them.

SIMON. God is my protection. May his good angel guard
our house in my absence! Good day, Matrena!

MATRENA. Good day, Simon!

[*He goes out, closing the door. She looks after him
affectionately, then goes to the closet and taking an iron pot
from the shelf hangs it before the fire. Seeing that all is
well, she crosses and goes into the inner room. The basement is but dimly lighted. The* LITTLE DEVIL, *after peering
into the window to see that the coast is clear, comes in from
the street, closing the door after him. He moves quickly
and is merry as though about to reap some reward for his
efforts. From out the curtains by the stairs, steps the figure
of* THE GUARDIAN ANGEL *in long flowing garments. The*
ANGEL *remains in the shadows and is never clearly visible.*]

ANGEL. Why are you here?

[THE DEVIL *goes to the hearth and sits in front of the fire.
He shows no surprise at being spoken to by the* ANGEL, *and
does not look in his direction as he answers.*]

DEVIL. To try my luck to see if I can win old Simon with
my dice. He has begun to ask credit and if he stops for
vodka, as I shall see that he does, that will be one more step
in my direction.

ANGEL. His faith is strong.

DEVIL. So are my dice, ha! ha! [*He throws them.*]
Three, six, nine! Good! The three means that he will have a
little luck: it will make him drink vodka and forget his wife.
Six, he will prosper, and when a man prospers in *this* world
he forgets the next. Nine, nine, that is not so well. Nine

means that I shall get him—if—yet "if's" are so little in my way. So I shall get him, unless——

ANGEL. Unless?

DEVIL [*rising*]. Unless a greater than thou come into his home to protect him.

ANGEL. I am his Guardian Angel.

DEVIL [*on the stairs*]. I shall make the roubles jingle in his pockets so that he shall not hear the voice of the Guardian Angel. If nine had been twelve—but we shall see. I am off now to the home of the Baron, who long ago drowned the voice of his angel in vodka. I mixed his first glass. There was fox's blood to make him grow cunning, wolf's blood to make him grow cruel, and swine's blood to turn him into a pig. On my way, I shall mix a glass for Simon, to bring up in him all the beast blood there is.

ANGEL. His faith is great.

[*The* DEVIL *laughs derisively as he goes out and slams the door, and the* ANGEL *disappears again in the shadows. Feet go by the window and voices are heard. Then just as* MATRENA *comes in and goes to the fire, there is a knock.*]

MATRENA. Come in.

[*A comely woman of middle age enters. She is rather over-dressed in poor clothes that strive to imitate the rich. It is* ANNA MALOSKA.]

MATRENA. Ah, Anna Maloska, is it you? I thought I had the odor of smoke and I came to tend our fire. Come in.

ANNA [*sniffing*]. It smells like sulphur. That's bad luck. Who was it went out?

MATRENA. No one. Sit down. Simon has gone to buy a sheepskin. Is it cold out?

ANNA [*sitting and throwing back her wraps*]. Bitter cold. It was on just such a day my poor husband caught pneumonia.

MATRENA [*sitting on the other side of the fire and tending the porridge*]. I do hope Simon won't catch cold and I do hope the sheepskin seller won't cheat him. That man of mine is a regular simpleton.

ANNA [*patting her hair*]. They are all, poor dears.

MATRENA. Simon never cheats a soul himself, yet a little child can lead him by the nose. It's time he was back; he had no way to go.

ANNA. If it were poor dear Ivan, I should know he had stopped for a glass of vodka.

MATRENA [*walking to the window and looking out*]. I hope he hasn't gone making merry, that rascal of mine.

ANNA. Ah, Matrena, they are all rascals. Ivan drank himself into a drunken stupor every evening; then he would come home and beat me, and beat little Fifi, my dog, but I have to remember that he was a man and men are like that. I shall never be happy again, now that he is in his grave. [*She weeps.*]

MATRENA [*patting her shoulder*]. There, there, poor Anna!

ANNA [*brightening*]. Do you like my hat?

MATRENA. Aye, aye, it is very tasty; though if I might say, a trifle youthful.

ANNA. Why shouldn't a woman cheat Father Time if she can? He's the only man she can get even with. He liked my hat.

MATRENA. Ivan?

ANNA. Oh, no, the poor dear died without seeing it. I mean Martin Pakhom. I just met him at the door and he said, "Good-day, Anna, what a beautiful hat that is you're wearing."

MATRENA. They say Martin drinks like a trout.

ANNA. Ah, they all do, poor dears. [*Gathering up her basket.*] I must go on. Fifi will be wanting his supper, though neither of us have eaten anything since poor Ivan died. Fifi is so affectionate. We both cry an hour every morning. Sonka times us.

MATRENA. Poor Anna!

ANNA. Won't you walk a way with me?

MATRENA. Simon went out with all our clothes upon him and left me nothing to wear. Besides, I must have his supper ready, and clean out my sleeping-room.

ANNA [*at the stairs*]. I wish *I* had some one to get supper for. [*She goes up to the door.*] Matrena, Martin said something rather pointed just now.

MATRENA. What did he say, Anna?

ANNA. He said, "Marriage is a lottery!"

MATRENA. Aye, aye, so it is.

ANNA. I was just wondering——

MATRENA. Yes?

ANNA. I was wondering if Martin were thinking of taking a chance. Good-by, Matrena.

MATRENA. Good-by, Anna.

[ANNA *goes out.* MATRENA, *stirring her porridge, sits near the fire. The feet of two men pass the window. They belong to* SIMON *and a stranger. The men enter. The stranger is a young man, tall and slender, with fine clear-cut features and a mild gentle expression. He is without stockings, being clad in* SIMON'S *woolen slippers and kaftan. He stands hesitating at the foot of the steps.* MATRENA *has risen and regards the two men angrily.* "What tramp is this now, Simon has brought home?" *she is wondering. The old man approaches his wife fearfully.*]

SIMON. Well, Matrena, here we are home again. [MATRENA *after a scathing glance, turns her back on him, and tends her fire.*] We have brought our appetites with us. Get us some supper, will you? [*He takes off his sheepskin and cap, but still* MATRENA *does not respond. He motions the stranger to a chair at the right.*] Sit you down, brother, and we will have some supper. Have you anything cooked that you could give us?

MATRENA [*facing him in rage*]. Yes, I have something cooked, but not for you. I can see you have drunk your senses away. [*As he starts to protest.*] Do you think I can not smell your breath? Where is our sheepskin? Did you drink up all the three roubles?

[SIMON *goes to the stranger and reaching in the pocket of the kaftan takes out the roubles.*]

SIMON. No, Matrena, I did not get the sheepskin because the vender would not let me have one unless I brought all the

money. "Bring all the cash," he said, "and then you can
pick what skin you like. We all of us know how difficult it
is to get quit of a debt." But here are your roubles; I only
spent the two kopecks for the merest drop to send the blood
bubbling finely in my veins.

MATRENA [eyeing the man]. I have no supper for a pair
of drunkards like you. One cannot feed every drunkard
that comes along when one has not enough in the pot for two.

SIMON. Hold your tongue, Matrena. Give me time to
explain.

MATRENA. How much sense am I likely to hear from a
drunken fool, indeed! My mother gave me some linen—and
you drank it away! You go out to buy a sheepskin and
drink that away, too.

SIMON. But I did not——

MATRENA [beside herself with rage]. Give me my jacket!
It's the only one I have, yet you sneak it off while I stay
home for lack of clothes. [As she snatches off the jacket and
starts to the other room, her anger is burning off.] You,
you haven't told me who this fellow is.

SIMON. If you will give me a chance for a word, I will. I
saw this man lying by the chapel yonder, half-naked and
frozen. It is not summer time, you must remember. God
led me to him, else he must have perished. The Baron Av-
deitch drove up and I thought he would stop but he did not.
I started on, saying to myself the man could be up to no
good there and if I went back I might be robbed and murdered. Then, I said, "Fie, Simon, for shame! would you
let a man die for want of clothing and food at your very
door?" What could I do? I shared with him my covering
and brought him here. Calm your temper, Matrena, for to
give way to it is sinful. Remember we would all die, were
it not for God.

[MATRENA turns back from the door, sets a teapot on the
table and pours some kvass, laying knives and forks by the
places and serving the porridge.]

MATRENA. Here is kvass and porridge. There is no bread.

[*They eat humbly.* MATRENA *stops before the stranger.*]
What is your name?
MICHAEL [*lifting his serious eyes to her face*]. Michael.
MATRENA. Where do you come from?
MICHAEL. From another part than this.
MATRENA. How did you come to the chapel?
MICHAEL. I cannot say.
MATRENA. Some one must have assaulted you then?
MICHAEL. No, no one assaulted me. God was punishing me.
SIMON. Of course, all things come of God. Yet where were you bound for?
MICHAEL. For nowhere in particular.
SIMON. Do you know any trade?
MICHAEL. No, none.
MATRENA [*her heart warming within her*]. You could learn. I know, Simon, he could learn, if you would teach him. He might stay with us. There is enough straw for another bed in the hallway.
MICHAEL. The Lord be good to you! I was lying frozen and unclothed, when Simon saw and took compassion on me. He shared with me his clothing and brought me hither. You have given me food and drink and shown me great kindness.
MATRENA. No, I was not kind. I am ashamed of myself. [*She goes to the cupboard and brings out the one bit of bread.*] And I lied. I said there was no bread. There is one crust and you shall have half.
MICHAEL. But you?
MATRENA [*gently*]. Eat, we shall have enough. You are welcome to stay with us as long as you wish. [MICHAEL *turns and smiles radiantly on her.*] Let us eat.
MICHAEL. God's blessing on this house.

SCENE II

[*There is an air of greater prosperity than before. The cobbler's bench is new. There are flowers in the window-*

*box and on the mantel. It is spring outside. The sound of
hammering is heard within. The outer door opens and
MATRENA enters with ANNA MALOSKA. The two women
have been to market. MATRENA is well, though quietly
dressed; ANNA, as usual, in bright colors.*]

MATRENA. Come in, Anna.

ANNA. The men are not here. I wished to ask Simon
about my shoes.

MATRENA. They are inside, building another room. We
have needed it since Michael came. Michael made the new
bench.

ANNA. Michael seems to do everything well. Just like
poor Ivan.

MATRENA [*enthusiastically*]. Ah, he is wonderful. Everything that Simon teaches him he learns readily. The first
day he learned to twine and twist the thread, no easy task for
the apprentice. The third day, he was able to work as
though he had been a cobbler all his life. He never makes
mistakes, and eats no more than a sparrow.

[*They sit down at the table.*]

ANNA. He is woefully solemn.

MATRENA. Aye, he works all day, only resting for a moment to look upward. He never wishes to go out of doors;
never jests, nor laughs. He has only smiled once; it was the
night he came.

ANNA. Has he any family—a wife?

MATRENA. He never speaks of his own affairs.

ANNA. *I* should manage to worm it out of him, trust me.
Martin shall have no secrets that I don't know.

MATRENA. When are you to marry, Anna?

ANNA. Next month. It will be such a relief to let down.
I shan't wear these tight stays any longer, nor such close
boots. I can go to breakfast in my old wrapper and curl
papers. Now Martin has a way of dropping in to breakfast
and I have to keep on my sleekest dress.

MATRENA. Martin was in for shoes last week.

ANNA. Yes, he says no one sews so strongly and so neatly as Michael.

MATRENA. People come to Simon from all the country around. Since Michael came his business has increased ten-fold.

ANNA. Aye, Martin says the fame of Simon's apprentice has crept abroad. [*Regarding her own shoes.*] Martin has small feet. He told me last night he wore a number seven. But I must go.

MATRENA. Here comes Simon now.

[SIMON *and* MICHAEL *enter from the right. The latter is in simple workman's clothes. He bows gravely without speaking, and going to the bench bends over his work.* SIMON *approaches the women, who have risen.*]

SIMON. Ah, Anna Maloska, how fares the bride to-day?

ANNA. Well, thank you, Simon. I came to order some new shoes.

SIMON. Good, Anna. Shall we make them on the same last as before? Sixes, I believe?

ANNA. No, Simon, I wish sevens this time. Good-bye, Matrena. Good-bye, Simon.

SIMON and MATRENA. Farewell, Anna.

MATRENA. Come in again, Anna.

ANNA [*at the door*]. Simon, are Martin's shoes finished?

SIMON. No, Anna, but don't worry; they will be. I had to send for more leather. He wears large boots, you know.

ANNA [*turning on the steps*]. Large? Sevens?

SIMON. Elevens, Anna.

ANNA. Elevens, why—after all, Simon, I believe you may make my shoes nines. [*She opens the door.*]

SIMON. Very well, Anna.

ANNA [*looking out, becomes greatly excited*]. Oh, Matrena, a fine gentleman in a great-coat is getting out here. He has two coachmen and a footman. I think it is the Baron. I must run out of his way. [*She disappears.* SIMON *and* MATRENA *look out of the window.*]

MATRENA. It is the Baron Avedeitch, is n't it, Simon?

SIMON. There is no mistaking the Baron, and he is coming here.

[*The door has been left open and it is presently filled by a huge form that has to bow his great head to enter the low portal. The* BARON *has a ruddy, bibulous countenance, a neck like a bull's, and a figure of cast-iron. He straightens up just inside the door.*]

BARON [*in a loud pompous tone*]. Which of you is the master bootmaker?

SIMON [*stepping aside*]. I am, your honor.

BARON [*calling out the door*]. Hi, Thedka! Bring me the stuff here. [*He comes down into the room, followed by the footman, who places the bundle on the table.*] Untie it. [*The footman does so, disclosing two sheets of leather. He then withdraws.* MATRENA *curtsies every time anyone looks her direction, though no one heeds her.*] Look here, bootmaker. Do you see this?

SIMON. Yes, your nobility.

BARON. Do you know what it is?

SIMON. It is good leather.

BARON [*thundering for emphasis*]. Good leather, indeed! You blockhead, you have never seen such leather in your life before. It is of northern make and cost twenty roubles. Could you make me a pair of boots out of it?

SIMON. Possibly so, your honor.

BARON. "Possibly so!" Well, first, listen. I want a pair of boots that shall last a year, will never tread over, and never split at the seams. If you can make such boots, then set to work and cut out at once, but if you cannot, do neither of these things. I tell you beforehand that if the new pair should split or tread over before the year is out, I will clap you in prison.

MATRENA. Oh, your honor.

BARON [*ignoring her*]. But, if they should not do so, then I will pay you ten roubles for your work.

SIMON [*turning to* MICHAEL]. What do you think about it, brother?

MICHAEL. Take the work, Simon.

SIMON. Very well, sir.

BARON [*he sits and extends his foot*]. Hi, Thedka.

[*The footman advances and draws off the boot. The* BARON *then motions to* SIMON. MICHAEL *has advanced.*]

BARON. Take my measure. [MICHAEL *kneels and takes the measure of the sole and of the instep. He has to fasten on an extra piece of paper to measure the calf as the muscles of the* BARON'S *leg are as thick as a beam.*] Take care you don't make them too tight in the leg. [*As* MICHAEL *draws back, the footman replaces the boot on his master's foot, then withdraws again to the door.*]

BARON [*indicating* MICHAEL]. Who is this you have with you?

SIMON. That is my skilled workman who will sew your boots.

BARON [*standing and stamping into his boot*]. Look you sharp, then, and remember this—that you are to sew them so that they will last a year. [MICHAEL *does not respond but stands gazing past the* BARON *as though he saw some one back of him. His face suddenly breaks into a smile and he brightens all over. The* BARON, *irritated, glances back of him, then scowls at* MICHAEL.] What are you grinning at, you fool? I see no one back of me to grin at. You had better see that the boots are ready when I want them. [*He stalks up the steps.*]

MICHAEL. They will be ready when you need them.

[*The* BARON *goes out. The footman follows, closing the door.*]

MATRENA. What a man!

SIMON. He is as hard as a flint stone.

MATRENA. Why wouldn't he get hardened with the life he leads? Even death itself would not take such an iron rivet of a man.

SIMON [*taking the leather to* MICHAEL *at the bench*]. Well, Michael, we have undertaken the work and we must take care not to go amiss over it. This leather is valuable stuff.

MATRENA. And the gentleman is short-tempered.

SIMON. Aye, there must be no mistakes. You have the sharper eyes, as well as the greatest skill in your fingers, so take these measures and cut out the stuff, while I finish sewing those toe-caps.

MICHAEL. I will make them according to your needs.

[*The men sit working while* MATRENA *busies herself with the housework.*]

MATRENA. Oh, Simon, I forgot to tell you, Sonia Ivanich is coming by to get shoes for her two little girls. The little Nikita is hard to fit, but Madame has heard that Michael can fit even a lame foot.

[MICHAEL *drops his work and leans forward.*]

MICHAEL. A lame child?

MATRENA. Yes, poor little thing—but hush, I hear the clamp, clamp of a wooden foot. Come, Simon, and greet her. Madame has money; you are getting all the best trade now.

[SIMON *puts down his work and comes forward.* MATRENA *hastens up to the door and holds it open. A gentle, good-looking lady enters with two pretty little girls. They have round wide eyes, rosy cheeks and wear smart little shawls and dresses.*]

SONIA. Good day to you, mistress.

MATRENA. The same to you, madame, and the young misses. Won't you sit down?

[SONIA *sits by the table, the two little girls burying their faces in her skirts from timidity. She pats them tolerantly.* MICHAEL *keeps regarding them, though he works.*]

SONIA. Thank you. Is this Master Simon?

SIMON. It is, mistress. What can we do for you?

SONIA. I wish a pair of boots made for each of these little girls to wear for the spring.

SIMON. Very well, madame. Will you have them leather throughout or lined with linen?

SONIA. I believe linen will be softer. [*The lame child has slipped over to* MICHAEL *and he takes her on his knee.*] Well, will you see Nikita? I have never known her to take to a stranger so.

MATRENA. All the children love Michael. He is Simon's skilled workman. He will take the measures.
[MICHAEL *measures the little feet. The child pats his head.*]
NIKITA. I love you. Have you a little dirl?
MICHAEL [*gently*]. No, I have no little girl.
SONIA. Take both sets of measures from this little girl and make one bashmak [1] for the crooked foot and three ordinary ones. The two children take the same size: they are twins.
MATRENA. How came she to be lame? Such a pretty little lady.
SONIA. Her mother fell over her as she was dying.
MATRENA [*surprised*]. Then you are not their mother.
SONIA. No, I adopted them. But I love them as much as though they were my own and they are as happy as the day is long; they know no difference.
SIMON. Whose children were they?
SONIA. The children of peasants. The father died on a Tuesday from the felling of a tree. The mother died that Friday, just after the twins were born. She was all alone and in her death agony she threw herself across the baby and crushed its foot. When we found her, she was stiff in death but the children were alive.
MATRENA. Poor little mother!
SONIA. I was the only one in the village with a young child, so they were given to me to nurse. God took my own little one unto Himself, but I have come to love these like my own flesh. I could not live without them. They are to me as wax is to the candle.
SIMON. It is a true saying which reads, "Without father and mother we may live, but without God—never."
[*All are drawn to look toward* MICHAEL *who, sitting with his hands folded on his knees, is gazing upward and smiling as though at some one unseen by the others.*]
SONIA [*rising*]. Good-day, master. Come, Nikita, we will stop in again to try the boots.

1 Bashmak—boot.

SIMON. In seven days, mistress. We thank you.

NIKITA. Good-bye, man!

MICHAEL. Good-bye, little one!

SONIA. Well, I never! The little dear! [*She goes out with the children.*]

SIMON. Michael, if you will bring me the awl from the other room, I, too, will work. [*He approaches the bench as* MICHAEL *goes into the other room for the awl. He suddenly cries aloud in dismay.*] What has he done? What can ail the fellow?

MATRENA. What is it? [*She hastens to his side.*]

SIMON [*groaning*]. Oh! How is it that Michael who has lived with me for a whole year without making a single mistake, should now make such a blunder as this? The baron ordered high boots and Michael has gone and sewed a pair of soleless slippers and spoiled the leather.

MATRENA [*aghast*]. Michael has done this!

SIMON. Alas, yes, and you heard what the gentleman said. I could replace an ordinary skin, but one does not see leather like this every day. [MICHAEL *returns with the awl.*] My good fellow, what have you done? You have simply ruined me! The gentleman ordered high boots, but what have you gone and made instead?

[*Before* MICHAEL *has a chance to respond, there is a loud knock at the door.*]

SIMON. Come in!

[*The door is opened and* THEDKA, *the footman of the* BARON, *enters.* SIMON *pushes the slipper back of him.*]

THEDKA. Good-day to you.

SIMON [*uneasily*]. Good-day. What can we do for you?

THEDKA. My mistress sent me about the boots.

SIMON. Yes? What about them?

[MICHAEL, *unseen by the others, goes into the other room.*]

THEDKA. My master will not want them now. He is dead.

MATRENA. What are you saying!

THEDKA. He died on the way home. When we went to

help him alight, he lay limp as a meal-sack on the floor of the carriage.

MATRENA. God help us!

THEDKA. My mistress sent me to tell the bootmaker to use the leather for a pair of slippers for the corpse and to make them as quickly as he can.

[MATRENA and SIMON *look at each other with wonderment in their eyes. They turn to where* MICHAEL *stood by the inner door, but he has disappeared.*]

SIMON. You shall have them in an hour.

THEDKA. I shall return. Good day, my master, and good luck to you.

SIMON. And to you.

[THEDKA *goes out, leaving* SIMON *and* MATRENA *gazing at each other in awe.*]

MATRENA. Michael is no ordinary being. We might have guessed before this.

SIMON. You remember how he smiled?

MATRENA. He has smiled three times.

SIMON. Let us see what he is doing.

MATRENA. You do not suppose he would go from us without a word, do you?

[*They go into the other room. Immediately The* LITTLE DEVIL *appears in the doorway at the back and The* GUARDIAN ANGEL *is seen in the shadow of the curtains at the left.*]

ANGEL. You have lost!

DEVIL [*with a stamp of his foot*]. I have lost Simon's soul, but I have the Baron. He shall be my torch this night in hell.

ANGEL. The faith of Simon was great.

DEVIL. *Thou* didst not save him!

ANGEL. One greater than I saved Simon. It was God!

[*At the word, the* DEVIL *stamps his foot again, slams the door and goes. The* ANGEL *disappears. From the other room come* MATRENA *and* SIMON, *crossing to the hearth.*]

SIMON. He was in prayer.

MATRENA. His face was illumined and such a light shone

from him that at first I thought it was a fire. Oh, Simon,
who is this that has dwelt with us?

[MICHAEL *comes in from the other room, goes to the steps,
where he turns and faces them.*]

MICHAEL. God has pardoned me, good master and mistress. Do you also pardon me?

SIMON. Tell us, Michael, who you are and why God punished you.

MICHAEL. I was an angel in Heaven and God punished me
because I disobeyed Him. He sent me to earth to bear away
a woman's soul. But the woman who had given birth to
twin babies cried to me, "Angel of God, I can not leave them.
They will die, I have no kin to care for them. Do not take
away my soul. Children cannot live without mother or
father!" So I hearkened to the mother and flew back to
God, saying, "Little children cannot live without mother or
father, so I did not take away the mother's soul." Then
God said to me, "Go thou and fetch away the soul of the
chiding woman, and before thou return to Heaven, thou shalt
learn three words. Thou shalt learn both what that is which
dwelleth in men, and what that is which is not given to men
to know, and what that is whereby men live. When thou hast
learned these words thou mayst return to Heaven."

MATRENA. Tell us what you did, Michael.

MICHAEL. I went to earth and took the soul of the chiding
woman, then I rose above the village and tried to bear the
soul to God, but a wind caught me, so that my wings hung
down and were blown from me. The soul returned alone to
God, while I fell to earth along the roadside.

[SIMON *and* MATRENA *marvel:* SIMON *speaks.*]

SIMON. Tell me, Michael, why you smiled three times, and
what were the three words of God.

MICHAEL. When you, Simon, took me to your home and
Matrena's heart prompted her to share her last crust, I
smiled because I knew the first word of God. "Thou shalt
learn what that is which dwelleth in men," and I knew by
your goodness that what dwelleth in men is Love. I felt glad
that God had seen fit to reveal this to me, and I smiled.

MATRENA. What was it you saw over the shoulder of the Baron that made you smile?

MICHAEL. I saw the Angel of Death. No one but I saw him, and I thought, here is this man planning for boots that shall last a year, when he is to die before the nightfall. Then I smiled when I remembered that God had said, ''Thou shalt learn what it is not given to men to know.''

SIMON. What was it made you smile at the story of the good Sonia Ivanich?

MICHAEL. I recognized in the children the twins that I had thought would die. Yet this woman had fed them and loved them. I beheld in her, love and pity for the living God, and understood what that is whereby men live. And I smiled. This much do I tell you to repay your kindness, that men only appear to live by taking thought of themselves; in reality, they live by Love alone. He that dwelleth in Love dwelleth in God and God in him; for God is Love.

[*The room is suddenly black with night. Then a hymn bursts forth as though from a great choir of voices, and in the doorway* MICHAEL, *bathed in light, stands looking upward. Before him, at the foot of the stairs, kneel the two peasants.*]

SUGGESTIVE QUESTIONS

1. Point out passages in the dialogue that do most to indicate Russia as the scene of the play.
2. Point out stage settings that indicate Russia.
3. Suppose Simon had been a young man. What would be the loss, or the gain, in dramatic value?
4. What parts of the dialogue most illustrate Simon's character?
5. How much does the use of supernatural characters add to, or take from, the dramatic value of the play?
6. What is the most vividly dramatic section of the play?
7. What is the most realistic section?
8. What section of the play does most to arouse emotion?
9. How does Scene II differ from Scene I?
10. What subordinate stories are made part of the plot?

11. What emotions does the play produce?
12. Compare or contrast the presentation of *What Men Live By*
    with the presentation of a puppet play.

SUGGESTIONS FOR WRITTEN IMITATION

1. Write a scenario for a play based on humble life in the United
   States. Aim to emphasize a single theme, a worthy principle
   of life.
2. Write a dialogue between two humble working people, one of
   whom has a simple nature and a sincere desire to help others.
3. Write a dialogue, with stage directions, emphasizing some
   weakness common in everyday life.
4. In such modern plays as *Peter Pan* and *The Bluebird* there are
   characters foreign to ordinary life. Write a scenario for a
   play that will make use of such unusual characters.
5. Write a dialogue in which the characters show real love for
   children.

DIRECTIONS FOR WRITING

Make every effort to emphasize theme without sacrificing reality.
Draw your material from daily life. Use everyday language, and
refer to everyday things.

ORAL WORK IN THE CLASS

1. Select from the play a section that is extremely realistic. Act
   that section.
2. Select from the play a section that expresses strong emotion.
   Act that section.
3. Read aloud Simon's speech, near the end of Scene I, beginning:
   "If you will give me a chance for a word, I will." Use voice
   and dramatic action in the most effective ways to make
   Simon's speech natural.

THE GREEN GODDESS

By William Archer

The Green Goddess is romance, pure and simple, a *tour de force* that suddenly sets people of the ordinary world, with their own life-problems, in the midst of entirely alien surroundings. There they meet a man like Jack London's "Sea Wolf," who has the learning and the exterior forms of civilization, but who has retained the soul of barbarism.

Such a situation gives ample opportunity for caustic dialogue, as well as for thrilling action. Side by side with the Asiatic who has kept much of his barbarism while gaining much of culture, the dramatist has placed a European who has degenerated into a renegade. In the characters of the two Englishmen who so unexpectedly land in a strange region he gives a further contrast: the one knowing that he is slowly slipping from manhood; the other, like Banquo in *Macbeth*, holding to honor.

Vividly objective, intense in situations, original in treatment, and so written that every word is made to count, *The Green Goddess* is a tale well told, a play that will interest every student. It makes no attempt to present an important message, nor to give a notable interpretation of life, but it does succeed in holding interest spellbound. It illustrates much that is best in dramatic construction. It is an interesting example of what a great dramatic critic does when he turns to creative writing.

William Archer, author of *The Green Goddess,* is distinguished as a dramatic critic and as a man of letters. In 1879, after studies at the University of Edinburgh, Mr.

Archer began that work in dramatic criticism for which he made himself famous.

In newspapers, magazines, and books, year after year, for nearly fifty years, Mr. Archer has upheld the high traditions of the theatre.

As a dramatic critic he wrote such books as: "About the Theatre" (1886); "Masks or Faces: a Study in the Psychology of Acting" (1888); "Study and Stage" (1899); "Playmaking: a Manual of Craftsmanship" (1912); "Old Drama and the New" (1923).

As a biographer he wrote: "English Dramatists of To-day (1882); "Henry Irving" (1883); "W. C. Macready" (1890); "The Life, Trial, and Death of Francisco Ferrer" (1911); "Allan Seeger" (1917).

As a translator he translated Henrik Ibsen's prose dramas, and Wallemar's *Life of Nansen*, and he assisted in translating several of Maeterlinck's plays.

To general literature Mr. Archer has contributed numerous important works, among which may be mentioned editions of the plays of William Congreve, and of George Farquhar: *America Today* (1899); *Real Conversations* (1904); *God and Mr. Wells* (1917), and *India and the Future* (1918).

INTRODUCTORY PROBLEMS

1. If you have read Jack London's *Sea Wolf* write a scenario for a play founded on the book.
2. If you have read Rudyard Kipling's *Captains Courageous* write a scenario for a play founded on the book.
3. Imagine that an American aviator fell into the hands of the enemy in the World War. Write a scenario that will tell of his being made prisoner, of the adventures that he had, and of his unexpected rescue at the moment of greatest danger.

PERSONS OF THE PLAY

THE RAJA OF RUKH (40)
WATKINS, *his valet* (35)
MAJOR ANTONY CRESPIN (40)

LUCILLA, his wife (28)
DOCTOR BASIL TRAHERNE (35)
LIEUTENANT DENIS CARDEW (23)
Priests, villagers, regular and irregular troops, servants and
an unseen multitude.

SCENE. A remote region at the back of the Himalayas.

ACT I

*A region of gaunt and almost treeless mountains, uni-
formly gray in tone, except in so far as the atmosphere lends
them color. Clinging to the mountain wall in the background, at an apparent distance of about a mile, is a vast
barbaric palace, with long stretches of unbroken masonry,
crowned by arcades and turrets.*

*The foreground consists of a small level space between two
masses of rock. In the rock on the right[1] a cave-temple has
been roughly hewn. Two thick and rudely-carved pillars
divide it into three sections. Between the pillars, in the
middle section, can be seen the seated figure of a six-armed
Goddess, of forbidding aspect, colored dark green. In front
of the figure is a low altar with five or six newly-severed
heads of goats lying at its base. The temple is decorated
with untidy and moldering wreaths and other floral
offerings.*

*The open space between the two rock masses forms a
rudely-paved forecourt to the temple. It is bordered by
small idols and three or four round-headed stone posts,
painted green.*

*Mountain paths wind off behind the rocks, and through
the low shrubs, both to right and left.*

*Projecting over the rock-mass on the left can be seen the
wing of an aeroplane, the nacelle and under-carriage hidden.
It has evidently just made a rather disastrous forced landing.
The pilot and two passengers are in the act of extricating*

---

[1] From the point of view of the audience.

*themselves from the wreck, and clambering down the cliff.
The pilot is* Dr. Basil Traherne; *the passengers are* Major
Antony Crespin *and his wife* Lucilla. Traherne (35) *is
a well-set-up man, vigorous and in good training.* Crespin
(40), *somewhat heavy and dissipated-looking, is in khaki.*
Lucilla (28), *is a tall, slight, athletic woman, wearing a
tailor-made tweed suit. All three on their first appearance
wear aviation helmets and leather coats. The coats they
take off as occasion offers.*

*Their proceedings are watched with wonder and fear by a
group of dark and rudely-clad natives, rather Mongolian in
feature. They chatter eagerly among themselves. A man
of higher stature and more Aryan type, the* Priest *of the
temple, seems to have some authority over them.*

As soon as all three newcomers have descended, the Priest
*gives some directions to a young man among the bystanders,
who makes off at great speed. He is a messenger to the
castle.*

Lucilla [*to* Crespin, *who is at a difficult point, and about
to jump*]. Take care, Antony! Let Dr. Traherne give you
a hand.

Traherne [*already on the ground*]. Yes.

Crespin. Hang it all, I 'm not such a crock as all that.
[*Jumps heavily, but safely.*]

Traherne. Are you all right, Mrs. Crespin? Not very
much shaken?

Lucilla. Not a bit.

Traherne. It was a nasty bump.

Lucilla. You managed splendidly.

Crespin. Come on, Lu—sit on that ledge, and I can swing
you down.

Traherne. Let me——

[Crespin *and* Traherne *support her as she jumps lightly
to the ground.*]

Lucilla. Thank you.

Crespin. That last ten minutes was pretty trying. I
don't mind owning that my nerves are all of a twitter.

[*Producing a pocket flask, and pouring some of its contents into the cup.*] Have a mouthful, Traherne?

TRAHERNE. No, thank you.

CRESPIN [*to* LUCILLA]. You won't, I know. I will. [*Drinks off the brandy, then pours and drinks again.*] That 's better!—And now—where are we, Doctor?

TRAHERNE. I have no notion.

CRESPIN. Let 's ask the populace.

[*The natives have been standing at some distance, awe-struck, but chattering eagerly among themselves. The* PRIEST, *intently watching, is silent.* CRESPIN *advances towards him, the natives meanwhile shrinking back in fear. The* PRIEST *salaams slightly and almost contemptuously.* CRESPIN *addresses him in Hindustani, which he evidently does not understand. He in turn pours forth a speech of some length, pointing to the temple and the palace.* CRESPIN *can make nothing of it. While this is proceeding:*

TRAHERNE [*in a low voice, to* LUCILLA]. You were splendid, all through!

LUCILLA. I had perfect faith in you.

TRAHERNE. If I 'd had another pint of petrol, I might have headed for that sort of esplanade behind the castle——

LUCILLA. Yes, I saw it.

TRAHERNE. —and made an easy landing. But I simply had to try for this place, and trust to luck.

LUCILLA. It was n't luck, but your skill, that saved us.

TRAHERNE. You are very good to me.

CRESPIN [*turning*]. It 's no use—he does n't understand a word of Hindustani. You know Russian, don't you, Doctor?

TRAHERNE. A little.

CRESPIN. We must be well on towards Central Asia. Suppose you try him in Russian. Ask him where the deuce we are, and who owns the shooting-box up yonder.

[TRAHERNE *says something to the* PRIEST *in Russian.*]

THE PRIEST [*his face lighting up, points to the earth, and then makes an enveloping gesture to signify the whole country, saying*]. Rukh, Rukh, Rukh, Rukh.

CRESPIN. What the deuce is he Rooking about?

TRAHERNE. Goodness knows.

LUCILLA. I believe I know. Wait a minute. [*Feeling in her pockets.*] I thought I had the paper with me. I read in the *Leader*, just before we started, that the three men who murdered the Political Officer at Abdulabad came from a wild region at the back of the Himalayas, called Rukh.

TRAHERNE. Now that you mention it, I have heard of the place. [*He turns to the* PRIEST *and says a few more words in Russian, pointing to the Palace. The* PRIEST *replies "Raja Sahib" several times over.*]

CRESPIN. Oh, it's Windsor Castle, is it? Well, we'd better make tracks for it. Come, Lucilla.

[*The* PRIEST, *much excited, stops his way, pouring forth a stream of unintelligible language.* TRAHERNE *says something to him in Russian, whereupon he pauses and then says two or three words, slowly and with difficulty—one of them "Raja."*]

TRAHERNE. His Russian is even more limited than mine; but I gather that the Raja has been sent for and will come here.

CRESPIN [*lighting a cigarette*]. All right—then we'd better await developments. [*Seats himself on a green-painted stone. As the* PRIEST *sees this, he makes a rush, hustles* CRESPIN *off, with wild exclamations, and then, disregarding him, makes propitiatory gestures, and mutters formulas of deprecation, to the stone.*]

CRESPIN [*very angry, lays his hand on his revolver-case*]. Confound you, take care what you're doing! You'd better treat us civilly, or——

TRAHERNE [*laying a hand on his arm*]. Gently, gently, Major. This is evidently some sort of sacred enclosure, and you were sitting on one of the gods.

CRESPIN. Well, curse him, he might have told me——

TRAHERNE. If he had you wouldn't have understood. The fellow seems to be the priest—you see, he's begging the god's pardon.

CRESPIN. If I knew his confounded lingo I 'd jolly well make him beg mine.

TRAHERNE. We 'd better be careful not to tread on their corns. We have Mrs. Crespin to think of.

CRESPIN. Confound it, sir, do you think I don't know how to take care of my own wife?

TRAHERNE. I think you 're a little hasty, Major—that 's all. These are evidently queer people, and we 're dependent on them to get us out of our hobble.

LUCILLA [down, left]. Do you think I could sit on this stone without giving offence to the deities?

TRAHERNE. Oh yes, that seems safe enough. [After LU-CILLA is seated.] I don't know how to apologize for having got you into this mess.

LUCILLA. Don't talk nonsense, Dr. Traherne. Who can foresee a Himalayan fog?

TRAHERNE. The only thing to do was to get above it, and then, of course, my bearings were gone.

LUCILLA. Now that we 're safe, I should think it all great fun if it were n't for the children.

CRESPIN. Oh, they don't expect us for a week, and surely it won't take us more than that to get back to civilization.

TRAHERNE. Or, at all events, to a telegraph line.

LUCILLA. I suppose there 's no chance of flying back?

TRAHERNE. Not the slightest, I 'm afraid. I fancy the old 'bus is done for.

LUCILLA. Oh, Dr. Traherne, what a shame! And you 'd only had it a few weeks!

TRAHERNE. What does it matter so long as you are safe?

LUCILLA. What does it matter so long as we 're all safe?

CRESPIN. That 's not what Traherne said. Why pretend to be blind to his—chivalry?

TRAHERNE [trying to laugh it off]. Of course I 'm glad you 're all right, Major, and I 'm not sorry to be in a whole skin myself. But ladies first, you know.

CRESPIN. The perfect knight errant, in fact!

TRAHERNE. Decidedly "errant." I could n't well have gone more completely astray.

LUCILLA. Won't you look at the machine and see if it 's quite hopeless?

TRAHERNE. Yes, at once. [*He goes towards the wreck of the aeroplane and passes out of sight. The populace clustered in and around the temple on the right are intent upon the marvel of the aeroplane, but the* PRIEST *fixes his gaze upon* CRESPIN *and* LUCILLA.]

CRESPIN [*sits beside* LUCILLA *on the stone*]. Well, Lucilla!

LUCILLA. Well?

CRESPIN. That was a narrow squeak.

LUCILLA. Yes, I suppose so.

CRESPIN. All 's well that ends well, eh?

LUCILLA. Of course.

CRESPIN. You don't seem very grateful to Providence.

LUCILLA. For sending the fog?

CRESPIN. For getting us down safely—all three.

LUCILLA. It was Dr. Traherne's nerve that did that. If he had n't kept his head——

CRESPIN. We should have crashed. One or other of us would probably have broken his neck; and if Providence had played up, it might have been the right one.

LUCILLA. What do you mean?

CRESPIN. It might have been me. Then you 'd have thanked God, right enough!

LUCILLA. Why will you talk like this, Antony? If I had n't sent Dr. Traherne away just now, you 'd have been saying these things in his hearing.

CRESPIN. Well, why not? He 's quite one of the family! Don't tell me he does n't know all about the "state of our relations," as they say in the divorce court.

LUCILLA. If he does, it 's not from me. No doubt he knows what the whole station knows.

CRESPIN. And what does the whole station know? Why, that your deadly coldness drives me to drink. I 've lived for three years in an infernal clammy fog like that we passed through. Who's to blame if I take a whiskey-peg now and then, to keep the chill out?

LUCILLA. Oh, Antony, why go over it all again? You know very well it was drink—and other things—that came between us; not my coldness, as you call it, that drove you to drink.

CRESPIN. Oh, you good women! You patter after the parson, "Forgive us as we forgive those that trespass against us." But you don't know what forgiveness means.

LUCILLA. What's the use of it, Antony? Forgive? I have "forgiven" you. I don't try to take the children from you, though it might be better for them if I did. But to forgive is one thing, to forget another. When a woman has seen a man behave as you have behaved, do you think it is possible for her to forget it, and to love him afresh? There are women in novels, and perhaps in the slums, who have such short memories; but I am not one of them.

CRESPIN. No, by Jove, you're not! So a man's whole life is to be ruined——

LUCILLA. Do you think yours is the only life to be ruined?

CRESPIN. Ah, there we have it! I've not only offended your sensibilities; I am in your way. You love this other man, this model of all the virtues!

LUCILLA. You have no right to say that.

CRESPIN [disregarding her protest]. He's a paragon. He's a wonder. He's a mighty microbe-killer before the Lord; he's going to work Heaven knows what miracles, only he hasn't brought them off yet. And you're cursing the mistake you made in marrying a poor devil of a soldierman instead of a first-class scientific genius. Come! Make a clean breast of it! You may as well!

LUCILLA. I have nothing to answer. While I continue to live with you, I owe you an account of my actions—but not of my thoughts.

CRESPIN. Your actions? Oh, I know very well you're too cold—too confounded respectable—to kick over the traces. And then you have the children to think of.

LUCILLA. Yes; I have the children.

CRESPIN. Besides, there's no hurry. If you only have patience for a year or two, I'll do the right thing for once, and drink myself to death.

LUCILLA. You have only to keep yourself a little in hand to live to what they call "a good old age."

CRESPIN. 'Pon my soul, I've a mind to try to, though goodness knows my life is not worth living. I was a fool to come on this crazy expedition——

LUCILLA. Why, it was you yourself that jumped at Dr. Traherne's proposal.

CRESPIN. I thought we'd get to the kiddies a week earlier. They'd be glad to see me, poor little things. They don't despise their daddy.

LUCILLA. It shan't be my fault, Antony, if they ever do. But you don't make it easy to keep up appearances.

CRESPIN. Oh, Lu, Lu, if you would treat me like a human being—if you would help me and make life tolerable for me, instead of a thing that won't bear looking at except through the haze of drink—we might retrieve the early days. Heaven knows I never cared two pins for any woman but you——

LUCILLA. No, the others, I suppose, only helped you, like whiskey, to see the world through a haze. *I* saw the world through a haze when I married you; but you have dispelled it once for all. Don't force me to tell you how impossible it is for me to be your wife again. I am the mother of your children—that gives you a terrible hold over me. Be content with that.

TRAHERNE [*still unseen, calls*]: Oh, Mrs. Crespin! [*He appears, clambering down from the aeroplane.*] I've found in the wreck the newspaper you spoke of—you were right about Rukh.

CRESPIN [*as* TRAHERNE *comes forward*]. What does it say?

TRAHERNE [*reads*]. "Abdulabad, Tuesday. Sentence of death has been passed on the three men found guilty of the murder of Mr. Haredale. It appears that these miscreants are natives of Rukh, a small and little-known independent state among the northern spurs of the Himalayas."

LUCILLA. Yes, that 's what I read.

TRAHERNE. This news is n't the best possible passport for us in our present situation.

LUCILLA. But if we 're hundreds of miles from anywhere, it can't be known here yet.

CRESPIN [*lighting a cigarette*]. In any case, they would n't dare to molest us.

TRAHERNE. All the same it might be safest to burn this paragraph in case there 's anybody here that can read it. [*He tears a strip out of the paper, lights it at* CRESPIN'S *match, watches it burn till he has to drop the flaming remnant of it, upon which he stamps.* LUCILLA *takes the rest of the small local paper and lays it beside her leather coat on the stone, left. The* PRIEST *intently watches all these proceedings.*]

[*Meanwhile strange ululations, mingled with the throb of tom-toms and the clash of cymbals, have made themselves faintly heard from the direction of the mountain path, right.*]

CRESPIN. Hallo! What 's this?

TRAHERNE. Sounds like the march of the Great Panjandrum.

[*The sounds rapidly approach. The natives all run to the point where the path debouches on the open space. They prostrate themselves, some on each side of the way. A wild procession comes down the mountain path. It is headed by a gigantic negro flourishing two naked sabers, and gyrating in a barbaric war-dance. Then come half a dozen musicians with tom-toms and cymbals. Then a litter carried by four bearers. Through its gauze curtains the figure of the* RAJA *can be indistinctly seen. Immediately behind the litter comes* WATKINS, *an English valet, demure and correct, looking as if he had just strolled in from St. James Street. The procession closes with a number of the* RAJA'S *bodyguard, in the most fantastic, parti-coloured attire, and armed with antique match-locks, some of them with barrels six or seven feet long. The* RAJA'S *litter is set down in front of the temple.* WATKINS *opens the curtains and gives his arm to the* RAJA *as he alights. The* RAJA *makes a step towards the European party in silence.*]

*He is a tall, well-built man of forty, dressed in the extreme.
of Eastern gorgeousness.* CRESPIN *advances and salutes.*]

CRESPIN. Does Your Highness speak English?

RAJA. Oh, yes, a little. [*As a matter of fact he speaks it
irreproachably.*]

CRESPIN [*pulling himself together and speaking like a
soldier and a man of breeding*]. Then I have to apologize
for our landing uninvited in your territory.

RAJA. Uninvited, but, I assure you, not unwelcome.

CRESPIN. We are given to understand that this is the
State of Rukh.

RAJA. The kingdom of Rukh, Major—if I rightly read
the symbols on your cuff.

CRESPIN [*again salutes*]. Major Crespin. Permit me to
introduce my wife——

RAJA [*with a profound salaam*]. I am delighted, Madam,
to welcome you to my secluded dominions. You are the first
lady of your nation I have had the honour of receiving.

LUCILLA. Your Highness is very kind.

CRESPIN. And this is Dr. Basil Traherne, whose aeroplane
—or what is left of it—you see.

RAJA. Doctor Traherne? The Doctor Traherne, whose
name I have so often seen in the newspaper? "The Pasteur
of Malaria."

TRAHERNE. The newspapers make too much of my work.
It is very incomplete.

RAJA. But you are an aviator as well?

TRAHERNE. Only as an amateur.

RAJA. I presume it is some misadventure—a most fortunate misadventure for me—that has carried you so far into
the wilds of the Himalayas?

TRAHERNE. Yes—we got lost in the clouds. Major and
Mrs. Crespin were coming up from the plains to see their
children at a hill station——

RAJA. Pahari, no doubt?

TRAHERNE. Yes, Pahari—and I was rash enough to suggest that I might save them three days' traveling by taking
them up in my aeroplane.

RAJA. Madam is a sportswoman, then?

LUCILLA. Oh, I have been up many times.

CRESPIN [*with a tinge of sarcasm*]. Yes, many times.

LUCILLA. It was no fault of Dr. Traherne's that we went astray. The weather was impossible.

RAJA. Well, you have made a sensation here, I can assure you. My people have never seen an aeroplane. They are not sure—simple souls—whether you are gods or demons. But the fact of your having descended in the precincts of a temple of our local goddess—[*with a wave of his hand towards the idol*] allow me to introduce you to her—is considered highly significant.

CRESPIN. I hope, sir, that we shall find no difficulty in obtaining transport back to civ—to India.

RAJA. To civilization, you were going to say? Why hesitate, my dear sir? We know very well that we are barbarians. We are quite reconciled to the fact. We have had some five thousand years to accustom ourselves to it. This sword [*touching his scimitar*] is a barbarous weapon compared with your revolver; but it was worn by my ancestors when yours were daubing themselves blue and picking up a precarious livelihood in the woods. [*Breaking off hastily to prevent any reply.*] But Madam is standing all this time! Watkins, what are you thinking of? Some cushions. [WATKINS *piles some cushions from the litter so as to form a seat for* LUCILLA. *Meanwhile the* RAJA *continues.*] Another litter for Madam, and mountain-chairs for the gentlemen, will be here in a few minutes. Then I hope you will accept the hospitality of my poor house.

LUCILLA. We are giving a great deal of trouble, Your Highness.

RAJA. A great deal of pleasure, Madam.

CRESPIN. But I hope, sir, there will be no difficulty about transport back to—India.

RAJA. Time enough to talk of that, Major, when you have rested and recuperated after your adventure. You will do me the honor of dining with me this evening? I trust you will not find us altogether uncivilized.

LUCILLA [*lightly*]. Your Highness will have to excuse the barbarism of our attire. We have nothing to wear but what we stand up in.

RAJA. Oh, I think we can put that all right. Watkins!

WATKINS [*advancing*]. Your 'Ighness!

RAJA. You are in the confidence of our Mistress of the Robes. How does our wardrobe stand?

WATKINS. A fresh consignment of Paris models come in only last week, Your 'Ighness.

RAJA. Good! Then I hope, Madam, that you may find among them some rag that you will deign to wear.

LUCILLA. Paris models, Your Highness! And you talk of being uncivilized!

RAJA. We do what we can, Madam. I sometimes have the pleasure of entertaining European ladies—though not, hitherto, Englishwomen—in my solitudes; and I like to mitigate the terrors of exile for them. Then, as for civilization, you know, I have always at my elbow one of its most finished products. Watkins!

WATKINS [*stepping forward*]. Your 'Ighness!

RAJA. You will recognize in Watkins, gentleman, another representative of the Ruling Race. [WATKINS, *with downcast eyes, touches his hat to* CRESPIN *and* TRAHERNE.] I assure you he rules me with an iron hand—not always in a velvet glove. Eh, Watkins?

WATKINS. Your 'Ighness will 'ave your joke.

RAJA. He is my Prime Minister and all my Cabinet—but more particularly my Lord Chamberlain. No one can touch him at mixing a cocktail or making a salad. My entire household trembles at his nod; even my *chef* quails before him. Nothing comes amiss to him; for he is, like myself, a man without prejudices. You may be surprised at my praising him to his face in this fashion; you may foresee some danger of—what shall I say?—swelled head. But I know my Watkins; there is not the slightest risk of his outgrowing that modest bowler. He knows his value to me, and he knows that he would never be equally appreciated elsewhere. I have guarantees for his fidelity—eh, Watkins?

WATKINS. I know when I 'm well off, if that 's what Your 'Ighness means.

RAJA. I mean a little more than that—but no matter. I have sometimes thought of instituting a peerage, in order that I might raise Watkins to it. But I must n't let my admiration for British institutions carry me too far. —Those scoundrels of bearers are taking a long time, Watkins.

WATKINS. The lady's litter 'ad to 'ave fresh curtains, Your 'Ighness. They won't be a minute, now.

RAJA. You were speaking of transport, Major—is your machine past repair, Dr. Traherne?

TRAHERNE. Utterly, I 'm afraid.

RAJA. Let us look at it. [*Turns and finds that his body-guards are all clustered on the path, looking at it. He gives a sharp word of command. They scamper into a sort of loose order, up, right.*] Ah, yes—propeller smashed—planes crumpled up——

TRAHERNE. Under-carriage wrecked——

RAJA. I 'm afraid we can't offer to repair the damage for you.

TRAHERNE. I 'm afraid not, sir.

RAJA. A wonderful machine! Yes, Europe has something to boast of. I wonder what the Priest here thinks of it. [*He says a few words to the* PRIEST, *who salaams, and replies volubly at some length.*] He says it is the great roc —the giant bird, you know, of our Eastern stories. And he declares that he plainly saw his Goddess hovering over you as you descended, and guiding you towards her temple.

TRAHERNE. I wish she could have guided us towards the level ground I saw behind your castle. I could have made a safe landing there.

RAJA. No doubt—on my parade ground—almost the only level spot in my dominions.

LUCILLA. These, I suppose, are your bodyguards?

RAJA. My household troops, Madam.

LUCILLA. How picturesque they are!

RAJA. Oh, a relic of barbarism, I know. I can quite

understand the contempt with which my friend the Major is at this moment regarding them.

CRESPIN. Irregular troops, Raja. Often first-class fighting men.

RAJA. And you think that, if irregularity is the virtue of irregular troops, these—what is the expression, Watkins?

WATKINS. Tyke the cyke, Your 'Ighness?

RAJA. That 's it—take the cake—that is what you are thinking?

CRESPIN. Well, they would be hard to beat, sir.

RAJA. I repeat—a relic of barbarism. You see, I have strong conservative instincts—I cling to the fashions of my fathers—and my people would be restive if I did n't. I maintain these fellows, as his Majesty the King-Emperor keeps up the Beefeaters in the Tower. But I also like to move with the times, as perhaps you will allow me to show you. [*He blows two short blasts on a silver whistle hanging round his neck. Instantly from behind every rock and shrub—from every bit of cover—there emerges a soldier, in spick-and-span European uniform (Russian in style), armed with the latest brand of magazine rifles. They stand like statues at attention.*]

CRESPIN. Good Lord!

TRAHERNE. Hallo!

RAJA [*to* LUCILLA, *who makes no move*]. I trust I did not startle you, Madam?

LUCILLA. Oh, not at all. I 'm not nervous.

RAJA. You, of course, realize that this effect is not original. I have plagiarized it from the excellent Walter Scott:

> "These are Clan-Alpine's wariors true,
> And, Saxon, I am Roderick Dhu!"

But I think you 'll admit, Major, that my men know how to take cover.

CRESPIN. By the Lord, sir, they must move like cats—for you can't have planted them there before we arrived.

RAJA. No, you had given me no notice of your coming.

LUCILLA. Perhaps the Goddess did.

RAJA. Not she, Madam. She keeps her own counsel. These men followed me down from the palace and have taken up position while we have been speaking. [*The* RAJA *gives a word of command, and the men rapidly assemble and form in two ranks, an officer on their flank.*]

CRESPIN. A very smart body of men, Raja. Allow me to congratulate you on their training.

RAJA. I am greatly flattered, Major. I superintend it myself.—Ah, here comes the litter. [*Down the path comes a litter borne, like the* RAJA'*s, by four men. It is followed by two mountain-chairs carried by two men apiece.*] Permit me, Madam, to hand you to your palanquin. [*He offers* LUCILLA *his hand. As she rises she picks up her leather coat, and the newspaper falls to the ground. The* RAJA *notices it.*] Forgive me, Madam. [*Picks up the paper and looks at it.*] A newspaper, only two days old! This is such a rarity you must allow me to glance at it. [*He opens the paper and sees that a strip has been torn out from the back page.*] Ah! the telegraphic news gone! What a pity! In my seclusion, I hunger for tidings from the civilized world. [*The* PRIEST *comes forward and speaks to him eagerly, suggesting in pantomime* TRAHERNE'S *action in burning the paper, and pointing to the ashes on the ground, at which the* RAJA *looks.*] You burned this column?

TRAHERNE. Unfortunately, I did.

RAJA. Ah! [*Pause.*] I know your motive, Dr. Traherne, and I appreciate it. You destroyed it out of consideration for my feelings, wishing to spare me a painful piece of intelligence. That was very thoughtful—but quite unnecessary. I already know what you tried to conceal.

CRESPIN. You know—!

TRAHERNE. Your Highness knows——!

[*Simultaneously.*]

RAJA. I know that three of my subjects, accused of a political crime, have been sentenced to death.

TRAHERNE. How is it possible—?

RAJA. Bad news flies fast, Dr. Traherne. But one thing

you can perhaps tell me—is there any chance of their sentences being remitted?

TRAHERNE. I am afraid not, Your Highness.

CRESPIN. Remitted? I should rather say not. It was a cold-blooded, unprovoked murder.

RAJA. Unprovoked, you think? Well, I won't argue the point. And the execution is to be——?

TRAHERNE. I think tomorrow—or the day after.

RAJA. Tomorrow or the day after—yes. [*Turning to* LUCILLA.] Forgive me, Madam—I have kept you waiting.

TRAHERNE. Does Your Highness know anything of these men?

RAJA [*over his shoulder, as he hands* LUCILLA *into the litter*]. Know them? Oh, yes—they are my brothers. [*He seats himself on his own litter and claps his hands twice. Both litters are raised and move off,* LUCILLA'S *first. The regular soldiers line the way, in single rank. They salute as the litters pass.* WATKINS *follows the* ₁RAJA'S. CRESPIN *and* TRAHERNE *seat themselves in their chairs. As they do so:*]

CRESPIN. His brothers? What did he mean?

TRAHERNE [*shrugging his shoulders*]. Heaven knows!

CRESPIN. I don't half like our host, Traherne. There's too much of the cat about him.

TRAHERNE. Or of the tiger. And how the mischief had he got the news?

[*As the two chairs move off,* CRESPIN *first, the two ranks of soldiers close round them. The irregulars and musicians, headed by the dancing negro, bring up the rear. The* PRIEST *prostrates himself, as if in thanksgiving, before the Goddess.*]

ACT II

A spacious and well-proportioned room, opening at the back upon a wide loggia. Beyond the loggia can be seen distant snow-peaks and a strip of sky. Late afternoon light.

The room is furnished in a once splendid but now very old-
fashioned and faded style. Furniture of black picked out
with gold, and upholstered in yellow damask. A great
crystal chandelier in the middle of the ceiling, and under it a
circular ottoman. Right, a large two-leaved door; left, a
handsome marble fireplace, with a mirror over it. Candle-
sticks with crystal pendants at each end of the mantelpiece,
and in the middle a bronze statuette, some eighteen inches
high, representing the many-armed Goddess. A wood fire
laid, but unlighted. Near the fireplace, two quite modern
saddle-bag armchairs, out of keeping with the stiffness of the
remaining furniture. A small table near the door, right,
with modern English and French books on it. A handsome
gramophone in the corner, right. On the walls, left and
right, some very bad paintings of fine-looking Orientals in
gorgeous attire. Electric lights.

TRAHERNE *discovered at back, center, looking out over the*
landscape. He does not go out upon the loggia (which can
be entered both right and left without passing through the
room) because two turbaned servants are there, under the
direction of an old and dignified Major-domo, arranging a
luxurious dinner table, with four covers. TRAHERNE *stands*
motionless for a moment. Then enters CRESPIN *by the door,*
right, ushered in by a servant, who salaams and retires.

CRESPIN. Ah, there you are, Doctor.

TRAHERNE [*turning*]. Hullo! How did you get on?

CRESPIN. All right. Had a capital tub. And you?

TRAHERNE. Feeling more like a human being. And what
about Mrs. Crespin? I hope she's all right.

CRESPIN. She was taken off by an ayah as soon as we got
in—presumably to the women's quarters.

TRAHERNE. And you let her go off alone?

CRESPIN. What the blazes could I do? I couldn't thrust
myself into the women's quarters.

TRAHERNE. You could have kept her with you.

CRESPIN. Do you think she'd have stayed? And, come
to that, what business is it of yours?

TRAHERNE. It 's any man's business to be concerned for a woman's safety.

CRESPIN. Well, well—all right. But there was nothing I could have done or that she would let me do. And I don't think there 's any danger.

TRAHERNE. Let us hope not.

CRESPIN. It 's a vast shanty this.

TRAHERNE. It 's a palace and a fortress in one.

CRESPIN. A devilish strong place before the days of big guns. But a couple of howitzers would soon make it look pretty foolish.

TRAHERNE. No doubt; but how would you get them here?

CRESPIN [*looking at the dinner table*]. I say—it looks as if our friend were going to do us well. [*One of the servants comes in with a wine-cooler. When the man has gone,* CRESPIN *picks up the bottle and looks at the label.*] Perrier Jouet, nineteen-o-six, by the lord! [*He strolls over to the ottoman, and seats himself, facing the fireplace.*] It 's a rum start this, Traherne. I suppose you intellectual chaps would call it romantic.

TRAHERNE [*examining the figure of the Goddess on the mantelpiece.*] More romantic than agreeable, I should say. I don't like the looks of this lady.

CRESPIN. What is she?

TRAHERNE. The same figure we saw in the little temple, where we landed.

CRESPIN. How many arms has she got?

TRAHERNE. Six.

CRESPIN. She could give you a jolly good hug, anyway.

TRAHERNE. You would n't want another.

CRESPIN. Where do you suppose we really are, Traherne?

TRAHERNE. On the map, you mean?

CRESPIN. Of course.

TRAHERNE. Oh, in the never-never land. Somewhere on the way to Bokhara. I 've been searching my memory for all I ever heard about Rukh. I fancy very little is known, except .that it seems to send forth a peculiarly poisonous breed of fanatics.

CRESPIN. Like those who did poor Haredale in?

TRAHERNE. Precisely.

CRESPIN. D'you think our host was serious when he said they were his brothers? Or was he only pulling our leg, curse his impudence?

TRAHERNE. He probably meant caste-brothers, or simply men of the same race. But, even so, it's awkward.

CRESPIN. I don't see what these beggars, living at the back of the north wind, have got to do with Indian politics. We've never interfered with them.

TRAHERNE. Oh, it's a case of Asia for the Asians. Ever since the Japanese beat the Russians, the whole continent has been itching to kick us out.

CRESPIN. So that they may cut each other's throats at leisure, eh?

TRAHERNE. We Westerners never cut each other's throats, do we?

[WATKINS *has entered at the back, right, carrying a silver center-piece for the table. He sets it down and is going out to the left, when* CRESPIN *catches sight of him and hails him.*]

CRESPIN. Hallo! You there! What's your name!

[WATKINS *stops.*] Just come here a minute, will you?

WATKINS. Meaning me, sir? [*He advances into the room. There is a touch of covert insolence in his manner.*]

CRESPIN. Yes, you, Mr.——? Mr——?

WATKINS. Watkins is my name, sir.

CRESPIN. Right ho! Watkins. Can you tell us where we are, Watkins?

WATKINS. They calls the place Rukh, sir.

CRESPIN. Yes, yes, we know that. But where is Rukh?

WATKINS. I hunderstand these mountains is called the 'Imalayas, sir.

CRESPIN. Confound it, sir, we don't want a lesson in geography!

WATKINS. No, sir? My mistake, sir.

TRAHERNE. Major Crespin means that we want to know how far we are from the nearest point in India.

WATKINS. I really could n't say, sir. Not so very far, I dessay, as the crow flies.

TRAHERNE. Unfortunately we 're not in a position to fly with the crow. How long does the journey take?

WATKINS. They tell me it takes about three weeks to Cashmere.

CRESPIN. They tell you! Surely you must remember how long it took you?

WATKINS. No, sir, excuse me, sir—I 've never been in India.

CRESPIN. Not been in India? And I was just thinking, as I looked at you, that I seemed to have seen you before.

WATKINS. Not in India, sir. We might 'ave met in England, but I don 't call to mind having that pleasure.

CRESPIN. But if you have n't been in India, how the mischief did you get here?

WATKINS. I came with 'Is 'Ighness, sir, by way of Tashkent. All our dealin 's with Europe is by way of Russia.

TRAHERNE. But it 's possible to get to India direct, and not by way of Central Asia?

WATKINS. Oh, yes, it 's done, sir. But I 'm told there are some very tight places to negotiate—like the camel and the needle 's eye, as you might say.

TRAHERNE. Difficult travelling for a lady, eh?

WATKINS. Next door to himpossible, I should guess, sir.

CRESPIN. A nice look-out, Traherne! [*To* WATKINS.] Tell me, my man—is His Highness—h 'm—married?

WATKINS. Oh, yessir—very much so, sir.

CRESPIN. Children?

WATKINS. He has fifteen sons, sir.

CRESPIN. The daughters don 't count, eh?

WATKINS. I 've never 'ad a hopportunity of counting 'em, sir.

TRAHERNE. He said the men accused of assassinating a political officer were his brothers——

WATKINS [*quickly*]. Did 'e say that, sir?

TRAHERNE. Did n't you hear him? What did he mean?

WATKINS. I 'm sure I could n't say, sir. 'Is 'Ighness is what you 'd call a very playful gentleman, sir.

TRAHERNE. But I don't see the joke in saying that.

WATKINS. No, sir? P'raps 'Is 'Ighness 'll explain, sir. [*A pause.*]

CRESPIN. Your master spoke of visits from European ladies—do they come from Russia?

WATKINS. From various parts, I understand, sir.

CRESPIN. Any here now?

WATKINS. I really could n't say, sir.

TRAHERNE. They don't dine with His Highness?

WATKINS. Oh no, sir. 'Is 'Ighness sometimes sups with them.

CRESPIN. And my wife—Mrs. Crespin——?

WATKINS. Make your mind easy, sir—the lady won't meet any hundesirable characters, sir. I give strict orders to the —the female what took charge of the lady.

TRAHERNE. She is to be trusted?

WATKINS. Habsolutely, sir. She is—in a manner of speakin',—my wife, sir.

CRESPIN. Mrs. Watkins, eh?

WATKINS. Yessir—I suppose you would say so.

TRAHERNE. But now look here, Watkins—you say we 're three weeks away from Cashmere—yet the Raja knew of the sentence passed on these subjects of his, who were tried only three days ago. How do you account for that?

WATKINS. I can't sir. All I can say is, there 's queer things goes on here.

TRAHERNE. Queer things? What do you mean?

WATKINS. Well, sir, them priests you know—they goes in a lot for what 'Is 'Ighness calls magic——

TRAHERNE. Oh come, Watkins—you don't believe in that!

WATKINS. Well, sir, p'raps not. I don't, not to say, believe in it. But there 's queer things goes on. I can't say no more, nor I can't say no less. If you 'll excuse me, sir, I must just run my eye over the dinner-table. 'Is 'Ighness will be here directly. [*He retires, inspects the table, makes one or two changes, and presently goes out by the back, left.*]

CRESPIN. That fellow's either a cunning rascal or a cursed fool. Which do you think?

TRAHERNE. I don't believe he's the fool he'd like us to take him for.—Ah, here is Mrs. Crespin.

[*Enter* LUCILLA, *right, ushered in by a handsome* AYAH. *She is dressed in a gauzy gown of quite recent style, dark blue or crimson. Not in the least décolletée. At most the sleeves might be open, so as to show her arms to the elbow. No ornaments except a gold locket on a little gold chain round her neck. The costume is absolutely plain, but in striking contrast to her traveling dress. Her hair is beautifully arranged.*]

LUCILLA [*to the* AYAH]. Thank you. [*The* AYAH *disappears.* LUCILLA *advances, holding out her skirt a little.*] Behold the Paris model!

CRESPIN. My eye, Lu, what a ripping frock!

TRAHERNE. Talk of magic, Major! There's something in what our friend says.

LUCILLA. What is that? What about magic?

CRESPIN. We'll tell you afterwards. Let's have your adventures first.

LUCILLA. No adventures precisely—only a little excursion into the Arabian Nights.

TRAHERNE. Do tell us!

LUCILLA [*evidently a little nervous, yet not without enjoyment of the experience*]. Well, my guide—the woman you saw—led me along corridor after corridor, and upstairs and downstairs, till we came to a heavy bronze door where two villainous-looking blacks, with crooked swords, were on guard. I didn't like the looks of them a bit; but I was in for it and had to go on. They drew their swords and flourished a sort of salute, grinning with all their teeth. Then the ayah clapped her hands twice, some one inspected us through a grating in the door, and the ayah said a word or two——

TRAHERNE. No doubt "Open sesame!"

LUCILLA. The door was opened by a hideous, humpbacked old woman, just like the wicked fairy in a pantomime. She did n't actually bite me, but she looked as if she 'd like to—and we passed on. More corridors, with curtained doorways, where I had a feeling that furtive eyes were watching me—though I can't positively say I saw them. But I 'm sure I heard whisperings and titterings——

CRESPIN. Good Lord! If I 'd thought they were going to treat you like that, I 'd have——

LUCILLA. Oh, there was nothing you could have done; and, you see, no harm came of it. At last the woman led me into a large sort of wardrobe room, lighted from above, and almost entirely lined with glazed presses full of frocks. Then she slid back a panel, and there was a marble-lined bath room!—a deep pool, with a trickle of water flowing into it from a dolphin's head of gold—just enough to make the surface ripple and dance. And all around were the latest Bond Street luxuries—shampooing bowls and brushes, bottles of essences, towels on hot rails and all the rest of it. The only thing that was disagreeable was a sickly odor from some burning pastilles—oh, and a coal-black bath-woman.

TRAHERNE. It suggests a Royal Academy picture—''The Odalisque's Pool.''

CRESPIN. Or a soap advertisement.

TRAHERNE. Same thing.

LUCILLA. Well, I was n't sorry to play the odalisque for once; and when I had finished, lo and behold! the ayah had laid out for me half-a-dozen gorgeous and distinctly risky dinner-gowns. I had to explain to her in gestures that I could n't live up to any of them, and would rather put on my old travelling dress. She seemed quite frightened at the idea——

CRESPIN. Ha ha! She 'd probably have got the sack—perhaps literally—if she 'd let you do that.

LUCILLA. Anyway, she at last produced this comparatively inoffensive frock. She did my hair, and wanted to finish me off with all sorts of necklaces and bangles, but I stuck to my old locket with the babies' heads.

CRESPIN. Well, all 's well that ends well, I suppose. But

if I 'd foreseen all this "Secrets of the Zenana" business,
I 'm dashed if I would n't——

LUCILLA [cutting him short]. What were you saying
about magic when I came in?

TRAHERNE. Only that this man, Watkins—he 's the husband of your ayah, by the way—says queer things go on
here, and pretends to believe in magic.

LUCILLA. Do you know, Antony, when the Raja was
speaking about him down there, it seemed to me that his
face was somehow familiar to me.

CRESPIN. There, Doctor! What did I say? I knew I 'd
seen him before, but I 'm blowed if I can place him.

LUCILLA. I wish I could get a good look at him.

[WATKINS enters, back, left, with something for the
table.]

TRAHERNE. There he is. Shall I call him in?

LUCILLA. Say I want him to thank his wife from me.

TRAHERNE [calls]. Watkins!

WATKINS. Sir?

TRAHERNE. Mrs. Crespin would like to speak to you.
[WATKINS comes forward.]

LUCILLA. I hear, Watkins, that the ayah who so kindly
attended to me is your wife.

WATKINS. That 's right, ma 'am.

LUCILLA. She gave me most efficient assistance, and, as
she seems to know no English, I could n't thank her. Will
you be good enough to tell her how much I appreciated all
she did for me?

WATKINS. Thank you kindly, ma 'am. She 'll be proud
to hear it. [Pause.] Is that all, ma 'am?

LUCILLA. That 's all, thank you, Watkins.

[He returns to the loggia, but goes to the other side of
the dinner-table and keeps an eye on the three.]

CRESPIN. You 've a good memory for faces, Lu. Do you
spot him?

LUCILLA. Don't let him see we 're talking about him. I
believe I do know him, but I 'm not quite sure. Do you remember, the first year we were in India, there was a man of

the Dorsets that used often to be on guard outside the mess-room?

CRESPIN. By heaven, you 've hit it!

TRAHERNE. Take care! He 's watching.

LUCILLA. You remember he deserted, and was suspected of having murdered a woman in the bazaar.

CRESPIN. I believe it 's the very man.

LUCILLA. It 's certainly very like him.

CRESPIN. And he swears he 's never been in India!

TRAHERNE. Under the circumstances, he naturally would.

LUCILLA. At all events, he 's not a man to be trusted.

[*At this moment the* RAJA *enters by the door, right. He is in faultless European evening dress—white waistcoat, white tie, etc. No jewels, except the ribbon and star of a Russian order. Nothing oriental about him except his turban and his complexion.*]

RAJA [*as he enters*]. Pray forgive me, Madam, for being the last to appear. The fact is, I had to hold a sort of Cabinet Council—or shall I say a conclave of prelates?—with regard to questions arising out of your most welcome arrival.

CRESPIN. May we hope, Raja, that you were laying a dawk for our return?

RAJA. Pray, pray, Major, let us postpone that question for the moment. First, let us fortify ourselves; after dinner we will talk seriously. If you are in too great a hurry to desert me, must I not conclude, Madam, that you are dis-satisfied with your reception?

LUCILLA. How could we possibly be so ungrateful, Your Highness? Your hospitality overwhelms us.

RAJA. I trust my Mistress of the Robes furnished you with all you required?

LUCILLA. With all and more than all. She offered me quite a bewildering array of gorgeous apparel.

RAJA. Oh, I am glad. I had hoped that perhaps your choice might have fallen on something more—[*He indicates by gestures, "décolleté".*] But no—I was wrong—Madam's taste is irreproachable.

[*A servant enters from behind with cocktails on a silver salver.* LUCILLA *refuses. The men accept.* LUCILLA *picks up a yellow French book on one of the tables.*]

RAJA. You see, Madam, we fall behind the age here. We are still in the Anatole France period. If he bores you, here [*picking up another book*] is a Maurice Barrès that you may find more amusing.

LUCILLA. Oh, I too am in the Anatole France period, I assure you. [*Reads.*] "Sur la Pierre Blanche"—is n't that the one you were recommending to me, Dr. Traherne?

TRAHERNE. Yes, I like it better than some of his later books.

RAJA [*picking up a silver-grey book*]. As for Bernard Shaw, I suppose he 's quite a back number; but I confess his impudence entertains me. What do you say, Major?

CRESPIN. Never read a line of the fellow—except in *John Bull.*

LUCILLA and TRAHERNE [*simultaneously*]. In *John Bull!*

CRESPIN. Somebody told me he wrote in *John Bull*—does n't he?

RAJA. Are you fond of music, Mrs. Crespin? [*Goes to the gramophone, and turns over some records, till he finds one which he lays on the top of the pile.*] Suppose we have some during dinner. [WATKINS *enters from the back, left.*] Watkins, just start this top record, will you. [WATKINS *does so.*]

[*At this moment the* MAJOR-DOMO *enters from the back, and says a few words.*]

RAJA. Ah! *Madame est servie!* Allow me— [*He offers* LUCILLA *his arm and leads her to the table. The others follow.*] Will you take this seat, Madam? You here, Major—Dr. Traherne! [*He himself sits to the left of the table;* LUCILLA *on his right;* TRAHERNE *opposite him; and* CRESPIN *opposite* LUCILLA, *with his back to the sunset, which is now flooding the scene.*]

[*As the servants offer dishes.*] I can recommend this caviar, Major—and you 'll take a glass of maraschino with it—Russian fashion.

[*Just as they sit down the gramophone reels out the first bars of a piece of music.*]

LUCILLA [*after listening a moment*]. Oh, what is that?

RAJA. Don't you know it?

LUCILLA. Oh yes, but I can't think what it is.

RAJA. Gounod's "Funeral March of a Marionette"—a most humorous composition. May I pour you a glass of maraschino? [*He goes on talking as*

THE CURTAIN FALLS

When it rises again, the glow has faded, and some big stars are pulsing in the strip of purple sky. The party is just finishing dinner. Dessert is on the table, which is lighted by electric lamps. WATKINS *stands behind the* RAJA'S *chair. The* MAJOR-DOMO *and other servants hover round. The* RAJA *has just finished a story, at which all laugh. A short pause.*]

LUCILLA. What a heavenly night!

RAJA. Yes, our summer climate is far from bad.

LUCILLA. The air is like champagne.

RAJA. A little over frappé for some tastes. What do you say, Madam? Shall we have coffee indoors? There is an edge to the air at these altitudes, as soon as the sun has gone down.

LUCILLA [*shivers slightly*]. Yes, I do feel a little chilly.

RAJA. Watkins, send for a shawl for Madam. [*Rising.*] And ah—let us have the fire lighted. [WATKINS *goes off to the left. The* RAJA *says a word to the* MAJOR-DOMO, *who touches a switch in one of the pillars of the loggia opening. The chandelier and wall-lamps of the salon burst into brilliant light.*]

RAJA [*offering his arms to* LUCILLA]. Let me find you a comfortable seat, Madam. [*He leads her to the farther back of the two arm-chairs.*] When the fire is lighted, I think you will find this quite pleasant. Take the other chair, Major. [CRESPIN *does so.*] I must really refurnish this salon. My ancestors had no notion of comfort. To tell the truth, I use the room only on state occasions, like the present. [*Bowing to* LUCILLA.] I have a much more modern snuggery upstairs, which I hope you will see tomorrow.

[*Servants hand round coffee, liqueurs, cigars, cigarettes, during what follows. One of them lights the fire, of aromatic wood.*]

RAJA [*to* TRAHERNE *who has remained at the loggia opening, looking out into the night.*] Star-gazing, Dr. Traherne?

TRAHERNE. I beg your pardon. [*Comes forward.*]

LUCILLA. Dr. Traherne is quite an astronomer.

RAJA. As much at home with the telescope as with the microscope, eh?

TRAHERNE. Oh no. I'm no astronomer. I can pick out a few of the constellations,—that's all.

RAJA. For my part, I look at the stars as little as possible. As a spectacle they're monotonous, and they don't bear thinking of.

[*The* AYAH, *entering by door, right, brings* LUCILLA *a shawl, which the* RAJA *places on her shoulders.*]

LUCILLA. What an exquisite shawl!

RAJA. And most becoming—don't you think so, Doctor? [TRAHERNE *is gazing at* LUCILLA.] My Mistress of the Robes has chosen well! [*He makes a motion of noiseless applause to the* AYAH, *who grins and exit, right.*]

LUCILLA. Why won't the stars bear thinking of, Raja?

RAJA. Well, dear lady, don't you think they're rather ostentatious? *I* was guilty of a little showing-off today, when I played that foolish trick with my regular troops. But think of the Maharaja up yonder [*pointing upwards*] who night after night whistles up his glittering legions, and puts them through their deadly punctual drill, as much as to say, "See what a devil of a fellow *I* am!" Do you think it quite in good taste, Madam?

TRAHERNE [*laughing*]. I'm afraid you're jealous, Raja. You don't like having to play second fiddle to a still more absolute ruler.

RAJA. Perhaps you're right, Doctor—perhaps it's partly

that. But there's something more to it. I can't help resenting— [*To* CRESPIN, *to whom a servant is offering liqueurs.*] Let me recommend the kümmel, Major. I think you 'll find it excellent.

TRAHERNE. What is it you resent?

RAJA. Oh, the respect paid to mere size—to the immensity, as they call it, of the universe. Are we to worship a god because he's big?

TRAHERNE. If you resent his bigness, what do you say to his littleness? The microscope, you know, reveals him no less than the telescope.

RAJA. And reveals him in the form of death-dealing specks of matter, which you, I understand, Doctor, are impiously proposing to exterminate.

TRAHERNE. I am trying to marshal the life-saving against the death-dealing powers.

RAJA. To marshal God's right hand against his left, eh? or *vice versa?* But I admit you have the pull of the astronomers, in so far as you deal in life, not in dead mechanism. [*Killing a gnat on the back of his hand*]. This mosquito that I have just killed—I am glad to see you smoke, Madam: it helps to keep them off—this mosquito, or any smallest thing that has life in it, is to me far more admirable than a whole lifeless universe. What do you say, Major?

CRESPIN [*smoking a cigar*]. I say, Raja, that if you 'll tell that fellow to give me another glass of kümmel, I 'll let you have your own way about the universe. [*The* RAJA *says a word to one of the servants, who refills* CRESPIN'*s glass.*]

LUCILLA. But what if the mechanism, as you call it, isn't dead? What if the stars are swarming with life?

TRAHERNE. Yes—suppose there are planets, which of course we can't see, circling round each of the great suns we do see? And suppose they are all inhabited?

RAJA. I 'd rather not suppose it. Isn't one inhabited world bad enough? Do we want it multiplied by millions?

LUCILLA. Haven't you just been telling us that a living gnat is more wonderful than a dead universe?

RAJA. Wonderful? Yes, by all means—wonderful as a

device for torturing and being tortured. Oh, I 'm neither a saint nor an ascetic—I take life as I find it—I am tortured and I torture. But there 's one thing I 'm really proud of —I 'm proud to belong to the race of the Buddha, who first found out that life was a colossal blunder.

LUCILLA [*in a low voice*]. Should you like the sky to be starless? That seems to me—forgive me, Prince—the last word of impiety.

RAJA. Possibly, Madam. How my esteemed fellow-creatures were ever bluffed into piety is a mystery to me. Not that I 'm complaining. If men could not be bluffed by the Raja above, much less would they be bluffed by us Rajas below. And though life is a contemptible business, I don't deny that power is the best part of it.

TRAHERNE. In short, your Highness is a Superman.

RAJA. Ah, you read Nietzsche? Yes, if I were n't of the kindred of the Buddha, I should like to be of the race of that great man.

[*The servants have now all withdrawn.*]

LUCILLA [*looking out*]. There is the moon rising over the snowfields. I hope you would n't banish her from the heavens?

RAJA. Oh no—I like her silly, good-natured face. And she 's useful to lovers and brigands and other lawless vagabonds, with whom I have great sympathy. Besides, I don't know that she 's so silly either. She seems to be for ever raising her eyebrows in mild astonishment at human folly.

CRESPIN. All this is out of my depths, your Highness. We 've had a rather fatiguing day. Might n't we——?

RAJA. To be sure. I only waited till the servants had gone. Now, are you all quite comfortable?

LUCILLA. Quite.

TRAHERNE. Perfectly, thank you.

CRESPIN. Perfectly.

RAJA [*smoking a cigar, and standing with his back to the fire*]. Then we 'll go into committee upon your position here.

CRESPIN. If you please, sir.

RAJA. I 'm afraid you may find it rather disagreeable.

CRESPIN. Communications bad, eh? We have a difficult journey before us?

RAJA. A long journey, I fear—yet not precisely difficult.

CRESPIN. It surely can't be so very far, since you had heard of the sentence passed on those assassins.

RAJA. I am glad, Major, that you have so tactfully spared me the pain of re-opening that subject. We should have had to come to it, sooner or later. [*An embarrassed pause.*]

TRAHERNE. When your Highness said they were your brothers, you were, of course, speaking figuratively. You meant your tribesmen?

RAJA. Not at all. They are sons of my father—not of my mother.

LUCILLA. And we intrude upon you at such a time! How dreadful!

RAJA. Oh, pray don't apologize. Believe me, your arrival has given great satisfaction.

TRAHERNE. How do you mean?

RAJA. I'll explain presently. But first——

CRESPIN [*interrupting*]. First, let us understand each other. You surely can't approve of this abominable crime?

RAJA. My brothers are fanatics, and there is no fanaticism in me.

LUCILLA. How do they come to be so different from you?

RAJA. That is just what I was going to tell you. I was my father's eldest son, by his favorite wife. Through my mother's influence (my poor mother—how I loved her!) I was sent to Europe. My education was wholly European. I shed all my prejudices. I became the open-minded citizen of the world whom I hope you recognize in me. My brothers, on the other hand, turned to India for their culture. The religion of our people has always been a primitive idolatry. My brothers naturally fell in with adherents of the same superstition, and they worked each other up to a high pitch of frenzy against the European exploitation of Asia.

TRAHERNE. Had you no restraining influence upon them?

RAJA. Of course I might have imprisoned them—or had

them strangled—the traditional form of argument in our family. But why should I? As I said, I have no prejudices —least of all in favor of the British raj. We are of Indian race, though long severed from the Motherland—and I do not love her tyrants.

CRESPIN [*who has had quite enough to drink*]. In short, sir, you defend this wicked murder?

RAJA. Oh no—I think it foolish and futile. But there is a romantic as well as a practical side to my nature, and, from the romantic point of view, I rather admire it.

CRESPIN [*rising*]. Then, sir, the less we intrude on your hospitality the better. If you will be good enough to furnish us with transport tomorrow morning——

RAJA. That is just where the difficulty arises——

CRESPIN. No transport, hey?

RAJA. Materially it might be managed; but morally I fear it is—excuse the colloquialism, Madam—no go.

CRESPIN. What the blazes do you mean, sir——?

LUCILLA [*trying to cover his bluster*]. Will your Highness be good enough to explain?

RAJA. I mentioned that the religion of my people is a primitive superstition? Well, since the news has spread that three Feringhis have dropped from the skies precisely at the time when three princes of the royal house are threatened with death at the hands of the Feringhi government,—and dropped, moreover, in the precincts of a temple—my subjects have got it into their heads that you have been personally conducted hither by the Goddess whom they especially worship.

LUCILLA. The Goddess——?

RAJA [*turning to the statuette*]. Here is her portrait on the mantelpiece—much admired by connoisseurs. [LUCILLA *cannot repress a shudder.*] I need not say that I am far from sharing the popular illusion. Your arrival is, of course, the merest coincidence—for me, a charming coincidence. But my people hold unphilosophic views. I understand that even in England the vulgar are apt to see the Finger of

Providence in particularly fortunate—or unfortunate—occurrences.

CRESPIN. Then the upshot of all this palaver is that you propose to hold us as hostages, to exchange for your brothers?

RAJA. That is not precisely the idea, my dear sir. My theologians do not hold that an exchange is what the Goddess decrees. Nor, to be quite frank, would it altogether suit my book.

LUCILLA. Not to get your brothers back again?

RAJA. You may have noted in history, Madam, that family affection is seldom the strong point of Princes. Is it not Pope who remarks on their lack of enthusiasm for "a brother near the throne?" My sons are mere children, and were I to die—we are all mortal—there might be trouble about the succession. In our family, uncles seldom love nephews.

LUCILLA. So you would raise no finger to save your brothers?

RAJA. That is not my only reason. Supposing it possible that I could bully the Government of India into giving up my relatives, do you think it would sit calmly down under the humiliation? No, no, dear lady. It might wait a few years to find some decent pretext, but assuredly we should have a punitive expedition. It would cost thousands of lives and millions of money, but what would that matter? Prestige would be restored, and I should end my days in a maisonette in Petrograd. It wouldn't suit me at all. Hitherto I have escaped the notice of your Government by a policy of masterly inactivity, and I propose to adhere to that policy.

CRESPIN. Then I don't see how——

TRAHERNE [simultaneously]. Surely you don't mean——?

RAJA. We are approaching the crux of the matter—a point which I fear you may have some difficulty in appreciating. I would beg you to remember that, though I am what is commonly called an autocrat, there is no such thing under the sun as real despotism. All government is government by consent of the people. It is very stupid of them to consent—but they do. I have studied the question—I took a pretty good degree at Cambridge, in Moral and Political Science—and I assure you that, though I have absolute power of life and death over my subjects, it is only their acquiescence that gives me that power. If I defied their prejudices or their passions, they could upset my throne tomorrow.

CRESPIN [*angrily*]. Will you be so kind as to come to the point, sir?

RAJA. Gently, Major! We shall reach it soon enough. [*To* LUCILLA.] Please remember, too, Madam, that an autocracy is generally a theocracy to boot, and mine is a case in point. I am a slave to theology. The clerical party can do what it pleases with me, for there is no other party to oppose it. True, I am my own Archbishop of Canterbury—but "I have a partner: Mr. Jorkins"—I have a terribly exacting Archbishop of York. I fear I may have to introduce you to him tomorrow.

LUCILLA. You are torturing us, your Highness. Like my husband, I beg you to come to the point.

RAJA. The point is, dear lady, that the theology on which, as I say, my whole power is founded, has not yet emerged from the Mosaic stage of development: it demands an eye for an eye, a tooth for a tooth—

[*A long pause.*]

a life for a life.

[*Another pause.*]

TRAHERNE. You mean to say——

RAJA. Unfortunately, I do.

LUCILLA. You would kill us——?

RAJA. Not I, Madam—the clerical party. And only if my brothers are executed. If not, I will merely demand your word of honor that what has passed between us shall never be mentioned to any human soul—and you shall go free.

CRESPIN. But if your brother assassins are hanged—as assuredly they will be—you will put to death in cold blood——

RAJA [*interrupting*]. Oh, not in cold blood, Major. There

TRAHERNE. Wireless!

CRESPIN [*much excited*]. Wireless, by Jupiter! They're sending out a message.

TRAHERNE. That accounts for it! They're in wireless communication with India!

LUCILLA [*to* TRAHERNE]. Antony knows all about wireless.

CRESPIN. I should rather think so! Wasn't it my job all through the war! If I could hear more distinctly now—and if they're transmitting in clear—I could read their message.

TRAHERNE. That may be our salvation!

CRESPIN. If we could get control of the wireless for five minutes, and call up the aerodrome at Amil-Serai——

LUCILLA. What then?

CRESPIN. Why, we'd soon bring the Raja to his senses.

LUCILLA [*to* CRESPIN]. Where do you suppose the installation is?

CRESPIN. Somewhere overhead I should say.

TRAHERNE. We must go very cautiously, Major. We must on no account let the Raja suspect that we know anything about wireless telegraphy, else he'd take care we should never get near the installation.

CRESPIN. Right you are, Traherne—I'll lie very low.

LUCILLA [*tearing off the shawl*]. And how are we to behave to that horrible man?

CRESPIN. We must keep a stiff upper lip, and play the game.

LUCILLA. You mean pretend to take part in his ghastly comedy of hospitality and politeness?

TRAHERNE. If you can, it would be wisest. His delight in showing off his European polish is all in our favor. But for that he might separate us and lock us up. We must avoid that at all costs.

LUCILLA. Oh, yes, yes——

CRESPIN. You've always had plenty of pluck, Lu—. Now's the time to show it.

LUCILLA [*putting on the shawl again*]. You can trust me.

The thought of the children knocked me over at first; but I 'm not afraid to die. [*The chittering sound ceases, and the lights suddenly go up again*]. The noise has stopped.

CRESPIN. Yes, they 've left off transmitting, and ceased to draw on the electric current.

TRAHERNE. He 'll be back presently. Don't let us seem to be consulting.

[TRAHERNE *seats himself in an easy chair.* LUCILLA *sits on the ottoman.* CRESPIN *lights a cigar and takes the* RAJA'S *place before the fire.*]

CRESPIN. Curse it! I can't remember the wave-length and the call for Amil-Serai. I was constantly using it at one time.

TRAHERNE. It 'll come back to you.

CRESPIN. I pray to the Lord it may!

[*The* RAJA *enters, right.*]

RAJA. I promised you news, and it has come.

CRESPIN. What news?

RAJA. My brothers' execution is fixed for the day after tomorrow.

LUCILLA. Then the day after tomorrow——?

RAJA. Yes—at sunset. [*A pause.*] But meanwhile I hope you will regard my poor house as your own. This is Liberty Hall. My tennis courts, my billiard-room, my library are all at your disposal. I should not advise you to pass the palace gates—it would not be safe, for popular feeling, I must warn you, runs very high. Besides, where could you go? There are three hundred miles of almost impassable country between you and the nearest British post.

TRAHERNE. In that case, Prince, how do you communicate with India? How has this news reached you?

RAJA. Does that puzzle you?

TRAHERNE. Naturally.

RAJA. You don't guess?

TRAHERNE. We have been trying to. The only thing we could think of was that you must be in wireless communication.

RAJA. You observed nothing to confirm the idea?

TRAHERNE. Why, no.

RAJA. Did you not notice that the lights suddenly went down?

TRAHERNE. Yes, and at the same time we heard a peculiar hissing sound.

RAJA. None of you knew what it meant?

TRAHERNE. No.

RAJA. Then you have no knowledge of wireless telegraphy?

TRAHERNE. None.

RAJA. I may tell you, then, that that hissing is the sound of wireless transmission. I am in communication with India.

TRAHERNE [to the others]. You see, I was right.

CRESPIN. You have a wireless expert here then?

RAJA. Watkins,—that invaluable fellow—he is my operator.

TRAHERNE. And with whom do you communicate?

RAJA. Do you think that quite a fair question, Doctor? Does it show your usual tact? I have my agents— I can say no more. [Pause.] Shall I ring for the ayah, Madam, to see you to your room?

LUCILLA. If you please. [As he has his finger on the bell, she says.] No; stay a moment. [Rises and advances towards him.] Prince, I have two children. If it weren't for them, don't imagine that any of us would beg a favor at your hands. But for their sakes won't you instruct your agent to communicate with Simla and try to bring about an exchange—your brothers' lives for ours?

RAJA. I am sorry, Madam, but I have already told you why that is impossible. Even if your Government agreed, it would assuredly take revenge on me for having extorted such a concession. No whisper of your presence here must ever reach India, or—again forgive the vulgarism—my goose is cooked.

LUCILLA. The thought of my children does not move you?

RAJA. My brothers have children—does the thought of

them move the Government of India? No, Madam, I am
desolated to have to refuse you, but you must not ask for
the impossible. [*He presses the bell.*]

LUCILLA. Does it not strike you that, if you drive us to
desperation, we may find means of cheating your Goddess?
What is to prevent me, for instance, from throwing myself
from that loggia?

RAJA. Nothing, dear lady, except that clinging to the
known, and shrinking from the unknown, that all of us feel,
even while we despise it. Besides, it would be foolishly pre-
cipitate, in every sense of the word. While there is life
there is hope. You can't read my mind. For aught you
can tell, I may have no intention of proceeding to extremities,
and may only be playing a little joke upon you. I hope you
have observed that I have a sense of humor. [*The* AYAH
enters.] Ah, here is the ayah. Good night, Madam; sleep
well. [*Bows her to the door. Exit* LUCILLA *with* AYAH.]
Gentlemen, a whiskey and soda. No? Then good night,
good night. [*Exeunt* CRESPIN *and* TRAHERNE.]

[*The* RAJA *takes from the table a powerful electric torch,
and switches it on. Then he switches off the lights of the
room, which is totally dark except for the now moonlit background. He goes up to the idol on the mantelpiece, throws
the light of the torch upon it, and makes it an ironic salaam.
Then he lights himself towards the door, left, as*]

THE CURTAIN FALLS

ACT III

The RAJA'S *Snuggery. An entirely European and modern room; its comfort contrasting with the old-fashioned,
comfortless splendor of the scene of Act II.*

*A door in front, left, opens on the billiard-room; another,
a little farther back, leads to the rest of the palace. A large
and solid folding door in the back wall, centre. To the right,
a large open window with a shallow balcony, which has the*

effect of being at a great height, and commands a view across the valley to the snow peaks beyond.

On the right, near the window, a handsome pedestal writing table, with a large and heavy swivel chair behind it. Silver fittings on the table, all in perfect order. Close to the nearer end of the writing table, a revolving bookcase, containing the Encyclopaedia Britannica and other books of reference. On the top of it a tantalus with a syphon and glasses. Close up to the writing table, and about of equal length, a deeply upholstered green leather sofa. Further over towards the left, a small table with smoking appliances. On each side of the table a comfortable green leather arm-chair. No small chairs. Low bookcases, filled with serious-looking modern books, against the walls, wherever there is space for them. On the top of one of the bookcases, a large bronze bust of Napoleon. A black and white portrait of Nietzsche on the wall, along with some sporting prints.

CRESPIN discovered alone, wandering around the room, nervous and irritable. He tries the door at back; it is locked. Opens the door down left, and closes it, muttering "Billiards, begad!" Crosses to the writing table, examines the articles upon it, and picks up a paper which proves to be "La Vie Parisienne." He throws it down with the comment, "French muck!" Notices a paper on the couch, picks it up and says with disgust, "Russian." Then he comes down to the revolving bookcase, glances at the books and spins it angrily. After a moment's hesitation, he pours some whiskey into a tumbler and fills it from the siphon. Is on the point of drinking, but hesitates, then says, "No!" Goes to the balcony and throws out the contents of the glass. As he is setting the glass down, TRAHERNE enters, second door left, ushered in by a SOLDIER, who salutes and exit.

CRESPIN. There! You think you 've caught me!

TRAHERNE. Caught you?

CRESPIN. Lushing. But I have n't been. I threw the stuff out of the window. For Lucilla's sake, I must keep all my wits about me.

TRAHERNE. Yes, if we can all do that, we may pull through yet.

CRESPIN. Did you sleep?

TRAHERNE. Not a wink. And you?

CRESPIN. Dozed and woke again fifteen times in a minute. A beast of a night!

TRAHERNE. Have you news of Mrs. Crespin?

CRESPIN. She sent me this *chit*. [*Hands him a scrap of paper.*]

TRAHERNE [*reads*]. "Have slept and am feeling better. Keep the flag flying." What pluck she has!

CRESPIN. Yes, she's game—always was.

TRAHERNE. She reminds me of the women in the French Revolution. We might all be in the Conciergerie, waiting to hear the tumbrils.

CRESPIN. It would be more endurable if we were in prison. It's this appearance of freedom—the scoundrel's cursed airs of politeness and hospitality—that makes the thing such a nightmare. [*Mechanically mixing himself a whiskey and soda.*] Do you believe we're really awake, Traherne? If I were alone, I'd think the whole thing was a blasted nightmare; but Lucilla and you seem to be dreaming it too. [*Raising the glass to his lips, he remembers and puts it down again, saying:*] Curse it!

TRAHERNE. Some day we may look back upon it as on a bad dream.

CRESPIN. He does you well, curse him! They served me a most dainty *chota hazri* this morning, and with it a glass of rare old *fine champagne*.

TRAHERNE [*pointing to the door, down left*]. Where does that door lead?

CRESPIN. To the billiard-room. Billiards! Ha, ha!

TRAHERNE [*at door, centre*]. And this one?

CRESPIN. I don't know. It's locked—and a very solid door, too.

TRAHERNE. Do you know what I think?

CRESPIN. Yes, and I agree with you.

TRAHERNE. Opening off the fellow's own sanctum——

CRESPIN. It 's probably the wireless room.

[*They exchange significant glances.*]

TRAHERNE [*indicating the window*]. And what 's out here?

CRESPIN. Take a look.

TRAHERNE [*looking over*]. A sheer drop of a hundred feet.

CRESPIN. And a dry torrent below. How if we were to pick up our host, Traherne, and gently drop him on those razor-edged rocks?

TRAHERNE [*shrugs his shoulders*]. As he said last night, they 'd only tear us to pieces the quicker.

CRESPIN. If it were n't for Lucilla, I 'm cursed if I would n't do it all the same.

[*The* RAJA *enters, second door left, dressed in spick-and-span up-to-date riding attire. He crosses to the writing table.*]

RAJA. Good morning, Major; good morning, Doctor. How do you like my snuggery? I hope you have slept well? [*They make no answer.*] No? Ah, perhaps you find this altitude trying? Never mind. We have methods of dealing with insomnia.

CRESPIN. Come now, Raja, a joke 's a joke, but this cat-and-mouse business gets on one's nerves. Make arrangements to send us back to the nearest British outpost, and we 'll give you our Bible oath to say nothing about the—pleasantry you 've played on us.

RAJA. Send you back, my dear Major? I assure you, if I were ever so willing, it would be as much as my place is worth. You don't know how my faithful subjects are looking forward to tomorrow's ceremony. If I tried to cancel it, there would be a revolution. You must be reasonable, my dear sir.

CRESPIN. Do you think we would truckle to you, curse you, if it were n't for my wife's sake? But for her we 'll make any concession—promise you anything.

RAJA. What can you promise that is worth a brass farthing to me? [*With sudden ferocity.*] No. Asia has a long score against you swaggering, blustering, whey-faced lords of creation, and, by all the gods! I mean to see some of it

paid tomorrow! [*Resuming his suave manner.*] But in
the meantime there is no reason why we should n't behave
like civilized beings. How would you like to pass the morning? I 'm sorry I can't offer you any shooting. I must n't
lead you into temptation. What do you say to billiards?
It soothes the nerves. [*Opening the door.*] Here is the
billiard-room. I have a littlè business to attend to, but I 'll
join you presently.

CRESPIN. Of all the infernal purring devils——!

RAJA. Dignity, Major, dignity!

[TRAHERNE *interposes and shepherds the* MAJOR *off. The
click of billiard-balls is presently heard. The* RAJA *seats
himself at the writing table and presses a bell. Then he takes
up a pad of paper and pencil, and taps his teeth, cogitating
what to write. In a few moments* WATKINS *enters.*]

WATKINS. Your Highness rang?

RAJA. Come in, Watkins. Just close the billiard-room
door, will you?

[WATKINS *looks into the billiard-room and then closes the
door.*]

WATKINS. They 're good pluck'd uns, sir; I will say that.

RAJA. Yes, there 's some satisfaction in handling them.
I 'm glad they 're not abject—it would quite spoil the sport.

WATKINS. Quite so, sir.

RAJA. But it has occurred to me, Watkins, that perhaps
it 's not quite safe to have them so near the wireless room.
Their one chance would be to get into communication with
India. They appeared last night to know nothing about the
wireless, but I have my doubts. Tell me, Watkins—have
they made any attempt to bribe you?

WATKINS. Not yet, sir.

RAJA. Ha, that looks bad. It looks as if they had something else up their sleeves, and were leaving bribery to the
last resort. I want to test their ignorance of wireless. I
want you, in their presence, to send out some message that is
bound to startle or enrage them, and see if they show any
sign of understanding it.

WATKINS [*grinning*]. That 's a notion, sir.

RAJA. But I can't think of a message.
[*The* AYAH *opens the second door, left, ushers in* LUCILLA, *and exit.* LUCILLA *has resumed her travelling dress. The* RAJA *has been examining the lock of the wireless room, and is thus partly concealed by the entrance door as it opens, so that* LUCILLA *is well into the room before she observes him. He comes forward.*]
RAJA. Ah, Mrs. Crespin, I was just thinking of you. Think of angels and you hear their wings. Won't you sit down?
LUCILLA [*ignoring his invitation*]. I thought my husband was here.
RAJA. He 's not far off. [*To* WATKINS, *pointing to the center door.*] Just wait in there for a few minutes; I may have instructions for you.
[WATKINS *produces a key-ring, selects a key, unlocks the door of the wireless-room, and goes in, closing the door behind him.*]
RAJA [*to* LUCILLA, *who has stood motionless*]. Do, pray, sit down. I want so much to have a chat with you. [LU-CILLA *seats herself, in silence.*] I hope you had everything you required?
LUCILLA. Everything.
RAJA. The ayah?
LUCILLA. Was most attentive.
RAJA. And you slept——?
LUCILLA. More or less.
RAJA. More rather than less, if one may judge by your looks.
LUCILLA. Does it matter?
RAJA. What can matter more than the looks of a beautiful woman?
LUCILLA [*listening*]. What 's that?
RAJA. The click of billiard-balls. Your husband and Dr. Traherne are passing the time.
LUCILLA [*rising*]. If you 'll excuse me, I 'll join them.
RAJA. Oh, pray spare me a few moments. I want to speak to you seriously.

LUCILLA [*sitting down again*]. Well—I am listening.

RAJA. You are very curt, Mrs. Crespin. I 'm afraid you bear me malice,—you hold me responsible for the doubtless trying situation in which you find yourself.

LUCILLA. Who else is responsible?

RAJA. Who? Why chance, fate, the gods, Providence— whoever, or whatever, pulls the strings of this unaccountable puppet-show. Did *I* bring you here? Did *I* conjure up the fog? Could I have prevented your dropping from the skies? And when once you had set foot in the Goddess's precinct, it was utterly out of my power to save you—at any rate the men of your party. If I raised a finger to thwart the Goddess, it would be the end of my rule—perhaps of my life.

LUCILLA. You know that is not true. You could easily smuggle us away, and then face the people out. What about your troops?

RAJA. A handful, dear lady—a toy army. It amuses me to play at soldiers. They could do nothing against priests and people, even if they were to be depended upon. And they, too, worship the Goddess.

LUCILLA. What you really mean, Raja, is that you dare not risk it—you have n't the courage.

RAJA. You take a mean advantage, Madam. You abuse the privilege of your sex in order to taunt me with cowardice.

LUCILLA. Let us say, then, that you have n't the will to save us.

RAJA. Reflect one moment, Madam—why should I have the will, at the risk of all I possess, to save Major Crespin and Dr. Traherne? Major Crespin is your husband—does that recommend him to me? Forgive me if I venture to guess that it does n't greatly recommend him to you. He is an only too typical specimen of a breed I detest: pigheaded, bullnecked, blustering, overbearing. Dr. Traherne is an agreeable man enough—I daresay a man of genius——

LUCILLA. If you kill him—if you cut short his work—you kill millions of your own race, whom he would have saved.

RAJA. I don 't know that I care very much about the mil-

lions you speak of. Life is a weed that grows again as fast
as death mows it down. At all events, he is an Englishman,
a Feringhi—and, may I add, without indiscretion, that the
interest you take in him—oh, the merest friendly interest, I
am sure—does not endear him to me. One is, after all, a
man, and the favor shown to another man by a beautiful
woman—[Lucilla *rises and moves toward the billiard-
room. The* Raja *interposes.*] Please, please, Mrs. Crespin,
bear with me if I transgress your Western conventions. Can
I help being an Oriental? Believe me, I mean no harm; I
wanted to talk to you about——

Lucilla. Well?

Raja. You spoke last night of—your children. [Lucilla
turns away, her self-control wavering.] I think you said—
a boy and a little girl.

Lucilla [*throws herself down on the couch in a fit of weeping*]. My babies, my babies!

Raja. I feel for you, Mrs. Crespin, I do indeed. I would
do anything——

Lucilla [*looking up, vehemently*]. Prince, if I write
them a letter of farewell, will you give me your word of
honor that it shall reach them?

Raja. Ah, there, Madam, you must pardon me! I have
already said that the last thing I desire is to attract the
attention of the Government of India.

Lucilla. I will say nothing to show where I am, or what
has befallen me. You shall read it yourself.

Raja. An ingenious idea! You would have it come fluttering down out of the blue upon your children's heads, like
a message from a Mahatma. But, the strength of my position, you see, is that no one will ever know what has become
of you. You will simply disappear in the uncharted sea of
the Himalayas, as a ship sinks with all hands in the ocean.
If I permitted any word from you to reach India, the
detective instinct, so deeply implanted in your race, would be
awakened, and the Himalayas would be combed out with a
tooth-comb. No, Madam, I cannot risk it.

LUCILLA [*her calm recovered*]. Cannot? You dare not!
But you can and dare kill defenseless men and women.
Raja, you are a pitiful coward.

RAJA. Forgive me if I smile at your tactics. You want to
goad me into chivalry. If every man were a coward who
took life without risking his own, where would your British
sportsmen be?

LUCILLA. I beg your pardon—a savage is not necessarily
a coward. And now let me go to my husband.

RAJA. Not yet, Mrs. Crespin—one more word. You are
a brave woman, and I sincerely admire you——

LUCILLA. Please—please——

RAJA. Listen to me. It will be worth your while. I
could not undertake to send a letter to your children—but
it would be very easy for me to have them carried off and
brought to you here.

LUCILLA [*starts, and faces him*]. What do you mean?

RAJA. I mean that, in less than a month, you may have
your children in your arms, uninjured, unsuspecting,
happy—if——

LUCILLA. If?

RAJA. If—oh, in your own time, of your own free will—
you will accept the homage it would be my privilege to offer
you.

LUCILLA. That!

RAJA. You have the courage to die, dear lady—why not
have the courage to live?

[*Pause.*]

You believe, I daresay, that tomorrow, when the ordeal is
over, you will awaken in a new life, and that there your
children will rejoin you. Suppose it were so: suppose that
in forty—fifty—sixty years, they passed over to you: would
they be your children? Can God Himself give you back
their childhood? What I offer you is a new life, not
problematical, but assured; a new life, without passing
through the shadow of death; a future utterly cut off from
the past, except that your children will be with you, not as
vague shades, but living and loving. They must be quite

young; they would soon forget all that had gone before. They would grow to manhood and womanhood under your eyes; and ultimately, perhaps, when the whole story was forgotten, you might, if you wished it, return with them to what you call civilization.

And meanwhile, you are only on the threshold of the best years of your life. You would pass them, not as a memsahib in a paltry Indian cantonment, but as the absolute queen of an absolute king. I do not talk to you of romantic love. I respect you too much to think you accessible to silly sentiment. But that is just it: I respect as much as I admire you; and I have never pretended to respect any other woman. Therefore I say you should be my first and only Queen. Your son, if you gave me one, should be the prince of princes; my other sons should all bow down to him and serve him. For, though I hate the arrogance of Europe, I believe that from a blending of the flower of the East with the flower of the West, the man of the future—the Superman—may be born.

[LUCILLA *has sat motionless through all this speech, her elbows on the end of the couch, twisting her handkerchief in her hands and gazing straight in front of her. There is now a perceptible pause before she speaks in a toneless voice.*]

LUCILLA. Is that all? Have you quite done?

RAJA. I beg you to answer.

LUCILLA. I can't answer the greater part of what you have been saying, for I have not heard it; at least I have not understood it. All I have heard is "In less than a month you may have your children in your arms," and then again, "Can God Himself give you back their childhood?" These words have kept hammering at my brain till—[*showing her handkerchief*] you see—I have bit my lip to keep from shrieking aloud. I think the devil must have put them in your mouth——

RAJA. Pooh! You don't believe in these old bugbears.

LUCILLA. Perhaps not. But there is such a thing as diabolical temptation, and you have stumbled upon the secret of it.

RAJA. Stumbled!

LUCILLA. Mastered the art of it, if you like—but not in your long harangue. All I can think of is, "Can God Himself give you back their childhood?" and "In a month you may have them in your arms."

RAJA [*eagerly*]. Yes, yes—think of that. In three or four weeks you may have your little ones——

LUCILLA [*rising and interrupting him vehemently*]. Yes —but on what conditions? That I should desert my husband and my friend—should let them go alone to their death— should cower in some back room of this murderous house of yours, listening to the ticking of the clock, and thinking, "Now—now—the stroke has fallen"—stopping my ears so as not to hear the yells of your bloodthirsty savages—and yet, perhaps, hearing nothing else to my dying day. No, prince!—you said something about not passing through the shadow of death; but if I did this I should not pass through it, but live in it, and bring my children into it as well. What would be the good of having them in my arms if I could not look them in the face? [*She passes to the billiard-room door.*]

RAJA. That is your answer?

LUCILLA. The only possible answer. [*She enters the billiard-room and closes the door.*]

RAJA [*looking after her, to himself*]. But not the last word, my lady! [*He sits at the writing table, and begins to write, at the same time calling, not very loudly, "*WATKINS!"* The valet immediately appears, center.*]

WATKINS. Yessir?

RAJA [*tearing a sheet off the pad and handing it to him.*] Read that.

WATKINS. A message to be sent out, sir?

RAJA. Yes.

WATKINS [*reading*]. "The lady has come to terms. She will enter His Highness's household." Quite so, sir. What suite will she occupy?

RAJA. My innocent Watkins! Do you think it's true? What have I to do with a stuck-up Englishwoman? It's only a bait for the Feringhis. You shall send it out in their hearing, and if either of them can read the Morse code, the mischief 's in it if he does n't give himself away.

WATKINS. Beg pardon, sir; I did n't quite catch on.

RAJA. If they move an eyelash I 'll take care they never see the inside of this room again.

WATKINS. Am I to send this to India, sir?

RAJA. To anywhere or nowhere. Reduce the current, so that no one can pick it up. So long as it 's heard in this room, that 's all I want.

WATKINS. But when am I to send it, sir?

RAJA. Listen. I 'll get them in here on the pretext of a little wireless demonstration, and then I 'll tell you to send out an order to Tashkent for champagne. That 'll be your cue. Go ahead—and send slowly.

WATKINS. Shall I ask you whether I 'm to code it, sir?

RAJA. You may as well. It 'll give artistic finish to the thing.

WATKINS. Very good, Your 'Ighness. But afterwards, —if, as you was saying, they was to try to corrupt me, sir——

RAJA. Corrupt you? That would be painting the lily with a vengeance.

WATKINS [*with a touch of annoyance*]. Suppose they tries to get at me, sir—what are your instructions?

RAJA. How do you mean?

WATKINS. Shall I let on to take the bait?

RAJA. You may do exactly as you please. I have the most implicit confidence in you, Watkins.

WATKINS. You are very good, sir.

RAJA. I know that anything they can offer you would have to be paid either in England or in India, and that you dare n't show your nose in either country. You have a very comfortable job here——

WATKINS. My grateful thanks to you, sir.

RAJA. And you don't want to give the hangman a job, either in Lahore or in London.

WATKINS. The case in a nutshell, sir. But I thought if I

was to pretend to send a message for them, it might keep them quiet-like.

RAJA. Very true, Watkins. It would not only keep them quiet, but the illusion of security would raise their spirits, which would be a humane action. I am always on the side of humanity.

WATKINS. Just so, sir. Then I 'll humor them.

RAJA. Yes, if they want you to send a message. If they try to "get at," not only you, but the instrument, call the guard and let me know at once.

WATKINS. Certainly, sir.

RAJA. Now open the door and stand by. You have the message?

WATKINS [*producing the slip from his pocket, reads*]: "The lady has come to terms. She—"

RAJA [*interrupting*]. Yes, that 's right. [*As* WATKINS *is opening the door.*] Oh, look here—when you 've finished, you 'd better lock the door, and say, "Any orders, sir?" If I say "No orders, Watkins," it 'll mean I 'm satisfied they don't understand. If I think they do understand, I 'll give you what orders I think necessary.

WATKINS. Very good, sir. [*He opens the folding doors wide, revealing a small room, in which is a wireless installation.*]

RAJA [*at billiard-room door*]. Oh, Major, you were saying you had no experience of wireless. If you 've finished your game, it might amuse you to see it at work. Watkins is just going to send out a message. Would Mrs. Crespin care to come?

CRESPIN [*at door*]. Yes—why not? Will you come, Lucilla?

[CRESPIN *enters, followed by* LUCILLA *and* TRAHERNE. *The* RAJA *eyes them closely so that they have no opportunity to make any sign to each other.*]

RAJA. This, you see, is the apparatus. All ready, Watkins? [*To the others.*] Won't you sit down? [*To* WATKINS.] You have the order for Tashkent?

WATKINS [*producing paper*]. Yes, Your 'Ighness; but I have n't coded it.

RAJA. Oh, never mind; send it in clear. Even if some outsider does pick it up, I daresay we can order three cases of champagne without causing international complications.

[*CRESPIN and TRAHERNE sit in the arm-chairs, left. LUCILLA is about to sit on the couch, but seeing the RAJA make a move to sit beside her, she passes behind the writing table and sits in the swivel chair. The RAJA sits on the sofa. WATKINS begins to transmit—pauses.*]

RAJA. He 's waiting for the reply signal.

[*A pause.*]

CRESPIN. May I take one of your excellent cigars, Raja?

RAJA. By all means.

[*CRESPIN lights a cigar.*]

WATKINS. I 've got them. [*Proceeds to send the message: "The lady has come to terms," etc.*]

CRESPIN [*a moment after the transmission has begun, says in a low voice to the RAJA.*] May we speak?

RAJA. Oh, yes—you won't be heard in Tashkent.

CRESPIN [*holding out his cigarette case*]. Have a cigarette, Traherne.

TRAHERNE. Thanks. [*He takes a cigarette. CRESPIN strikes a match and lights the cigarette, saying meanwhile:*]

CRESPIN. Let us smoke and drink, for tomorrow we—— [*Blows out the match.*]

[*Silence until the transmission ends.*]

RAJA. That 's how it 's done!

TRAHERNE. How many words did he send?

RAJA. What was it, Watkins? "Forward by tomorrow's caravan twelve cases champagne. Usual brand. Charge our account"; was that it?

WATKINS. That 's right, sir.

RAJA. Twelve words.

CRESPIN. And can they really make sense out of these fireworks?

RAJA. I hope so—else we shall run short of champagne.

WATKINS [*locking the folding door*]. Any orders, Your 'Ighness?

RAJA. No orders, Watkins.

[*As he is going out,* WATKINS *meets at the door a* SOLDIER, *who says a few words to him.*]

WATKINS [*turning*]. The 'Igh Priest is waiting to see Your 'Ighness.

RAJA. Oh, show him in.

[WATKINS *ushers in the* HIGH PRIEST OF THE GODDESS, *and then exit. The* HIGH PRIEST'S *personality is unmistakably sinister. The* RAJA, *after a word of greeting, turns to the others.*]

RAJA. I mentioned my Archbishop of York. This is he. Allow me to introduce you. Your Grace, Mrs. Crespin— Major Crespin—Dr. Traherne.

[*The* PRIEST, *understanding the situation, makes a sort of contemptuous salaam.*]

The Archbishop's manners are not good. You will excuse him. He regards you, I regret to say, as unclean creatures, whose very presence means pollution. He would be a mine of information for an anthropologist. [*He exchanges a few words with the* PRIEST, *and turns again to his guests.*]

His Grace reminds me of some arrangements for to-morrow's ceremony, which, as Archbishop of Canterbury, I must attend to in person. You will excuse me for half an hour? Pray make yourselves at home. Tiffin at half past twelve. [*He speaks a few words to the* PRIEST, *who replies in a sort of growl.*] His grace says *au revoir*—and so do I.

[*Exit, followed by the* PRIEST. *Both* TRAHERNE *and* LUCILLA *are about to speak.* CRESPIN *motions them to be cautious. He goes to the billiard-room, opens the door, looks around and closes it again.* LUCILLA *examines the balcony.* TRAHERNE *slips up to the center door and noiselessly tests it.*]

TRAHERNE [*to* CRESPIN]. What was the message?

CRESPIN. It said that the lady had accepted her life— on his terms.

TRAHERNE. Oh!—a trap for us.

CRESPIN. Yes. A put-up job.

LUCILLA. You gave no sign, Antony. I think he must have been reassured.

TRAHERNE. Evidently; or he would n't have left us here.

CRESPIN. What to do now?

TRAHERNE. Can we break open the door?

CRESPIN. No good. It would make a noise. We 'd be interrupted, and then it would be all up.

TRAHERNE. Well, then, the next step is to try to bribe Watkins.

CRESPIN. I don't believe it 's a bit of good.

TRAHERNE. Nor I. The fellow 's a thorough-paced scoundrel. But we might succeed, and if we don't even try they 'll suspect that we 're plotting something else. If we can convince them that we 're at our wits' end, we 've the better chance of taking them off their guard.

LUCILLA. Yes—you see that, Antony?

CRESPIN. Perhaps you 're right. But, even if the cursed scoundrel can be bought, what good is it if I can't remember the wave-length and the call for Amil-Serai?

LUCILLA. You 'll think of it all of a sudden.

CRESPIN. Not if I keep racking my brains for it. If I could get my mind off it, the cursed thing might come back to me.

TRAHERNE. All the more reason for action. But first, we must settle what message to send if we get the chance.

LUCILLA [sits at writing-table]. Dictate—I 'll write.

TRAHERNE. What about this? "Major Crespin, wife, Traherne imprisoned, Rukh, Raja's palace, lives in danger."

[LUCILLA writes on an envelope which she takes from the paper-case.]

CRESPIN. We want something more definite.

LUCILLA. How would this do? "Death threatened to-morrow evening. Rescue urgent."

TRAHERNE. Excellent.

[LUCILLA finishes the message, and hands it to CRESPIN.]

CRESPIN [reads]. "Major Crespin, wife, Traherne, imprisoned, Rukh, Raja's palace. Death threatened tomorrow evening. Rescue urgent.'' [*Takes the paper.*] Right. I 'll keep it ready.

TRAHERNE. Now, how to get hold of Watkins?

LUCILLA [*at the table*]. There 's a bell there. Shall I try it?

TRAHERNE. Hold on a moment. We have to decide what to do if he won't take money, and we have to use force in order to get his keys.

CRESPIN [*looking around*]. There 's nothing here to knock him on the head with—not even a chair you can lift——

TRAHERNE. Not a curtain cord to truss him up with——

LUCILLA. The first thing would be to gag him, would n't it? [*Takes off her scarf.*] Would this do for that?

TRAHERNE. Capital! [*Takes the scarf, ties a knot in it, and places it on the upper end of the sofa.*]

CRESPIN. What about a billiard cue?

TRAHERNE. If he saw it around he 'd smell a rat.

CRESPIN. Then there 's only one thing——

TRAHERNE. What?

[CRESPIN *points to the balcony, and makes a significant gesture.*]

LUCILLA. Oh! [*Shrinks away from the window.*]

TRAHERNE. I 'm afraid it can't be helped. There 's a drop of a good hundred feet.

CRESPIN. None too much for him.

TRAHERNE. When he locked that door he put the key in his trousers pocket. We must remember to get it before——

LUCILLA. But if you kill him and still don't remember the call, we shall be no better off than we are now.

TRAHERNE. We shall be no worse off.

CRESPIN. Better, by Jove! For if I can get three minutes at that instrument, the Raja can't tell whether we have communicated or not. [*He takes up the glass of whiskey-and-soda which he has poured out before.*]

LUCILLA. Oh, Antony!

CRESPIN. Don't be a fool, Lu. [*Gulps down the drink, and says as he pours out more whiskey:*] It 's because I 'm so unnaturally sober that my brain won't work. [*Drinks the whiskey raw.*] Now ring that bell. [LUCILLA *does so.*] You do the talking, Traherne. The fellow's cursed insolence gets on my nerves.

TRAHERNE. All right. [*Sits at the writing table.*]

CRESPIN. Look out——

[*Enter* WATKINS, *second door, left.*]

WATKINS. You rang, sir? [*Standing by the door.*]

TRAHERNE. Yes, Watkins, we want a few words with you. Do you mind coming over here? We don't want to speak loud.

WATKINS. There's no one understands English, sir.

TRAHERNE. Please oblige me, all the same.

WATKINS [*coming forward*]. Now, sir!

TRAHERNE. I daresay you can guess what we want with you.

WATKINS. I'm no 'and at guessin', sir. I'd rather you'd put it plain.

TRAHERNE. Well, you know that we've fallen into the hands of bloodthirsty savages? You know what is proposed for tomorrow?

WATKINS. I've 'eard as your numbers is up.

TRAHERNE. You surely don't intend to stand by and see us murdered—three of your own people, and one of them a lady?

WATKINS. My own people, is it? And a lady—!

LUCILLA. A woman, then, Watkins.

WATKINS. What has my own people ever done for me— or women either—that I should lose a cushy job and risk my neck for the sake of the three of you? I wouldn't do it for all your bloomin' England, I tell you straight.

CRESPIN. It's no good, Traherne. Come down to tin tacks.

TRAHERNE. Only a sighting shot, Major. It was just possible we might have misread our man.

WATKINS. You did if you took 'im for a V.C. 'ero wot 'ud lay down his life for England, 'ome and beauty. The first thing England ever done for me was to 'ave me sent to a

reformatory for pinching a silver rattle off of a young
haristocrat in a p'rambulator. That, and the likes of that,
is wot I've got to thank England for. And why did I do
it? Because my mother would have bashed my face in if
I'd have come back empty-handed. That's wot 'ome and
beauty has meant for me. W'y should I care more for a
woman being scragged than what I do for a man?

TRAHERNE. Ah, yes, I quite see your point of view. But
the question now is: What 'll you take to get us out of
this?

WATKINS. Get out of this! If you was to offer me
millions, 'ow could I do that?

TRAHERNE. By going into that room and sending this
message through to the Amil-Serai aerodrome.

[CRESPIN *hands* WATKINS *the message. He reads it
through and places it on the table.*]

WATKINS. So that's the game, is it?

TRAHERNE. That, as you say, is the game.

WATKINS. You know what you 're riskin'?

TRAHERNE. What do you mean?

WATKINS. W'y, if the Guv'nor suspected as you 'd got a
word through to India, ten to one he 'd wipe you off the slate
like that [*snapping his fingers*] without waiting for tomorrow.

CRESPIN. That makes no difference. We 've got to face it.

TRAHERNE. Come now! On your own showing, Mr. Watkins, loyalty to your master ought n't to stand in your way.
I don't suppose gratitude is one of your weaknesses.

WATKINS. Gratitude! To 'im? What for? I 'm not
badly off here, to be sure, but it 's nothing to wot I does
for 'im; and I 'ate 'im for 'is funny little ways. D'you
think I don't see that he 's always pulling my leg?

TRAHERNE. Well, then, you won't mind selling him.
We 've only to settle the price.

WATKINS. That 's all very fine, sir; but what price 'ave
you gents to offer?

TRAHERNE. Nothing down—no spot cash—that 's clear.

You 'll have to take our word for whatever bargain we come to.

WATKINS. Your word! How do I know——?

TRAHERNE. Oh, our written word. We 'll give it to you in writing.

WATKINS [*after thinking for a moment*]. If I was to 'elp you out, there must be no more fairy-tales about any of you 'avin' seen me in India.

TRAHERNE. All right. We accept your assurance that you never were there.

WATKINS. And see here, Dr. Traherne—you know very well I could n't stay here after I 'd helped you to escape—leastways, if I stayed, it 'd be in my grave. You 'll 'ave to take me with you—and for that I can only have your word. Supposing you could get the message through, and the English was to come, no writing could bind you if you chose to leave me in the lurch.

TRAHERNE. Quite true. I 'm afraid you 'll have to trust us for that. But I give you my word of honor that we would be as careful of your safety as if you were one of ourselves. I suppose you know that, strange as you may think it, there are people in the world that would rather die than break a solemn promise.

CRESPIN. Even to a hound like you, Watkins.

WATKINS. I advise you to keep a civil tongue in yer 'ead, Major. Don't forget that I 'ave you in the 'ollow of my 'and.

TRAHERNE. True, Watkins; and the hollow of your hand is a very disagreeable place to be in. That 's why we 're willing to pay well to get out of it. Come, now, what shall we say?

WATKINS. Well, what about a little first instalment? You ain't quite on your uppers, are you, now? You could come down with something, be it ever so humble?

TRAHERNE [*examining his pocket-book*.] I have 300 rupees and five ten-pound notes. [*Places the money on the table.*]

WATKINS. And you, Major?

CRESPIN. Two hundred and fifty rupees. [*Crosses and lays the notes on the table.*] Oh, and some loose change.

WATKINS [*nobly*]. Oh, never mind the chicken-feed! And the lady?

LUCILLA. I gave my last rupee to your wife, Watkins.

WATKINS. Well, that 's about £120 to go on with.

TRAHERNE [*placing his hand on the heap of notes*]. There. That 's your first instalment. Now what about the balance? Shall we say £1000 apiece?

WATKINS. A thousand apiece! Three thousand pounds! You 're joking, Dr. Traherne! Wot would £3000 be to me in England? W'y, I 'd 'ave to take to valetting again. No, no, sir! If I 'm to do this job, I must 'ave enough to make a gentleman of me.

[CRESPIN, TRAHERNE *and* LUCILLA *burst out laughing.*]

WATKINS. Well, you are the queerest lot as ever I come across. Your lives is 'anging by a 'air, and yet you can larf!

LUCILLA [*hysterically*]. It 's your own fault, Watkins. Why will you be so funny? [*Her laughter turns to tears and she buries her face in the end of the couch, shaken with sobs.*]

TRAHERNE. I 'm afraid what you ask is beyond our means, Watkins. But I double my bid—two thousand apiece.

WATKINS. You 'll 'ave to double it again sir, and a little more. You write me out an I. O. U. for fifteen thousand pounds, and I 'll see wot can be done.

CRESPIN. Well, you are the most consummate——

WATKINS. If your lives ain't worth five thousand apiece to you, there 's nothing doing. For my place here is worth fifteen thousand to me. And there 's all the risk, too—I 'm not charging you nothing for that.

TRAHERNE. We appreciate your generosity, Watkins. Fifteen thousand be it!

WATKINS. Now you 're talking.

[TRAHERNE *rapidly writes and signs the I. O. U. and hands it to* WATKINS.]

WATKINS. That's right, sir; but the Major must sign it, too.

CRESPIN [*crosses to the table, on which* WATKINS *places the paper, writes, throws down the pen.*] There you are, curse you!

TRAHERNE. Now get to work quick, and call up Amil-Serai.

WATKINS. Right you are, sir. [*Picks up the envelope and begins, in a leisurely way, unlocking the center door.*]

CRESPIN. Isn't there some special call you must send out to get Amil-Serai?

WATKINS. Oh, yes, sir, I know it.

[WATKINS *takes his seat at the instrument, with his back to the snuggery, and begins to work it.*]

CRESPIN [*whispers*]. That's not a service call.

[*A pause.*]

WATKINS. Right! Got them, sir. Now the message.

CRESPIN [*as* WATKINS *works the key,* CRESPIN *spells out*]. "The—white—goats—are—ready—for—'' [*To* TRAHERNE.] No, but the black sheep is! Come on!

[CRESPIN *tiptoes up toward* WATKINS *followed by* TRA-HERNE. *As he passes the upper end of the sofa* CRESPIN *picks up* LUCILLA'S *scarf and hands it to* TRAHERNE, *meantime producing his own handkerchief.* LUCILLA *rises, her hand pressed to her mouth. The men steal up close behind* WAT-KINS. *Suddenly* TRAHERNE *jams the gag in* WATKINS'S *mouth, and ties the ends of the scarf.* WATKINS *attempts a cry, but it trails off into a gurgle.* CRESPIN *meantime grips* WATKINS'S *arms behind, and ties the wrists with his handkerchief.* TRAHERNE *makes fast the gag, and the two lift him, struggling, and carry him towards the window.* WAT-KINS'S *head falls back, and his terror-stricken eyes can be seen over the swathing gag. They rest him for a moment on the balustrade.*]

TRAHERNE. Must we——?

CRESPIN. Nothing else for it—one, two, three! [*They heave him over.* LUCILLA, *who has been watching, petrified, gives a gasping cry.*]

CRESPIN. At least we have n't taken it lying down! [*He pours out some whiskey and is about to drink when he pauses, puts down the glass, and then cries in great excitement.*] Hold on! Don't speak! [*A pause.*] I have it! [*Another pause.*] Yes, by Jupiter, I have it! I 've remembered the call! Can you lock that door?

LUCILLA [*at second door left*]. No key this side!

TRAHERNE [*whispering, and running to the door*]. Don't open it. There are soldiers in the passage. I 'll hold it. [*He stations himself before the door.* CRESPIN *rushes to the instrument and rapidly examines it.*]

CRESPIN. The scoundrel had reduced the current. [*Makes an adjustment with feverish haste.*] Now the wave length! [*More adjustment. He begins to transmit. A pause.*]

TRAHERNE. Do you get any answer?

CRESPIN. No, no; I don't expect any—I 'm sure they have n't the power. But it 's an even chance that I get them all the same. [*He goes on transmitting hurriedly while* TRAHERNE *and* LUCILLA *stand breathless,* TRAHERNE *with his shoulder to the door.*]

TRAHERNE. Some one 's coming up the passage! Go on! Go on! I 'll hold the door.

[*Another slight pause, while* CRESPIN *transmits feverishly. Suddenly* TRAHERNE *braces himself against the door, gripping the handle. After a moment, there is a word of command outside, the sound of shoulders heaved against the door, and it is gradually pushed open by three guards.* TRAHERNE *is shoved back by its motion.*]

[*The* RAJA *enters, rushes forward and grasps the situation.*]

RAJA. Ah! When the cat 's away—— [*He whips out a revolver and fires.*]

CRESPIN. Got me, by Heaven! [*He falls forward over the instrument, but immediately recovers himself, and rapidly un-*

makes the adjustments. LUCILLA *and* TRAHERNE *catch him as he staggers back from the instrument, and lay him on the couch.*]

TRAHERNE [*kneeling and supporting him*]. Brandy!

[LUCILLA *gets the glass. They put it to his lips.*]

[*The* RAJA *meanwhile goes to the wireless table, sees the draft message and reads it.*]

RAJA [*holding out the paper*]. How much of this did you get through?

CRESPIN [*raising himself a little*]. Curse you—none! [*Falls back dead.*]

LUCILLA [*crying out*]. Antony!

RAJA. All over, eh?

[TRAHERNE, *still kneeling, makes an affirmative sign.*]

[*At this moment a noise is heard outside, and three soldiers burst open the door and rush in. One of them speaks to the* RAJA, *pointing to the window, the other two rush up to* TRAHERNE, *seize him and drag him over to the left.* LUCILLA *remains kneeling by* CRESPIN'S *body. The* RAJA *goes calmly over to the window and looks out.*]

RAJA [*returning to the center*]. Tut tut—most inconvenient. And foolish on your part—for now, if my brothers should be reprieved, we cannot hear of it. [*Looks at the message reflectively.*] Otherwise, the situation remains unchanged. We adhere to our program for tomorrow. The Major has only a few hours' start of you.

CURTAIN

ACT IV

A gloomy hall, its roof supported by four wooden columns, two in a row, rudely carved with distorted animal and human figures. The walls are also of rudely-carved wood, and are pierced all round, at the height of about twelve feet, by a sort of clerestory—a series of oblong slits or unglazed windows through which the sky can be seen. The general tone of the wood is dark brown, but the interstices between the

*carvings have here and there been filled in with dull red.
There is a high curtained doorway, left, leading to a sort of
robing-room. Opposite to it, right, a two-leaved wooden
door, closed with a heavy wooden bolt. An oblong hole in the
door, with a sliding shutter, enables the guard within to inspect whoever approaches from without. At the back, center,
is a wide opening, curtained at the beginning of the Act.
When the curtains are withdrawn, they reveal a sort of balcony or tribune, raised by two steps above the level of the
hall, over the balustrade of which can be seen the head and
shoulders of a colossal image of the Goddess, apparently at a
distance of some fifty yards. Between the two foremost
columns, on a dais of two steps, a wide throne, which has for
its backing a figure of the Goddess carved in high relief, amid
a good deal of barbaric tracery. The figure is green, but
there are touches of gold in her crown, her ornaments, and
in the tracery. A low brazier rests on the ground in front
of the throne.*

*The hall is a sort of anteroom to the public place of
sacrifice without.*

*Late afternoon light comes in through the clerestory on
the left.*

*When the curtain rises, a group of Priests is gathered
round the doorway, left, while the* CHIEF PRIEST *stands at
the center, holding the curtains a little way apart and looking out. A Priest is on guard at the door, right.*

*For a moment after the rise of the curtain, there is a
regular and subdued murmur from the crowd without.
Then it swells into a chorus of execrations. The* CHIEF
PRIEST *gives an order to the other Priests, left, one of whom
goes off through the doorway. The guard at the door, right,
slips back the shutter and looks out, then unbolts the door,
and admits* TRAHERNE, *strapped to a mountain chair, and
guarded by two soldiers, who withdraw. At the same time,
the* RAJA, *in splendid Eastern attire, enters, left.*

RAJA. Well, Doctor, it does n't appear that any "god
from the machine" is going to interfere with our program.

TRAHERNE. You are bringing a terrible vengeance upon yourself.

RAJA. Think, my dear Doctor. If, as the Major said, he did not get your S. O. S. through, I have nothing to fear. If he lied, and did get it through, nothing can ultimately save me, and I may as well be hung for a sheep as for a lamb.

TRAHERNE [*writhing in his bonds*]. You might have spared me this.

RAJA. A ritual detail, Doctor; not quite without reason. Persons lacking in self-control might throw themselves to the ground or otherwise disarrange the ceremony. [*He speaks a word, and the bearers promptly release* TRAHERNE, *and carry the chair out, right.*]

TRAHERNE. What have you done with Mrs. Crespin?

RAJA. Don't be alarmed. She'll be here in due time.

TRAHERNE. Listen to me, Raja. Do what you will with me, but let Mrs. Crespin go. Send her to India or to Russia, and I am sure, for her children's sake, she will swear to keep absolute silence as to her husband's fate and mine.

RAJA. You don't believe, then, that I couldn't save you if I would?

TRAHERNE. Believe it? No!

RAJA. You are quite right, my dear Doctor. I am not a High Priest for nothing. I might work the oracle. I might get a command from the Goddess to hurt no hair upon your heads.

TRAHERNE. Then what devilish pleasure do you find in putting us to death?

RAJA. Pleasure? The pleasure of a double vengeance. Vengeance for today—my brothers—and vengeance for centuries of subjection and insult. Do you know what brought you here? It was not blind chance, any more than it was the Goddess. It was my will, my craving for revenge, that drew you here by a subtle, irresistible magnetism. My will is my religion—my god. And by that god I have sworn that you shall not escape me. [*Yells from the crowd outside.*] Ah, they are bringing Mrs. Crespin.

[*The* PRIEST *unbolts the door, right, and* LUCILLA *is carried in.*]

RAJA. I apologize, Madam, for the manners of my people. Their fanaticism is beyond my control. [*He says a word to the bearers, who release* LUCILLA. TRAHERNE *gives her his hand, and she steps from the chair, which the bearers remove, right.*]

TRAHERNE. How long have we left?

RAJA. Till the sun's rim touches the crest of the mountain. A blast of our great mountain horn will announce the appointed hour, and you will be led out to the sacred enclosure. You saw the colossal image of the Goddess out yonder? [*He points to the back. They look at each other in silence.*]

TRAHERNE. Will you grant us one last request?

RAJA. By all means, if it is in my power. In spite of your inconsiderate action of yesterday——

TRAHERNE. Inconsiderate——?

RAJA. Watkins, you know—poor Watkins—a great loss to me! But *à la guerre comme à la guerre!* I bear no malice for a fair act of war. I am anxious to show you every consideration.

TRAHERNE. Then you will leave us alone for the time that remains to us.

RAJA. Why, by all means. And oh, by the way, you need have no fear of the ceremony—being protracted. It will be brief and—I—trust—painless. The High Church Party are not incapable of cruelty; but I have resolutely set my face against it. [LUCILLA *has meanwhile stood stonily gazing in front of her. The* RAJA *reflects for a moment, and then goes up to her.*] Before I go, Madam, may I remind you of my offer of yesterday? It is not yet too late. [LUCILLA *takes no notice.*] Is it just to your children to refuse? [*She looks at him stonily, saying nothing. After a pause.*] Immovable? So be it! [*He turns to go. At this moment a great yell of triumphant hatred goes up from the populace.*]

RAJA. Your husband's body, Madam. They are laying it at the feet of the Goddess.

LUCILLA. You promised me——

RAJA. That it should be burnt. I will keep my promise. But you see I had three brothers—a head for a head. [*He goes into the inner chamber, encircled by his Priests. Only the* GUARD *at the door, right, remains, half hidden by the door jamb.*]

[LUCILLA *and* TRAHERNE *are left alone.* LUCILLA *sinks down upon the broad base of the foremost pillar, left.*]

LUCILLA. So this is the end!

TRAHERNE. What offer did that devil make you?

LUCILLA. Oh, I did n't mean to tell you, but I may as well. He is an ingenious tormentor. He offered yesterday to let me live, and to kidnap the children and bring them here to me—you know on what terms.

TRAHERNE. To bring the children here?

LUCILLA. He said in a month I might have them in my arms. Think of it! Ronny and Iris in my arms!

[*A pause.* TRAHERNE *stands with his back to her.*]

TRAHERNE [*in a low and unsteady voice.*] Are you sure you did right to refuse?

LUCILLA. Do you mean——?

TRAHERNE [*louder and almost harshly*]. Are you sure it is not wrong to refuse?

LUCILLA. Oh, how can you—? Right? Wrong? What are right and wrong to me now? If I could see my children again, would any scruple of "right" or "wrong" make me shrink from anything that was possible? But this is so utterly, utterly impossible.

TRAHERNE. Forgive me. You know it would add an unspeakable horror to death if I had to leave you here. But I felt I must ask you whether you had fully considered——

LUCILLA. I have thought of nothing else through all these torturing hours.

TRAHERNE. How brave you are!

LUCILLA. Not brave, not brave. If I could live, I would—there, I confess it! But I should die of shame and misery, and leave my children—to that man. Or, if I did live, what sort of a mother should I be to them? They would be much better without me! Oh my precious, precious darlings!

[*She clasps her arms across her breast, and rocks herself in agony. A short silence.*]

TRAHERNE [*lays his hand on her shoulder*]. Lucilla!

LUCILLA [*looking up*]. Oh, Basil, say you think it won't be altogether bad for them! They will never know anything of their father now, but what was good. And their mother will simply have vanished into the skies. They will think she has flown away to heaven—and who knows but it may be true? There may be something beyond this hell.

TRAHERNE. We shall know soon, Lucilla.

LUCILLA. But to go away and leave them without a word—! Poor little things, poor little things.

TRAHERNE. They will remember you as something very dear and beautiful. The very mystery will be like a halo about you.

LUCILLA. Shall I see them again, Basil? Tell me that.

[*A pause.*]

TRAHERNE. Who knows? Even to comfort you, I won't say I am certain. But I do sincerely think you may.

LUCILLA [*smiling woefully*]. You think there is a sporting chance?

TRAHERNE. More than that. This life is such a miracle—could any other be more incredible?

LUCILLA. But even if I should meet them in another world, they would not be my Ronny and Iris, but a strange man and a strange woman, built up of experiences in which I had had no share. Oh, it was cunning, cunning, what that devil said to me! He said "God Himself cannot give you back their childhood."

TRAHERNE. How do you know that God is going to take their childhood from you? You may be with them this very night—with them, unseen, but perhaps not unfelt, all the days of their life.

LUCILLA. You are saying that to make what poor Antony called a "haze" for me—to soften the horror of darkness that is waiting for us? Don't give me "dope," Basil—I can face things without it.

TRAHERNE. I mean every word of it. [*A pause.*] Why do you smile?

LUCILLA. At a thought that came to me—the thought of poor Antony as a filmy, purified spirit. It seems so unthinkable.

TRAHERNE. Why unthinkable? Why may he not still exist, though he has left behind him the nerves, the cravings, that tormented him—and you. You have often told me that there was something fine in the depths of his nature; and you know how he showed it yesterday.

LUCILLA. Oh, if I could only tell the children how he died!

TRAHERNE. But his true self was chained to a machine that was hopelessly out of gear. The chain is broken: the machine lies out there—scrapped. Do you think that he was just that machine, and nothing else?

LUCILLA. I don't know. I only feel that Antony spiritualized would not be Antony. And you, Basil—if Antony leaves his—failings, you must leave behind your work. Do you want another life in which there is no work to be done— no disease to be rooted out? [*With a mournful smile.*] Don't tell me you don't long to take your microscope with you wherever you may be going.

TRAHERNE. Perhaps there are microscopes awaiting me there.

LUCILLA. Spirit microscopes for spirit microbes? You don't believe that, Basil.

TRAHERNE. I neither believe nor disbelieve. In all we can say of another life we are like children blind from birth, trying to picture the form and colors of the rainbow.

LUCILLA. But if the forms and colors we know are of no use to us, what comforts are we to find in formless, colorless possibilities? If we are freed from all human selfishness, shall I love my children more than any other woman's? Can I love a child I cannot kiss, that cannot look into my eyes and kiss me back again?

TRAHERNE [*starting up*]. Oh, Lucilla, don't!

LUCILLA. What do you mean?

TRAHERNE. Don't remind me of all we are losing! I meant to leave it all unspoken—the thought of him lying out there seemed to tie my tongue. But we have only one moment on this side of eternity. Lucilla, shall I go on? [*After a perceptible pause,* LUCILLA *bows her head.*] Do you think it is with a light heart that I turn my back upon the life of earth and all it might have meant for you and me—for you and me, Lucilla!

LUCILLA. Yes, Basil, for you and me.

TRAHERNE. Rather than live without you, I am glad to die with you; but oh, what a wretched gladness compared with that of living with you and loving you! I wonder if you guess what it has meant to me, ever since we met at Dehra Dun, to see you as another man's wife, bound to him by ties I couldn't ask you to break. It has been hell, hell! [*Looking up with a mournful smile.*] My love has not been quite selfish, Lucilla, since I can say I really do love your children, though I know they have stood between me and heaven.

LUCILLA. Yes, Basil, I know. I have known from the beginning.

TRAHERNE. Oh, Lucilla, have we not been fools, fools? We have sacrificed to an idol as senseless as that—[*with a gesture towards the image*] all the glory and beauty of life! What do I care for a bloodless, shadowy life—life in the abstract, with all the senses extinct? Is there not something in the depths of our heart that cries out "We don't want it! Better eternal sleep!"?

LUCILLA. Oh, Basil—you are going back on your own wisdom.

TRAHERNE. Wisdom! What has wisdom to say to love, thwarted and unfulfilled? You were right when you said that it is a mockery to speak of love without hands to clasp, without lips to kiss. We may be going to some pale parody of life; but in our cowardice we have killed love for ever and ever.

LUCILLA. No, Basil, don't call it cowardice. I, too, regret —perhaps as much as you—that things were—as they were. But not even your love could have made up to me for my

LUCILLA. No, no, he would n't—but he must have no choice. That is part of the bargain. Send him—bound hand and foot, if need be—down to Kashmir, and put him over the frontier——

RAJA. You don't care what he thinks of you?

LUCILLA. He will know what to think.

RAJA. And I, too, Madam, know what to think. [*Kneeling with one knee on the throne, he seizes her by the shoulders and turns her face towards him.*] Come, look me in the eyes and tell me that you honestly intend to fulfil your bargain! [*Her head droops.*] I knew it! You are playing with me! But the confiding barbarian is not so simple as you imagine. No woman has ever tried to fool me that has not repented it. You think, when you have to pay up, you will fob me off with your dead body. Let me tell you, I have no use for you dead—I want you with all the blood in your veins, with all the pride in that cursed sly brain of yours. I want to make my plaything of your beauty, my mockery of your pride. I want to strip off the delicate English lady, and come down to the elemental woman, the handmaid and the instrument of man. [*Changing his tone.*]

Come now, I 'll make you a plain offer. I will put Dr. Traherne over the frontier, and, as they set him free, my people shall hand him a letter written by you at my dictation. You will tell him that you have determined to accept my protection and make this your home. Consequently, you wish to have your children conveyed to you here——

LUCILLA. Never—never—never! I will make no bargain that involves my children.

RAJA. You see! You will give me no hostages for the fulfilment of your bond. But a pledge of your good faith I must have. For without a pledge, Madam, I don't believe in it one little bit.

LUCILLA. What pledge?

RAJA. Only one is left—Dr. Traherne himself. I may—though it will strain my power to the uttermost—save his life, while keeping him in prison. Then, when you have fulfilled your bond I will let him go free. But the moment you attempt to evade your pledge, by death or by escape, I will hand him over to the priests to work their will with; and I will put no restraint upon their savage instincts. [*Pause.*] Choose, my dear lady, choose!

[*The subdued murmur of the crowd below, which has been faintly audible during the foregoing scene, ceases, and in the silence is heard a faint, but rapidly increasing, whirr and throb.*]

[LUCILLA, *who has been crouching on the steps of the throne, looks up slowly, hope dawning in her face. For a few seconds she says nothing, waiting to assure herself that she can believe her ears. Then she says in a low voice, with a sort of sob of relief:*]

LUCILLA. Aeroplanes! [*She spring up with a shriek.*] The aeroplanes! Basil! Basil! The aeroplanes! [*She rushes out through the doorway, left, thrusting aside the incoming Priests, who are too amazed to oppose her.*]

[*The* RAJA *does not at first alter his attitude but looks up and listens intently. The curtains shutting off the balcony at the back are violently torn apart by the guard outside, who shout to the* RAJA *and point upward. Sounds of consternation and terror proceed from the unseen crowd.*]

[*The* RAJA *goes to the back and looks out. At the same moment* LUCILLA *and* TRAHERNE *rush in from the doorway, left.*]

LUCILLA. See! See! They are circling lower and lower! Is it true, Basil? Are we saved?

TRAHERNE. Yes, Lucilla, we are saved.

LUCILLA. Oh, thank God! I shall see my babies again! [*She sways, almost fainting.* TRAHERNE *supports her.*]

RAJA. So the Major lied like a gentleman! Good old Major! I did n't think he had it in him.

[*The Guards call his attention; he looks out from the balcony, and gives an order, then turns down again.*]

One of the machines has landed. An officer is coming this way—he looks a mere boy.

TRAHERNE. The conquerors of the air have all been mere boys.

RAJA. I have given orders that he shall be brought here unharmed. Perhaps I had better receive him with some ceremony. [*He goes back to the throne and seats himself, cross-legged. At his command the Priests range themselves about him.*]

RAJA. You said just now, Dr. Traherne, that you were saved. Are you so certain of that?

TRAHERNE. Certain?

RAJA. How many men does each of these humming-birds carry?

TRAHERNE. Two or three, but——

RAJA. I counted six planes—say at the outside, twenty men. Even my toy army can cope with that number.

[*There is a growing clamor outside. The* RAJA *gives an order to the Priest at the door, right. He throws it wide open.*]

[FLIGHT-LIEUTENANT CARDEW *saunters in, escorted by three soldiers.*]

RAJA. Who are you, sir?

CARDEW. One moment! [*Crosses to* LUCILLA, *who holds out both her hands. He takes them cordially but coolly.*] Mrs. Crespin! I'm very glad we're in time. [*Turns to* TRAHERNE.] Dr. Traherne, I presume? [*Shakes hands with him.*] And Major Crespin?

TRAHERNE. Shot while transmitting our message.

CARDEW. I'm so sorry, Mrs. Crespin. [*To* TRAHERNE.] By whom? [TRAHERNE *indicates the* RAJA, *who has meanwhile watched the scene impassively.*]

RAJA. I am sorry to interrupt these effusions, but——

CARDEW. Who are you, sir?

RAJA. I am the Raja of Rukh. And you?

CARDEW. Flight-Lieutenant Cardew. I have the honor to represent his Majesty, the King-Emperor.

RAJA. The King-Emperor? Who is that, pray? We live so out of the world here, I don't seem to have heard of him.

CARDEW. You will in a minute, Raja, if you don't instantly hand over his subjects.

RAJA. His subjects? Ah, I see you mean the King of England. What terms does his Majesty propose?

CARDEW. We make no terms with cut-throats. [*Looks at his wrist watch.*] If I do not signal your submission within three minutes of our landing——

[*A bomb is heard to fall at some distance. Great consternation among the Priests, etc.*]

RAJA [*unperturbed*]. Ah! bombs!

CARDEW. Precisely.

RAJA. I fancied your Government affected some scruples as to the slaughter of innocent civilians.

CARDEW. There has been no slaughter—as yet. That bomb fell in the ravine, where it could do no harm. So will the next one— [*Bomb—nearer. Increasing hubbub without.*] But the third—well, if you 're wise you 'll throw up the sponge, and there won't be a third.

RAJA. Throw up the sponge, Lieutenant—? I did n't quite catch your name?

CARDEW. Cardew.

RAJA. Ah, yes, Lieutenant Cardew. Why on earth should I throw up the sponge? Your comrades up yonder can no doubt massacre quite a number of my subjects—a brave exploit!—but when they 've spent their thunderbolts, they 'll just have to fly away again—if they can. A bomb may drop on this temple, you say? In that case, you and your friends will escort me—in fragments—to my last abode. Does that prospect allure you? I call your bluff, Lieutenant Cardew. [*A third bomb—very loud.*]

[*The Priests rush up to the* RAJA, *and fall before him in panic-stricken supplication, with voluble remonstrances, pointing to the Idol in the background. The* RAJA *hesitates for a moment, then proceeds.*]

RAJA. My priests, however, have a superstitious dread of these eggs of the Great Roc. They fear injury to the Sacred Image. For myself, I am always averse from bloodshed.

You may, if you please, signal to your squadron commander my acceptance of your terms.

CARDEW. I thought you would come to reason. [*Shaking out his flag in preparation for signaling, he hurries across to where the white beam of a searchlight is visible outside the doorway, right. He disappears for a moment.*]

RAJA. This comes of falling behind the times. If I had had anti-aircraft guns——

TRAHERNE. Thank your stars you had n't!

CARDEW [*returning*]. All clear for the moment, Raja. You have no further immediate consequences to fear.

RAJA. What am I to conclude from your emphasis on immediate?

CARDEW [*after whispering to* TRAHERNE]. I need scarcely remind you, sir, that you can only hand over the body of one of your prisoners.

RAJA. Major Crespin murdered a faithful servant of mine. His death at my hands was a fair act of war.

CARDEW. His Majesty's Government will scarcely view it in that light.

RAJA. His Majesty's Government has today, I believe, taken the lives of three kinsmen of mine. Your side has the best of the transaction by four lives to one.

CARDEW [*shrugging his shoulders*]. Will you assign us an escort through the crowd?

RAJA. Certainly. [*Gives an order to the officer of regulars, who hurries out, right.*] The escort will be here in a moment. [*To* LUCILLA *and* TRAHERNE.] It only remains for me to speed the parting guest. I hope we may one day renew our acquaintance—oh, not here! I plainly foresee that I shall have to join the other Kings in Exile. Perhaps we may meet at Homburg or Monte Carlo, and talk over old times. Ah, here is the escort.

[*The escort has formed at the door, right.* TRAHERNE, LUCILLA *and* CARDEW *cross to it, the* RAJA *following them up.*]

Good-bye, dear lady. I lament the Major's end. Perhaps I was hasty; but, you know, " 'T is better to have loved and lost," etc. And oh—Mrs. Crespin! [*As she is going out,* LUCILLA *looks back at him with horror.*] My love to the children!

[*The Priests and others are all clustered on the balcony, looking at the aeroplanes. The* RAJA *turns back from the door, lights a cigarette at the brazier, takes a puff, and says:*] Well, well—she 'd probably have been a deuce of a nuisance.

CURTAIN

SUGGESTIVE QUESTIONS

1. What different dramatic means make the opening of the play peculiarly effective?
2. Would the opening dialogue have been better if it had given more explanation? Explain your answer.
3. How much of character is given immediately?
4. What plot values are mentioned immediately?
5. What foreshadowing is made immediately?
6. How much does the subordinate plot of the relations between Major Crespin and Lucilla, and between that couple and Dr. Traherne, add to the dramatic values of the play?
7. By what different dramatic means does the author indicate the character of the Raja?
8. Why is Watkins necessary in the play?
9. What effects are produced by references to literature and to learning?
10. What foreshadowing appears in Act I?
11. What parts of the stage setting do most to increase dramatic effects?
12. Point out the different means by which the play presents the character of Watkins?
13. What dramatic advantages are gained by the break in Act II?
14. Analyze the character of the Raja.
15. Tell the past history of the Raja. How does the play tell the Raja's past?
16. By what means does the Raja keep his power over his people? How is that related to the plot of the play?

17. What is the importance of the conclusion of Act II?
18. What is the atmosphere of the play? Point out all the means by which it is produced.
19. What character developments occur in the play? How are they related to the producing of dramatic effects, or the awakening of emotions?
20. What does most to create dramatic suspense?
21. Point out the different antagonisms and contests of cleverness on which the play is based. Which of these gives most powerful effects?
22. What different emotions does the play arouse? Point out the places of most intense emotion.
23. At what points does the play most deeply appeal to the sympathies of the audience?
24. Point out moments of inner conflict. What emotions do they arouse in the audience?
25. Tell the full story of the life of Watkins. How is that story revealed? What dramatic purposes does the revelation of Watkins' story fulfil?
26. How does the death of the Major affect the audience?
27. What purpose does Act IV fulfil?
28. What admirable characteristics does Act IV emphasize?
29. What are the most notable dramatic effects produced in Act IV?
30. How do the stage directions contribute to the effects that are produced in Act IV?
31. What does Lieutenant Cardew add to the play?
32. Show that the conclusion of the play is in full keeping with the character of the Raja.
33. Make a diagram of the play, showing its moments of greatest dramatic power.
34. What dramatic values does *The Green Goddess* illustrate?
35. Select any important part of the play; by means of a series of carefully chosen adjectives, describe the characters as vividly as possible, with regard to action, appearance, and state of mind.

SUBJECTS FOR WRITTEN IMITATION

1. American explorers, in aeroplanes flew over unexplored regions of the Orinoko and the Amazon, a land of fierce savages and head hunters. Write a scenario for a play that

will tell of startling adventures, and that will, at the same time, make strong use of characterization.
2. Suggest several somewhat similar situations that might be used as bases for dramatic work.
3. Write directions for stage setting and for costumes, for the play suggested.
4. Write a dialogue in which you show a person of a cynical nature.
5. Write directions for unusual and startling stage setting.
6. Write a dialogue in which you reveal somewhat of the past history of a man who has put aside the best traditions of his kind.
7. Write a dialogue in which you show a person struggling between two alternatives.
8. Write a dialogue in which you show an unexpected rescue. Make full use of stage directions.

Directions for Writing

Write with the greatest possible condensation, but do not sacrifice naturalness of situation or of dialogue. Think primarily of character, but aim at originality of action. Indicate important stage business.

Oral Work in Class

1. Read aloud, or act with others, any part of your own writing.
2. Make a selection of the Raja's important speeches. Read two or three of them aloud, using proper intonation and action.
3. Select associates, and act any important scene in the play.
4. Select associates, and act one of the dialogues in which Watkins takes part.
5. Read aloud, as dramatically as you can, the part of the play that pleases you most.
6. Select associates, and act one of the dialogues in which Lucilla displays unusual emotion.

OFF NAGS HEAD

OR

THE BELL BUOY

A Tragedy of the North Carolina Coast

By Dougald MacMillan

Off Nags Head is a remarkably powerful example of folk-play. As a basis for it the author took the tragic story of Mrs. Theodosia Burr Alston, daughter of Aaron Burr, who sailed on a small boat, *The Patriot*, from Georgetown, South Carolina, December 30, 1812, and was never heard of again. The fate of the boat and of its passengers was never learned. In 1869, fifty-seven years later, a doctor, visiting an old fisherwoman near Nags Head, found in her house a portrait of Theodosia Burr. The local story of Nags Head was that in 1812 a wrecked and abandoned boat, containing the portrait, had drifted ashore. At that time the coast was inhabited by wreckers who used false lights to lure vessels to destruction. Sometimes they placed a light on a horse's head, and led the horse along the beach, thus deceiving mariners into thinking that the light was on a vessel proceeding in safe waters. Possibly such false lights lured to destruction *The Patriot*, on which Theodosia Burr sailed.

Taking fact and legend, the dramatist conceived a strong situation by assuming that the woman, the owner of the portrait, was Theodosia Burr Alston herself, old and demented, and that she heard in the noise of an unusual storm the cry of the child she had lost at sea fifty-seven years before. The dramatist then made the situation more powerful by assuming that the fisherman in whose hut the woman lived, was among those who had wrecked *The Patriot*.

The hypnotic effect of a storm; re-awakened memories; longing for a dead child, these are the moving forces in the play. The graphic outlining of characters; the quick, vivid, natural dialogue, breathless in the tensity of its emotion; suggestions concerning the past; steady growth to a powerful climax; and atmospheric effects produced by the insistent clanging of a bell buoy, the roar of the surf, and the sound of the wind in a great storm, made *Off Nags Head* a powerful play.

Off Nags Head, written by Dougald MacMillan, is a representative production of The Carolina Playmakers, Inc., of which Frederick H. Koch, Professor of Dramatic Literature in the University of North Carolina, is the Founder and Director.

Throughout the United States numerous Little Theater and Community groups strongly influence the advancement of the drama. In New York City alone over fifty Little Theater groups work actively. In the United States over five hundred well-organized, well-directed groups of interested students of the drama actively study, write, and produce plays. Such a widespread movement for the uplift of the drama means much.

Although commercial forces cheapen the stage by multiplying the appeal to the eye, and by decreasing the appeal to the brain and to the heart, other forces, represented by the Little Theaters and Community groups, do important work to increase interest in the drama of the better sort.

Through the influence of Little Theater groups the one-act play is now an art form of notable importance.

INTRODUCTORY PROBLEMS

1. Write a scenario for a play based on any legend of your community or State.

2. Write a scenario for a play based on any story of kidnaping, such as the story of the kidnaping of Charlie Ross in 1874.
3. Write a dialogue in which you make surprising revelations concerning the past history of one of the characters.

CHARACTERS

An Old Fisherman
The "Gal," *his daughter*
The Sick Woman, *the fisherman's wife*
The Doctor
The Old Woman

Scene: A fisherman's hut on the sand dunes of Nags Head on the North Carolina Coast.

Time: September, 1869. A stormy night.

SCENE

The roar of the surf and the distant clanging of the bell buoy can be heard before the curtain rises on a room furnished meagerly, and not very neat in appearance. There is a door at the back to the left, opening out on the beach; to the right a small window, closed by a rough shutter. Between the door and the window, on the back wall, hangs an old portrait in a tarnished gilded frame. It is a handsome painting of a young woman. At the beginning of the play it is covered by a coarse woolen cloth.

There is a fireplace in the left side wall and in that corner a table with a water bucket. On the right a door opens into the adjoining room. A lantern, hung on a nail by the fireplace, gives a flickering light.

It is nearly dark on an evening in September and a storm is piling up mountains of spray in the surf, some distance

*across the beach. Throughout the entire action the roar of
the surf and the ringing of the bell buoy can be heard. It is
far away, but you could hear it at any time; only, when some
one is talking, you do not notice the distant clanging. From
time to time the wind howls around the house, and every
now and then the smoke blows out of the fireplace, in which
a fire of driftwood is struggling to overcome the draft down
the chimney.*

*A woman is lying on a low bed in the corner of the room
to the right. She is moaning as if she were suffering acutely.
The old* FISHERMAN *is standing by the bed with a conch-shell
of water in his hand. He touches the woman on the shoulder.*

FISHERMAN.   Here, want a drink o' water?

[*The woman moans and raises her head slightly. The*
FISHERMAN *holds the shell to her lips. She drinks a swallow
and sinks back on the bed. The* FISHERMAN *puts the shell
on top of the water bucket and, crossing to the fireplace, begins to mend a shrimp-seine lying across a chair. He sits
down with the seine in his lap. The* SICK WOMAN *moans
again and moves restlessly. He turns toward her.*]

Doctor Wright 'll be here purty soon. The gal 's been
gone long enough to be back.

[*After a moment of silence the door at the back opens and
the* GIRL *comes in with an apron full of driftwood that she
has picked up on the beach. She has a shawl drawn tightly
around her shoulders and her colorless hair has been blown
into wisps about her freckled face. She whines in a nasal
drawl when she talks. Dragging her heels, she shuffles over
to the fireplace and drops the wood in a pile on the hearth.
The* FISHERMAN *turns to the door as she comes, speaking
anxiously.*]

Is he comin'?

GIRL.   Doctor Wright 's gone over to Jug Neck an' won't
be back till to-morrow. I foun' a docto' at ol' man Stokes's,
though. He come thar to-day from Raleigh. He 's comin'.
[*She hangs her shawl on a hook behind the door and goes
to the* SICK WOMAN.]   Is it bad?

[*The* SICK WOMAN *groans.*]

FISHERMAN. Did you see the ol' 'oman?

GIRL. Naw. Is she gone?

FISHERMAN. Been gone 'bout an hour.

GIRL. Which way 'd she go?

FISHERMAN. Toward the inlet.

GIRL [*she rises from bending over the* SICK WOMAN *and goes to the door for her shawl*]. M . . . hm. Time she was back. I 'll go hunt 'er.

FISHERMAN. Wait. Maybe she 'll come in in a minute. I 'll go hunt. How high is the tide now?

GIRL [*hangs up her shawl again but speaks anxiously*]. Them stakes fo' Jones's shack is covered an' it 's washin' up under the seine racks.

FISHERMAN. M . . . hm. Purty bad.

GIRL. An' it 's so misty you can't see the Topsail Light. [*She goes to the fireplace and crouches there, warming her hands.*]

FISHERMAN. Huh. This is a worse storm 'n we 've had in a long time. [*He goes to the door and looks out. The bell buoy clangs.*]

GIRL. Listen to that bell buoy. It makes me feel so quar. [*She shivers.*]

FISHERMAN. Don' you take on like that. The ol' 'oman 's bad enough.

GIRL [*takes an old, round, iron kettle and fills it with water from the bucket by the door*]. She 's been bad all day —like she was las' storm we had when she tried to jump off 'n the landin'! She might try again. We better look for 'er. [*She hangs the kettle over the fire and crosses to the* SICK WOMAN.]

FISHERMAN. I reckon so. You look out for yo' ma.

GIRL. The ol' 'oman 's been a-doin' like she done that day when she tried to run in the surf with the picter.

FISHERMAN. Has she? [*As though he doesn't quite understand why.*] She sets a lot o' store by that picter.

GIRL. I 'm kind o' skeered she 'll do somethin' bad some day.

FISHERMAN. She ain't gonna jump in the surf no more.
Not on a col' night like this un. You take care o' yo' ma
thar. I 'll hunt th' other un. [*He starts toward the door
and opens it. The* OLD WOMAN *is seen outside just coming
in. She has been tall and might have been imperious. She
speaks with a more refined accent than the others. She is
demented and they humor her. The* FISHERMAN *speaks
to her from the doorway.*] Well, we was jest a-comin' to
look fo' you! Thought you might 'a' fallen overboard or
sumpthin'. [*He sits down again by the fire. The* GIRL *takes
the* OLD WOMAN'S *shawl from her shoulders and hangs it by
the fireplace to dry. The* OLD WOMAN *does not seem to
notice the others but speaks as though to herself.*]

OLD WOMAN. I 've had so much to do.

FISHERMAN. Well, now that 's bad. You must n't work
too hard. It 's bad for you.

OLD WOMAN. It 's better to work than to think. [*She
smiles in a vague sort of way. Her eyes are expressionless.*]
There are times when I think and I hear things. They keep
calling me on the boat and the bell buoy rings——

GIRL [*to the* FISHERMAN]. Ain't it time the doctor was
comin'?

OLD WOMAN. I see many things. There is the cheery
crowd on the boat and they keep calling, for all is dark and
everything reels—the light comes close and all is dark again.
Listen! my baby boy calls—the water roars and we all get
wet. . . . But I still have my work. I must not give up—I
still have my child and my pictures to work for. [*She goes
toward the curtained portrait.*] My dead boy and you—
[*She pulls the curtain aside, displaying the beautiful old
painting. Her voice is more cheerful and less troubled as
she speaks to the* FISHERMAN.*] It is a picture of me! Don't
you think it is good? It was done by the best artist. I am
taking it to my father in New York.

FISHERMAN [*humoring her*]. Yes, yes. You done tol' us
that a lot o' times.

GIRL [*to the* FISHERMAN]. I wonder why the doctor ain't
come.

OLD WOMAN [*interrupting and still speaking to the* FISHERMAN]. So I have—so I have. Well, I must keep on working. I've had a message from my father. [*More brightly.*] I'm going to leave soon. [*She starts toward the room at the right, then turns to the* FISHERMAN, *speaking anxiously.*] Take care of her. Don't let anyone get her. [*Speaking to the portrait.*] I am going to take you with me when I go to New York to see my father. [*She goes out, glancing back from the door at the portrait.*] I'm coming back soon.

FISHERMAN. She's so scared someun's gonna steal her picter. . . . Is the lamp lit in thar?

GIRL. Yeah. I lit it. [*There is a knock on the door.*] It must be the new doctor. [*She opens the door and the* DOCTOR *comes in. He is an elderly man, wearing a long cloak and carrying a satchel. His manner is brisk and cheerful and he is rather talkative, the old family doctor type.*]

FISHERMAN. Come in.

DOCTOR. Thank you. I had some trouble finding the house. There is so much mist you can't see very well. I believe this is the worst storm I ever saw.

FISHERMAN. Yeah. It's bad. You can't even see the Topsail Light.

DOCTOR [*taking off his hat and cloak and laying them on a chair by the fire*]. Do you often have storms like this one? This is my first trip down here. Mr. Stokes asked me down to go fishing with him.

FISHERMAN. This un is right bad.

DOCTOR. Now, where is the sick woman?

FISHERMAN [*pointing to the bed*]. Here.

DOCTOR. Oh, yes! Your wife?

FISHERMAN. Yes, suh.

DOCTOR [*sitting by the bed*]. How do you feel?

[*The* SICK WOMAN *moans.*]

FISHERMAN. She don' say nothin'. She's got a misery in her chist.

DOCTOR. I see. How long has she been this way?

FISHERMAN. Since this mornin'.

DOCTOR [*to the* GIRL, *who stands by the door to the next room*] Will you bring me some water, please.

[*She goes out. He opens his satchel and takes out a bottle, pouring some medicine into the cup which the* GIRL *brings him, and gives it to the sick woman to drink. The* FISHERMAN *and the* GIRL *look on in silence. He speaks reassuringly.*]

She 'll be comfortable in a few minutes. It is not serious this time, but she must not work too hard. [*He rises and crosses to the fireplace for his cloak.*]

FISHERMAN. Will you set down an' rest yourself an' git dry? It 's a long walk back to Stokes's.

DOCTOR. Why, thank you, I believe I will.

[*They sit before the fire and light their pipes. The* GIRL *goes out.*]

FISHERMAN. You ain't been here befo', Doctor?

DOCTOR. No. This is my first trip. I 've always wanted to come but never had a chance before. There are lots of interestin' tales told about your beaches and islands around here.

FISHERMAN. Yeah. I reckon thar 's a lot o' tales.

DOCTOR. Captain Kidd is said to have buried money on every island on the coast.

FISHERMAN. Yes, suh. Right over thar on Haw's Hammock my pa dug up a chist.

DOCTOR. Was there anything in it?

FISHERMAN. No. [*He smiles.*]

DOCTOR. That 's often the way. [*He laughs, then stops to listen to the wind, which is increasing in volume and intensity.*] Listen to that! This would be a good night for the land pirates that used to be around here. Did you know any of them?

FISHERMAN. I don't know what you mean.

DOCTOR. Oh, is that so? Why, they say there used to be a band of men around here that hung lights on a horse's head and drove the horse down the beach. From a distance it looked like a ship. Ships at sea were often fooled by it and ran aground. When they did, the men on shore plundered them and killed the crew. That's how Nags Head got its name.

FISHERMAN [*showing some confusion*]. Is that right?

DOCTOR. Why, you are old enough to know about that. I'm surprised that you didn't know some of those old rascals.

FISHERMAN [*turning away*]. We don't talk much in these parts.

DOCTOR [*becoming interested in his tale*]. A very famous case, I remember—one that has been talked about for a long time—I heard it from my mother, was that of a boat named the . . . *The Patriot*. She was bound for New York from Georgetown, I believe. An illustrious lady, Theodosia Burr, was on board—the daughter of Aaron Burr. The boat disappeared somewhere along this coast. That was about fifty years ago, and none of the crew has been heard of since. [*The* FISHERMAN *is silent, looking into the fire. The* DOCTOR *rises.*] Well, let's have another look at the patient. I'll have to get back pretty soon. Stokes gets me out early these days to get the blue fish on the right time o' the tide. [*He knocks out his pipe against the chimney and turns toward the bed. The* FISHERMAN *rises. The* OLD WOMAN *enters unnoticed, crosses to the fireplace and stands there watching the others. The* DOCTOR *starts to the bed but stops suddenly, astonished. He has seen the portrait!*] Why, hello, what's that?

FISHERMAN. What?

DOCTOR. The portrait. Where did it come from?

FISHERMAN. Oh, we found it on a derelict that drifted in one day.

DOCTOR [*becoming excited*]. Why that looks like the picture that was on *The Patriot*. I remember distinctly, I once saw a copy of the lost portrait. It must be the portrait of Theodosia Burr!

[*The* OLD WOMAN *watches them intently.*]

FISHERMAN. Who 's she?

DOCTOR. The woman that was lost. Where were the crew and passengers on the boat?

FISHERMAN. I don' recollect no people on 'er. I reckon thar wan't no people on 'er.

DOCTOR. Where were they?

FISHERMAN. I don' know.

DOCTOR. Was the boat named *The Patriot?*

FISHERMAN. I can't say, 'cause I don' exactly know. She might 'a' been *The Patriot* or she might 'a' been the *Mary Ann*—I can't say. [*He has become sullen.*]

DOCTOR. Come, now. Tell me about it.

FISHERMAN. I don' know no more. We jest found it. [*He turns away.*]

DOCTOR. Then I must have the portrait. I 'm sure it 's the key to the Theodosia Burr mystery. Will you sell it?

[*The* OLD WOMAN *watches him, frightened.*]

FISHERMAN. I dunno as how we would. We sets a lot o' store by that picter.

DOCTOR. I 'll pay you for it. How much do you want? [*He starts to take the picture from the wall. The* OLD WOMAN, *who has been moving toward it, seizes his arm, excitedly.*]

OLD WOMAN. Sell her! Sell my picture! She is one of the things I work for—my dead boy and my pictures. You shall not take them from me. [*She lifts the portrait from its place and holds it tightly in her arms, talking to it.*] I am taking you to my father in New York. He wants it. [*More wildly, speaking to the* DOCTOR.] You shan't have it. . . . They shan't take you from me. . . . It is all that I have. I 've been cruelly treated. My baby boy died. He is out there. . . . [*She points to the sea.*] He often calls me to come to him but I must stay here, for I still have my picture to work for. [*She turns away.*]

DOCTOR. Who are you?

OLD WOMAN [*smiling. She seems to look at something far away*]. Ah. . . .

DOCTOR. Who are you? What do you know about the picture? It must be a portrait of Theodosia Burr!

OLD WOMAN. Burr? Theodosia Burr? [*Almost frenzied as she suddenly remembers her identity.*] Why, she 's the person that I stand for! I 've been thinking—she keeps talking to me. That 's who I stand for!

DOCTOR. What?

FISHERMAN [*with a significant nod*]. Don't mind her. She ain't right.

OLD WOMAN. I must be going now. They are tired of waiting. I 've stayed here long enough. . . . I 'm coming, father. [*She starts to go into the next room.*]

DOCTOR [*stepping in front of the door, he speaks gently*]. Where are you going?

OLD WOMAN [*turning back into the room*]. Maybe the boat 's fixed now. I wonder where the others are.

DOCTOR [*persuasively*]. Yes, tell us where the others are.

OLD WOMAN. Oh, I remember. They 're gone. They were killed. Hush, don't you hear them . . . listen! . . . *They* took all the things on the boat, but I have saved you. [*She clasps the picture closer and stares before her.*] It was an awful storm like this one. A false light; we ran on the beach. It was horrible! Yes . . . yes, *they* were there —*they,* they killed them all!

DOCTOR. Yes, yes! Don't get excited. We 'll fix everything all right. Don't let it worry you. Sit down and tell us all about it.

OLD WOMAN [*moving to the right of the room*]. I am going away very soon now. . . . I saw a sign to-day. I have been sent for. They have sent for me to come to see my father in New York. He has been waiting so long. I must go—— [*She goes out into the adjoining room, muttering. The* DOCTOR *turns to the* FISHERMAN.]

DOCTOR. What do you know about this?

FISHERMAN. Nothin', I tol' you.

DOCTOR. How did she get here?

FISHERMAN. We took 'er in one time. [*He speaks sullenly.*]

DOCTOR. Yes, but where did she come from? You know more about this, and you 're going to tell me. If you don't, I 'll have you arrested on suspicion. You 'll be tried and maybe you 'll be hanged. Now, tell me what you know.

FISHERMAN. Wait— [*He is beginning to be afraid.*]—I don't know nothin', I tol' you.

DOCTOR [*threateningly*]. Yes, you do. Do you want to get into court?

FISHERMAN. No! No!

DOCTOR [*raising his voice*]. Then tell me what you know about it. I 'll——

FISHERMAN [*interrupting*]. Be quiet, I 'll tell you. Don' make no noise . . . I was a boy . . . they used to hang a lantern on a horse . . . then when the ship run aground they got all the stuff off'n 'er . . .

DOCTOR. Land pirates! I thought you knew! Go on.

FISHERMAN. That 's all.

DOCTOR. What became of the people on these boats?

FISHERMAN. They got drownded.

DOCTOR. How? Don't take so long.

FISHERMAN. Jes' drownded.

DOCTOR. Did you kill them?

FISHERMAN. No. They was jes' drownded.

DOCTOR. And where did the old woman and the portrait come from?

FISHERMAN. They was on one o' the boats an' we took 'em in. She ain't been right in 'er head sence. Her baby boy died that night.

DOCTOR. Where did she go? I want to talk to her again. [*He goes toward the door.*]

FISHERMAN. You ain't a-goin' t'——

DOCTOR [*interrupting*]. No, I won't send you to jail. Go get the old woman. [*He moves to the fireplace.*]

FISHERMAN. She went in thar. [*He goes to the door and looks into the next room.*] She ain't in thar now.

DOCTOR. Then where could she be?

FISHERMAN. I dunno.

[*The* GIRL *comes in, very much excited and frightened.*

*She enters by the door at the back and as she opens it the
roar of the surf and the ringing of the bell buoy may be
heard more distinctly.*]

GIRL. I tried to stop 'er, but she jest went on! I can't
do nothin' with 'er.

DOCTOR. What do you mean?

GIRL. She run out a-huggin' that picter. I could n't stop
'er. She said she was goin' away!

FISHERMAN. Where did she go?

GIRL. I dunno. She 's been so bad all day, a-talkin' 'bout
the bell buoy a-ringin' for 'er— [*She goes to the* FISHERMAN.]
I 'm skeered o' what she 'll do!

[*Above the roar of the surf can be heard faintly but
clearly, a high-pitched, distant cry.*]

DOCTOR. What 's that?

FISHERMAN. I dunno . . .

GIRL. I wonder if it 's . . .

[*The* DOCTOR *and* FISHERMAN *go to the door at the back.*]

DOCTOR. We 'd better go look for her.

FISHERMAN [*as they run out into the darkness across the
beach*]. I hope she ain't . . .

[*The* GIRL *stands in the open door watching them. The*
SICK WOMAN *moans. The roar of the surf and the ringing
of the bell buoy are heard more distinctly. After a moment
the* FISHERMAN *comes in, breathless and wild-eyed.*]

FISHERMAN. Gi' me the lantern! She 's run in the surf
an' it a-bilin'.

GIRL [*taking the lighted lantern from a nail by the fireplace*]. She said the bell was a-ringin' for 'er. . . . Is
she . . .

FISHERMAN [*takes the lantern, pausing a moment in the
doorway*]. She 's drownded! She done washed ashore!

[*The* FISHERMAN *goes out and the light from his lantern
disappears in the night. As the* GIRL *stands in the doorway
looking toward the sea, the bell buoy can still be heard above
the storm.*]

CURTAIN

SUGGESTIVE QUESTIONS

1. By what means does the dramatist give the play its strong atmospheric effects?
2. What different emotions does the play arouse?
3. What appeals to the eye, and what appeals to the ear, does the setting make?
4. What parts of the stage setting do most to increase the dramatic effects?
5. Show that the play has unity in all respects.
6. Trace the development of the play to its climax.
7. Point out various examples of foreshadowing.
8. What part in the play does the storm take?
9. What different means does the dramatist use in order to produce striking effects?
10. Tell the story of the Old Woman's past.
11. By what means does the dramatist reveal that story?
12. Tell the story of the Fisherman's past.
13. By what means does the dramatist reveal that story?
14. What purpose does the Doctor fulfil in the play?
15. Compare the dialogue in which the Doctor takes part, with the dialogue in *Macbeth* in which a Doctor also takes part.
16. Point out places where the play strongly stimulates the imagination.
17. Point out places where the play strongly awakens emotion.
18. What makes the ending of the play effective?

SUBJECTS FOR WRITTEN IMITATION

1. Write a dialogue that takes place in a forest camp during a great storm.
2. Write a dialogue that takes place in a dwelling house during a thunder storm.
3. Write a dialogue in which a half-crazed person speaks.
4. Write a dialogue in which you make the characters reveal much about the past.
5. Write a scenario for a play based on storm and tragedy.
6. Write directions for stage setting for a play based on storm and tragedy.

Directions for Writing

Make full use of appeals to the emotion, but make the appeals comparatively simple. Do not let your work fall into mere sentimentality, or into mere melodrama. Use everyday language. Make your sentences short and emphatic. Write all the necessary stage directions.

Oral Work in Class

1. Read aloud any part of your own written work.
2. Read aloud, with appropriate dramatic action, all of the Old Woman's speeches.
3. Point out that part of the play that interests you most. Select associates, and act that part.
4. Act any one of the brisk dialogues in the play.

BUSHIDO

Adapted from Terakoya or The Village School, otherwise called Matsu, the Pine-Tree

BY TAKEDA IDZUMO

1746

In 1900 Professor Karl Florenz, of the Imperial University of Tokio, translated from Japanese into French the one-act play now called *Bushido*, one of the most remarkable of all Japanese plays. In the original Japanese, *Bushido* was part of a famous long play by the great eighteenth century dramatist, Takeda Idzumo.

In 1916, Mr. M. C. Marcus translated from Japanese into English the same section of the long Japanese play. In 1916 the Washington Square Players, in New York City, produced the play. Thus, while *Bushido* first appeared in 1746, it only recently came to the attention of the people of Europe and of the United States.

The version that appears in this book is a translation from the French.

The drama in Japan, like the drama in England, grew from religious beginnings. Even before the eighth century religious pantomimes added to the force of religious teaching. In the fourteenth century these pantomimes led to dialogues and written plays.

Dramatic story telling, and especially, the giving of

marionette plays, in which the Japanese excelled, likewise led toward a type of drama like our own.

Just at the beginning of the eighteenth century two famous dramatists, Chikamatsu Monzayemon, and Takeda Idzumo, became popular writers. Chikamatsu, who died in 1734, wrote no less than 74 plays founded on history, and 37 plays concerning people in his own period. He was the first really great Japanese dramatist.

Takeda Idzumo, who died in 1756, was a partner with Chikamatsu Monzayemon in the management of one of the most popular marionette theatres. Idzumo collaborated with others in writing great historical plays that throw into the light of high tragedy some of the most noble characteristics of humankind.

One of these long five-act plays tells of dramatic events in the life of Sugawara Michizane, a poet and famous Chancellor who lived about A.D. 900. The play lays stress on loyalty at all costs. That part of the long play, which is included in this book, is called *Bushido,* the Japanese word for *loyalty to one's superior.*

According to Japanese tradition, Michizane had three trees that he loved, a plum tree, a cherry tree, and a pine tree. Michizane, therefore, expressed delight when his most faithful retainer named three sons, in honor of their lord, "Plum Tree," "Cherry Tree," and "Pine Tree" (Matsuo).

It happened that "Pine Tree" (Matsuo) gained employment with a great lord named Shihei, and that this great lord, later on, conquered Michizane and wished to kill all of Michizane's heirs.

"Cherry Tree" died in battle, fighting for his lord; "Plum Tree" remained with his lord in flight and hiding. "Pine Tree" (Matsuo), sad at heart, stayed with the conqueror.

One day "Pine Tree" (Matsuo) learned that Shihei had discovered that an old warrior who kept a school, was sheltering the eight year old son and heir of Michizane, pretending that the boy was his own son. He learned that Shihei planned to have "Pine Tree" (Matsuo) identify the boy, and then to have the child killed. "Pine Tree" (Matsuo) substituted his own son, and saved the heir of Michizane. The touching, almost too-tragic story, is the basis of the plot of *Bushido,* a story of loyalty. One thinks at once of Abraham's willingness to sacrifice Isaac; of Sidney Carton's taking the place of Charles Darnay; and of the Gold Star Mothers sending their sons to die for the sake of their country. One thinks, too, of the whole theme of sacrifice, that has played so great a part in all religions, and in all lands, from ancient times down to the present.

The simplicity, the brevity, and the naturalness of the dialogue, make the characters vividly real. Their emotions are genuine. When one accepts the code of the Japanese, he sees that there is not a false note in the play. *Bushido* is a work of real art, emphasizing a noble theme.

The large, revolving stages of the Japanese theaters permit the actors to appear in settings that are full of detail, complete in every respect. "The Flower Path" that leads down among the audience, a device that has been imitated in some American theaters, makes possible the most heartfelt interpretation of parts. Every slight movement, every shade of expression, every breath, carries emotion. The manner of acting of the Japanese is slow, giving to every movement a sort of fatality. Facial expression is so controlled that there seems to be no change at all; but the slight flickering of an eyelid, the faintest movement of a muscle, is made to tell volumes. In our own land Sessue Hayokawa, the Japanese moving picture actor, has shown the possibilites for interpretation that may be given to even the slightest muscular change.

With this attention to facial expression and the importance of minutely detailed acting, the Japanese of the past combined the weird music of Japanese stringed instruments, like guitars, the music rising and falling with the emotions of the play.

The men chanted their parts in deep, bass voices, in harmony with the music; the women spoke in voices higher than natural; both paid much attention to gesticulation with hands and especially with fans, and to the production of startlingly effective pantomime pictures.

The great Japanese drama, like the great Greek drama, or even the Elizabethan drama, deals too much with violence to suit modern American taste, but when one accepts the conventions of the Japanese stage, when one becomes, for the moment, Japanese in spirit, then he sees the high art of such work as *Bushido*. Then, too, one may look upon *Bushido* as a dramatization of a Japanese tradition. No child thinks of *Jack, the Giant Killer* as gruesome. He looks upon it as "just a fairy story."

INTRODUCTORY PROBLEMS

1. Write a scenario for a play that will tell of self-sacrifice for the sake of loyalty to team or school. Plan to have your play call for action.
2. Write a scenario for a play about Nathan Hale. Plan to emphasize self-sacrifice.
3. How did the Elizabethan stage affect the Elizabethan drama?
4. How did the Japanese stage affect the Japanese drama?
5. How does our modern stage affect our modern drama?

STAGING

The stage is in two levels. The upper stage, all across the rear, is nine or ten inches higher than the lower stage in front, and about six feet behind the curtain line. Six feet back from its edge, in turn, is a wall of *shoji* or sliding panels, the middle one of which remains open throughout, forming a doorway. Through this, several feet yet farther back, is shown a similar wall, but of a lighter color. Characters going out by this center door turn to their right, stage left.

The side walls are sharply slanting; the length of the back wall is, in fact, barely three-fifths of the proscenium width. That on the left is a continuation of the back wall, with a similar door, open onto the lower stage. That on the right, however, is a lattice-work of one-inch-square wood, the interstices two inches wide by twelve high. The down-stage half of it contains a gate that can slide up behind the up-stage half, wide enough to admit easily the litter presently to be described. It can be bolted with a kind of hook. Through the grating is seen a courtyard with three trees. The tree farthest up-stage, visible to almost every spectator, is a Japanese pine. Farthest down-stage, perhaps only its branches visible, drooping over the gateway, is a plum-tree. Between them, but separated from the pine by a wall or fence, is a cherry-tree in bloom. These trees stand out, plastic and real, against a blue sky. The path to the gate leads between the cherry and the plum trees, and characters entering so may be seen approaching by the audience; but the gate can also be reached, of course, from down-stage, without warning.

The colors of the scene are all pale, harmonious and pretty. The floor of the lower stage may be light brown, of the upper stage pale green in front, pale purplish gray behind the door. The *shoji* show variations of these tints, perhaps light gray in front, light blue within. The woodwork—both the right wall and the edges of the upper stage, the door-frames, etc., —keeps its natural, unpainted buff.

The tables that serve Ghenzo's pupils as desks are of varying shades of brown, from russet to violet, stronger than the scene tints. They are not more than a foot wide and are low enough to be comfortable for a child sitting cross-legged on the floor. They stand not on legs but on hourglass-shaped boards, beyond which their ends project as far as a child's comfortable arm-spread and terminate in a bit of molding that gives them a turned-up appearance. Four of them stand at the edge of the upper stage, about two feet apart, and are occupied by Shusai, the Dunce, Iwama, and Toku. On the lower stage, in the space to the left of each of these, are the other four, or three, if that number proves more convenient. Later, the Dunce is set at Shusai's right on the lower level, and Kotaro on the upper. At Ghenzo's command the boys put their tables close together along the back wall, Kotaro's, Shusai's, the Dunce's, and Choma's right of the center door, and the other five or four on the left, but leaving a foot or two of free space on either side of the doorway.

the yellow fan he carries in his right hand. His complexion is not Mongolian or porcelain-white, but flushed. His expression is wholly sinister. His voice and laugh are harsh.

MATSUO, the Pine-tree, a samurai of Shihei's court, but of a family long vassals to the house of Mitchizaneh.
His is the most exacting part in the play. His voice is very deep and powerful. His face is white, his eyes and eyebrows very slanting, his nose aquiline, his thin mouth turned down, all as in old Japanese pictures. He has a great bushy mass of hair that overhangs a purple fillet and is tied in a tuft behind with a white bow. His undergarments are white, his outer kimono gray-blue dotted with white specks and larger clouds upon which is a design of green pine needles. His socks and the thick round cord about his waist are white—the tufted ends of the cord tied in a big loop in front—and his swords have white-and-gold handles and gold-studded scabbards. At his second entrance he appears all in black and green—the dark, glossy green of the pine-tree—a green kimono with a wide black border and an open black kimono covering its upper part. The purple fillet is gone, the waist cord is thinner and brown like a pine's branch, and the socks are black. Showing at his throat and sleeve ends are the mourning garments that he reveals just before the curtain: a pure white kimono with a clear sky-blue train, wide on the shoulders, drawn down to the girdle in a deep narrow V in front, falling down his back and spreading in folds on the floor but caught up under the green kimono until the moment of discovery.

CHIYO, his Wife. She looks like all the ladies in Japanese pictures, with gold pins in her elaborate coiffure. Her under-dress is a white mourning kimono like Matsuo's, with a blue sash instead of his train. Over it she wears a black kimono, lined and edged with light blue, with four round white spots: two on the sleeves, two above the breasts.

Her deep sash, tied with a big bow in front, is light brown lined with pale blue, with a faint daisy pattern in darker brown. Her stockings are white, her fan light blue.

KOTARO, their Son, eight years old. He very much resembles Shusai, but he wears a skirt of striped brown and gray-blue, and a short, lilac-colored kimono over it with white spots like his mother's and a lining of rose-pink. The under-dress, showing in front, is light green. His *tabi* are white.

GHENZO, the Master of the Village School, formerly a samurai of Mitchizaneh's. His is the outstanding part after Matsuo's. That he is a samurai can be seen by his two swords; that he is in poor circumstances, by the plainness of his dress. His feet are bare; his kimono is dull red, lined with vivid blue-green, with a dark pine-green sash and round white spots on the sleeves; his open outer kimono is of better material, black, with similar white spots. He had donned this to go to the Mayor's and discards it the first time he leaves the stage. At the same time he loops up his sleeves with a blue cord around his neck, that is fastened to the short sword,—as shown in our frontispiece. His crown is shaved like Ghemba's,—but not colored. The hair is drawn up into the conventional tuft, in this case more like a queue, looped forward and stuck down in the middle of the bald spot. His face is stern, hard-pressed and strained, his voice flexible and strong.

TONAMI, his Wife. She looks just like Chiyo. Her undergarment is lilac, her kimono gray-green, bordered with black and lined with light blue, and her sash is black, tied in an enormous bow behind. She has the round white spot on the sleeve. Her feet, like Ghenzo's, are bare.

FIVE MEN-AT-ARMS, Retainers of Shihei. Their heads are shaved around a central tuft which is drawn back and tied to the back hair with a white bow, and they wear light red-brown fillets, tied with a bow in front. Their undergarments, showing at the throat V and as trousers on thigh and knee, are pale blue or light vermilion or perhaps canary yellow like Ghemba's feet, and their scalps are colored light blue like Ghemba's. Their short, coat-like kimonos are slate-gray with red-brown belt and white tape round the back of the neck, under the arms, crossed at the back, and tied in a bow in front just above the belt, to keep their kimono sleeves out of the way. Above the elbow, their arms are bare in these loose, drawn-back sleeves; below, they wear a sort of mitt, slate-gray, tied round the wrist. Their stockings or puttees are slate-gray, tied just below the knee. They wear sandal soles, with black strings. Their weapon is a kind of short, blunt sword with no hilt but with a long catch or hook at the side by which to swing naked in their belts.

SANZUKEI, attendant upon Chiyo and Kotaro. He is elderly, bald though with a small queue looped like Ghenzo's, with a black under-vest, a short kimono without deep sleeves, of blue-gray cotton dotted with white, an over-vest of horizontally striped material, pine-green and dark gray, long blue trousers with a big white patch on one knee, and white socks. The table he carries is like the other boys', but obviously brand-new. The box with it, that Chiyo later seizes for a shield, is black, lined with yellow.

Two COOLIES, Litter-bearers for Matsuo. They are dressed like the Men-at-arms except that their trousers and coats are light and dark grayish-blue respectively, and they lack the white tape, the mitts, and the weapons. On their heads they have buff-colored, almost flat conical hats, tied under the chin.

SIX or SEVEN PEASANTS. They are mostly middle-aged, some elderly; and mostly bald, though one or two may have a little queue at the crown. They all wear long kimonos and short, open, over-kimonos of quiet, harmonious colors, without patterns or figures. Some are barefoot, some in white socks.

Six or Seven Boys, Pupils in Ghenzo's School. They are
all barefoot, clad in little kimonos of checked or striped
brown, gray, or blue material, with gay sashes of red, pink,
or lilac. Their hair is done in various queer ways,—odd
areas shaved, and tufts and topknots tied up in several
shapes. In age they range from seven to thirteen. The
oldest is the Dunce, a big baby in a bib, terribly ink-stained
all over. Iwama is about ten, round-faced and good-
natured. Toku and Choma are Shusai's age, homely and
ink-marked. They are all "cabbage-heads," as Ghemba
calls them: low-caste features, dark complexions, loud
voices, vulgar manners, in sharp contrast to Shusai and
Kotaro.

SCENE

Shusai and the six or seven other pupils of Ghenzo are
sitting on their heels or on their crossed legs behind little
brown tables or desks, writing Japanese characters. They
write down the paper, beginning at the upper right-hand
corner, and the written sheets hang down from the pad over
the front of the desk, the black characters showing through
the thin paper. At each boy's right, on the table, is a box
containing brushes and india ink, and at his left are the
small sheets of characters to be copied. None of the desks is
as spotless as Shusai's, the farthest right; and that of the
Dunce, who sits beside him on the upper stage, is a filthy
mass of spilled ink. The contrast between the boys themselves is just as marked: Shusai's smooth, white complexion,
aristocratic features, and plain but immaculate purple kimono,
are totally unlike the yellow, vulgar faces and dun, soiled
garments of the rest. The Dunce wears a bright brown bib,
black-stained. He and some of the others have cheeks
smutted and fingers clotted with ink, and their exercises are
blotted and blurred.

The Dunce [suddenly interrupting the silence, loudly].
Why do you keep on working when teacher is n't here?

[SHUSAI *gives him a scornful glance; but some of the others, on the lower stage, stop working and turn toward him.*] Look! I 've drawn a bonze, a bald-head! [*He holds up his crude picture. All except* SHUSAI *laugh and get up and crowd around to look.*]

SHUSAI [*not ceasing to write*]. Huh, silly!—you 'd better use your time for something besides *drawing,* and making fun of holy men. Are n't you ashamed not to be able to write the simplest syllables, at your age?

THE DUNCE. Aw, listen to teacher's pet, the wise guy!

IWAMA [*on the other side, the left, of the* DUNCE]. Don't call him names, Duncy, or I 'll— [*He gives him a light crack on the head with his brush.*]

THE DUNCE [*forcing a cry*]. Stop! He 's hitting me! [*With childish wails he throws ink in the boy's face.*]

CHOMA [*below him*]. Sissy. He 's the biggest, and he starts to bawl when any one touches him!

ANOTHER BOY [*beside* CHOMA]. Let 's give him a lesson for once that he *will* remember!

[*They pull the* DUNCE, *overturning his table, down on to the lower stage, where all except* SHUSAI—*who remains sedate at his desk—proceed to attack him. Uproar, of course, ensues, in the midst of which appears, down left,* TONAMI, *the schoolmaster's wife.*]

TONAMI. Children, children! Stop fighting! Quiet! [*She is quickly obeyed; only the* DUNCE *continues to cry.*] Go back to your places and do your lesson. The schoolmaster will be here in a minute, and if you 're good perhaps he will let you all go home early this afternoon.

THE BOYS. Oh, good! Let 's get it done quick!

[*Talking ad lib., they restore order and resume their work.* TONAMI *comforts the* DUNCE, *sets up his table on the lower stage, down right of* SHUSAI, *and runs in and out the left door, providing him with new ink and paper; then squats beside him, her back to the right, and helps him. A scholastic drone begins: the boys as they write murmur the syllable each character represents*—Ee, ro, ha, nee, ho ka, to, *etc.*]

410   MODERN PLAYS: SHORT AND LONG

[*Into the yard outside, up right, comes* SANZUKEI, *carrying a little table upside down and on it a rather large box— presumably of books and school accessories, but closed—and two small parcels.* CHIYO *follows him, leading her little son,* KOTARO, *by the hand.*]

SANZUKEI [*knocking at the gate*]. Excuse me. May we come in?

TONAMI [*popping up; politely*]. Certainly! Please!

[SANZUKEI *slides back the gate, and stays outside it while* CHIYO *and* KOTARO *enter, the boy clinging to his mother's right hand. The two ladies bow obsequiously to each other.*]

CHIYO. Master Ghenzo was pleased to return a favorable answer by the messenger [*with a slight gesture at* SANZUKEI] I sent to him this morning. Since he is willing to take my boy under his care, I have brought my son along: this is he.

TONAMI. Ah [*smiling at* KOTARO], your son? We are glad to see him. He looks unusually bright and spirited.

CHIYO. You are very sweet. I hope he will not be too much trouble. We have only been a few days in this village, 'way at the other end. I was very much pleased when I learned you had a boy of the same age. Is he among these——?

TONAMI. Yes. [*Turning left to* SHUSAI.] This is he. [*To him.*] Stand up and say how do you do to the lady.

[SHUSAI *rises and bows low, but does not descend to the lower stage.* CHIYO *crosses* TONAMI, *introduces* KOTARO *to* SHUSAI, *and stands back comparing them earnestly.*]

CHIYO. What a beautiful child. . . . But [*catching herself up*] I do not see Master Ghenzo here. Is he— [*She pauses politely*]?

TONAMI. I am sorry. He is away. He was called to the Mayor's this morning, on some very important matter. It's so far from here, I'm afraid it'll be a little time before he gets back. Still, if you wish to speak to him——

[*She crosses* CHIYO *as though to lead the way off, left.*]

CHIYO. No, no. I don't want to bother you. [TONAMI *stops, center.*] I have got to do an errand in the next village, still; and on my way back perhaps I may have the honor to see Master Ghenzo. [*Going to* SANZUKEI.] Sanzukei! The packages. [SANZUKEI *gives her the two small parcels. One, wrapped in white paper and adorned with a token of remembrance, she respectfully presents to* TONAMI.] I hope you will please accept this little present,—merely as a souvenir of this day.

TONAMI [*with a low bow*]. You are too kind; indeed . . . [*She takes it.*]

CHIYO [*deprecatingly*]. Oh, don't speak of it. It's nothing.—Here [*presenting the other box*] are some sweets for all the boys to share.

TONAMI [*laying her gifts on the edge of the upper stage*]. A thousand thanks for your thoughtfulness. My husband will indeed be——

CHIYO. Now I must go. Please take care of my son while I am gone: I trust him to you.—[*Crossing to her son and squatting by him tenderly.*] Be a good child, Kotaro. I am just going to the next village; I'll come back soon. [*But as she rises and turns from him,* KOTARO *seizes her kimono.*]

KOTARO [*fearfully*]. Don't leave me here! Take me with you!

CHIYO [*unclasping his hand*]. Aren't you ashamed, Kotaro! To be afraid! [*To* TONAMI.] You see, he's just a *little* boy. He's been too much with his mother. [*Caressing his head.*] You're my own dear child. Stay here and be good. I'll come back in a few minutes. [*She goes, but turns in the gateway and looks back upon* KOTARO *with passionate love. He sees the look and turns, his face rigidly controlled, to* SHUSAI, *who smiles kindly.* CHIYO *disappears, down right.* TONAMI *goes and takes from* SANZUKEI *the box and the little table, and sets them up in the right corner of the upper stage, her back to the audience.* SANZUKEI *shuts the gate and disappears. Then* CHIYO *returns, but stands outside.*] Pardon me for disturbing you again. I must have forgotten my fan.

[TONAMI *looks for the fan. All the boys look about on the floor, but don't get up except the* DUNCE, *who under a pretense of looking under the parcels appropriates the candy box, hides it in his sleeve, and sits down again. Meanwhile* CHIYO *gazes with unspeakable, sorrowful tenderness at* KOTARO, *who does not dare to look towards her.*]

TONAMI [*suddenly*]. But you have it in your hand—your fan!

CHIYO [*starting*]. So I have! What was I thinking of! Pardon me. [*Still looking back through the bars, she passes out of the yard and is gone.* KOTARO *suppresses a sob.* TONAMI *hastens to him.*]

TONAMI. Come, dear. Don't mind. This little boy will show you all about it. Let me . . . [*With her back to the gate, she tries to divert* KOTARO, *talking softly, ad lib.* SHUSAI *also helps to start him at his writing. The other boys resume their interrupted lesson, except the* DUNCE *who eats candy on the sly till* GHENZO'S *entrance terrifies and stops him.*]

[GHENZO *suddenly appears in the yard, quietly opens the gate, and stands down right, stock-still, examining with a sorely troubled expression the faces of his pupils. Naturally, he does not see* KOTARO, *and he pays no attention to the* DUNCE.]

GHENZO [*to himself, bitterly*]. Peasant faces,—only low, peasant heads! Too coarse, too vulgar,—idle for my purpose! [*At his voice,* TONAMI *starts, turns, looks at him anxiously.*]

TONAMI [*after a moment's pause, approaching him respectfully*]. Why are you pale? Why are you so excited? What did they mean—those words you spoke just now? [GHENZO *darts a severe glance at her; then peers again at each pupil.*] Why do you look so sharply at the children? What angers you? You frighten them. Please stop! [GHENZO *strides away from her, crosses the front of the stage, and comes back pacing like a trapped beast.*] Calm yourself: all the more because we 've just received a new pupil, a wonderful child. [*She indicates* KOTARO, *up on her left.*] Look at him, won't you? Give him a friendly smile. [*To* KOTARO.] Come here, Kotaro, and meet your schoolmaster.

[GHENZO, *who knew another pupil was expected, hardly looks at him.* KOTARO *comes down timidly and gazes earnestly into* GHENZO'S *face, then bows low before him.*]

KOTARO. You are very good to take me under your protection.

GHENZO [*absently*]. Thank you. Go back to your place. [*He sits down on his heels on the floor, just where he is, down center.* KOTARO *goes back to his place and* SHUSAI *helps him: they are very close together.* GHENZO, *looking up desperately from brooding on the floor, suddenly notes the striking resemblance between them.*] But, what's this? [*All look up startled at his tone.*] Come here, Kotaro. [*As* KOTARO *obeys.*] It is well, it is well: this is the one for me! [*To* KOTARO.] Look in my face. [*He studies* KOTARO'S *face, with an occasional glance at* SHUSAI. KOTARO *is wide-eyed but quiet.*] You are a well-born child, Kotaro,—well bred, of a good stock. That is seen at a glance, isn't it, Tonami?

TONAMI. That was what struck me when I first saw him. I'm glad he makes the same impression on you. The clouds that hung upon your forehead have disappeared as by enchantment since you looked at him. He will be a good scholar! Just now when his mother brought him——

GHENZO. His mother, ha? His mother—is *she* here?

TONAMI. No; she was in some haste; important business called her. She has gone to the next village, but she will come back this way. It will not be long before she comes.

GHENZO [*more and more constrained*]. It will not be long?—Ah! [*He rises.*] Listen, Tonami: I am concerned just now. It is most grave.—Take the children in to the farthest room, and let them play there as they please so long as they do not disturb me. [*Turning up-stage to the children.*] Put your things away carefully, and set your desks and boxes by the wall. You [*with a meaningful accent on the word*] may make holiday this afternoon.

[*With uproar and tumult the boys—their fear dispelled—line the rear wall on either side of the center door with their little tables, and rush off, center, with boisterous glee.*

TONAMI *takes the hands of* KOTARO *and* SHUSAI *and follows the others out.* GHENZO *watches these three intently: he goes up to the door and sees them off; then, facing front, he sits down on his heels again, on the upper stage. Presently* TONAMI *returns. He looks up at her, somberly intense.*]
TONAMI. What, dark looks again? You make me afraid. [*She sits on her heels beside him.*] Just now, when I saw your face brighten at the sight of the little stranger, the new pupil,—I wondered if we were not threatened with some danger. [GHENZO'S *looks assent.*] What is it? Speak!
GHENZO. It is true. We are threatened. Nay, we are betrayed! Shihei, the persecutor of our lord and all his household, *knows* that Shusai is not, as we pretend, our own son, but, in fact, is our young lord,—the last scion of the house of Mitchizaneh. He knows, and fears he will avenge his father, later. He orders me to bring him Shusai's head.
TONAMI [*exclaiming*]. Oh, no! [*Then, lower.*] I felt it coming.—How were you told, Shihei——
GHENZO. This conference with the Mayor was nothing but a trap—a bait they offered to keep us from escaping. Hardly had I arrived when Ghemba, Shihei's representative, appeared, at the head of a hundred men or more, and said to me, "We know all. Deliver to us this child whom you pretend to call your son. He is none other than young lord Shusai! How darest thou, impudent, protect Shusai, the enemy of Chancellor Shihei? Harkee: if in two hours thou bring us not the head of this Shusai, we will by force enter your house and take it for ourselves! My lord Shihei commands us."—How I longed to answer with a sword-blow! But I stood alone, against a host. I had to bow [*slowly*] before foul Ghemba, and cast about—some trick, some ruse! . . . Well, I avowed all; only asked the necessary time to execute the orler—thinking— Then I saw Matsuo the Pine-tree, the only one of Shihei's men who knows Shusai! He is with them, and on him they must depend to recognize the head: he [*with growing passion*] must confirm the death of *his young lord,*—forgetting, oh, the ingrate! all the good the house of Mitchizaneh heaped on him in olden days,—the exile

and the death of his twin brothers, faithful to their lord,—
[*Overcome with fiery indignation, he breaks down.*]

TONAMI [*softly*]. Remember,—he took service with Shihei
before the feud began—when all were friends.

GHENZO. I blame him not for that, but that he dares to
seek the life of the last son of his old liege, his father's liege,
who named him! *He* betrayed Shusai!—he came to see the
child assuredly killed. He is sick—so feeble that he scarce
can stand upright. Only his hate—perverse, incredible hate!
—gives him the strength to carry through this base, cowardly
—Oh— [*His feelings again overcome him; but with his left
hand he restrains* TONAMI *from speaking, and resumes, low
and tense.*] Listen, Tonami, what I thought to do. We are
surrounded here by Sheihei's men. Flight is impossible.
Some head—*some head*—must be delivered that is like
Shusai's, or they themselves will find and finish him. I
pondered, as I came just now, what one of our few school-
boys has a face like his? Not one!—their base-born features
cannot pass, one moment, for his little noble's face! In
chilled despair I sat; when, like a ray from heaven, the new
child struck my eye! His face! Tonami, 't is the image of
Shusai's! To save our little liege, the gods themselves have
led to us this boy, at the very instant when peril was most
pressing. [TONAMI *covers her face.*]   —It is sad, but hesitate
we cannot: he must die. His head once rendered up, we may
escape with Shusai still, and in a few hours reach the frontier
of Kawachi, and be safe!

TONAMI. Oh, horrible!—Are we constrained at last even
to shed innocent blood, this little child's blood? We know
that loyalty to our young lord comes before all, excuses everything, though the whole world perish!—But will this awful
act serve any end at last? Matsuo knows too well the linea-
ments of Lord Shusai. His eyes, his memory, will never
fail him at the critical moment when he looks at the head!
He will perceive the cheat, and then——

GHENZO. He 'll die! I 'll scrutinize his face so constantly
that if he shows the slightest tremor of doubt I 'll send his
own beard rolling on the floor with one stroke of my sword

—then fling myself [*rising*] upon the rest, and massacre them all! Let me not live if my young lord must die! A faithful servant, I will go with him at least to the next world! [*To her as she gets up, too, more calmly and consolingly.*] But reassure yourself, Tonami. Matsuo never will divine the cheat. The resemblance of the children is too close—and death will wipe out every difference. What I most apprehend [*with a glance at the gate*] is the return of this child's mother. If she comes too soon and calls for him, or if not finding him she raises an alarm—'t will jeopardize our flight!—Well, in that case, I will cut down her, too! [*He strides down to the lower stage.*]

TONAMI. Ghenzo! You terrify me. [*He turns up to her.*] No, [*coming down to him*] let me inveigle her away. While you escape with Shusai, I will entertain her.

GHENZO. Impossible! She will have learned already: the village will be humming with the news of these extraordinary happenings here, and in her fright she will demand to see her son.—No, no, Tonami, your good heart will only serve to ruin us.—This woman, if she comes back, must die!—Courage! We are condemned to commit crimes: let us go through with them! The safety of our little lord exacts it. [*He paces to the left door, with set lips, and turns there.*]

TONAMI. So be it, O Gods! since fate will have it so. Let us recoil at nothing! Oh, poor child, poor mother! This very day to have entrusted him whom she holds most dear to us!—and we, miserable! compelled to sacrifice a child to whom we should be father and mother! [*She covers her face with her sleeve and, sobbing, sinks down on her heels, down left center. GHENZO remains standing, impassive, left. There are sounds of many clog-soled feet approaching, off right, and the querulous, timid clamors of the peasants are heard. A procession enters the yard: GHEMBA'S resplendent figure first, then a retainer carrying a round wooden box for the head, then two coolies bearing MATSUO in his closed litter, and up-stage of them, four more men-at-arms, and finally six or seven anxious peasants, middle-aged or elderly. One old peasant runs ahead to the gate and without asking the leave*]

*of those within or seeming to notice them pulls it open and
squats obsequiously by it.* GHEMBA *pays no attention to him,
but with a cold, keen glance at* TONAMI *and* GHENZO, *enters
and goes up to the upper stage, just to the right of the
center door. His hand on his sword,* GHENZO, *followed by*
TONAMI, *goes up to the left side of the door as though to
prevent* GHEMBA *from penetrating farther. They eye each
other across the doorway. Meanwhile, the two foremost retainers—the one with the box down-stage—enter and stand
guard on either side of the gateway as* MATSUI'S *litter is
carried across and set down by the left door. The three other
retainers follow it and stand in the corner, up right. The
crowd of peasants stops at the gate, not daring to come in.*]

THE PEASANTS [*during all this*]. Mercy, noble lords!
Our children are there, too! *Our* boys are in this house!

ONE PEASANT. Mine is just beginning to write! Let him
go, let him come out, my lord!

ANOTHER. My nephew, sirs! If you should cut off *his*
head by mistake, you could never put it back! Let me have
him!

A THIRD. For Heaven's sake, don't go and take my son for
the young lord! They 're just the same age! Let me go in
and find him!

SEVERAL [*at the gate now*]. Let us come in, your lordship!

GHEMBA [*turning upon them savagely, from his place up
by the center door*]. Go to the devil! Enough of this! No
one can hear! Away!—We 'll be careful not to touch your
silly brats! [*He turns his back on them and speaks to*
MATSUO, *but for* GHENZO'S *ears.*] What presumption! The
churls imagine one can confound a peasant's face with the
features of a samurai! [*He laughs harshly.*]

MATSUO [*who has meanwhile been painfully emerging
from his litter, supporting himself on his great sword, and
now moves with slow, tragic dignity towards the gate.*]
Nevertheless, Ghemba, let them not go too lightly. 'T is not
impossible one of these churls is party to the plot, and will
make off with young Shusai as his. I, who must answer for
all, will not neglect the meagerest precaution. [*To the*

peasants, almost with a touch of sympathy for their parental anxiety.] Calm yourselves, my good fellows: you shall have your own children presently. Call them.

THE PEASANTS [*all together*]. Iwama! Toku-san! Choma! Heiko! [*Etc.*]

MATSUO [*thunderously*]. Peace! One by one!

[*All remain absolutely still while the invisible chorus of three or four singers, accompanied by two shamisen—instruments not unlike banjos but with only three strings—sing:*

"With a hand of iron he guards the gate.
His piercing glances every one shuns.
His voice of thunder stuns like fate
The pair, from whose hearts the chilled blood runs . . .
And without, gray-haired, disconsolate, wait
The peasants for their imperil'd sons."]

A PEASANT [*after a moment, timidly*]. Choma! Choma!

GHENZO [*speaking tensely but quietly into the rear room*]. Choma! Come here.

[CHOMA *appears at the door, winces from* GHEMBA'S *glare, sees the crowd, and is frightened. The peasant, his arms out, tries to go to him but is barred by the retainers at the gate.* MATSUO, *midway between them, scans the boy closely.*]

MATSUO. One of them has so blotted his face with his ink-brush, he is well disguised. However, it is not he. [*To the guard.*] Let him run.

[CHOMA *jumps off the upper stage, flies into the peasant's arms, and they disappear.*]

AN OLD PEASANT. Iwama! Is Iwama there?

IWAMA [*popping out before* GHENZO *can repeat his name*]. Yes, Grandpa! Here I am!

MATSUO [*promptly*]. A better-looking rogue, but too round-faced. March!

[IWAMA *bows and runs to his grandfather, who takes him away pickaback.*]

ANOTHER PEASANT [*unusually dull-looking*]. Baby! Baby!

[*The* DUNCE *responds, in time to see* IWAMA *disappear.*]

THE DUNCE. Papa! Take me pickaback too! [*He notices* GHEMBA *and* MATSUO *sneering at him, and begins to cry.* MATSUO *contemptuously signs to his papa to come and take him. The* DUNCE *climbs on his father's back from the upper stage, and is borne off, still crying, amid smiles of scorn.*]

GHEMBA [*meanwhile*]. I find myself in thorough agreement with you, Matsuo! A fine noble, truly: the little brute with his monkey howl and bow-legs! Good Lord, the old fool takes the young one off on his back like a treasure sack!

A FOURTH PEASANT [*he who had run ahead to open the gate*]. Toku! Toku! Toku-san! [TOKU *appears: he is almost as inky and ugly as the* DUNCE.] Pray you, my lords, don't take *him* for the young noble. He is very handsome.

[TOKU *tries to hide his face in embarrassment, and slips down to the lower stage.*]

MATSUO [*with a flick of his sword*]. Stop, little fool! [*With the tip of the scabbard under* TOKU'S *chin he raises his face and scans it.*] You seem to have an uneasy conscience. Look me in the face. [*Then with a snort of disgust.*] Huh! A melon-head, and dirty withal! [*Tapping* TOKU *on the head.*] Be off with you!

[TOKU *and the peasant run away.*]

GHEMBA. Master Ghenzo, call the other little peasants all out at once. By the specimens we've just seen, I could identify 'em in a moment. It's cabbage heads grow from cabbages! [GHENZO *calls two or three names—say,* SERA, HAMI, *or* CHANO. *The boys appear, are scanned by* GHEMBA *and* MATSUO, *and cross to their joyful relatives, who hasten away with them. At a nod from* GHEMBA, *the retainer with the box goes up to him, behind* MATSUO; *and the other man-at-arms shuts the gate and remains guarding it.*] Well, Ghenzo; keep your word. Cut off Shusai's head, and bring it to me. [*Tendering him the box.*] Go. Hurry!

GHENZO [*in even tones, that only his eyes, in his tense mask, belie*]. Think you one can cut off a noble daimio's head with no more ceremony than one would take to stick a dog? Be patient for a minute, and grant me time to carry out an act of so much weight. [*As he starts to go out the center door, MATSUO's deep, strained tone stops him short.*]

MATSUO. One moment, Ghenzo. Make no attempt to cheat us or elude us! If, while we wait you here, you seek to fly out of some other door—you will be foiled. More than a hundred swords enring your house and nothing can escape. Renounce as well the idea that you can bring some other head, imagining that death will wipe away all difference. That is too old a ruse,—and would cost you too dear.

GHENZO [*his face working with his efforts to control himself*]. Spare yourself all these vain anxieties. Keep your reflections to yourself. I 'll bring the very head.

GHEMBA [*impatient*]. 'T is well. Enough. Go. [*Giving him the box.*] Do what you must do.

[GHENZO *goes out, center.* GHEMBA *assigns the guarding of the center door to his retainer, and crosses to the door down left, behind the litter, peering off. Meanwhile* TONAMI, *left of the center door, listens, with strained and anxious face; and* MATSUO, *down right center, turns his back on the audience and counts the desks along the back wall.*]

MATSUO. Hm! Strange! Incomprehensible!—[*Toward* GHEMBA, *but not turning.*] The little devils whom we 've just dismissed,—were they not seven? How comes this *extra* table [*pointing with his left hand at* KOTARO's] there? [*To* TONAMI.] Whose is it?

TONAMI [*much troubled*]. The new —— —— Pardon! I am distraught! The table, you are speaking of? It is Shusai's! I promise you! Believe me, it is!

MATSUO. 'T is well. I *will* believe it. [*He goes, weakly, toward* GHEMBA, *left.*] But why will not this Ghenzo make more haste? I am so ill that I can scarcely— [*He sinks back against the upper stage, a trifle left of center.* TONAMI *moves away from him, as though loathing and fearing him, down right. There comes the sound, behind, of a little body falling.* MATSUO *stands erect with a shudder.* TONAMI

*turns, makes as if to go to the door and see, but stands power-
less . . .* GHENZO *enters, formally, center. He comes down
and deposits the closed box before* MATSUO, *who sinks down
on his crossed legs, looking at it blankly.*]

GHENZO. What you commanded is performed. The head!
[*Backing away, right, and sitting on his heels just before*
TONAMI, *who sinks down likewise.*] Study it closely, O right
noble Matsuo! Assure yourself it is indeed Shusai's! [*He
grasps the handle of his sword and peers fixedly into* MAT-
SUO'S *face.* MATSUO *waves to the three men-at-arms up right,
who when* GHEMBA *repeats the signal come forward.*]

MATSUO [*to them*]. Stand there, and keep your eyes on
them. [*The three stand over* TONAMI *and* GHENZI, *poised to
strike them down.* MATSUO *shuts his eyes—opens the box.
He need not take the head out—the physical horror of it
would, with a Western audience, lessen the necessary concen-
tration on his tragic face. Slowly, as if in a dream, he opens
his eyes, looks motionlessly at the head, extends a tremulous
hand and touches it; and for a second a shadow of his agony
fleets across his rigid face. Then he speaks, deeply.*] There
is no doubt. It is Kwan Shusai's head. [*He shuts the box
and bears down heavily on the lid.* GHENZO *darts a glance
over his right shoulder at* TONAMI. GHEMBA, *who has been
standing at* MATSUO'S *left, leaning forward tensely, straightens up exultant.*]

GHEMBA. At last! We have it! . . . —You have been
firm and faithful, Master Ghenzo,—and merit some reward.
The pain of death had been decreed against you, for concealing the son of Mitchizaneh in your home; but in beheading
him with your own hands, you have made reparation: you
may live. [*He waves the retainers back and extends a hand
to* MATSUO, *to help him up.*] Come, let us go, Matsuo, and
announce our enterprise's success to Lord Shihei. He will be
waiting for us.

MATSUO [*not rising*]. Ay—go on, Ghemba, with all speed.
Take the happy news to him—and, take the head. [*With a
scarcely perceptible reluctance he puts the box into* GHEMBA'S

hands.] But—for my part—I am sore sick: far worse than I appear. [*He struggles to his feet.*] Excuse me to him. Get permission for me to quit his service altogether.

GHEMBA. Well, be it as you please. Go home and guard your health. Your great task is accomplished. [*Crossing to the gate.*] Open! [*The gate is opened.*] Come! [*He goes out with the box, the five men after him. MATSUO meanwhile gets feebly into his litter. GHENZO and TONAMI stand up; MATSUO is carried out, past them, right; and they are left alone.*]

GHENZO [*after a marveling pause*]. The gods be thankful! Mindful of Mitchizaneh's piety they granted us this boon, and for his sake made blind Matsuo's eyes! [*He goes and looks out, still almost incredulous, after MATSUO's litter; then shuts the gate and bolts it.*] Rejoice, Tonami! Long life to our young lord!

TONAMI [*who has been prostrating herself in thankful worship*]. Is it a dream? Shusai's protecting angel must have vexed Matsuo's vision! or perhaps the head of the poor child itself was the good spirit! He was no common stone, to be confused with the real jewel! Oh, I thank the gods!

[*In the midst of their rejoicings, CHIYO appears at the gate, and knocks.*]

CHIYO. Open the gate! It is I, the mother of the new pupil!

TONAMI [*seizing GHENZO, hiding behind him from CHIYO*]. It's the mother! Ghenzo, we're lost! What'll we do? What'll we say?

CHIYO. Open the gate!

GHENZO [*to TONAMI, low and stern*]. Be quiet, fool! Did I not foresee this? Keep still. We will finish with her, too, somehow or other! [*He unbolts the gate. CHIYO shoves it aside and enters with hardly an attempt at the formal greeting.*]

CHIYO. Ah! Are your Master Ghenzo, my son's teacher? [*As GHENZO looks blank in an effort to gain time for quick thought.*] I left him here just a little while ago! Where is he?

GHENZO [*smoothly, in great contrast with her excitement*].
Your son is in the next room, playing with the other scholars.
Do you wish to see him?

CHIYO. Yes, take me to him! I want him to come home
with me!

GHENZO. Very well. Follow me. This way, if you please.
[*He takes her to the center, across* TONAMI *who cannot look*
CHIYO *in the face, and indicates that she is to precede him up
to the center door. As she picks up her clothes to step up
onto the upper stage, he draws his sword like a flash of
lightning and strikes down at her head. But she appears to
have been ready for the attempt: she dodges to the right (her
left), and as the blow crashes upon the upper stage she flees
to the right corner and there snatches up the box that she
had brought for her son.* GHENZO *pursues her along the upper stage, his sword above his head.*]

CHIYO. Stop! Stop!

GHENZO. Die! [*His sword crashes down on the box that*
CHIYO *holds up as a shield; the box falls open, and out of
it streams one of the white robes used in Japan as shrouds,
with fluttering paper prayers and other funeral objects.*
GHENZO, *his sword poised for a third blow, stops, astounded.*]
Ha? What does all that mean?!

CHIYO [*on her knees, lowering the box and sobbing*]. Tell
me—I beseech you—my son—is he dead? Has he laid down
his life for his lord Shusai? I implore you, do not hide the
truth from me!

GHENZO [*stupefied*]. What? For his lord Shusai? Your
son?—So it was by design you brought him——?

CHIYO [*tears in her voice*]. Oh, my boy, my only child!
. . . Yes—we sacrificed him to save his liege lord's life! As
you see, here is the robe of death, the funeral prayers, the
invocation, "Namu Amida Butsu"—all will prove it to
you!

GHENZO [*low, almost awe-struck*]. I do not understand.
Who are you? Who is your husband?

[*In the gateway suddenly* MATSUO *stands.* GHENZO *starts
back, again raising his sword; but* MATSUO, *with a grave ges-*

*ture that bids him be still and listen, moves rhythmically to
left center, chanting softly.*]

MATSUO. "The Plum-tree has followed me into exile:
    The Cherry-tree died for my cause:
    Should the Pine-tree alone be false and vile,
    Ignoring Bushido's laws?''

[*Turning toward his wife.*] Rejoice, Chiyo! Our son is
dead to save his young lord's life! [CHIYO *covers her face
and cries.*] Weep, sorrow-stricken Chiyo! Give free rein to
your mother's grief: you may mourn him without shame!—
Your pardon, Ghenzo. A mother's heart!

GHENZO [*still standing, sword in hand, on the upper stage,
between them*]. I do not yet understand. Is it a dream?
Is it reality? What! you, Matsuo, Shihei's samurai,—are
you not our enemy? Did you not long since break the bonds
that linked you with the house of Mitchizaneh? Yet volun-
tarily have you sacrificed your own son for his son, Shusai?
I know not what to think!

MATSUO. Your astonishment is natural. Alas! a bitter
fate divided me from faith, tore me from the true path, set
me in vassalage under a lord who came to hate and harry all
that from childhood I had held most sacred: my master Mitchizaneh, the patron of my house, the benefactor of my father and my brothers!—Ah, what I suffered, thus to see myself cut off from all I cherished—to hear myself denounced—
ingrate and traitor! Yet how else could I have kept my oath
of homage to Shihei? . . . To have deserved such punishment I must have sinned in some precedent life unutterably!
. . . Well, my strength failed me. To quit Shihei, at any
cost, I feigned an illness and requested a release. Just at
that moment burst on us the news that Shusai still was living, as your son. Shihei gave orders instantly to seize him—
to kill him ere you could escape with him—and bring his head
in proof. Of all his train, I only knew the face of Mitchizaneh's, of my godfather's, son! On me then fell the need to
verify the head to be presented as Shusai's: on this condition
my release was given me; and you have seen how I fulfilled

the task.—I thank the gods to be delivered now from the sore burden that so long oppressed me! . . . Ghenzo, I know that you would stop at nothing to save Shusai from death—of that, believe me, I needed no convincing—but, how could you? Flight was impossible, and to present a vulgar head would only ruin you. So I perceived the time had come for *me;* and losing not a moment, my brave wife brought you our son to take Lord Shusai's place. I left the rest to heaven and to you. But when I counted at the fatal instant that row of desks, and recognized my son's,—I knew. . . . "Should the Pine-tree alone be false and vile, ignoring Bushido's laws?" —Those verses that my unforgotten liege, Lord Mitchizaneh, aimed at me have rung continually in my ears: I seemed to hear on every hand that "false and vile." You can imagine what it meant to me; and had I had no son to expiate his sire's dishonor and disloyalty,—I, and my heirs, and theirs, had been accursed and infamous forever!—Oh, my son! Through thee I was permitted to atone! Thou hast preserved the honor of our house!

CHIYO [*still kneeling, up right*]. Aye, he has saved our honor, and for that his memory shall be graven in our hearts forever!—Dear child! when I left him here he tried so hard to follow me, my heart bled, for I was abandoning him to certain death!—Oh, let me hold his body in my arms one last time more! My little boy! [*She breaks down again, puts her face to the floor and sobs.*]

TONAMI [*going up to her*]. Dear mother, let me share your grief. I did not know your son, but I can still hear perfectly his gentle little voice telling my husband he was very good to take him under his protection! A cold shudder runs through me when I think of it!

MATSUO. Master your grief, good Chiyo. Let us bear, unyielding, the disasters of our lot.—Ghenzo, the boy knew that he was to die. [CHIYO *looks up.*] I told him, Chiyo, before I parted from him; and he, a little boy scarce nine years old, without a tremor let me send him here. How did he die, Ghenzo? Not asking mercy?

GHENZO. No. Like a hero. 'Twere impossible more

coolly to face death. I drew my sword and told him 'twas for him, and with a smile he raised his chin to let me strike his neck.

MATSUO. Brave child! 'Twas even so my brother died, the Cherry-tree, in Mitchizaneh's cause. What joy must have been theirs to meet each other in the next world! What bliss is their reward for their heroic deaths! [*He weeps.*] Pardon me, Ghenzo: I can no longer struggle with my tears!

[SHUSAI, *hearing the deep sobs, appears in the center door.*]

SHUSAI. Oh, was this murder done in *my* behalf? [*To* GHENZO.] Why didn't you tell me? I should never have let another perish in my place! What horror! What shame for me!

MATSUO [*looking out, right, where the litter is seen again approaching, and bowing deeply to* SHUSAI]. Noble lord, in presenting myself before you I bring with me a gift that you would not have dared to hope for. Look.

[*The litter has stopped outside the gate. Out of it steps the mother of* SHUSAI, *and enters.*]

SHUSAI. Why, mother! Mother!

HIS MOTHER [*hastening gracefully to him*]. Son! Shusai! My son!

[*They embrace, she on the lower stage, he on the upper.*]

GHENZO. Do I see right? Noble lady, is it you? Oh, happy meeting! We have searched everywhere, but could not find you. Who gave you such safe shelter?

[*The lady turns toward* MATSUO. *In renewed astonishment,* GHENZO *steps down to the lower stage, facing* MATSUO *across her.*]

MATSUO [*bowing his head in confirmation*]. When bloody Shihei threatened to annihilate the entire family of Mitchizaneh, I took the noble lady home to Saga. But straightway she was recognized. I donned a cowl and like a monk conducted her through a thousand dangers hither, and, but now discharged, sent her my litter.—But lose no time! Fly with all speed till the frontier be crossed! And in Kawachi you will find your daughter and [*to* SHUSAI] sister, anxiously awaiting you. [GHENZO *conducts the lady and the boy to the litter, which they enter, and, instructing the coolies, sees them carried off.*] For us, dear Chiyo, it remains to inter all that is left us of our beloved son, and make the offerings to his spirit that are due.

[TONAMI *goes out, center, to fetch the body.* CHIYO *follows her to the door.*]

GHENZO. No, Matsuo,—we will not have the heart, now when your grief is still so strong upon you, to leave you with this solemn task alone. My wife and I——

MATSUO [*with the deep authority that once more stills* GHENZO]. Suffer me. [*He and* CHIYO *remove their outer kimonos and appear in mourning garments of white and sky-blue.* TONAMI *reënters between them, with the body, close-wrapped in white.* CHIYO *holds out her arms for it, but* MATSUO *steps up on to the upper stage*]. Let me do it. [*He takes the body.*] In the world's eyes, remember, it is not my son I bury, but the heir of Mitchizaneh.

[*The other three bow their heads, but* MATSUO *lifts his face, nobly impassive.*]

CURTAIN

SUGGESTIVE QUESTIONS

1. How much does stage setting, and how much does costuming, add to the effect of *Bushido?*
2. What advantage is gained by introducing school children in the opening of the play, instead of introducing more serious characters?
3. What is the effect of differentiating Shusai immediately?
4. What foreshadowings of tragedy appear in the early part of the play?
5. What deep emotions does the early part of the play emphasize?
6. Point out, throughout the play, how evidences of human weakness are made to increase respect for human strength of character.
7. At what point in the play is the plot fully disclosed?
8. How does the dramatist make tragic action seem natural?

9. Point out places where stage business increases the effect of the play.
10. In what way does music increase the effect?
11. What is the moment of greatest suspense?
12. What is the moment of most poignant emotion?
13. What is the moment when the dramatist most appeals to our sympathies?
14. What stage business is most effective?
15. What dramatic values would have been lost if the play had ended with the departure of Ghemba?
16. What is the effect of re-introducing Chiyo and Matsuo?
17. How much of the value of the play depends upon outward event, and how much upon the revelation of inner emotion?
18. What dramatic skill does the conclusion of the play show?
19. What sort of acting does the play make necessary?

SUGGESTIONS FOR WRITTEN IMITATION

1. Write a dialogue that has for its setting any modern school room.
2. Write a dialogue that will show genuine mother-love.
3. Write a dialogue, with full stage directions, to show nobility on the part of a child.
4. Write a dialogue between a mother and her only son, an aviator who is about to sail for France to take part in the World War.
5. Write a dialogue, with full stage directions, in which a man and a woman plan hastily to take steps to fulfil some duty, when circumstance seems against their fulfilling it.
6. Write a dialogue, with full stage directions, concerning any tragic moment in the World War.
7. Write a dialogue in which you show how a Gold Star Mother learns, for the first time, how her son met death in the World War.
8. Write a scenario for a play that will strongly emphasize sacrifice.

DIRECTIONS FOR WRITING

Aim to emphasize inner life rather than outer event. At the same time, give your work plenty of simple, natural action. Base all your work on deep and true emotions. Make your stage directions call for stage business that will aid in interpreting character and in producing emotion.

ORAL WORK IN CLASS

1. Read aloud, effectively, all that you wrote.
2. Select associates, and act the school-room scene, and the introduction of the new pupil.
3. Read aloud, in dramatic manner, the part of the play that most pleases you.
4. Read aloud Matsuo's speech in which he explains all that he did to fulfil his sense of loyalty.
5. Read aloud the closing scene of *Bushido*, beginning with the entrance of Shusai's mother.

THE END